Ecological Politics Ecofeminists and the Greens

Ecological Politics

Ecofeminists and the Greens

Greta Gaard

Temple University Press *Philadelphia*

Temple University Press, Philadelphia 19122

Copyright © 1998 by Temple University. All rights reserved

Published 1998

Printed in the United States of America

60%
TOTAL RECOVERED FIBER
10% POST-CONSUMER WASTE

This book is printed on acid-free paper
for greater longevity

Text design by Will Boehm

Library of Congress Cataloging-in-Publication Data
Gaard, Greta Claire.
    Ecological politics : ecofeminists and the Greens / Greta Gaard.
        p.   cm.
    Includes bibliographical references and index.
        ISBN 1-56639-569-0 (cl. : alk. paper). — ISBN 1-56639-570-4 (pbk. : alk.
paper)
        1. Green movement—United States.   2. Ecofeminism—United States.
    3. Environmental policy—United States.   4. Environmental ethics—
    United States.   I. Title.
    GE197.G33   1998
    363.7'0525—dc21   97-12413

To the next generation of social movement activists

Contents

Appendixes

Acknowledgments

On the shores of Lake Superior, while I was working on the actions and interviews that would find expression in this book, Jan Hartley was working out many of these same ideas in her art. In 1989, Jan gave up her commercial art work and began painting the images that came to her in meditation. Though all her work addresses issues of environmental concern, I was drawn to her Spirit Cape series, which refers to the destruction and possible rebirth of the earth's ecosystems. Each of the twelve images in the series carries symbols on the wings of birds, symbols representing the habitat destruction of the bird portrayed as well as the hope that the viewer will respond by taking action. Jan writes, "I am concerned that the circle of life and death, male and female, night and day, good and evil (all the opposites that we hold in our mind) is being torn apart by our dualistic thinking. Instead of seeing holistically, we are separating the part from the whole, causing dissension and dis-ease." In "Spirit Cape of the Gemini," crow and dove give birth to the ancient completeness that exists in all creation. Like this book, it presents an image of hope. I am grateful to Jan Hartley for offering her "Spirit Cape of the Gemini" for the cover of this book's paperback edition.

Ecological Politics was made possible by the many ecofeminists and Greens who participated in this research, allowing me to videotape or interview them without compensation for their time or inconvenience: Margo Adair, Carol Adams, Lourdes Arguëlles, Lois Arkin, Judi Bari, Amy Belanger, Dee Berry, Keiko Bonk, Walt Bresette, David Conley, Jan Conley, Deane Curtin, Debbie

Domal, Josephine Donovan, Riane Eisler, Regina Endrizzi, Hugh Esco, Carolyn Estes, Mike Feinstein, Margaret Garcia, Annie Goeke, Winston Gordon, Elizabeth Dodson Gray, Lori Gruen, JoAnn Haberman, Chaia Heller, Lydia Herbert, Tricia Hoffman, Marti Kheel, Ynestra King, Erica Bremer Kneipp, Winona LaDuke, Stephanie Lahar, Linda Martin, Cathleen McGuire, Susan Meeker-Lowry, Ross Mirkarimi, Lowell Nelson, Gloria Orenstein, John Rensenbrink, Ira Rohter, Julia Scofield Russell, Connie Salamone, Lorna Salzman, Catriona Sandilands, Laura Schere, Vandana Shiva, Joel Sipress, Charlene Spretnak, Penelope Starr-Karlin, Brian Tokar, Karen Warren, Laura Winton, and Toni Wurst. I am truly indebted to Dan Coleman, Chaia Heller, Laura Schere, and John Schrafnaugel, who trusted me with their books and archives of grassroots materials on ecofeminism and Green politics; to George Franklin of *Green Letter* and Don Fitz of *Synthesis/Regeneration* for supplying me with back issues of their publications when I could not find them anywhere else; and to Shea Howell for informative conversations. I am particularly grateful to those who read chapters of this manuscript in its various drafts: Beth Bartlett, Chaia Heller, Johann Moore, Lowell Nelson, Laura Schere, Joel Sipress, and Brian Tokar. The University of Minnesota supported this research by awarding me a single-quarter leave and later a year's sabbatical, during which I completed most of this writing. Common Ground Vipassana Meditation Center provided me with glimpses of equanimity and a steadfast spiritual community. Beverly Gaard Gherardi assisted me in recording several interviews and offered me immeasurable support through weekly telephone conversations. Finally, I am grateful to Shawn Boeser, whose patience, steadiness, and support make everything possible.

Ecological Politics Ecofeminists and the Greens

Introduction

Every history is an act of interpretation. Originally, my goal in this book was to tell the story of ecofeminist activism and participation within the U.S. Green movement and to chronicle the history and development of the Greens from movement to party. As I wrote, I kept photographs of the activists and theorists near my writing table. Since many of them disagreed with one another, and I had positions of agreement and disagreement with each of them as well, I decided to tell this history not once but several times, once from each viewpoint. As I shifted through the various constituencies, I imagined myself sitting with members of each group, telling their story from their perspective and in their presence. Would they feel that I had done justice to their viewpoint? Where we disagreed, I imagined us arguing face to face, making certain concessions to one another's viewpoints and yet holding firmly to our own. Although writing may be a solitary endeavor, the histories in this book grew out of experiences within particular communities, and they will be read by activists and scholars from those communities, as well as others interested in social movement histories, women's studies, and environmental activism. In this retelling, then, I hope to have provided a more thorough history of ecofeminism and Green politics in the United States than has been available in the past, thus benefiting readers who may agree or disagree with my interpretations. For in the process of writing, I found that I was unable to tell these histories without interpretation; in fact, I doubt that anyone could. With the guidance of feminist methodologies, I decided my best alternative would be to allow these activists to speak in their own words wherever possible and to discard any claims of objectivity in favor of distinguishing specific viewpoints from one another and from my own interpretations and theorizing as well. Here I offer my own activist history as a way of eschewing objectivity and providing both an intellectual and a personal framework for the interpretations that follow.

The roots of my ecofeminism and Green politics lie in animal liberation. Although I participated in antinuclear protests at Diablo Canyon Nuclear Power Plant in 1977 and 1978, distributed cards and flyers opposing California's homophobic Briggs Initiative in 1978, and was sexually harassed by Sierra Club trip leaders on my first backpacking trip to the Sierras in 1976, none of these separate incidents led me to become a full-blown activist. I simply didn't see the connections. In 1984, while visiting friends at their cabin home in Vermont, one of my hosts, Bonnie Dodson, urged me to read Peter Singer's *Animal Liberation*.[1] The book provided me with one of those revolutionary moments of insight after which there is no turning back. Later that same year, at a conference organized by the Animal Rights Coalition in Minneapolis, I picked up a reprint of Aviva Cantor's stunning essay linking the oppression of women with the oppression of animals, and promptly subscribed to a grassroots newsletter published by Feminists for Animal Rights.[2] It would be a decade later before I learned that Peter Singer and I were both part of an international Green movement that brought together our shared commitment to animals, to the earth, and to social justice.

After several years of working on issues of animal rights, my life experiences took another illuminating turn. In 1987, I began a graduate minor in women's studies, and in the summer of 1988 I signed up for a two-week wilderness skills course with the National Outdoor Leadership School (NOLS) in Lander, Wyoming. The two weeks I spent in the Wind River Mountains with thirteen others (as one of only three women) overwhelmed me with sensory, emotional, psychological, and ethical information it would take me years to sort through.[3] I was surprised to find that although NOLS taught environmental ethics for the wilderness—"no trace" camping, acute observation of our physical health and our surroundings, ecological techniques for depositing human wastes—the organization remained virtually silent about bringing those techniques into our daily lives. My vision had shifted on that wilderness expedition, and I was finding evidence of "wilderness" everywhere I looked; hence, I wanted a more inclusive ethical practice, a way to achieve a minimum impact lifestyle suitable for all parts of nature. When I returned home, my friend Dan Seifert (an eco-dude in the very classic sense, who had actually driven me to

Lander and hitchhiked home to St. Paul just to be sure I would go on the NOLS course) handed me a book by Bill Devall and George Sessions, *Deep Ecology: Living as if Nature Mattered*.[4] Although the book was sadly negligent on issues concerning feminism, it had enough of an index to provide me with leads to other sources, and for several months I used the book as a virtual treasure map to recent environmental theory. From the NOLS course and the Devall and Sessions book, I started making the connections that would provide the foundation of my ecofeminism: ecology, animal liberation, and feminism.

At the National Women's Studies Association (NWSA) convention in 1989, I presented my first essay on ecofeminism, titled "Feminists, Animals, and the Environment: The Transformative Potential of Feminist Theory," and met Stephanie Lahar and Ariel Salleh on the first panel to address ecofeminism in the history of the NWSA. Sandra Eisdorfer, senior editor at the University of North Carolina Press, invited me to write a book on ecofeminism after listening to my paper, but I declined, arguing that a single-author book would not do justice to such a multivocal grassroots movement. After much discussion, we agreed that I would edit a collection, and it was with her encouragement and support that I began what would become *Ecofeminism: Women, Animals, Nature* (published by Temple in 1993). At that same conference, Judith Plant's new anthology, *Healing the Wounds: The Promise of Ecofeminism*, was available for the first time, and from it I learned that others before me had made these same connections.[5] When Noël Sturgeon, Marti Kheel (cofounder of Feminists for Animal Rights), and Linda Vance presented another panel on ecofeminism at that conference, I realized we were part of a movement. With about forty other women, we established an Ecofeminist Caucus within NWSA, and Sturgeon agreed to publish our newsletter. It was both humorous and frustrating to discover that so many of us, working alone in our separate parts of the country, thought we had invented these ideas ourselves. Yet the more I learned of our history—from Rachel Carson's *Silent Spring*, Léonie Caldecott and Stephanie Leland's *Reclaim the Earth: Women Speak Out for Life on Earth*,[6] the Women and Life on Earth conference, the Women's Pentagon Action, Greenham Common, and the chipko movement—the more I realized that we were part of an international ecofeminist movement whose ideas were being discovered and articulated by women unknown to one another around the world.

But, at least in the United States, that seemed to be all we were doing. Certainly there were feminist peace activists camping on military bases, and feminists for animal rights working to free women and animals from our shared oppression, but I could not find a group of activists who self-identified as ecofeminists and whose activism included the many concerns addressed by an ecofeminist analysis. At the same time, I was becoming overextended by too many meetings—meetings for my environmental activism, my animal rights activism, my feminist activism—meetings at which I felt like an outsider. The feminists discussed battered women's issues over hamburgers delivered on Styrofoam plates, and my protests about the oppression of animals and the environment were rebuffed or ignored; the animal liberationists and the environmentalists trivialized the concerns of women, telling me our needs were less pressing than those of the animals, who had no voice, or the environment, which was being polluted, clearcut, and despoiled at an alarming rate. It was at this time that I discovered the Green movement in Minneapolis.

As an activist with the Greens, I learned about the connections between racism and environmental degradation, and between economics and environment as well. At the Prairie Island nuclear power plant in Minnesota, Northern States Power is generating power and storing highly radioactive waste in metal casks less than a mile from homes on the Mdewakanton reservation. Emissions from the power plant release enough radiation to cause a cancer risk six times above Minnesota's policy guideline, a clear example of environmental racism. The Twin Cities Greens were an active member of the Prairie Island Coalition Against Nuclear Storage and the fight to halt additional cask storage, but the people couldn't stop NSP—this time. With the Lake Superior Greens, I attended the Protect the Earth gathering at the Mole Lake Sokaogon Chippewa reservation and met activists from the Indigenous Environmental Network; there I learned about corporate mining interests on native lands and the destruction mining causes to both the land and the people living on the land. Also in 1994, I worked with the Fair Trade Coalition and the Institute for Agriculture and Trade Policy as part of an ongoing Green opposition to the General Agreement on Tariffs and Trade (GATT). Like NAFTA, GATT promised to undermine numerous environmental laws, jeopardize food safety, eliminate more than one million textile and apparel jobs, put more family farmers out of work, threaten the sovereignty of indigenous people, and create a World Trade Organization with the power to overrule federal, state, and local laws. The connections linking corporate power, racism, sexism, and the destruction of the earth were clarified for me as a result of my activism with the Greens.

I joined the Greens as a way to enact my ecofeminism, and I have been a Greens member since 1988. Because my work relocated me from Minneapolis to Duluth, I have been part of the Twin Cities Greens, the Northwoods Greens in Duluth, and the Lake Superior Greens in Superior, Wisconsin, and I have served on the founding and coordinating committee of the Green Party of Minnesota. I participated in the decision to develop the Minnesota Greens from a movement to a political party, and I have served as cofounder of the Duluth Area Green Party. I have attended national gatherings of the U.S. Greens in Minneapolis (1992), Syracuse (1993), Albuquerque (1995), and Los Angeles (1996). During all that time, I was surprised by how few people within the Greens or within ecofeminist circles knew of or considered the intersections between these two movements. In the fall of 1992, nine months after completing and recovering from my work on *Ecofeminism*, I decided to undertake a four-year research project that would explore these intersections, motivated by the expectation that a coalition between ecofeminist and Green activists would strengthen and broaden both movements. From the seed idea of this research to the project's completion, I have been guided by feminist research methodologies, whose principles deserve a brief review.

Unlike traditional academic researchers, whose expressed goals are publication and the increase of knowledge in the field but whose implicit purposes may be to obtain scientific or scholarly data in support of the status quo, feminist researchers take liberation as our explicit goal.[7] Communication is another purpose: feminist research is intended to empower women and must be presented in a way that is understandable, not just to the research community but primarily to the women for whose benefit it is intended. Rejecting traditional methods of scholarship that create a hierarchical relationship between researcher and researched, scholar and subject, knower and known, feminist methodology guides researchers to create situations in which authority is shared as much as possible, and all participants have subject rather than object status. Naming as inauthentic the "objectivity" of the traditional researcher, feminist research methodology requires each scholar to describe her unique subjectivity and suggests that the best scholars are also full participants themselves in the projects they are studying. Often feminist research is collaborative or multivocal, since feminist methodologies require each project to acknowledge the diversity of women in terms of race, class, and sexualities, and to situate the research project within a specific historic, cultural, and economic context. Feminist scholarship maintains that "there must be a relationship between theory and practice which not only sees these as inextricably interwoven, but which sees experience and practice as the basis of theory, and theory as the means of changing practice."[8] Hence, feminist research is characterized by an action orientation.

Guided by these principles of feminist methodology, my purpose in undertaking this project was to reveal a broader base for a feminist, ecological, and liberatory movement. I imagined my audience as activists and scholars in both movements who would use these findings to collaborate on shared goals and to broaden their movements for social and ecological justice. My approach to the question of coalition would involve seeking common ground between ecofeminist and Green theories: evaluating Green politics from an ecofeminist perspective and ecofeminism from a Green perspective. In each context, I felt I played the role of "outsider within":[9] in Green communities, I was seen variously as an ecofeminist, an animal liberation advocate, an academic scholar, and a Green; in ecofeminist circles, I was seen as an activist, a Green, and an ecofeminist theorist. In each movement I have felt both at home and invisible at different times, and I have used these different experiences to inform my research.

Since little of the research on ecofeminism and Green politics addressed the topic of coalition between these movements, I decided to conduct interviews with key theorists and activists in both movements, attempting to gain a representative sample of speakers across the United States. From June through November 1993, and at various times in 1994 and 1995, I conducted thirty-seven individual, paired, and group interviews with ecofeminists and Greens in Hawai'i, California, Arizona, Kansas, Colorado, Minnesota, Wisconsin, Pennsylvania, Georgia, New York, Massachusetts, Vermont, New Hampshire, and Maine.[10] In each of these interviews, I asked a standard set of questions that I had formulated based on the work of feminist activist and scholar Charlotte Bunch. In her essay "Not by Degrees: Feminist Theory and Education," Bunch describes a four-part model for developing theory that will lead to activism: describing what exists (description), analyzing why that reality exists (analysis), determining what should exist (vision), and hypothesizing how to change what is to what should be (strategy).[11] Interviews took participants through these four steps and asked specific questions about movement history, composition, conflicts, goals, and actions. In each interview, I also answered the participants' questions of me, and I solicited additional information beyond the structured questions of the interview.

As a means of communicating my findings to the greatest number of activists and scholars most likely to use them, I decided to videotape the interviews, rather than audiotaping them or taking notes, and to use the videotaped interviews as the raw material for producing a documentary video. At the outset of this project, it seemed to me that the activists who most needed the findings of theory had the least amount of time to spare. I doubted that a book that explored these findings in full academic detail would be useful to or read by those activists, and I was committed then and now to providing activists with further tools for our shared work. I liked the idea of a documentary because the medium would allow the participants to speak for themselves; it was inherently collaborative and inclusive of diversity; and it would welcome newcomers to these movements by putting faces on scholars and activists they might have heard about or whose work they had read, thereby encouraging new activists to see themselves as part of a larger movement.

With these ideas, I took some courses in documentary filmmaking, studied the technical editing equipment at the local cable access television stations, purchased a hi-8 videocamera, and eventually produced two thirty-minute documentaries based on the interviews. "Thinking Green: Ecofeminists and the Greens" (1994) uses Bunch's four-part model to show that ecofeminists and Greens share many ideas about the interlocking structure of oppression, the origins of that structure, the characteristics of an ecological society, and the practical strategies for social transformation.[12] "Ecofeminism Now!" (1996) offers an overview of the several sources and present aspects of ecofeminist theory, along with a sampling of ecofeminist activism to date. Although the videos are essentially grassroots productions with no budget for technological niceties, publicity, or distribution, more than four hundred copies are already being used by college educators and community activists. In addition to diversifying and broadening my audience, the videos helped me obtain and record valuable information for my research; their production forced me to reflect on and articulate, in a concise way, my research findings at each stage of the project; and finally, these projects made me eager to return to the medium of written research, for only a full-length book would allow me the space to describe and explore the ideas generated from this research.

This exploration of the intersections between ecofeminism and Green politics begins by describing the origins and development of each movement (Chapters 1 and 2, respectively). Chapter 1, "Ecofeminist Roots," examines the various paths that have drawn women (and a few men) to make the connections that form the foundation of ecofeminism. Activism in environmental causes, the feminist peace movement, the feminist spirituality movement, the animal liberation movement, and the antitoxics movement, as well as personal experiences of interconnectedness, has led women to articulate an ecofeminist perspective. The various routes that lead women to ecofeminism—whether paths of activism or streams of feminist theory—of necessity shape and influence the several varieties of ecofeminist theory as well. During the 1980s, as ecofeminism took shape as a theory and a movement, scholars and activists celebrated the diversity within ecofeminism but did not distinguish among its several branches. By the 1990s, however, amid charges of "incoherence" and "internal inconsistency," it became apparent that the time had come to name the several branches of ecofeminist thought: liberal, "animal," radical cultural, spiritual/cultural, socialist, and social ecofeminism. As I demonstrate in Chapter 4, these distinctions are also useful in describing ecofeminist activism within the Green movement. To supplement this discussion, I have included a chronology of developments within ecofeminism as Appendix A.

Chapter 2, "The U.S. Greens: From Movement to Party," describes the development of the U.S. Green movement on the national level. This overview provides a necessary framework for understanding the various factions that developed within the Greens, and how their differences and their struggles influenced the direction of the movement and led almost inevitably to the debates that unfolded in the 1996 Nader presidential campaign. To supplement this discussion, I have included a chronology of the U.S. Green movement as Appendix B and a list of the original Ten Key Values of the U.S. Greens (Appendix C). Chapter 3, "The U.S. Greens as a Social Movement," augments the narrative of Chapter 2 by drawing on the social movement theories of Sidney Tarrow, Marta Fuentes and Andre Gunder Frank, Frances Fox Piven and Richard Cloward, and several others. Here I describe the various factions that developed within or departed from the Green movement: the Left Greens, the Youth Greens, and the Green Politics Network. I argue that the formation, popularity, and (in at least two cases) decline of these three groups can be seen most productively as different stages of a single social movement. Taken together, they outline the development of Green politics in the United States. The transition from a leftist and sometimes anarchist politics of movement building and local campaigning as advocated by the Left Green Network and the Youth Greens to the emphasis on statewide and national electoral politics as affirmed by the Green Politics Network places the U.S. Green movement within the pattern of social movements around the world. To clarify the differences among these several Green groups, I supply a list of their pillars, values, and principles as Appendix D.

Chapter 4, "Ecofeminists in the Greens," discusses the presence and participation of feminists and ecofeminists within the Greens nationally and within the various Green factions. Drawing on the distinctions among ecofeminisms explained in Chapter 1, I argue that the Ten Key Values of the U.S. Green movement were shaped within a cultural ecofeminist framework. Building on Chapters 2 and 3, I examine the influence of social ecofeminists in shaping the development of the Left Green Network and the Youth Greens. "Animal" eco-feminists came to the Greens and contributed to the life forms plank of the Greens' national platform, but most of these ecofeminists departed when their concerns were not heeded. Ecofeminists from the WomanEarth Feminist Peace Institute also delivered statements for consideration in the Greens' national platform, and several ecofeminists have been active with both the Greens and WomanEarth, although these ecofeminists too have vanished from the Greens as a result of persistent problems with patriarchal behaviors. Finally, social eco-feminists drew on activism from the Women's Pentagon Action to contribute to the Earth Day Wall Street Action in 1990 but later disappeared from the Green movement as the Greens moved closer to electoral politics, leaving only cultural ecofeminists and liberal feminists within the Greens at the time of the Nader presidential campaign. I believe this history reveals a disturbing compatibility among patriarchal politics, liberal feminism, and cultural ecofeminism, an issue I explore in greater depth in Chapter 6.

Chapter 5, "Divisions among the Greens," takes a closer look at the groups that came together to form the Greens and why or how many of these groups withdrew from the Greens when their particular issues were not addressed. The contentious debates within the Green movement before 1992 were not unique to the Greens; versions of these same debates had been ongoing battles within the New Left, the radical ecology movement, and the various movements for social justice. The Green movement was simply one attempt to bring all these various movements together. To describe the internal divisions, I divide my discussion into three general areas: conflicts dealing with philosophy, a section that summarizes the deep ecology/social ecology debate and the debates involving ecofeminist and animal liberation theories; conflicts over the representation of various constituencies, focusing primarily on people of color, gay/lesbian/bisexual/transgendered persons, and labor activists; and conflicts over strategy, beginning with bioregionalism and issue-based activism, developing into the movement versus party debates, and ending in a de facto resolution for a strategy concentrating mainly on electoral politics. It is my argument that these struggles within the Greens show that to achieve lasting social change a social movement must operate on many levels, transcending distinctions of public/private and personal/political. Social transformation of the kind envisioned by radical Greens and ecofeminists alike must involve both a structural transformation of economics and politics and a cultural transformation affecting social values, interpersonal relations, and intrapsychic processes.

Chapter 6, "Democracy, Ecofeminism, and the Nader Presidential Campaign," discusses the first national electoral campaign of the U.S. Greens, the presidential candidacy of Ralph Nader and his chosen running mate, Winona LaDuke, and uses that campaign as a departure point for developing an eco-feminist theory of democracy. Here it is my argument that the practice of national electoral politics restricts and rearticulates democracy within the framework of liberalism. Drawing on feminist critiques of liberal democracy, I argue that the version of democracy articulated by Nader in the Concord Principles and supported by the U.S. Greens in the theory and practice of the Nader presidential campaign is a populist form of liberal democracy that fundamentally betrays both ecofeminism and Green philosophy. As an alternative, I survey the various social ecofeminist critiques of liberal democracy and offer some preliminary remarks toward the development of an ecofeminist theory of radical democracy. Finally, in the Conclusion, I summarize the argument that has developed in the preceding chapters and speculate on the possible future directions for Green politics and for ecofeminism.

1 • Ecofeminist Roots

Although it hardly seems likely in a decade characterized by an overwhelming assault on the gains of the feminist movement in television, print media, education, and the workplace, the 1980s marked the birth and coming of age of ecofeminism in the United States. The decade was bookended by two events that signify the direction and development of ecofeminism: on one end was the April 1980 conference "Women and Life on Earth: Eco-Feminism in the '80s," followed in seven months by the Women's Pentagon Action in November; on the other end was the publication of the first North American ecofeminist anthology, Judith Plant's *Healing the Wounds: The Promise of Ecofeminism*,[1] and the formation in June 1989 of the Ecofeminist Caucus of the National Women's Studies Association. Between these two events was the process of a movement becoming self-conscious, naming itself, and distinguishing its views from its parent movements like any rebellious offspring. But by the end of the decade what had begun as a movement anchored in both activism and education seemed to be caught midstride, as more energy was spent on articulating and refining a theory that could provide the foundations or communicate the intentions and implications of that activism.[2] One of my intentions here, and throughout this book, is to examine how and why ecofeminism as a movement has faltered and to speculate about what might get it moving again.

During the eighties, the definition of ecofeminism had multiple meanings, as women from various backgrounds and affiliations used the word to describe their own activities and beliefs. Although outsiders could discern an ecofeminist commitment to both feminism and ecology, based on the belief that these two systems were somehow connected, the character of that connection was explained in widely various ways: Did it mean women were somehow "closer" to nature—and if so, what were the implications for men? Did it mean women and nature had experienced similar treatment under patriarchal systems? Or did it mean women who were active in both feminist and environmental movements now had a name for their dual involvements? Through the dialogue among ecofeminists addressing each of these questions, the several branches of ecofeminist thought developed. Ecofeminism has been a theory-in-process for nearly twenty years, and it is only in the mid-1990s that theorists are beginning to name the various branches of ecofeminist thought. During that developmental process, ecofeminists have been plagued by philosophers and political theorists who call the theory "internally contradictory" or "incoherent," demanding that we make up our minds on its singular definition and create a set of universal rules (a tactic antithetical to ecofeminism), or worse yet, creating taxonomies of ecofeminism and organizing our thoughts for us, without invitation. External assaults were often mirrored as internal debates, and in some cases ideological differences among ecofeminists tore at the movement, leading some people to disassociate themselves from it entirely.

What's in a Name?

Probably the most serious difficulty attending any discussion of ecofeminism is deciding whom to include: if scholars or activists do not claim the term "ecofeminism" to describe themselves or their work, is it accurate, respectful, or responsible for ecofeminists to include such people nonetheless? Many of the early texts that laid the foundation for ecofeminism—Susan Griffin's *Woman and Nature* (1978), Mary Daly's *Gyn/Ecology* (1978), Rosemary Radford Ruether's *New Woman, New Earth* (1975), Elizabeth Dodson Gray's *Green Paradise Lost* (1979), Carolyn Merchant's *The Death of Nature* (1980)[3]—did not use the term "ecofeminist" to describe their approach, and yet these books are regularly named and even discussed at length as "early ecofeminist works" by some scholars. Because some of these writers later embraced the term "ecofeminism," such discussions, though anachronistic, may not be inherently problematic.

The problem becomes more noticeable when such naming is used to refer to the activism of those who have not claimed the term—and to name their activism as an articulation of ecofeminism. Because every action articulates a theory, however simple or complex, naming the activism of others in a way that they have not effectively puts words in their mouths; contradicts, silences, or erases their activist speech; and colonizes or appropriates their labor for the use of others. The problem becomes obvious, finally, when one realizes that the naming and appropriation is taking place across the lines of race, class, or nationality: that is, the activism most likely to be named as exemplifying eco-feminism is the activism of women or communities of color (i.e., the environ-mental justice movement), working-class or poor women (i.e., the antitoxics movement), or women in the third world (i.e., the chipko movement)—and those most likely to engage in such naming tend to be white, middle-class aca-demic women in industrialized nations.

This same problem is very much at work in the "origin stories" of eco-feminism. In 1988, an article in *Studies in the Humanities* attributed the cre-ation of the word "ecofeminism" to a French writer, Françoise d'Eaubonne, and her 1974 publication *Le féminisme ou la mort.*[4] From that point forward, many writers cited this attribution without verification, and the cumulative force of so many citations angered some and puzzled others, who felt certain they had learned the term elsewhere. In a 1991 review published in *Hypatia*, Ariel Salleh was the first writer to challenge the attribution in print, asserting that "the term 'ecofeminism' [appeared] spontaneously . . . across several continents during the 1970s" and that d'Eaubonne's 1974 text was not translated into English until fifteen years after its initial publication.[5] Some ecofeminists, perhaps anticipat-ing this charge, had claimed that the substance of d'Eaubonne's argument was found in translation, excerpted in Elaine Marks and Isabelle deCourtivron's an-thology *New French Feminisms*—but even if this is the case, the word "ecofemi-nism" still did not appear in the excerpted text.[6] Others, such as Carol Adams, claim they had learned the term "ecofeminism" from Mary Daly, whose work *Gyn/Ecology* had used it in 1978 and whose classes included a study of Françoise d'Eaubonne's text in its original language.[7] What none of these defenses of d'Eaubonne addresses is the different political implications of attributing the origin of the term (and, by implication, the movement and the ideas behind it) to a lone, white, first world scholar—or to the "spontaneous combustion" of many women around the globe.

Salleh comes closest to this speculation, when she observes that, "for politico-economic reasons, . . . ecofeminists working from more visible niches in the dominant English-speaking culture have tended to get their views broad-cast first—even feminism is touched by its imperialist context."[8] It would seem that the dispute over the lineage of "ecofeminism" has been to some extent a class war over whether the idea was born from a single woman laboring alone in the library or from many women laboring in the forests, the military bases, and the nuclear power plants. For ecofeminists who want to open up the movement in such a way that activists themselves will claim the term, a more populist origin for the word would seem to have better strategic appeal. Fortunately, it's also true.

In the United States, it seems, the term "ecofeminism"—both the concept and the movement—formally originated at the Institute for Social Ecology, where it was used as the title of summer courses offered there by Ynestra King, who notes:

> At the time that I wrote "Feminism and the Revolt of Nature" and began thinking about the relationship between these things, "ecofeminism" was a term that I came up with. It's sort of an obvious term, in a way; when you put these things together, that's the word that makes sense, that comes up to talk about them. I understood later that Françoise d'Eaubonne in France had also used this term, "ecofeminism," and Mary Daly came out with *Gyn/Ecology* in which she used the term "ecofeminism" as well, right around the same time.[9]

Throughout the eighties, many women thought they had invented the word "ecofeminism" themselves, to describe their activism and their way of thinking. Others who heard the word for the first time immediately recognized it as having deep resonance with their beliefs and values. Charlene Spretnak explains: "After the ecofeminist conference at USC in 1987, when *Ms.* had just a little write-up about it, they got all these letters saying, 'I've never heard of this, but I know this is for me.' 'Ecofeminism—yes! This is what I do in my community. I'm an ecofeminist.' It was just an amazing response. . . . The word had a lot of power to the people who heard it, because they had already thought through this connection."[10]

What is clear is that "ecofeminism" was not the brainchild of a single identifiable woman. The movement can trace its roots to the work of Rachel Carson, whose research on the effects of pesticides on lakes and birds was assailed by the chemical industry and whose own premature death from breast cancer foretold the entirely unromantic links connecting women, animals, and nature, links it would take ecofeminists thirty more years to uncover. The work of women gardeners (Bernadette Cozart, Mattie Davenport, Kate Sessions, Celia Thaxter) and illustrators (Grace Albee, Lucy Say, Deborah Passmore), the stories of Native American women (Paula Gunn Allen, Leslie Marmon Silko, Pauline Johnson) and African-American women (Zora Neale Hurston, Toni Morrison, Alice Walker), even the literary tradition of women regionalist and revolutionary writers (Sarah Orne Jewett, Willa Cather, Mary Austin, Mary Wilkins Freeman, Elizabeth Stuart Phelps, Meridel Le Seuer) all created a climate and a tradition that can be claimed as foundational to ecofeminism.[11] More immediately, however, ecofeminists themselves have named the paths that drew them to an expanded vision of the functioning of oppression and the need to liberate woman and nature simultaneously.

A Geography of Ecofeminisms

The idea for illustrating the various ecofeminisms came to me one summer in Wyoming, as I watched the late afternoon sun fall behind the Grand Tetons, casting their shadows across Jackson Lake. Although it was August, I could see glacier packs on the high slopes and from them could trace the paths the snow-melt might take as it poured into the lake. From my position on the land, I could see various trails that led toward the lake, both from the field around it and down from the mountains themselves. In the lake were several islands, and though I couldn't see them from where I stood, the map showed there were a few creeks feeding the lake on the north end and several possible outflows to the east and south. Figure 1 (p. 16) took shape for me from that landscape.

Women have arrived at ecofeminist insights through a variety of paths and perspectives. In this drawing, I have depicted the various paths of activism leading to the lake of ecofeminism as peace and antinuclear activism, feminist spirituality, animal liberation, environmentalism, and antitoxics work. Next to the paths leading to ecofeminism, I have taken care to draw some dry stream-beds. These lines represent the paths that might have led torrents of feminists to ecofeminism but that never drew more than a trickle—the streams of labor activism, civil rights activism, and the movement for gay/lesbian/bisexual/transgender (GLBT) liberation. Why didn't activists from these three movements feel drawn to ecofeminism?

For GLBT and civil rights activists, the immediate issues of human rights (i.e., fighting discrimination in employment and housing, combating violence, challenging oppressive legislation) have demanded tremendous efforts in mounting educational campaigns, drafting legislation, and building community—basic issues of survival and well-being that take precedence over all else.

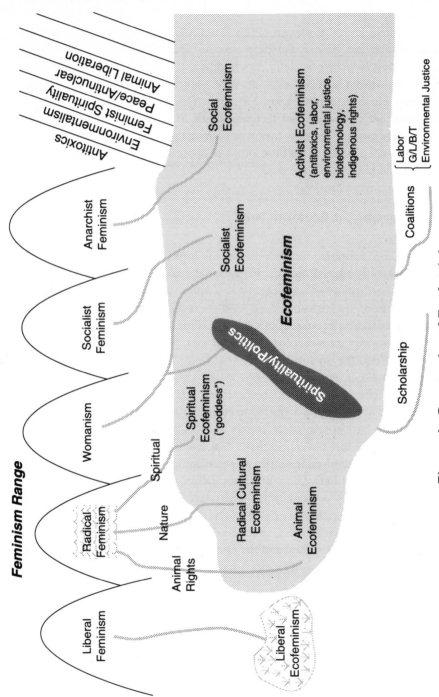

Figure 1: Geography of Ecofeminisms

In the nineties, however, more civil rights activists are confronting issues of environmental justice, as threats to human health and environmental health are most evident in poor communities and communities of color. This added dimension has given hope to social movement scholars and activists alike, for they see in the environmental justice movement the potential for a broad-based coalition powerful enough to resist oppression and to provide leadership for genuine social transformation.[12]

Similarly, labor activists have focused their efforts on resuscitating a labor movement in the United States, since union memberships declined after World War II, dropping from 34 percent in 1955 to 29 percent in 1975 and 18 percent in 1985, and in the 1990s have hovered around a mere 12 percent nationwide.[13] In 1996, with the creation of the Labor Party Advocates—a third party that requires each of its members to belong to a union—there has been new hope in rebuilding a labor movement as well. Because the concerns of labor, civil rights, and GLBT liberation movements are integral to ecofeminism, it is crucial that ecofeminists build conceptual and concrete alliances with these movements if ecofeminism is to participate in building the diverse and liberatory movement it envisions. At the bottom of the lake, then, I have drawn an outflow of coalitions between ecofeminism and these other liberatory movements.

This geography of ecofeminisms purposely distinguishes between paths and mountain streams as different sources. One shouldn't assume from this distinction that these paths didn't originate in feminist thought—indeed, they may have, from a path on the side of the mountains not depicted. But those activist paths brought in many women unfamiliar with feminist thought and introduced them to a particular form of activism that some may have followed on to ecofeminism. I want to emphasize the distinction between the route taken by the streams of thought and the route of vision channeled through activism and on to a new theoretical perspective. The various forms of activism are depicted as paths because each requires the embodied presence of participants; the lake is nestled against the base of the feminism range of mountains, because this relationship shapes the contours of the lake itself. Ecofeminism is fundamentally a feminist theory. I chose to depict ecofeminism as a lake because I like the metaphor of water: it is the base substance of all life. In many of the most ancient myths, the earth is covered with water "in the beginning" until a goddess begins creation. Our human bodies are said to be mostly water. Water both nourishes and replenishes the land. Finally, the water metaphor embodies the reality that all the various sources and emphases within ecofeminism flow together. Many ecofeminists have originated their work with one specific focus and then moved to another; the water metaphor captures that flexibility and movement. Using this geography as a departure point, I first discuss the paths of activism and then turn to a more detailed treatment of feminist theories and their influence on ecofeminist thought. Throughout this discussion, I point out what features of ecofeminism are not described by such a geography.

Peace and Antinuclear Activism

In the United States, the ecofeminist movement's most visible origin can be found in two events of 1980: the Women and Life on Earth conference and the Women's Pentagon Action. Both were shaped in the context of the feminist peace movement and were organized by feminists who had worked in the antinuclear Clamshell Alliance. Ynestra King, a principal organizer of both events, explains that the motivation for the conference was to bring together ecology and antimilitarism in a feminist framework, making it clear that these were feminist issues. Many women responded to the call for a conference, making it evident that the convergence of feminism, ecology, and peace was already apparent. Forced to limit the number of conference participants, organizers had to turn away many who expressed interest, and in the end more than eight hundred women attended. Out of that conference came the idea for a feminist action at the Pentagon.

The Women's Pentagon Action had elements of ritual and spirituality in its four components, but one of its most remarkable aspects was that there were no speakers or leaders; everyone participated equally.[14] After a series of workshops on the first day, the action of the second day was organized in four stages: mourning, rage, empowerment, defiance. For mourning, the women put on mourning veils and walked through Arlington National Cemetery, then planted cardboard gravestones at the Pentagon. These gravestones commemorated women who had died as a result of wars, rape, illegal abortions, and more. To express rage, the women shouted and ripped off their mourning veils, shaking their fists at the Pentagon. The empowerment segment involved encircling the Pentagon with a "ribbon of life" made of yarn, fabric, and ribbon, and entwined with photographs of loved ones, natural objects such as leaves and twigs, and pieces of paper inscribed with poems, messages, or the names of those women who wanted to be present but could not participate. During the final stage of the action, defiance, women engaged in civil disobedience by weaving closed the doors of the Pentagon with yarn and sitting on the steps in protest.

After a period in which the police repeatedly cut away the yarn and advised the protesters to move away from the entrance, there was a series of arrests. Meanwhile, others continued chanting or meditating on cracking the walls of the Pentagon and what those walls represented: "Witches from New York State created a large women's symbol with cornmeal; inside of it was a pentagram of cornmeal; inside of that was a pentagon of ashes, which they swept away into the pentagram."[15] According to King, only two thousand women participated in the action in 1980 and four thousand in 1981, but its message, particularly as articulated through the Unity Statement, influenced feminist peace activists around the world.[16]

The Unity Statement from the Women's Pentagon Action is probably the first—and possibly the only—ecofeminist "manifesto." The first half of the statement defines the problem to which the assembly is responding, and the second half lists the changes that must be made to solve that problem. Militarism, and its objective correlative, the Pentagon, is named as the force destroying life on earth: by channeling social wealth into the military instead of into maintaining the social infrastructure, by deploying nuclear weapons with the potential to destroy entire nations in a single blast, by creating toxic waste and storing it near those persons least able to resist, and by fostering relations of violence and domination, militarism is a force of annihilation, a "sickness transferred . . . through the fathers to the sons." The women demand an end to male violence in all its forms (warfare, poverty, educational deprivation and distortion, battering, rape, pornography, reproductive control, heterosexism, racism, nuclear power), an end to oppression, an end to warfare. In the last six paragraphs, the Unity Statement explicitly names women and ecology as forces opposed to militarism and corporatism.[17]

Authored primarily by Grace Paley and Ynestra King, the Unity Statement is an accurate snapshot of ecofeminism at its emergence and a forecast of its development over the next decade. The introductory emphasis on militarism as the root cause of the problem shows this first manifestation of ecofeminism as originating from the peace movement. There is no direct mention of women's spirituality, for example, or of the need for animal liberation; the military's destruction of nature is framed primarily in terms of its impact on humans rather than on the environment itself. And the connections between corporations and the military—connections that would move to the center of ecofeminist analysis as it developed a broader scope historically and internationally— are left to the end of the statement. Sexism, racism, classism, heterosexism, and colonialism are implied as sharing equal status as linked consequences of militarism. Later ecofeminists would name patriarchy in general, or the domination of women by men, as the root cause of oppression and then move away from analyses of root causes entirely, to focus on the present functioning and interconnections among various forms of oppression. But in the Unity Statement, many components of ecofeminist analysis were presented.

A 1981 anthology of primarily radical cultural feminist activism, *Fight Back! Feminist Resistance to Male Violence,* contained both the Unity Statement and an essay summarizing the Women's Pentagon Action. The essay's two authors, Tacie Dejanikus and Stella Dawson, critiqued the Unity Statement for its alleged essentialism (termed "biological determinism"), its crafting of feminist positions from feminine positions (women's status as mothers and as nurturers as a potential political position), and its naming of militarism (and later in the statement, corporatism and by implication capitalism) as a root cause.[18] Each of these points would be developed later by critics of ecofeminism, who argued that an appeal to essentialist connections between women and nature would do nothing to liberate men and thus nothing to stop the source of the problems ecofeminists describe (accepting for a moment the attribution of violence, corporatism, domination, and militarism primarily to men of a certain race and class). Moreover, arguments that appeal to the biological "closeness" of women and nature are more often used to justify women's "natural" role as caregivers and childbearers rather than as bricklayers or politicians. In sum, essentialist arguments have the tendency to become regressive, and they do nothing to challenge the dualisms of patriarchal thought, which associate men/reason/culture and define them in opposition to women/emotion/nature.

Throughout the second wave of feminism, theorists have repeatedly observed that liberatory, feminist positions cannot be created solely by revaluing the traditional and devalued roles or characteristics attributed to women: valuing rather than devaluing housework, for example, may lead to the liberal feminist demand of wages for housework, but it does not challenge the separate-spheres doctrine of liberalism, which sees housework as a primarily female occupation. Similarly, crafting a political theory from women's traditional roles as nurturers and caregivers—a strategy used most popularly by proponents of women's caring—has been challenged as the slippery slope leading back to women's subordination as compulsory caregivers, given that the cultural context of male not-caring has been a locus of male power. Finally, the attribution of "root cause" to any one system of subordination—whether patriarchal theology, sexism, capitalism, militarism, or the subordination of nature to humans—has the tendency to establish a hierarchy of oppression; that is, the liberation of one group or the termination of one oppressive system becomes the exclusive focus of emancipatory efforts, based on the belief that achieving this goal will have a ripple effect of liberating all other oppressed groups. As Dejanikus and Dawson state, "It is dangerous to believe that ending militarism will end the oppression of women, even though there is a link between them, just as it is misleading to believe that ending capitalism will end women's oppression, even though there is a link between them."[19] Not only have such beliefs proved to be inaccurate, but, from an activist perspective, the "root cause" rhetoric itself is flawed in that it provides a feeble means for building coalitions across difference: how many groups will be persuaded to work on issues that they perceive as tangential though related to their own, motivated by the promise that their own goals will be realized as an afterthought?

Each of these three challenges to the Unity Statement not only is defensible but previews a later and lengthier development within ecofeminism, articulating and responding to such challenges. Foreshadowing academic (primarily socialist) feminism's resistance to ecofeminism, Dejanikus and Dawson focus their strongest critique on the Unity Statement's inclusiveness of issues. That is, while claiming that "feminism has always been broad" (by which they seem to mean that radical feminism has contained an implicit critique of militarism, capitalism, naturism, and so on), the authors caution against broadening a feminist critique, on the grounds that women's issues will be "subsumed by so-called wider issues."[20] Thus, although ostensibly rejecting appeals to a "root cause" of oppression, the authors nonetheless maintain a hierarchical structure of thought which requires that genuine feminist activism be focused primarily on women, and they are unable to recognize an interconnected structure of thought in which women's oppression is one of many forms of oppression that are now so tightly interlinked that they must be challenged together. "We agree that women should work on the issue they feel most deeply about," they write, "but if as feminists [the Women's Pentagon activists] choose to work on militarism, then surely that work will be focused on how militarism specifically affects women. If that is not the primary focus," they continue, "the political work is not specifically feminist, even if the group chooses to work with women only to avoid sexism."[21] Just as ecofeminists would join deep ecologists in describing environmental problems as a result of anthropocentrism (but would refine that critique to its more specific form, androcentrism), so too ecofeminists would point out the femocentrism of standard radical feminist and socialist feminist critiques such as the one offered by Dejanikus and Dawson.

The WomanEarth Feminist Peace Institute was another form of ecofeminist activism that grew out of a feminist engagement with the peace movement.[22] Together, Ynestra King and Starhawk discussed the need for an ecofeminist educational institution that would focus on the connections linking feminist peace politics, ecology, and spirituality. Inspired by peace activist and lesbian feminist Barbara Deming, who told Ynestra King that feminism would never go forward without addressing the conflicts of race among women, King approached Barbara Smith of Kitchen Table Press for advice. Smith suggested the concept of racial parity as a foundation for the organization—meaning that an equal number of white women and women of color would be present as organizers and as participants at any organizational event—and made racial parity the condition for her participation. Thanks to Smith, other women of color were brought into the project, and out of their collaboration the idea for WomanEarth became a reality. In the three years (1986–89) that it was alive, WomanEarth sponsored only one public conference, though the organizers met a number of times during those years. During that time, however, the group experienced difficulties with funding and eventually dissolved, in part because of the different goals and expectations of the key organizers. At least one other problem may have been the organization's low profile and lack of publicity; the first essays to be written about it were published the same year WomanEarth disbanded.[23]

Feminist Spirituality

Another path to ecofeminism for many women was the feminist spirituality movement. Both the feminist peace movement and the women's spirituality movement emphasized the importance of recognizing connections among various forms of oppression and revaluing characteristics traditionally associated with women under patriarchy. The interconnections among these movements can be seen in the way both the people and the core philosophies intersect: for example, Starhawk, author of such books as *The Spiral Dance* (1979) and *Dreaming the Dark* (1982),[24] and promoter of witchcraft and pagan philosophy, worked closely with Ynestra King from 1984 to 1986, planning what would become WomanEarth Feminist Peace Institute. The two saw a symmetry between their cherished goals of fostering the connections among the ecology movement, the feminist peace movement (King), and the feminist spirituality movement (Starhawk). Both were committed to creating an ecofeminist institution that was antiracist. Luisah Teish, a Yoruban priestess who began teaching in 1977, and author of *Jambalaya* (1985), was one of the women who came on board the institute, and she came up with the name "WomanEarth" through a ritual chant.[25]

Women's spirituality gained increasing prominence in the 1970s, as archaeological discoveries reported in the sixties gained greater exposure and discussion. James Mellaart, the archaeologist in charge of the excavations at Çatal Hüyük, reported in 1967 that the findings there indicated a matriarchal society whose utopian character was unsurpassed: no signs of violence, warfare, or bloodshed were present, and there were no military fortifications of any kind.[26] Instead, countless figurines of the female body were found, and the supreme deity placed in each of the temples was a goddess; both discoveries were interpreted as evidence that women were held in high social esteem as incarnations of the divine. Digs at Hacilar, Mersin, and other sites around the Mediterranean yielded similar finds and pointed to the probability of a Neolithic civilization that was peaceful, agricultural, and matriarchal. These discoveries had a considerable impact on the budding feminist spirituality movement, which had already begun to connect the social, political, and religious devaluation and oppression of women. Books such as Elizabeth Gould Davis's *The First Sex* (1971), Mary Daly's *Beyond God the Father* (1973), Sheila Collins's *A Different Heaven and Earth* (1974), Merlin Stone's *When God Was a Woman* (1976), Marija Gimbutas's *The Gods and Goddesses of Old Europe* (1974), along with special issues of journals and many essays and speeches, represented an outpouring of interest in prepatriarchal history and its implications for a new feminist spirituality.[27] The goddess cultures also had significance for a new relationship with the earth and the animals of the earth: in these egalitarian cultures, animals were domesticated for companionship, milk, or wool, but the diet of the societies was primarily vegetarian.[28] Moreover, a peaceful relationship with the rest of nature seemed intricately connected to the status of women. Nature was perceived not as a force to be dominated but rather as a living being from which all life came and to which offerings and devotion were to be given. Although criticized by those feminists who viewed spirituality and politics as antithetical forces, the feminist spirituality movement was seen as crucial to the women's liberation movement and the ecology movement by its adherents. According to Charlene Spretnak, a leading advocate of feminist spirituality, "the largest mobilized force trying to defeat us" as feminists was the force of patriarchal religions; feminist spirituality was a strategic, political means of defense.[29] Advocates of feminist spirituality saw it as a source of empowerment that would fuel their liberatory struggles on behalf of women and the earth. The early insights of feminist spirituality seemed fundamentally compatible with those of ecofeminism.

In 1982, shortly after the Women's Pentagon Action and well before the formation of WomanEarth, Charlene Spretnak's anthology *The Politics of Women's Spirituality* appeared, containing an essay that described the Women's Pentagon Action and reprinted the Unity Statement. Spretnak herself has embodied the intersections of the various movements associated with ecofeminism: a prime mover in the feminist spirituality movement, contributor to both Plant's *Healing the Wounds* and Irene Diamond and Gloria Feman Orenstein's *Reweaving the World*, and a later affiliate of the WomanEarth Institute, Spretnak is also a central activist in the Green movement. Her book coauthored with Fritjof Capra, *Green Politics* (1984), her role in launching the Committees of Correspondence (forerunner to the Greens/Green Party U.S.A.) in 1984, and her authorship of *The Spiritual Dimension of Green Politics* all point to the intersections among these movements.[30]

Finally, the first major anthology on feminism and nonviolence, Pam McAllister's *Reweaving the Web of Life*, published the same year as Spretnak's anthology on feminist spirituality, demonstrated the theoretical connections among the movements feeding ecofeminism: on the cover was a photograph of "participants at the Women's Pentagon Action sit[ting] beneath their web of colorful strings and yarn woven as an act of empowerment, defiance and love"; inside, the anthology included seven essays on racism as violence, and essay on women and animal rights, and excerpts from the Women's Pentagon Action Unity Statement. While WomanEarth pursued these connections by emphasizing the fundamental violence of both racism and militarism, few of these ecofeminists recognized the similarities between violence against women and violence against animals. For other ecofeminists, however, vegetarianism appeared to be the logical way of bringing nonviolence home, from the direct action movement to the dinner table.

Animal Liberation Activism

When women active within the animal rights movement also became active within the women's movement and began examining their lives from a feminist perspective, they became aware of the gendered composition of the animal rights movement. As Josephine Donovan has remarked, "Certainly women are 70 to 80 percent of the animal rights movement. Much of the theory, of course, has been done by men, and many of the leadership positions of course are held by men. So here's an obvious case where feminism has something to say. If women really dominate the animals rights movement, then women's ideas, feminist ideas, and feminist leadership should too."[31] Instead, the theory of the animal rights movement had been articulated through the writings of philosophers such as Peter Singer and Tom Regan, who sought to ground animal liberation on a rational rather than an emotional foundation.[32] Yet their works did not articulate the motivations of the women who had constituted the majority of animal rights activists for the past century. In feminism's second wave, many of these animal rights feminists saw the oppression of animals as part of a larger oppression of nature and sought ways to link their activism on behalf of women, animals, and nature. The emergence of animal rights feminists into ecofeminism can be traced by the progression of essays addressing the connections between women's and animal liberation.

The first essay on feminism and vegetarianism to receive national distribution, Carol Adams's "The Oedible Complex," appeared in the 1975 publication of *The Lesbian Reader* and was followed in 1978 by Laurel Holliday's *The Violent Sex.*[33] In these texts, Adams and Holliday explicitly associated hunting and meat-eating with patriarchy and described both as quintessentially male behaviors. Throughout the 1970s, as feminists worked to establish a separate women's culture through businesses and social networks, the idea that feminists could also dissociate themselves from the male diet of violence inherent in carnivorism had definite persuasive appeal. In 1982, Marti Kheel and Tina Frisco founded Feminists for Animal Rights, a group committed to exploring connections between the exploitation of women and that of animals. Throughout the 1980s, essays by Ingrid Newkirk, Gena Corea, and Karen Davis linking the oppression of women with the oppression of animals appeared in the *Animals' Agenda,* a publication of the animal rights movement, in an attempt to encourage women animal rights activists to make the connection to feminism. From the other direction, feminists were encouraged to examine the links between sexism and speciesism through Aviva Cantor's essay "The Club, the Yoke, and the Leash: What We Can Learn from the Way a Culture Treats Animals," published in August 1983 in *Ms.* magazine.[34] Eight years after Carol Adams's initial exploratory essay written for a lesbian audience, Cantor's article brought animal liberation into an exclusively feminist context, offering a feminist critique of sexism and speciesism as interlocking, twin oppressions. But *Ms.* editors were not especially welcoming of animal rights feminists, and writers turned to other publications. When animal rights feminist Merle Hoffman became editor of the feminist newsjournal *On the Issues,* animal rights feminists gained access to another feminist publication. Meanwhile, animal rights feminists began making connections to other forms of oppression: several of Alice Walker's essays, such as "Am I Blue" and "Why Did the Balinese Chicken Cross the Road?" along with Marjorie Spiegel's *The Dreaded Comparison: Human and Animal Slavery*

(1988), extended the connections between sexism and speciesism to include racism as well.[35]

For many, the woman-animal connection led to ecofeminism when activists shifted their attention from the object of oppression to the structure of oppression itself. Carol Adams has explained her own path to ecofeminism in a way that exemplifies this progression:

> When I wrote *The Sexual Politics of Meat*, I didn't think of myself as an ecofeminist, and I didn't even realize there was a big debate going on about ecofeminism versus deep ecology. My roots were so strongly in the battered women's movement and the movement against violence against women; I knew animal rights language didn't speak to me, and I was looking for an alternate theory. But when *The Sexual Politics of Meat* was published, suddenly I began being written up as an ecofeminist and I realized I ought to figure that out: how did I relate to ecofeminism? And at first I resisted that, because like Catherine MacKinnon's book, *Feminism Unmodified*—why did feminism have to be "modified"? So I had to work that through for myself, and I realized that, yes, "eco-" is an appropriate modifier for feminism for a number of reasons—including the fact that women are often the people who have to mediate environmental exploitation, along with people of color and other nondominant people. Once I realized that my analysis inevitably led to the interconnections of human slavery, animal slavery, and women's oppression, then ecofeminism was the logical place from which I would articulate theory and articulate solutions.[36]

In some cases, animal rights feminists came to ecofeminism by mistakenly being associated with ecofeminism and taking that opportunity to examine their own relationship to ecofeminism. In other cases, animal rights feminists found themselves working with ecofeminist activists on specific projects and, through the exchange of ideas, adopted ecofeminism as a more comprehensive description for views they had already thought through for themselves.

Environmental Activism

> I guess people would probably call themselves ecofeminists if asked, but people don't really think of it in those terms. We're just a community that's defending the earth and battling against this corporation. You

know, we're defending both the human and nonhuman parts of our community against the assault of this corporation.

—Judi Bari, February 26, 1995

Another path into ecofeminism has been the route of environmental activism, as many women who had been active in various environmental organizations found themselves working side by side with men whose sexism they would have denounced in any other context. The kind of macho heroism first depicted in Edward Abbey's *Desert Solitaire* and *The Monkey Wrench Gang* has been no fiction in many radical environmental organizations.[37] Women working in these groups have struggled to make their voices heard and have yearned for a community in which their dual identities of feminist and environmentalist could find a home. In her northern California Earth First! group, Judi Bari and others have addressed these problems by occasionally holding women-only demonstrations and by engaging in debate within the pages of *Earth First! Journal.* Judi Bari described one such action:

The Albion Uprising occurred in 1992 when Louisiana Pacific tried to cut one of the last remaining relatively intact watersheds in our area. . . . We actually developed in particular one women's tactic there that was explicitly developed as a women's tactic. We had a solstice women's gathering, and we talked about, why are there not more women in these demonstrations, even though there were a lot of women, but not compared to the population. And we discussed the fact that, well, women can't just show up, they have to get child care. Can't risk arrest because they have to be to work the next day to take care of their kids. So we talked about it and we came up with specifically answering those needs: this tactic that was called yarning. And what we do is we take yarn and we go out at night so you can get child care and you can get everything arranged; there's a very low arrest risk. And we weave it in and out and in and out and in and out of the trees, and it may not sound like much, but it turned out to be, it really slowed them down. And all these tactics only slow them down, they don't stop them. Because when they come in and try to cut it with their chainsaw, the yarn wraps around the chainsaw and stalls the chainsaw out. And if they try to whack it with their logger's axe, which is always their next thing, the logger's axe bounces off. And actually the most efficient and aggressively nonmacho way to get rid of a web is to cut it with a scissors—but they won't do that, they use their knives instead, which takes longer.

So yarning became our symbol. We yarned everything. I mean, everything you can think of. Even if we'd block a truck in the middle of the road, we yarned the truck. So it totally became the symbol of the Albion Uprising, and along with it developed a mythology: we said to the loggers when they were getting ready to cut it, we said, "This is the web of life, and when the web is cut, the spell is cast." Just little things like that to freak them out.[38]

Although women-only actions may give feminist environmentalists a break from male sexism (though not women's sexism) within their movement, these and other examples of feminist activism do not necessarily indicate that activists have embraced the philosophy or the terminology of ecofeminism. In many situations, women environmentalists believe the urgency of their struggle requires that they subordinate their complaints about sexism within the movement in order to work more effectively with the men whose environmental goals they share. In such instances, these women environmentalists perceive the concepts and the language of ecofeminism to be more divisive than inclusive.

Antitoxics Activism

One time I was reading the newsletter from the Citizens' Clearinghouse for Hazardous Waste, and the president's column by Lois Gibbs was very ecofeminist. And so I just telephoned her out of the blue, and introduced myself, and I asked her, "Do you self-identify as an ecofeminist?" And Lois Gibbs said, "Oh yes, absolutely. But very few women in this national network do, because they don't like the word 'feminist'— they would say, 'Oh, those are people who hate men'—and they don't like the words 'ecologist' or 'environmentalist,' because they would say, 'Oh, those are people who care more about bunnies and deer than people.'" So many of them would identify as a community activist because they don't like the ecofeminist label. But she feels what they are doing is ecofeminist work as she understands it, and I agree.

—Charlene Spretnak, June 5, 1993

For other women, activism in the antitoxics movement and particularly the feminist movement around breast cancer has served to illuminate the connections between human health and environmental health, connections that lead to an ecofeminist critique. In the Great Lakes region, women discovered that chemicals such as chlorine and dioxin were directly linked to various diseases affecting the great bodies of water, fish bodies, and women's bodies. In a suburb of Niagara Falls named Love Canal, Lois Gibbs found connections between military waste and childhood illnesses such as leukemia, and her experiences led to the founding of the Citizens' Clearinghouse for Hazardous Waste.[39] Whether fighting breast cancer or chemical pollution, women activists have found a strong correlation between the siting of toxic waste and the economies of the communities where it is located: poor, working-class, or communities of color are most likely to be targeted as "dumps" for toxic waste and for polluting industries. In Canada and in England, the Stop the Whitewash campaign uncovered the hazardous links between chlorine bleaching of tampons and baby diapers and the high rates of cervical and uterine cancers among young women. The link connecting chlorine bleaching, asbestos, and tampons was first proclaimed to a feminist audience in *Ms.* and later to an ecofeminist audience in Ellen Bass's poem "Tampons."[40] In the 1990s, the environmental causes of breast cancer and the links among organochlorines, radioactive fallout, and hormones added to meat and dairy products all received greater attention in the writing of feminist activists. Terry Tempest Williams's short story, "The Clan of One-Breasted Women," links breast cancer and ecological destruction to the radioactive fallout from the nuclear bomb testing of the 1950s in southern Utah and Nevada.[41] Writers and activists Liane Clorfene-Casten, Judy Brady, and Joan D'Argo have all used the issue of breast cancer to address the links between women's health and environmental health.[42] Their arguments and activism articulate the fundamental insights of ecofeminism.

The Path of Lived Experiences

Finally, of course, women who may or may not have been activists began making the connections to ecofeminism from their own personal experiences. As Charlene Spretnak has explained, for some women, the postorgasmic sense of interconnection ("body parables") may have been their first insight; for others, it was earth-based spiritual practices, memories from childhood, or simply moments of deep insight into the interrelationship of all life on earth.[43] Ecological feminist philosopher Karen Warren describes her awakening to ecofeminism as one of these experiences:

It was actually personally for me a rock-climbing experience that made me an ecofeminist, where I realized that within the span of a few days not only had my beliefs and values changed, but my behavior toward a rock had changed. I had gone from climbing it—trying to conquer it, trying to make it to the top with speed and agility as an athlete—to just being with the rock, and noticing the lichen and noticing the fungus, and noticing where the cracks in the rock were wet, and listening to the hummingbirds off of Lake Superior. And when I climbed that way, I not only had a lovely climb, but I came to realize that even though the rock was probably oblivious to my existence, I could climb it in very different ways. And that my relationship to the rock was really up to me. That I could climb it as a conqueror or I could climb it as a friend; I could climb it as someone who cared about it.

And that's when I first realized in 1981 that I didn't have a language to describe the second way of climbing. That all of my training was in the conquering mode, the rationalistic conquering control mode. And if I started thinking about being reciprocal with the rock, I didn't have anywhere in the philosophical lexicon to go. So I just started working with it, and asking, What would an ethic look like if the relationship were central, and not the nature of the relators? That the question would not be, Is the rock a moral agent? but rather, How do you as a moral agent relate to the rock? . . . I realized that those kinds of concerns were exactly the kinds of concerns that women who called themselves ecofeminists were raising.[44]

For Lourdes Arguëlles, reading about ecofeminism gave her a language and a conceptual framework for insights and beliefs she had held for many years:

Ever since I was a child I felt very strongly connected spiritually with the nonhuman animal world. Although I didn't have the critical insights about my relations with that nonhuman animal world, the connection was there from the time I was a child. Ecofeminism resonated with memories from childhood, and enabled me, empowered me, encouraged me to reclaim those things that had started in childhood, perhaps never reached fruition. . . . [It] made the feelings conceptually clear.[45]

The paths of lived experiences are not drawn on this geography of ecofeminism, simply because they are too numerous: there are different paths for every person. What can be said is that activism and lived experiences are strong conduits to ecofeminism—just as strong as the streams of feminist theory that have shaped the intellectual and philosophical aspects of ecofeminism.

The Range of Feminist Theories and the Streams of Ecofeminisms

Some have wondered whether ecofeminism began as a feminist rebellion within environmentalism or as an environmentalist rebellion within feminism, but to me, this seems like the wrong question to ask. Ecofeminism is not a rebellion in any sense of the word but rather a coming together of insights gained from various movements and historical events; unlike a rebellion, ecofeminism offers both a critique of existing conditions and an alternative; it is both multiple and diverse. Hence, it seemed more descriptive to depict the varieties of feminism as a range of mountains against which the insights of various other liberatory movements have flowed and whose contours have shaped every variety of ecofeminism. Ecofeminism is a perspective growing out of the realization that there are fundamental similarities among the many structures of oppression. In its origins, development, and present directions, ecofeminism flows very clearly from feminist thought. Recalling the history of feminism in the United States, from the "first wave" of liberal feminism in the nineteenth century to the "second wave" of radical feminism in the 1960s and 1970s, some today have claimed that ecofeminism may be feminism's "third wave." Val Plumwood notes: "It is not a tsunami, a freak tidal wave which has appeared out of nowhere sweeping all before it, but rather is built on the work of other forms of feminism, and hence has a basis for partial agreement with each."[46]

Here I trace the influence of the several streams of feminism on the various forms of ecofeminism. Note that developing the theory or focusing one's activism on a particular aspect of ecofeminism has not prevented ecofeminists from understanding the connections among the varieties of ecofeminisms. Many scholars and activists are difficult to categorize for this very reason, that their work has addressed so many aspects of ecofeminism. Like any descriptive taxonomy, this classification scheme should be understood to have permeable boundaries (hence the water metaphor). The divisions among ecofeminisms are sometimes the result of a "focus" phenomenon, in which ecofeminists understand the range of ecofeminisms and simply choose to direct their activism and theorizing to one particular area about which they feel the most passionate or most competent; in other cases, there are deep-seated theoretical and practical differences among ecofeminisms, differences that are being explored and discussed. From the start, ecofeminists have celebrated the diversity within ecofeminism, arguing that plurality is vital to such a new theoretical perspective and must be encouraged. In 1990, Lee Quinby proclaimed, "I want to argue against these calls for coherence, comprehensiveness, and formalized agendas and cite ecofeminism as an example of theory and practice that has combated ecological destruction and patriarchal domination without succumbing to the totalizing impulses of masculinist politics." According to Quinby, "coherence in theory and centralization of practice make a social movement irrelevant or, worse, vulnerable, or—even more dangerous—participatory with forces of domination."[47] In the same year as Quinby's views were published, Karen Warren described eight "boundary conditions" of a feminist ethic and defined ecofeminism as a feminist ethic accordingly. Among those conditions was the fact that ecofeminism is "structurally pluralistic," "inclusivist," and "reconceives theory as theory in process"; moreover, ecofeminism "makes no attempt to provide an 'objective' point of view."[48] But shortly after these declarations, it seemed, the ecofeminist honeymoon ended, as ecofeminists and former ecofeminists began to challenge or criticize various forms of ecofeminism, and critics outside ecofeminism began to point out internal contradictions. It became apparent that the time had come to define our own terrain before others conclusively set the terms of the debate.

Liberal Ecofeminism

From the mountains of feminist thought, then, flow the streams of theory feeding the lake of ecofeminism. But right away, there's something unusual: the stream flowing from liberal feminism doesn't go directly into the lake but empties into an adjoining wetland, whose waters seep into the lake but do not become a full part of it. The reason for this representation is fairly straightforward: liberal feminism is a theory based on the idea that some group or groups have been excluded from a system that is basically functional. The goal of liberal feminism is to incorporate those excluded groups into the system as it currently exists and to extend rights to them based on characteristics they share with the enfranchised group. Historically, liberal feminism has been effective in addressing the concerns of white, middle-class, heterosexual women in the first world; however, it has overlooked the inequities produced by cultural and institutionalized racism in the United States and the poverty and environmental degradation created internationally by corporate capitalism, and it has tended to instrumentalize and subordinate nonhuman animals and nature. Unlike liberal feminism, ecofeminism is a theory and a movement based on the understanding that there are structural problems with the current system: social and economic inequities simply cannot be resolved within the system, because the system's functioning depends on the devaluation, oppression, and exclusion of the majority of the earth's inhabitants. Ecofeminists believe that a systemic transformation is needed if we are to achieve genuine social justice and ecological health. "Liberal ecofeminism," then, is a contradiction in terms. Yet there have been arguments for using liberal feminist strategies to address environmental problems.

For example, Australian philosopher Karen Green argues that liberal feminism offers a sufficient basis for an ethic that is both environmental and feminist. Dismissing ecofeminist claims that there are logical, conceptual, historical, and psychosexual connections between the subordination of women and the subordination of nature, Green maintains that there are nonetheless practical connections between women's emancipation and the achievement of important environmental goals. Her argument rests on the analysis that "at root, the environmental crisis is largely a crisis about overpopulation," a crisis that will be solved "when women are not forced to reproduce in order to eat, and when they are given the opportunity to fashion the world that their children will inherit along rational principles." Moreover, Green believes there is "evidence of some improvement of women's position due to the rise of capitalism," and that when women receive "education, training, and satisfying careers" within the capitalist economy, it will be possible to stabilize human populations and thus to maintain "species diversity, natural ecosystems, and the preservation of wilderness."[49] These beliefs profoundly misrepresent the problems of social injustice and environmental degradation, as many ecofeminists have repeatedly explained.[50] One of the clearest distinctions between deep ecologists and ecofeminists has been their different positions on the topic of population: whereas deep ecologists see overpopulation as a root cause of environmental degradation, ecofeminists find that all talk of population functions as a form of "blaming the victim" and furthermore does not describe the problem in a way that it can be solved. Instead, ecofeminists have suggested replacing discussions about population with analyses of first world overconsumption, the globalized operations of corporate capitalism, and the pervasiveness of sexism in denying women reproductive control, maternal and infant health care, food security, and eldercare, while simultaneously defining "real" masculinity as the ability to produce many offspring (preferably sons). Moreover, though cultural ecofeminists may have too readily spoken about "women's position," as Green does in her statement that capitalism has "improv[ed] women's position," most ecofeminists have problematized the concept of "women" and "women's position" as falsely unified categories. By uncovering the differences among women in their various positions internationally, ecofeminists have exposed the ways corporate capitalism operates to reinforce institutionalized racism and sexism, leaving the majority of the world's women overworked and impoverished while improving the position of a tiny percentage of already privileged women. In sum, the liberal feminist critique advanced by Green is inadequate for illuminating the social and ecological crises addressed through ecofeminism.

A more effective manifestation of liberal ecofeminism may be found in an organization whose founders do not use the words "feminism" or "ecofeminism." Founded in 1989 by Bella Abzug and other feminist political leaders, the Women's Environment and Development Organization (WEDO) works to incorporate the concerns of women and ecology into the governing, economic, and social systems of nations throughout the world. In November 1991, WEDO sponsored the World Women's Congress for a Healthy Planet, an international gathering of more than fifteen hundred women from eighty-three countries, to prepare a Women's Action Agenda 21 for presentation at the June 1992 United Nations Conference on Environment and Development in Brazil. Though ostensibly presented as a collaborative document, the Agenda 21 was a fairly elusive document to obtain or to amend during the congress; ecofeminists in attendance circulated a statement on factory farming, "rainforest" beef, and animal experimentation which obtained numerous signatures and yet never appeared in the final compilation.[51] Ecofeminists also deplored the essentialist rhetoric used by the WEDO organizers ("It's Time for Women to Mother Earth" and "Our Wounded Planet Needs Healing Touch of Women"), even though this rhetoric was employed strategically toward achieving feminist and ecological goals. Persistently, WEDO has maintained a multiracial (albeit elite) representation from women around the world on its International Policy Action Committee, and the issues addressed by WEDO—from breast cancer and environmental health to reproductive control, economic justice, and a living wage—touch the lives of women of all races, classes, and nationalities. In September 1995, at the UN Fourth World Conference on Women, WEDO sponsored a Second World Women's Congress and a Women's Linkage Caucus of some 1,320 nongovernmental organization (NGO) representatives.[52] All these actions indicate that WEDO is intent on becoming an effective force for improving the status of women and the health of the environment through the most powerful institutions available. Many of WEDO's goals are compatible with ecofeminism, though it would be inaccurate to describe WEDO as an ecofeminist organization (particularly since WEDO co-chairs have not claimed the term for themselves) or to maintain that WEDO's liberal strategies will necessarily lead to ecofeminist ends. Nonetheless, as Zillah Eisenstein has argued, even liberal strategies and reforms have radical implications, and there is no doubt that ecofeminists must use short-term, stop-gap reforms along the path to social transformation.[53] Because the lake of ecofeminist thought and activism takes the need for social and economic transformation as one of its defining contours, it is more accurate to locate liberal ecofeminism in the adjoining wetland.

Radical Ecofeminisms

On the mountain of radical feminism, I have drawn a glacier pack to emphasize the fact that, of all the feminist theories, radical feminism has made the strongest contributions to ecofeminism. That glacier pack is constituted of ideas articulated by Mary Daly's *Gyn/Ecology* and Susan Griffin's *Woman and Nature*. Published the same year (1978), these two extraordinary texts provided the foundation for radical ecofeminisms. Stylistically, each is determined to break the narrative of patriarchy: Griffin's book is written in a kind of postmodern poetic prose, alternating the voice of masculine culture and the voices of women/nature; Daly's book is replete with what is now seen as her trademark of fracturing and reclaiming language itself. Both books are concerned with reclaiming the silenced voices of women and nature. Griffin begins within the context of patriarchal spirituality and Platonic cosmology, exploring the woman/nature association first from the perspective of the male but progressively allowing the voice of women/nature to gain prominence. Daly makes explicit the connection between "the silencing of women and Silent Spring," remarking that Rachel Carson's findings were silenced just as the songbirds Carson defended were becoming silent. Both books name Western medicine, and particularly gynecology, as a method of patriarchal oppression of women. Griffin's "The Room of the Undressing" and "The Cave," along with Daly's "Sparking: The Fire of Female Friendship," locate the turning point that initiates women's resistance in women finding each other, believing each other, seeing each other, and in the process, of course, finally seeing and believing in themselves. Both books end in a kind of lesbian separatist utopian vision, which involves either erotic

union between women and with nature (Griffin) or a fanciful bringing to justice of the patriarchal fiends who have assailed women and nature, followed by
an erotic celebration among women-loving women (Daly). For too long it has
gone unremarked that both these authors were also lesbians—perhaps the fact
was so well known that it was overlooked, for not until recently have ecofeminists made the connection between the oppression of lesbians and the oppression of nature.[54] In clear contrast to Griffin and Daly, none of the ecofeminist
transformative visions or utopias offers an exclusively lesbian vision.[55] Some
aspects of these books, then, were left behind while other aspects were carried
forward into ecofeminism.

Apart from these similarities, *Woman and Nature* and *Gyn/Ecology* are
quite different. Whereas Griffin explores the oppression of women and nature
within patriarchal history, Daly, as a theologian, begins with the loss and dis-
placement of matriarchal goddess cultures by patriarchal culture and religion.
The body of Griffin's book develops somewhat chronologically, moving from
the early Christian fathers through the medieval era, the Renaissance, and the
scientific revolution, on to the advent of feminism and the reclaiming and
strengthening of women's perspectives. In contrast, after examining the dis-
placement of matriarchy by patriarchy, Daly's book develops cross-culturally,
describing the torture and oppression of women in various cultural traditions
and historical eras. And whereas Daly's liberatory vision seems to focus on
women, with animals and "the wild" as context, Griffin's concluding vision
emphasizes the interconnections among women, animals, and nature to such an
extent that it seems clear any liberation must involve all of them equally. Given
these utopian visions and the varieties of ecofeminism they have inspired, it is
nonetheless important to note that neither Daly nor Griffin has been an advocate for animal liberation, neither one is practicing a form of goddess spirituality, and both maintain diets that include the bodies of animals. The connections among ecofeminism, animal liberation, and goddess spirituality were made
explicit by radical ecofeminists, not by radical feminists Daly and Griffin.[56]

As the strongest voice within feminism's second wave, radical feminism
grew out of the experiences of women in the new social movements of the
1960s. Angered by their subordination as women within an ostensibly liberatory movement (the New Left), radical feminists retained a leftist critique of
class stratification and capitalist economics at the same time that they developed
a thoroughgoing analysis of the ways patriarchal culture affects every aspect of
society.[57] But as Alice Echols explains, radical feminism confronted difficulties—
internal schisms among activists and divisive conflicts over differences of class

and sexuality—and ultimately was unable to withstand the antifeminist backlash that closely followed its visibility and achievements. Whereas the long-term movement goals of radical feminism were not clearly defined but seemed to involve large-scale social and economic transformations that appeared difficult if not impossible to achieve, cultural feminism held out the promise of success by suggesting that individual liberation could be realized without transforming patriarchal culture. The solution was simply to separate cultural feminists from patriarchal culture and patriarchal values. Emphasizing women's essential commonalities rather than the differences revealed by radical feminism, cultural feminism promised to unify the movement. Echols details many more differences among radical feminists and between radical and cultural feminists, but what is important here is the fact that cultural feminism also involved an explicit rejection of the Left, which it described as inherently "male." From a cultural feminist perspective, creating a feminist revolution and a gynocratic culture would necessarily bring about changes in economics and social injustices, since these were simply manifestations of a patriarchal culture. The economic critiques of the male-dominated Left were unnecessary to cultural feminism, which saw race and class oppression, militarism and environmental degradation, interpersonal and institutional violence as various aspects of patriarchy that would be abolished in a gynocratic culture. Although radical feminism held the seeds of cultural feminism from its very beginning, cultural feminism did not gain ascendancy until after 1975, and as a result, "liberal feminism became the recognized voice of the women's movement."[58] Cultural feminism also offered a context and a biological ("essentialist") explanation for women's interest in ecology, the defense of animals, and the development of a woman-centered spirituality. As in radical feminism, so too in radical ecofeminisms: these varieties of ecofeminism have the seeds for both radical and cultural manifestations. One of the future tasks of ecofeminists is to examine the effectiveness and the shortcomings of these varieties of radical ecofeminism and to strengthen the movement accordingly.

From the glacial field on radical feminism, then, three prominent streams have been drawn. The animal rights stream is closest to liberal feminism, for many who are now ecofeminists first made the connections between the oppression of women and the oppression of animals but did not specifically address the broader oppression of nature or the linked oppressions of people of color and the working class. Their main goal was to see animals incorporated into a feminist critique; such an approach aligns them most closely with liberal feminism. Yet their feminism is also marked with characteristics of the time in which it was developed (the 1970s) and bears the influence of cultural feminism: a belief in the importance of revaluing attributes traditionally associated with women, a belief in the superior nature of women for nurturing and for ensuring health and survival, a valuing of women-identified culture and relationships, and the identification of patriarchy and the masculine psychological drive for dominance as instrumental forces perpetuating the dual oppression of women and animals. As Josephine Donovan has explained:

> In the history of feminism, there are a number of feminists who have been very concerned about animal issues. The concern about nature is more of a twentieth-century phenomenon. If you go back to someone like Mary Wollstonecraft, who is considered probably the first major Western feminist theorist, she was very concerned about animal issues. Nineteenth-century feminists, the majority of them were concerned about diet, vegetarianism, animal welfare issues. The antivivisection movement of the nineteenth century was largely populated by women. So there is a whole history there of feminist involvement and concern with animal issues. It's not something new.[59]

Donovan's essay "Animal Rights and Feminist Theory" details the rich heritage of cultural feminism and argues that "the basis for a feminist ethic for the treatment of animals" emerges out of "women's relational culture of caring and attentive love."[60] Articulating another aspect of radical cultural feminism, Marti Kheel notes, "Until you address the underlying roots, what I call the psychosexual roots of our environmental crisis, you're not going to be doing anything but piecemeal change."[61] Although most of the "animal" ecofeminists today have moved away from cultural feminism, writers whose early works fit into this paradigm include Carol Adams, Marti Kheel, Constantia (Connie) Salamone, and Josephine Donovan.

The second stream, nature feminism, leads to radical cultural ecofeminism. The text that best exemplifies this perspective is Andrée Collard and Joyce Contrucci's *Rape of the Wild*, published in 1988 with an introduction by Mary Daly.[62] *Rape of the Wild* takes up the gendered "biophilic/necrophilic" distinction from Daly and applies it to nature. After reviewing some of Daly's concerns, such as the destruction of matriarchal cultures and nature-based spiritualities by patriarchal cultures and deity, the control of language as a means of thought control, and the introduction of militarism, Collard and Contrucci develop a new ecofeminist reading of patriarchal culture's domination of nature through hunting, animal experimentation, reproductive technologies, and space

exploration. Their approach forecasts ecofeminism's later concerns with reproductive technologies—Irene Diamond's *Fertile Ground*[63]—and their concluding
chapter touches on wilderness, antinuclear critiques, population concerns, and
the question of fertility itself, all topics of ecofeminist concern. In effect, *Rape of
the Wild* and *Gyn/Ecology* could be read as companion texts, for whereas *Gyn/
Ecology* foregrounds the oppression and visualizes the liberation of women primarily, *Rape of the Wild* takes the need for women's liberation as a given and
focuses on the need to liberate animals and nature from patriarchal oppression.
Together the two books give a complete picture of the critique offered by radical
cultural ecofeminism.[64]

The third stream from radical feminism, spiritual ecofeminism, comes out
of the archaeological discoveries of ancient matriarchal cultures.[65] The unique
feature of those peaceful societies was that women were esteemed not only as
mothers but as spiritual and political leaders as well. Comparing matrifocal
cultures to modern patriarchal ones, radical feminists recognized the reinforcing links between religious, cultural, and political institutions, and concluded
that transforming patriarchal religions would be crucial to the success of feminism. Since then, spiritual ecofeminists have built upon these findings in a
variety of ways. Starhawk's *Spiral Dance* and *Dreaming the Dark* showed how
modern feminists could revivify ancient goddess spirituality through witchcraft.
Charlene Spretnak's anthology, *The Politics of Women's Spirituality,* included an
array of feminist spiritualities and effectively formed the foundation for spiritual ecofeminism. Riane Eisler's *The Chalice and the Blade* appeared in 1987,
and its wide popular appeal (which marked the apex of popularity for spiritual
ecofeminism) must be attributed to the two decades of thought that had gone
before it. More recently, Carol Adams's multicultural anthology *Ecofeminism
and the Sacred* (1993) explores a wide variety of ecofeminist spiritualities and
spiritual traditions in the United States, and Rosemary Radford Ruether's anthology *Women Healing Earth* (1996) collects essays on ecology, feminism, and
spirituality from women of the third world.[66]

After a solid beginning in the critique of patriarchal religions and the
discovery of prepatriarchal goddess cultures, however, ecofeminist spirituality
has gone in many divergent directions, some of which are inherently flawed. As
Heather Eaton has explained, some varieties of spirituality claiming to be ecofeminist are in fact marred by essentialist claims about the relationship between
women and nature. Some are apolitical or politically apathetic. Some take religious symbols and practices out of their historic and cultural contexts, and
some even propose metaphors for the earth as mother, sister, lover, or home,
effectively domesticating the sacred without questioning the implications these

metaphors may have for women.[67] These varieties of spirituality grow out of a fundamental misunderstanding of ecofeminism, and thus it seems that the intersection of ecofeminism and spirituality is still in the process of becoming fully developed. To guide that development, Eaton has suggested four "conditions for a political ecological-feminist spirituality."[68] First, it must be political, meaning that it will not provide an other-worldly escape but rather address injustices in this world. Second, it must be ecological, in that it will address the ecological crisis itself. Third, it must be feminist, working in solidarity with local and global liberation movements; moreover, it must understand that reclaiming feminine manifestations of the divine may or may not be part of an ecofeminist project. Finally, Eaton stipulates that ecofeminist spiritualities must be "genuine," by which she means that "spirituality mediates a relationship with the Sacred."[69] Ecofeminist spiritualities developed with these conditions in mind will be more attuned to both the political and the spiritual implications of ecofeminism.

Womanism and Ecofeminism

The term "womanist" comes from Alice Walker, who offers this definition at the start of her collection of essays *In Search of Our Mothers' Gardens:* "A black feminist or feminist of color. . . . A woman who loves other women, sexually and/or nonsexually. Appreciates and prefers women's culture, women's emotional flexibility (values tears as natural counter-balance of laughter), and women's strength. Sometimes loves individual men, sexually and/or nonsexually. Committed to survival and wholeness of entire people, male and female. Not a separatist, except periodically, for health."[70] In this geography, I am using the potential conjunction of womanism and ecofeminism to explore the relationship between women of color and ecofeminists exclusively in the United States; the quality of racism in the United States makes it theoretically useful to examine questions of international racial diversity separately. For example, excluding for a moment such a notable ecofeminist of color as Vandana Shiva allows one to examine more clearly the racial composition of ecofeminisms. Notice that though womanism is one of the great mountains of feminist thought, when the womanist rivers flow into the lake of ecofeminism, there is no corresponding category of "womanist ecofeminism." Certainly, one can find U.S. women of color who have foregrounded issues of race and class at the same time as they have embraced ecofeminism or have worked within an ecofeminist framework: Cynthia Hamilton, Rachel Bagby, Paula Gunn Allen, Andrea Smith, Lourdes Arguëlles, Luisah Teish. Owing entirely to the principle of racial parity in WomanEarth, women of color have also played a leading role in shaping the first ecofeminist educational institute in the United States. Finally, not all those who would claim the term "womanist ecofeminist" have written about ecofeminism, though they may have written widely and their activism articulates their vision as well. But even with these concessions, it is still accurate to say that in the United States, ecofeminism as a theory and a movement has been developed predominantly by white women, and that this is not simply a "feature" of ecofeminism but a significant factor in determining the future of this movement and its transformative potential. The streams from womanism are drawn here to suggest unrealized potentials for ecofeminism. As I have done with the paths, I am attempting in this geography both to represent the actual contours of ecofeminism and, by indicating the sections that are missing or not fully developed, to strengthen my analysis of ecofeminism and to suggest directions for the future.

One immediate possibility is suggested in the geography of ecofeminisms, where the streams from womanism flow on both sides of an island labeled "spirituality/politics." The island is there to represent one of the debates that has divided ecofeminists and that is discussed at greater length in the section on activist ecofeminism. Here it is worth noting that the spirituality/politics debate has also divided radical feminists from socialist feminists, and deep ecologists from social ecologists, and since these theoretical groups are populated predominantly by white people, it seems fair to wonder if this schism between spirituality and politics isn't itself a feature of white U.S. culture and ideology and not a transcendent reality at all. As Margo Adair has explained:

> There's a lot of people that come more out of the old Left traditions
> that have inherited the Marxist idea that spirituality is—first of all, they
> don't distinguish between spirituality and religion, and then say that re-
> ligion is the opiate of the people, which is a bit of an arrogant position
> on religion, much less spirituality. The role that religion has played in
> the African-American movement, the Native American movement—I
> mean, most disenfranchised folks of color don't have this split between
> spirituality and religion.[71]

Dealing effectively with racism within the United States and the racial divide within ecofeminism means not just that more women of color identify as ecofeminists or work in coalition with ecofeminists: it means that the theory itself must be developed and transformed.

Socialist Ecofeminism

I want to begin with what I don't see ecofeminism as. So if some of you are waiting to ask if I am an essentialist, I think it's just a luxury academic discussion. I personally believe that people like me, people like Maria Mies, and others . . . when we are simultaneously ecological and feminist, what we are trying to do is not look so much at what women are, but how dominant power perceives them and manipulates structures to exclude, violate, dominate . . . and to see how closely the attitudes toward women are related to attitudes toward nature, and how the violence against women and the ecological crisis mimic each other all the time, in each period anew.

—Vandana Shiva, March 11, 1994

Socialist ecofeminism is a later development than radical or social ecofeminism, gaining currency after 1986. Unlike radical ecofeminists, socialist ecofeminists do not explicitly address the spiritual aspects of ecofeminism and often subsume the question of animals under the question of nature generally. Instead, socialist ecofeminists draw on socialist feminism in bringing their concerns about the intersections of race, class, and gender oppression to an analysis of the oppression of nature. Socialist ecofeminists have addressed such concerns as colonialism, the mal/development of the South by multinational corporations, the global distribution of wealth, the racism and sexism behind discussions of overpopulation, and the critique of biotechnology. Though only Carolyn Merchant has explicitly claimed the term "socialist ecofeminist" to describe herself, ecofeminists whose practices and perspectives fit this category might include Vandana Shiva, Maria Mies, and Karen Warren.

Social Ecofeminism

If we really want to create an ecological society, it's got to be a society that is not just free of toxins and poisons and free of ecological devastation, but it's a society that is also free of the toxin of oppression, it's free of the toxin of racism, sexism, imperialism, capitalism. It's going to

be a big beautiful blue-green sphere that is free of the toxins of domination and hierarchy.

—Chaia Heller, August 17, 1993

Social ecofeminism is a theory that emerges from both anarchist feminism
and social ecology; it is an ecofeminism with very definite links to the legacy of
the Left. With other ecofeminisms, social ecofeminism examines the interconnections between the oppression of nature and the oppression of women, people of color, the poor, and the working class. Features unique to social ecofeminism include its emphasis on the functionings of capitalist economies in the
degradation of social justice and ecological health and its analysis of the hierarchical structure of oppression as even more descriptive than the specific forms
of oppression (racism, sexism, classism, naturism). From a social ecofeminist
perspective, emphasizing this hierarchical structure allows one to make more
easily the connections among the many different manifestations of oppression.
The main proponents of social ecofeminism have been Ynestra King, Chaia
Heller, and Janet Biehl, though each has articulated the theory in different ways.
For example, although her ecofeminism is deeply rooted in social ecology,
Ynestra King has never been comfortable with the idea of any kind of internal
classification scheme for ecofeminism and, like Maria Mies, believes that such
classification only serves to divide people who should be working together, thus
weakening the movement:

> This tendency to split ecofeminism into the social versus the spiri-
> tual is something that should be resisted at every level. . . . It's been
> forced on ecofeminism from people who are not necessarily sympa-
> thetic to ecofeminism as a way to get people to fight among them-
> selves, or to frame the issues. And I think if ecofeminism is to be a
> conversation among people who share certain assumptions, the peo-
> ple within the movement have to decide how to define what the
> important questions are, and which way differences are going to be
> articulated and worked out.[72]

Hence King has never used the term "social ecofeminism" to describe her
perspective, and in fact it was Chaia Heller who first created the term to distinguish an ecofeminism that originated in social ecology and that offered a critique of capitalism and of hierarchy itself, from ecofeminisms that seemed to
overlook or to subordinate questions of race and economics. Later the term was
understood as an attempt to distinguish politically oriented ecofeminists from

spiritually oriented (cultural) ecofeminists, as King alludes to above. Though different in many other respects, both King and Heller see no necessary opposition between various forms of spirituality and ecofeminist critiques of hierarchy and domination. Unfortunately, clarifications among the various forms of ecofeminism, their consistencies and their divergences from one another, were not forthcoming in the late 1980s and early 1990s when ecofeminism finally gained visibility as a theory and a movement. A number of misunderstandings and misrepresentations could have been prevented by such distinctions.

The critique offered by Janet Biehl is one such example. In 1988, Biehl adopted the term "social ecofeminism" in her essay "What Is Social Ecofeminism?" Three years later, Biehl repudiated any ties she had with ecofeminism and faulted the entire theory in her book *Rethinking Ecofeminist Politics*.[73] There she seems to be taking a distorted view of spiritual cultural ecofeminism and believes that this single branch is the only ecofeminism there is. Her book has been soundly criticized by ecofeminists for its use of straw woman arguments, its failure to consider ecofeminisms that show some convergence with social ecology, its uncritical celebration of reason and of Greek democracy, and its exclusion of feminist philosophy generally.[74] Biehl's book itself is one good argument for developing an internal taxonomy for ecofeminism, so that ecofeminists can be more precise about our differences and similarities and critics cannot misrepresent a part for the whole.

Activist Ecofeminism

Q: What do you think that feminist theorists could be doing more of?
A: Getting out in the woods and chaining themselves to something. There's too much theory with no practice. They don't know what they're talking about.
—Judi Bari, February 26, 1995

Activist ecofeminism is listed in the lake itself, for activism is an integral part of each of these approaches. Ecofeminists have been active in creating shelter for women and animals who are the targets of violence, organizing demonstrations that make explicit the links between women's and animals' oppression, blocking clearcutting and deforestation, leading women's spirituality groups and ecofeminist study groups, protesting and where possible halting the spread of biotechnology, and contributing to the women's health movement, the environmental justice movement, the Green movement, and the various movements for indigenous rights. As many ecofeminists have argued, ecofeminism is based on praxis, the unity of theory and practice. Yet some activist ecofeminists see a disjunction instead of a unity: these activists have observed a "fault line" within ecofeminism, dividing theorists from practitioners in ways that reinforce liberal dualisms such as mind over body, as well as social hierarchies of race and class (i.e., white academic women theorize, whereas working-class women and women of color take direct action). Other ecofeminists believe that creating theory, communicating ideas, and educating others is itself a form of practice; they argue that direct action, often seen as the only "true" activism, is also a form of theorizing, since every direct action is organized with the expressed intent of communicating a specific message. Catriona (Kate) Sandilands explains:

> In any discussion of activism, what you're going to hear is "we have to get the media there, we have to get the message out, we have to change people's minds, we have to educate people in alternative ways." And although I think that kind of activist campaign is tremendously important, what ends up happening is we reduce our theorizing to sound bites. We end up summarizing our movement in ten words or less so that it can make good newspaper copy. . . . I think theory itself needs to be democratized. And a lot of people who are really angry about the status of theory are not actually angry about theory, they're angry at the university as an institution for claiming to be the sole space for theory. That strikes me as being perfectly useful anger, but it's misplaced to say the problem is theory. We all theorize in our everyday lives. The problem is to make that critical, and systematic, and communicative.[75]

Nonetheless, it may be significant that it is those ecofeminists whose activism includes written theory who make this argument with Sandilands; ecofeminists who engage primarily in direct action and grassroots organizing agree more with Judi Bari, rejecting the claim that "it's all action" and demanding that academic feminists spend more time on the front lines, engaging in direct action. The theory/practice split within ecofeminism is a topic of ongoing dialogue.

In fact, the spirituality/politics island dividing ecofeminisms in this geography may itself be a manifestation of the theory/practice debate: that is, politically active ecofeminists worry that spiritually oriented ecofeminists will privilege their own inner transformations over the very necessary work of social and economic transformations. Although no ecofeminist essay has explicitly charged spiritual ecofeminists with dropping out of political activities, many of the essays within spiritual ecofeminism take on a defensive tone, arguing that spirituality is not antithetical to political activism but in fact seems to inform and renew activists in their work. This defensive posture is articulated even in the title of Spretnak's anthology, *The Politics of Women's Spirituality*, and a third of the book is devoted to essays addressing ways of "transforming the political." But the defensiveness of spiritual ecofeminists may be a response to accusations coming from outside ecofeminism and may exemplify one way ecofeminism is marked by its cultural, historical, and political context. Possibly deriving its impetus from the Marxist charge that "religion is the opiate of the people," the spirituality/politics debate is a legacy of the Left in U.S. politics; it is also reflected in the male radical environmentalists' split between deep ecology and social ecology. The debate is congruent as well with the cultural geography of the United States: the more spiritual branches of radical ecology, the deep ecologists and spiritual ecofeminists, have developed primarily on the West Coast, whereas the more political branches of social ecology and social ecofeminism have flourished on the East Coast. But these distinctions are far from absolute. For example, although the Marxist charge against religion may apply to many specific historical moments, it fails to describe the way spirituality has powered the many movements for social justice: the civil rights movement, the American Indian Movement, the Hawai'ian sovereignty movement, and so on. As spiritual feminists and ecofeminists have consistently explained, there is a difference between religion and spirituality: whereas religion is a way of organizing and structuring (usually hierarchically) the possibilities of spiritual experience, spirituality is a direct experience of the sacred.

Some spiritual ecofeminists have demonstrated the compatibility between spirituality and politics in their work. Elizabeth Dodson Gray's *Green Paradise Lost* (1979) is widely acknowledged as one of the early texts of spiritual ecofeminism, and yet it also defies categorization: Gray persistently emphasizes the relationships among sexism, speciesism, racism, classism, and heterosexism, and her version of ecofeminism thus shares elements of "animal" ecofeminism and socialist ecofeminism as well as radical ecofeminism. A heterosexual feminist theologian, Gray appears to be the first ecofeminist to theorize the relationship between heterosexism and the oppression of nature in patriarchal cultures.[76] Yet another example of spirituality and politics harmonized in ecofeminism, Ecofeminist Visions Emerging (EVE), a study group that met monthly in New York City for nearly three years, had as its motto "For a Spiritual Politic and a Political Spirituality." EVE activists easily negotiated the boundaries by participating in a monthly reading and discussion group, a Mary Daly read-aloud group, a Madison Avenue graffitti squad, and a menstrual circle (organized unproblematically by one of the women who had undergone a hysterectomy). It seems that the critiques of spiritual ecofeminism—as individualist and apolitical, lacking a critique of racism and classism—have some foundation only in terms of spiritual cultural ecofeminism. That there are other spiritual ecofeminisms which may be radical or even social has been overlooked, again because ecofeminists have chosen not to define our differences.

Finally, it's worth noting that although ecofeminists of every variety—animal, radical, spiritual, womanist, socialist, and social—have engaged in direct action, the wide popular appeal of ecofeminism comes through the radical ecofeminisms. It is also these ecofeminisms that are most frequently subjected to attack, as being essentialist, apolitical, anti-intellectual, internally contradictory, or just plain "soft." Sadly, this attack has not been confined to outsiders: several ecofeminist philosophers have been a little too eager to distinguish themselves from the "essentialist" forms of ecofeminism.[77] Regardless of how well-founded their critiques may be, such essays cross the line between healthy internal debate and intellectual assault. What these writers fail to realize is that they are sawing off the trunk of the tree from which their branch grows. Just as liberal feminists of the nineteenth century distanced themselves from women of color, and the women's liberation movement of the second wave distanced itself from lesbians, these philosopher ecofeminists are repeating a flaw within feminism by separating themselves from a vital constituency in their own movement. For ecofeminism, this rift is indeed life threatening: as more and more activist women complain that they can't understand what ecofeminists are saying, ecofeminism has the potential to lose popular appeal and become irrelevant. The future and vitality of ecofeminism depends on the ability of ecofeminists to communicate across differences (particularly differences of race and class) and to work in coalition with other liberatory movements whose goals we share. Diversity, popular appeal, and real political relevance—as well as academic visibility—are critical if ecofeminism is to make a genuine contribution to social transformation.

Ecofeminism: Developments and Debates

As a theory and a movement, ecofeminism achieved an identity during the decade of the 1980s (see Appendix A). What began with the Women and Life on Earth conference and the Women's Pentagon Action was soon followed by the first ecofeminist anthology, Léonie Caldecott and Stephanie Leland's *Reclaim the Earth: Women Speak Out for Life on Earth*, published in London in 1983. Unfortunately, this anthology was never widely available in the United States and was not reprinted in England, so the essays have not reached as wide an audience as have some of the later ecofeminist anthologies. To date, Caldecott and Leland's collection remains the only ecofeminist anthology of international scope, and it introduces a variety of concerns that ecofeminists would later develop with more detail. Topics include the peace and antinuclear movement roots of ecofeminism; theoretical connections between feminism and ecology; women's health care, homeopathy, and technologies for controlling pregnancy and birth; the Green Belt movement of Kenya; urban ecology and environmental justice; animal liberation; indigenous sovereignty movements; an ecofeminist critique and reconstruction of work, recreation, and economics; an assessment of nuclear power versus solar power; a discussion of strategies used by the Mothers of the Plaza de Mayo in Argentina; forestry and deforestation; militarism and its assault on women, people of color, and the environment; and food security and sustainable agriculture. The Caldecott and Leland anthology was only the beginning; by mid-decade, ecofeminism was being discussed within a variety of alternative and mainstream journals, and many journals devoted entire special issues to the subject.[78]

Meanwhile, ecofeminism was gaining greater visibility at the same time as were two other branches of radical environmentalism, social ecology and deep ecology.[79] It seemed inevitable that these theories would articulate their distinct positions through dialogue and debate with each other, but this debate was uneven. The social/deep ecology debates of the late 1980s, epitomized in the figures of Murray Bookchin and Dave Foreman, were thoroughly publicized, explored, facilitated, and finally recorded in the pages of *Defending the Earth*, published by South End Press in 1991.[80] (This aspect of the radical environmental movement is explored in greater detail in Chapter 3). With much less fanfare, the deep ecology/ecofeminism debates were recorded primarily in the pages of the journal *Environmental Ethics* and were characterized by the following charges: ecofeminists held that deep ecology's description of the root cause of Western culture's destruction of the natural world, anthropocentrism (human-centered thinking), should be more properly termed androcentrism (male-centered thinking), since women and people of color have been only marginally included in the white male domination of nature.[81] Ecofeminists also rejected the "deep ecological self" developed by deep ecologists to articulate their experience of oneness with nature as fundamentally narcissistic, androcentric, and colonizing.[82] Finally, ecofeminists criticized deep ecologists for re-connecting with wild nature through the violence of hunting, for omitting the analyses of feminists from the construction of their theories, and for construct-ing a theory that functioned merely as the unfolding of white middle-class environmentalism in its regard for wilderness but its utter disinterest in social justice and the functioning of capitalism both in the United States and interna-tionally. In claiming that environmental preservation and ecological health could be realized only in relation to the achievement of social justice, and in pointing out the ways deep ecology erased or silenced feminist insights, ecofem-inists distinguished their theory from deep ecology and effectively outlined the direction for future ecofeminist thought. It's worth remarking the irony in this, that a theory such as ecofeminism, which is based on the idea of relationship and interconnection, gained greater visibility by separating and distinguishing itself from another theory of radical environmentalism. Of course, such distinc-tions had to be made, since deep ecologists were fond of regarding ecofeminism as a subset of deep ecology and frequently claimed there was nothing unique about the findings of ecofeminism that deep ecologists hadn't already said.

In the history of ecofeminism, the forms that ecofeminist theory has taken are also significant, particularly in view of its origins in Griffin's and Daly's refusal to write and to theorize in straightforward academic discursive modes. Ynestra King's remarks on the politics of theorizing are particularly relevant:

> It depends on what you want to legitimate as theory. There are certain cultural, political, historical reasons why women with different cultural and economic backgrounds would work in certain formats. Poetry, for example, is one of the ways in which someone who doesn't have a lot of paper and a lot of time can work out different relationships and can speak and so forth. There are also various narratives, stories, people who grew up primarily in an oral tradition, and I think there are cer-tain understandings of the world that can be arrived at from a number of different directions. Depending on what you want to call "ecofemi-nism," a lot of these ideas are being arrived at from a number of differ-ent directions. Even the ideas, if you look at the development of art and literature. . . . But it's true: white women in developed countries with certain kinds of education and access to certain forums tend to use those forums to develop ecofeminist theory, and that's one kind of con-tribution. It depends on who gets to say what is ecofeminism. There needs to be a continuous awareness of theory as developing through all

kinds of mediums, and ways of thinking, and a way of legitimating different forms of theory other than what might be recognized in traditional academic circles or traditional Left circles as theory.[83]

By the mid-1990s, the academic essay had come to dominate the literature of ecofeminism, signifying a move away from the more popular forms of storytelling, fiction, poetry, interview, conversation, and experimental prose. Originally, ecofeminism was articulated through anthologies as a way of emphasizing the plurality of voices and the diversity of women involved, and poetry, narrative, and interview were placed alongside the academic essay. As the literature of ecofeminism has become more intellectualized, these popular forms of writing have vanished from the anthologies, and more single-author texts have appeared. Unless temporary, this shift will be a significant loss, for the presence of poetry, narrative, informal or personal essays, and interviews was positively correlated with the popular appeal of ecofeminism. As ecofeminism spreads to literary criticism in such organizations as the Association for the Study of Literature and Environment, perhaps ecofeminists will be able to reclaim the power of literature's popular appeal.

In the United States, ecofeminism has not been warmly received by academic feminists, who are largely influenced by socialist feminism.[84] One reason may be socialist feminism's hostility to nature, its belief that freedom for women can be found only in the social realm of culture, and its apprehension that any association of women with nature (an association that is foundational to patriarchal thought) is the prelude to mandated caregiving and compulsory motherhood and poses a threat to women's liberation. These fears are not unfounded, but they reveal a basic unfamiliarity with ecofeminism. Other potential bases for ecofeminism's chilly reception among feminists may have to do with the fact that ecofeminism suggests more changes than some feminists want to make. For example, there has been real resistance to the ecofeminist critique of sexism as interconnected with speciesism and the importance of animal liberation in ecofeminism. The leading journal of academic feminism, *Signs*, was willing to publish an essay arguing that feminists need not be vegetarians; it took quite a bit of persuasion to convince the journal's editors to publish essays exposing the misinformation and faulty reasoning of such an argument.[85] The interconnections of sexism and speciesism may be difficult for socialist feminists to accept because they interpret such connections as an additional concern for already overburdened feminists.[86] If this is the case, these feminists again misinterpret the aims of ecofeminists, who are striving to reveal the intercon-nections among numerous forms of oppression in order to expose the structure and functioning of hierarchy itself.

Unlike their professors, most students respond favorably to ecofeminism simply because it gives them a direction for action. Although it is empowering to learn the ways that sexism, racism, and classism interact to support the status quo, students may nonetheless feel disempowered if they see no means for transforming those systems. In contrast, ecofeminism offers many starting points for activism. Ynestra King comments:

> What interested people in ecofeminism during the eighties was its re-constructive or visionary or alternative possibilities in a context where a lot of the feminist theory that's been done is deconstructive, rather than reconstructive. Feminism needs, and any social movement needs, vision. You can't develop a whole social movement on opposition. In the con-temporary context, that demands some coming to terms with nonhu-man nature, relationships to plants, animals, trees, air, rocks, and to a global economy and ecology. In that way, ecofeminism has a kind of political relevance and sustained political commitments that a lot of ac-ademic feminism doesn't have at this point.[87]

As ecofeminism continues to develop, these tensions with other feminists will need to be resolved. Feminists and ecofeminists are quite clearly partners in struggle.

Finally, there must be avenues for ecofeminist activists to reach beyond their own constituencies and participate in a broad-based movement for social change. On the geography of ecofeminisms, just below the lake, I have drawn two outlets where ecofeminist energy and concerns flow out to other move-ments and other people. Certainly one outlet for ecofeminism has been schol-arship—the writing, speaking, educating, and conversing that is so important to spreading ideas. Another outlet involves building coalitions, and here I have specifically listed those constituencies that are not represented in the paths or streams contributing to ecofeminism. It is crucial to the future of ecofeminism that dialogue and alliances be built between ecofeminists and labor activists, ecofeminists and queer activists, and ecofeminists and activists within the envi-ronmental justice movement. Many ecofeminists have worked with the Green movement as a way of enacting their ecofeminist beliefs. Paradoxically, within the Green movement ecofeminists have found themselves facing the same questions as they have within the context of feminism, the same underrepresentation of labor, queers, and people of color, and the same need to build coalitions with these diverse constituencies. To understand the challenges ecofeminists have confronted while working in the Greens, one must first understand the history and development of the Green movement itself.

2. The U.S. Greens:

From Movement to Party

When Ronald Reagan took office as U.S. president in 1980, his election was hailed by many as the end of the dwindling influence of the Left and the coming of age of the Right. The final loss of the Equal Rights Amendment in 1982 was emblematic of an era characterized by regressive economic policies ("Reaganomics") that gave unprecedented tax breaks to the wealthy and eliminated the social safety net for the working classes. Three wars—the war on welfare, followed by the war on drugs and later by the war in the Persian Gulf—were waged to protect the accumulation of wealth in the hands of the elite and the corporations, wealth that was extracted from women and children, poor people and people of color, less industrialized nations, and the earth itself. It was an era marked by the rise of the Christian Coalition, whose well-organized network mobilized thousands of people to "love the sinner but hate the sin." Anything that undermined the authority of the white patriarchal family was constructed as a sin: feminism, homosexuality, reproductive rights, gun control, Aid to Families with Dependent Children (AFDC), child care centers, affirmative action legislation, animal liberation, environmental protection, alternative spiritualities (whether non-Western, earth-based, or feminist). As many progressives would later observe, the Christian Coalition had a much clearer picture than did any progressive group of how the agendas of the various progressive movements were interconnected and reinforcing. In her 1991 book *Backlash: The*

Undeclared War against American Women, Susan Faludi chronicles the decade's right-wing assault on feminism and human rights through the popular media and the subtle and not-so-subtle shifts in popular opinion.[1] Internationally, the collapse of the Soviet Union in 1989 and its leaders' embrace of capitalism seemed like the final blow to those liberatory movements of the New Left that had begun with such vision and ended in such repression.

At first glance, the Republican regime seemed to have ended with the 1996 presidential election of Bill Clinton and Al Gore, two Democrats who had come of age with the sixties and whose campaign included promises of environmental protection, women's rights, gay/lesbian rights, and reparations for the working classes. But within a year of the election, all their most enticing campaign promises had been broken. The Clinton/Gore presidency saw passage of the North American Free Trade Agreement (NAFTA) and the General Agreement on Tariffs and Trade (GATT), international trade agreements favoring multinational corporations and jeopardizing or eliminating numerous environmental protections, worker safety protections, and fair wage compensations; the legalized use of recombinant Bovine Growth Hormone (rBGH), or as its advocates prefer to call it, Bovine Somatotrophin (BST); the passage of a salvage logging rider that authorized unprecedented increases in logging of ancient public forests and critical watersheds; the approval of a welfare reform bill that instituted a "five years and off" policy against women and children; the institution of a "don't ask, don't tell" policy for gays in the military, along with the passage of the Defense of Marriage Act restricting the economic benefits of marriage to certified heterosexuals and the defeat of the Employment Non-Discrimination Act, which would have prohibited employment practices discriminating against gays and lesbians; the signing of the Panama Declaration, which undermines protection of marine mammals, weakening the Endangered Species Act through changes in its rules and regulations, and opening even more wildlife refuges to hunting and fishing. What the Republicans could not accomplish in the 1980s was completed under the Clinton/Gore administration. It was in this context of escalating assaults on the environment, on workers, women, people of color, animals, and third world countries that the Green movement took root in the United States.

After the initial surge of countercultural movements of the sixties—Black Power, the women's movement, the American Indian Movement, the gay liberation movement, the peace movement—which was on the wane by 1972 or 1973, progressive activists turned to spreading movement ideas throughout the larger culture.[2] The seventies were marked by the back-to-the-land movement and the affiliated movement toward intentional communities; the peace movement became the antinuclear movement, responding to the fact that more and more nuclear power plants and nuclear weapons were being designed and built; the animal rights movement took shape; the environmental movement succeeded in obtaining passage of significant environmental protections; and the women's movement blossomed with radical feminism, though it was marked by many internal debates about race, sexuality, and class—debates that would erupt in the eighties. At the same time, a lot of activists lost heart or dismissed their earlier radicalism as youthful idealism and turned to the "adult" business of making money and raising children.

In the 1980s, progressives and intellectuals observed a "paradigm shift," by which they meant a change in the metaphor that dominates popular thought. Dramatic social changes of the past had often been characterized by paradigm shifts; for example, the Copernican revolution entailed a shift from the idea of a geocentric to a heliocentric universe. Fritjof Capra's *The Turning Point* (1982) described this paradigm shift in science, from a Newtonian worldview that imagined nature as a machine, composed of many intricate but interactive parts operating according to fixed laws, to a worldview shaped by the discoveries of quantum physics.[3] Ostensibly, the implications of quantum physics could be applied to everything, including politics.[4] Other writers describe this paradigm shift as simply a shift from a machine model of nature to the metaphor of an interconnected web.[5] Descendants of the sixties counterculture, intellectuals in every discipline heralded the advent of a new progressive politics in the 1980s.[6]

In 1984, Charlene Spretnak and Fritjof Capra's *Green Politics: The Global Promise* introduced Green politics to U.S. readers by describing Spretnak and Capra's tour of the West German Green movement.[7] According to Spretnak and Capra, the first Green party was not the West German Greens but the Values Party of New Zealand, founded in the late 1960s.[8] Its 1975 election manifesto, titled "Beyond Tomorrow," inspired ecologists and futurists around the world with its explicit statements about "the need for a steady-state population and economy, new industrial and economic relations, ecological thinking, human-centered technology, soft-path energy systems, decentralization of government, equality for women, and rights of native peoples, as well as for valuing the traits traditionally considered feminine: cooperation, nurturing, healing, cherishing, and peace-making" (p. 172). Like so many other progressive movements, the Values Party was weakened by internal bickering and effectively disappeared after 1981. In Europe, the Green movement came together with the 1979 elections for the European Parliament, using the antinuclear issue as a catalyst for building coalitions among citizens' groups to address social and environmental issues. Although none of the Green parties gained seats in the parliament from that election, their campaigns brought visibility to the movement, and in West Germany the Greens won 3.2 percent of the vote, qualifying them to receive roughly $1.3 million in federal funds, which in turn assisted their rise to visibility (p. 174). Although Green parties and alliances had been established or formed in most European countries—namely, Austria, Britain, Denmark, Finland, France, Greece, Ireland, Luxembourg, Spain, Sweden, and Switzerland—the West German Greens attracted the most attention because of their early success.[9] Hence, it was the West German Greens that Spretnak and Capra observed and described enthusiastically in 1984.

At the end of *Green Politics*, Spretnak and Capra conclude that the condition of U.S. politics is fertile ground for a Green movement, and they envision five possible configurations for such a movement: a Green network, linking decentralized groups so they could focus on the political system; a Green movement, which would formulate a coherent worldview and present proposals to the two major parties but would not run candidates for office; a Green caucus within the movement, functioning as an arm of the larger Green movement by providing candidates for either of the two parties; a national Green caucus, which people of either party could join; or a Green Party, which "would legitimize the movement," they believe (pp. 200–202). Acknowledging the hazards of moving into electoral politics prematurely, as well as the difficulties for third-party organizing without the benefit of proportional representation, Spretnak and Capra go on to suggest bioregional ways of organizing a Green movement and possible areas in which Greens could develop policy statements. All these suggestions are framed by cautionary statements. Before describing the possible configurations for a U.S. Green movement, Spretnak and Capra detail the many lessons to be learned from the German Greens' experiences. Then, following their description of Green policy statements, they list the internal and external problems a Green movement will face. They conclude with a possible agenda for the founding meeting of a Green movement and impart a sense of urgency. The organizaton of their concluding chapter, if not the message itself, is decidedly ambivalent.

But the public response was not. Soon after the book's publication, Spretnak and Capra received letters and phone calls from people around the United States, asking them to create a Green organization. From the outset, Capra decided not to get personally involved in politics but to offer the resources of the Elmwood Institute, which he had founded in 1983 with Spretnak and others. Spretnak, on the other hand, felt somewhat responsible for initiating a Green movement, after all she had done to publicize its possibilities in their book. As their new chapter in the 1986 edition describes it, Spretnak invited four others to form an organizing committee with her: "Harry Boyte, author of *Community Is Possible* and *The Backyard Revolution;* Catherine Burton, cofounder of Earth Bank; Gloria Goldberg, an associate of the Institute for Social Ecology; [and] David Haenke, coordinator of the first North American Bioregional Congress" (p. 228). Together the five-member committee invited two hundred activists, organizers, and theorists from twenty-seven issue areas to a founding meeting on the campus of Macalester College in St. Paul, Minnesota, on August 10–12, 1984. Of those invited, sixty-two attended, and the U.S. Green movement was formed.[10]

A somewhat different story is told by other Green writers. According to Brian Tokar's *The Green Alternative,* the first step toward creating a Green organization in the United States was taken at the North American Bioregional Congress, held in the Ozarks in May 1984.[11] There a group of people interested in building a Green movement met for several days and eventually drafted a statement of Green principles, signing it as the Green Movement Committee. Later in the summer, members of that working group invited "a larger group of people to St. Paul, Minnesota, to continue the discussions begun in May."[12] According to John Rensenbrink, the Maine Greens had been founded in January 1984 as both a party and a movement and may well be the first Green organization in the United States.[13] Like ecofeminists, Greens have a few different "origin stories" for their movement.

Greens generally concur, however, that their organizing meeting in St. Paul was "rocky": disagreements about national structure, strategy, and even the name of the organization were at issue. Some participants wanted to establish a single national organization, while others believed local and regional alliances needed to be formed first. Some wanted to found a national Green party within the coming year, while others felt the group was not yet sufficiently representative and the movement not sufficiently grounded. Some wanted to call the movement "Green," while others maintained that such a name would connote white, middle-class environmentalism devoid of social justice concerns. In the end, the group created a single national clearinghouse in St. Paul and named their organization the "Committees of Correspondence" (CoC), after the network of people in the thirteen colonies who had sparked the U.S. Revolution— a name that (the group clearly did not recognize) institutionalized the exclusion of Native Americans and other non-Europeans just as much as if not more than the name "Green" ever would. An Interregional Committee (IC) was formed from representatives of the various parts of the country and charged with building the movement at the local, regional, and national levels. The best-known result of the meeting, of course, was the statement of Ten Key Values, which participants created as a means of introducing Green values, generating discussion, and guiding the development of the movement.

The Ten Key Values of the U.S. Greens were derived from the Four Pillars of the West German Greens: *ecology, democracy, nonviolence,* and *social responsibility.* Even these Four Pillars were somewhat modified at the outset: *ecology* became *ecological wisdom* in deference to the deep ecologists and spiritually minded people present, and *social responsibility* became *personal and social responsibility* to emphasize the role of both the individual and the society in creating change. To expand on and clarify the meaning of the Four Pillars, six values were added: *decentralization, community-based economics, postpatriarchal values, respect for diversity, global responsibility,* and *future focus.* As a way of defining the key values, the founding committee chose to offer not statements but a series of questions for each one. Strategically, it was a brilliant device: organizers who distributed these values offered newcomers a way of becoming immediately engaged by inviting them to think about ways of answering these questions. The questions gave real meaning to the claim that the movement was just beginning, that new ideas were welcome, and that there was the opportunity for individuals to contribute their vision to an evolving statement.[14] Most important was the fact that none of these values stood alone: from a Green perspective, ecological health depended on grassroots democracy, community-based economies, and social justice; in turn, true democracy could not be achieved without postpatriarchal values. As Greens have been fond of saying, the Ten Key Values are not a menu from which we can select our portions—that is, "I'd like some *ecological wisdom* but please hold the *nonviolence* and *decentralization.*" The Green vision is founded on the understanding that all these values are interconnected, such that social justice and ecological justice go hand in hand. This understanding separates the Green movement from other environmental movements before it, which have been predominantly white, middle-class efforts to protect nature; it also distinguishes the Greens from other movements for social or economic justice, which have focused entirely on human interactions and overlooked their environmental consequences. Given this holistic vision, Greens predictably had some difficulty establishing priorities and getting started.

In 1985, after some problems with getting under way in St. Paul, the clearinghouse was moved to Kansas City when the Green local there agreed to provide basic services and Dee Berry, who lived in Kansas City, offered to serve as coordinator. For the next few years until the summer of 1991, the Interregional Committee met three times annually to assist in local and regional organizing, exchange information, and plan the national gatherings. The *IC Bulletin* was mailed monthly to the various locals, and a quarterly newsletter (*Green Letter*) and journal (*Green Synthesis*) were mailed to all members of the Committees of Correspondence. Between 1985 and 1991, membership in locals affiliated with the national movement fluctuated between two thousand and three thousand.[15] Eventually, the IC meetings became burdensome for both the representatives and the regions, which were charged with providing travel expenses for their delegates. Moreover, the locals that hosted the meetings quit participating in the IC after serving as hosts, due to frustrations in planning, organization, and communications. Eventually only 35 percent of the locals on the CoC mailing lists were dues-paying members of the organization, and few subscribed to the *IC Bulletin*.[16] Hence, the best way to get an overview of the evolution of the Greens is to trace their development through the annual gatherings.

The Educational Gatherings, 1987–1988

One theme characterizes the reports on the Greens' national gatherings: the theme of growing up. In her description of the first national Green gathering in Amherst, Massachusetts, in 1987, aptly titled "Coming of Age with the Greens," Ynestra King describes the New Left of the sixties and seventies as "utopian" and "infantile" but suggests that the Greens are "potentially the new left come of age."[17] Writing from the perspective of a sixties activist now in his forties, Mark Satin introduces his report on the second national gathering in Eugene, Oregon, with the claim that the Greens represent "our generation's last chance to affect the mainstream political debate." "The planet itself is at stake," Satin concludes, "and is calling upon us to grow up, already."[18] As captured in the title of Howie Hawkins's retrospective on the Green movement in the winter of 1992—"North American Greens Come of Age"—the call to "grow up" takes a twist in meaning after the 1991 gathering in Elkins, West Virginia: initially used as an imperative to "get real" by pulling together the various constituencies of the sixties into a coherent leftist and ecological movement, after 1991 it is used specifically to mean engaging in electoral politics on a grand scale.[19] For example, John Rensenbrink's *The Greens and the Politics of Transformation* (1992) turns on the distinction between transformative politics ("growing up") and the politics of protest, which Rensenbrink sees as "ineradicably immature." According to Rensenbrink, the protest politics of the sixties reveal "a lack of confidence and a lack of willingness to take responsibility for running the store." Sixties protesters embodied "an attitude toward authority much like that of an angry child who suddenly one day rebels against the perceived authority of the parent. The child demands that the parent do something or get out of the way. He or she has not yet reached a mature decision to let the parent know that it is time for the nature of the relationship to change fundamentally."[20] At the 1991 national gathering of Greens in Elkins, participants finalized a national program and a revised national structure; according to one reporter, these developments meant the Greens "finally came of age."[21] One year later, an article summarizing events at the 1992 national gathering in Minneapolis concluded, "The Greens have grown up."[22] But the evaluation was not universally shared: in her keynote address to the 1995 national gathering in Albuquerque, Keiko Bonk, Hawai'i County Council chair for the Big Island, opened with the challenge, "It is time for the Greens to grow up."[23] What did it mean for the Greens to "grow up" or "come of age"? How has the meaning of maturity changed from speaker to speaker? And how have the Greens "grown up" since their founding in 1984?

For Ynestra King in 1987, "coming of age" seemed to mean retaining the insights of the old Left and the New Left but leaving behind the problems that destroyed those movements. In her report on the first national gathering, King saw the potential for the Greens to combine "two of the most powerful movements in history," feminism and ecology, "into a coherent, political critique and program for transforming the social and economic structures which threaten the survival of all species on the planet, including the human one."[24] According to King, insights gleaned from the old Left included the lesson "that workerism, authoritarianism, and economism do not work as ways to think about, or transform the world"; from the New Left, "new revolutionary subjects—youth, women, Blacks, Native Americans—emerged," transcending the old Left's singular focus on the proletariat. These insights would have to be brought forward in tandem with the insights of feminism and ecology. In addition, Greens would need to surmount the problems that defeated the New Left: "sexism, anti-intellectualism, a dearth of political experience, and a lack of critical historical perspective." Greens would also have to transcend the organizational problems that characterized the New Left—that is, "small groups regularly evaporated and large national organizations became arenas for old left-style political power struggles."[25] These problems in substance and structure are what King calls "infantile." In the context of the first national gathering, then, "coming of age" meant building a social and ecological movement that was structurally functional, composed of individuals from a diversity of communities who would bring their political experience and historical perspectives together in feminist process.

From King's perspective, the chances of the Greens succeeding were a coin toss; the markers for their success or failure were equally present. King noted a number of elders at the gathering—"half of the heads were gray"—and recognized many activists as "veterans" from earlier struggles for social or ecological justice. The opening speakers also reflected a diversity of experience and perspectives: along with King, there was social ecologist Murray Bookchin, African-American activist James Boggs, and Mohawk midwife Katsi Cook. Throughout the six-day gathering, King recognized many people from various groups on the Left, "people who had remained committed activists since the radical heyday of the sixties." Also present was the potential for repeating former mistakes: the gathering was nearly split by the conflict King describes as a "major philosophical struggle" between deep ecology and social ecology.[26] Her report spends a good deal of time criticizing the "pseudo-spirituality of deep ecology" and its spokesman, Dave Foreman, for what King calls an "eco-macho" approach to nature, in which being "for" nature means being "against" human beings. Some deep ecologists had welcomed famine in Africa and the AIDS epidemic as means of reducing population; they had opposed sanctuary for Central American refugees because such people "belong to their own bioregion"; and deep ecologists generally made no distinction among human beings in terms of gender, race, or global location. What is curious about King's description, however, is that Dave Foreman was not present at the Amherst gathering: the tensions between spirituality and leftist politics, which were observed and reported on by several others in attendance, were symbolically resolved by the end of the gathering when Murray Bookchin and Charlene Spretnak embraced in front of a crowd of participants. Targeting Spretnak—possibly for her spiritual and political views, articulated in *The Spiritual Dimension of Green Politics*[27]—Bookchin had deplored the New Age element of the Greens for its indifference to leftist political theory. Described by some as a deep ecology/social ecology conflict, though observably manifested as a spiritual ecofeminism/social ecology conflict, the conflict over spirituality within the Greens receded in importance after a few years. And as King's account concluded, ecofeminism, as "an autonomous feminist movement, and as part of the green movement," offers "potentially the most powerful integrative approach in green politics."[28] Alternative journals that reported on the gathering described it favorably, and the Greens were off to an upbeat start.[29]

The following year, a similar gathering was held in northern California to introduce Green politics to the West. Titled "Greening the West," this regional gathering was held at Jones Gulch YMCA Camp the weekend of September 30 through October 2, 1988, and was attended by more than nine hundred people.[30] Advance publicity for the gathering had urged participants to register early because of limited space, and the warnings proved to be true: more than three dozen latecomers had to be turned away, and on Sunday morning the entire water system of the camp ran dry.[31] Why wasn't a larger site chosen? Perhaps there was something attractive to the organizers about meeting in the redwoods just south of San Francisco. As one reporter commented, the fact that this location was "adjacent to the town of La Honda—where Ken Kesey and The Merry Pranksters, the early '60s avant/literary/LSD progenitors of the East Coast counter-culture, first dropped acid—gained greater meaning as the conference weekend progressed."[32] The theme of "growing up," now implying an ability to leave behind trappings from the sixties counterculture, continued in full force.

But though both the Greens and The Merry Pranksters saw sociocultural change as both a personal and a group process, The Merry Pranksters had no coherent political view. One of the workshops at the gathering, aptly titled "Lessons from the Sixties," featured Barbara Epstein, who explained that the student movements of the sixties collapsed in part because of a lack of firm theoretical grounding.[33] In contrast, the Greens represented a confluence of cultural, political, and metaphysical activism and thought. Only one report on the gathering defined maturity as a willingness to engage in electoral politics: the fact that some Greens felt the movement should stay out of electoral politics was characterized as an "unlikely return to the Eden of the 60s [which] showed what had evolved—and what hadn't—over the past 25-plus years of U.S. social movements."[34] Two of the three reports noted, as one of them put it, that "the proportion of people of color among the total participants was as disappointing as it has been at past Green gatherings around the country."[35] For the next decade, however, the Green movement remained predominantly white, reflecting the racial segregation of the United States in spite of repeated exhortations to build multiracial coalitions.

"Greening the West" differed from the Amherst gathering in a way that parallels the cultural geography of the United States. The East Coast gathering, held on a college campus and funded primarily through Hampshire College's Social Ecology Endowment Fund, had a predominance of leftists and intellectuals as well as social and environmental activists: for example, Kim Bartlett, Janet Biehl, Murray Bookchin, Dan Chodorkoff, Ward Churchill, Betsy Hartmann, Howie Hawkins, Chaia Heller, Alex Hershaft, Ynestra King, Grace Paley, David Rothenberg, and Rick Whaley attended only the Amherst conference.[36] In contrast, the West Coast gathering was held at a YMCA camp and was populated more by eco-activists and scholars with a cultural or spiritual approach: Peter Berg, David Brower, Ernest Callenbach, Fritjof Capra, Bill Devall, Jerry Mander, Deena Metzger, Julia Russell, Starhawk, and George Sessions attended only the West Coast event. Of course, many Greens attended both conferences, among them Margo Adair, Rachel Bagby, Carl Boggs, Irene Diamond, Barbara Epstein, Marti Kheel, Danny Moses, Charlene Spretnak, and Brian Tokar. As conference reports of "Greening the West" acknowledged, this wide divergence of philosophies among Greens had not yet coalesced into an agreed-on strategy. It was a diversity that would have to find some common ground if the Greens were to go forward together.

The various statements from Greens following the Amherst gathering expressed this problem clearly. "This conference shows the remarkable diversity of political, personal, cultural interests that are melding together in this country to form the embryonic beginnings of a green alternative," said Paul Cumar, from the New York Green Network. "People came to the perspective that the green movement is not seamless," said Don Alexander, from *Kick It Over* magazine in Toronto. "There are a lot of important issues that need to be thrashed out." Ecofeminist Rachel Bagby also expressed a tempered optimism: "This conference is a very necessary first step and my other foot is still in the air." Mark Satin was more critical: "There's been a cornucopia of ideological banter, but a poverty of realistic discussion about how to build a movement that can challenge the power structure." Perhaps the most pointed call to action was expressed by Bruce Shur from New Hampshire: "We have to start getting practical, cut out this air-headed bullshit, and come up with strategies now."[37] At a point so early in the movement, people generally had faith that through dialogue they could either resolve these differences or find a way toward peaceful coexistence. But all shared a sense that there was no time to lose.

In the very next mailing Greens received from the clearinghouse, there was a proposal for follow-up to the Amherst gathering.[38] Over the next three years, three gatherings would develop a Green program: a miniconference in 1988, a Green Continental Program conference in 1989, and a Green Continental Congress in 1990, which would serve as a more inclusive founding convention. To start the process, Greens were invited to define key areas for strategy and policy and to generate statements that developed and explained policies for each area. These statements on strategic and policy approaches in key areas (known as SPAKA) represent a truly amazing effort to educate and generate agreement through a participatory, grassroots, and democratic process of collaborative writing. Not surprisingly, the process had flaws. What is notable is that it was attempted at all, given the standard pitfalls of collaborative writing; yet, when the program was finished, the document was actually a coherent summary of Green philosophy.

SPAKA Gatherings, 1989–1990

Between the 1987 Amherst gathering and the June 1989 gathering in Eugene, Greens on the Interregional Committee set in motion a process of drafting a national statement of Green values, which came to be known as the SPAKA documents.[39] Through a series of articles in *Green Letter,* John Rensenbrink, the coordinator of the SPAKA process, regularly communicated the evolution of the documents to the Green readership.[40] In response to an invitation to define the key areas, thirty out of one hundred locals sent in statements that were narrowed down to eleven key areas: ecology, sustainable economics, politics, social justice, personal values, human needs, peace and nonviolence, community, organizing and internal organization, strategy, and common action proposals. These eleven key areas were then sent back to all one hundred or more locals, with the invitation to create definitions and statements. All this idea generation was done to make the 1989 Eugene gathering more productive and the search for common ground more likely to be successful.

The Eugene gathering was planned not as an open or educational gathering but as a working meeting. Each local would be invited to send two representatives, preferably gender balanced, and to bring one other person from their area who was not a member of the CoC but was active in other groups working for peace, social justice, or environmental concerns. All Green caucuses would also send one representative. Finally, the working group would invite one person from approximately fifty different activist organizations, such as ACORN (Association of Community Organizations for Reform Now), Pledge of Resistance, Greenpeace, the North American Bioregional Congress, United Farm Workers, the American Indian Movement, the Center for Economic Conversion, the Rainbow Coalition, the Ecofeminist network, and Witness for Peace. The document produced at Eugene would be returned to the locals for more discussion and revision and brought back to a national founding convention in 1990 or 1991.

By spring 1989, just a few months before the gathering, problems in the process had begun to surface. For one thing, the eleven key areas had grown into nineteen. While social justice, politics, community, peace and nonviolence, organizing, and strategy had remained consistent, the other five areas had been replaced with thirteen more specific divisions: ecology expanded into energy, forest and forestry, life forms, materials use and waste management, and water/air; economics became general economic analysis and finance; personal values was replaced by eco-philosophy and by spirituality; human needs became education, health, and food and agriculture; and common actions was subsumed under strategy. Two hundred papers, totaling more than six hundred pages, had been written on these nineteen key areas and were available to locals at the price of five dollars per each key area, or ninety-five dollars in all. Ideally, the SPAKA documents were to be sent to each local, but by this point there was neither the staff nor the money to support such distribution. A northern California Green, Jon Li, condensed all six hundred pages into a forty-three-page document, uploaded the excerpts onto the Internet, and organized a regional conference in May to discuss them.[41] Other than this preparation, many Greens arrived at Eugene without having seen all the SPAKA documents.

For five years, Greens had been working with the Ten Key Values and the questions "defining" them as their only vehicle for organizing. The SPAKAs would provide something more specific, more concrete. According to Jeff Land, site organizer for the gathering, the conference itself would have six goals: "To state a brief yet holistic vision for a reconstructed Green society; to identify the major values and principles that can unite people, making this vision a reality; to develop policy by applying these principles and values to issues; to discover appropriate strategies by working together at the gathering; to combine policy and strategy into action plans"; and to enjoy the process itself, which involved meeting Greens and creating a temporary Green community at the gathering. But even six months before the gathering, Land expressed some concerns with "the lack of response on questions of internal organization," fearing that "the as yet indeterminate and fluid nature of our own structure and decision-making process" might undermine efforts to formulate policy statements. And what was the point of making these vision statements without the "person power or money or clout" to carry them out?[42] Apparently, Greens were beginning to operate on the premise that "if you build it, they will come." This premise was to dominate in later years.

About three hundred people, two hundred fifty of whom were delegates, attended the second national gathering in Eugene in June 1989. Because of the smaller size, or perhaps because of the shared task, participants experienced the gathering as less contentious than the Amherst gathering of two years past. Perhaps the increased amiability could be credited to the absence of the perceived spokespersons of the most prominent ideological battle from Amherst, social ecology versus spiritual ecofeminism. Without charismatic leaders to rally around, people tended to address issues more than personalities. Nonetheless, some of the debates that would later deepen and tear at the Green movement were already being shaped.

One central tension within the Greens had to do with economics. In the two years between the Amherst and Eugene gatherings, a group of social ecologists had formed the Left Green Network with the expressed intent of ensuring that Green politics articulated an anticapitalist critique. At the Eugene gathering, the Left Green Network held workshops on economics that lasted far into the night and were attended by as many as one hundred people. There, and throughout the gathering, Greens debated whether it was capitalism, industrialism, or both that created the structural problems ensuring that Western economies depend on the exploitation of both humans and nature. Although many Greens advocated small-scale enterprise and worker control of the means of production, some Greens resisted using any language about "capitalism," because it bore connotations of communism, because they feared it would not appeal to a wider public, or because they believed capitalism was not inherently antiecological. The Greens' failure to reach a unified position on economics was soundly criticized by some observers, who felt that until the Greens achieved clarity on this single point, they would have difficulty progressing as a movement.[43]

Other conflicts were more immediately resolved—or people agreed that these were indeed problems that needed to be resolved.[44] In terms of strategy, the question whether to work on national politics or to focus on building a local, grassroots base was decided in favor of the latter, in spite of the urging of West German Green Wilhelm Knabe and a few U.S. Greens who were becoming impatient with the movement's slow pace of growth. Mark Satin, one of the "New Age" and more conservative participants, suggested that Greens needed to leave behind some classic characteristics of the sixties counterculture: namely, their fears of money, hierarchy, authority, and leadership. Satin felt the Greens would need both fundraising skills and a more coherent structure in order to get their message out to a broad base of the population.

Many Greens voiced concerns about diversity in terms of race and class. Participants noted the overwhelmingly white and middle-class composition of the gathering, along with its registration fees ($250 per person) and its location in one of the ten whitest cities in the United States. Wilmette Brown, a black veteran of the civil rights movement and director of a London-based women's organization, addressed the gathering and emphasized the need to make connections with the larger ecology movements, led and populated by women and people of color.[45] Bharat Patankar, an environmental activist from India, remarked on the absence of a farmer or labor perspective in the Greens, along with its overwhelmingly white population and the predominance of men. In the process sessions following the gathering, some ecofeminists observed that Green men liked the *idea* of gender balance more than the women's actual influence, and one woman noted that many men cared more about being heard than about listening to others. The problem of diversifying the Greens' race, class, and gender composition was generally perceived as an important one, though no reports of concrete plans for addressing this problem were made.

Nevertheless, the gathering accomplished what it set out to do. The name of the movement was changed to include the word "Green" in Green Committees of Correspondence (GCoC), reflecting the popular usage of that term. Participants spent free time exploring the Eugene environs, networking with other delegates, and exchanging ideas and strategies. Most central to the gathering's goals, the SPAKA documents were distributed, reviewed, and discussed throughout the gathering. Aided by the availability of numerous computers, participants compiled revisions and reports of the SPAKAs' developments throughout each day and published them each morning in the gathering's newspaper, *Green Tidings*. By Sunday afternoon, all the statements had been revised and presented to the gathering at large, with the understanding that the SPAKAs would be circulated among the locals during the following year and then brought to a final vote at the next gathering, already scheduled for Estes Park, Colorado.

Presenting the SPAKA documents at Eugene, each group could choose whether to ask for consensus on all or any part of its text; if the group did not request a call for consensus, the paper was simply "received." If consensus was not achieved when requested, a straw poll was taken of everyone present and later from the delegates exclusively. The matter of voting and the process of decision making itself were somewhat contentious among the Greens. Most Greens agreed with the idea that consensus decision making was more democratic in that it required everyone to participate in the decision: people could advocate, support, disagree, or block a decision. Those who blocked were required to write down their reasons, with the understanding that the documents would be published along with those statements so that all Greens would know exactly what the problems were, along with who had blocked a particular decision.[46] Opponents of consensus decision making described the process as cumbersome, time-consuming, ineffectual, and ultimately antidemocratic. According to the *L.A. Weekly*, the antidemocratic aspects of consensus decision making were nowhere more evident than in the document that was defeated in a 72 to 2 vote—by the two voting against it. Others expressed reservations that seeking consensus would translate into an incapacity to act on anything. One Youth Green who favored the 66 percent majority rule described the consensus process as a product of a middle-class fear of conflict: "They [the Greens] seem to think if you keep talking and talking, people will eventually agree. But they won't. Different groups have different interests. So all that happens is that you never act."[47] But in the case of the SPAKAs, at least, this despairing assessment was inaccurate. Captured so deftly in the titles of summary articles describing the gathering—"Can America Learn from the Greens? They're Right. But Is That Enough?" and "Last Chance Saloon"—participants left the Eugene gathering with a sense of urgency, believing that the project of program writing, along with the larger Green movement, had to go forward.

Immediately after the gathering in Eugene, John Rensenbrink, who had almost single-handedly coordinated the SPAKA process until that point, recruited Christa Slaton from the American Political Science Association and Margo Adair from the *Green Letter* editorial collective to help coordinate the upcoming year's SPAKA writing process. Together the three worked out a timeline for getting the Eugene SPAKA proposals printed in *Green Letter* and distributed to the locals, receiving feedback, incorporating those suggestions into an edited draft, and redistributing the draft to the locals prior to the next gathering in Estes Park. As before, the coordinators published regular reports of their progress in *Green Letter*, soliciting input and encouraging locals to be punctual in the submission of their revisions.[48] But the level of participation and response was lower than desired: in November, only a third of the working groups had responded to requests for updated information; only two met the year-end deadline for revisions, and the deadline had to be extended. Then it was discovered that only 35 percent of the locals were current in their dues payments to the national GCoC (a mere ten dollars per person annually), which meant that 65 percent of the locals would not be receiving the updated revisions of the SPAKAs issued regularly through *Green Letter*. By the summer of 1990, just months before the gathering in Estes Park, Christa Slaton prefaced the most up-to-date version of the SPAKAs with an article analyzing the unforeseen problems in the process along with her best attempts to address them. From her perspective, most of the problems occurred at the level of the working-group coordinators, who had no experience and no guidelines for working together or participating in a collaborative writing project of this magnitude. Accordingly, Slaton created a five-part format for articulating the results of each working group: this format would distinguish between policy proposals, strategy statements, and philosophical analysis about causes and solutions. At the gathering, delegates would vote only on policy proposals, striving for consensus but using a fall-back vote requiring 75 percent approval. Slaton concluded her article by enumerating the tasks she had completed in the eight months she had served as coordinator: "I sent out 908 letters and detailed information packets. . . . I made 112 phone calls and received 142 calls in efforts to inform and assist coordinators. . . . Yet I faced repeated travails when the process was ignored or bypassed."[49] She ended her report with a reference to Kahlil Gibran and an attempt at optimism.

But at the gathering in Estes Park that September, Slaton's optimism reached an end. To some, it seemed Slaton was caught in the middle of personal battles that had begun brewing well before she appeared; perhaps, as a woman in a supposedly ideological (rather than personal) power struggle between men, she was an easy target, or perhaps her leadership prominence simply made her vulnerable. But after eight months of attempting to keep the Greens to their deadlines and still foster a grassroots, democratic process, Slaton was in no mood to hear charges that she was being "manipulative" and "antidemocratic" at the gathering. On Friday afternoon, only two days into the event, she quit.

The conflict to which Slaton responded was intensified by requests from a group of Left Greens calling themselves "Greens for Democracy," estimated as numbering ten or twelve people out of the three hundred attending the gathering, though with a following that extended well beyond their own membership.[50] Their objections were presented in August, barely a month before the gathering, and focused on four main points: they believed the SPAKA process was antidemocratic because new ideas could not be presented at Estes Park, and they demanded that any decisions be sent back to the locals for ratification; they wanted time at the gathering allocated for a new proposal to restructure the national GCoC, which had become unwieldy and ineffectual; they wanted time allocated for action proposals; and they objected to the $250 registration fee, which would prevent many people from attending. Yet, as Left Green Howie Hawkins reports, all these requests were satisfied by the end of the gathering.

Action proposals came forward on the last day; a restructuring committee was elected to prepare a proposal that would be sent to the locals; the decision-making process was "as democratic as one could have hoped for"; and an alternative campsite was found where approximately forty Greens stayed, at 5 to 10 percent of the cost of the food and lodging at the gathering site.[51] The process through which the requests were satisfied, however, was upsetting to many and was described as "dysfunctional" and "patriarchal" by at least one Green writer.[52]

One of the controversial observations some Greens had begun to make based on the Estes Park gathering was that changing society was going to require some personal transformation on the part of Green activists as well. As Daniel Solnit explained, "To continue to ignore our 'process' is to reproduce patterns of oppression and domination in our movement. This is not a prerequisite to the 'real' work; this is the work."[53] Two years after the gathering, Slaton published an article corroborating Solnit's assessment and concluding that insofar as Greens around the globe had failed to "move established politics much beyond its destructive ways and means . . . the major reason has been a failure to integrate the major green values in a new politics among themselves."[54] Of course, not everyone agreed on the importance of personal transformation. For instance, Left Green Howie Hawkins seemed to experience the gathering differently: "There were no compulsory rituals nor any dogmatic advocates of personal lifestyle change as the one true path of Green politics—aspects of previous national conferences that have turned so many left activists off to the Greens."[55] In view of the interpersonal dynamics at Estes Park, both Hawkins's report of the gathering in *Left Green Notes* and the acount of Margo Adair (the third SPAKA coordinator) in *Green Letter* are remarkably upbeat. Hawkins makes no mention of Slaton at all, and though Adair alludes to "an untenable situation" that was "gruelling for everyone," she too concludes with what seems to be characteristic Green optimism in the face of glaring evidence to the contrary. Not too surprisingly, she echoes a theme of the Green movement: "One thing for sure," writes Adair, "is we Greens are maturing."[56]

Mark Satin, author of *New Age Politics* and a member of the Greens from the first meeting in Minneapolis, interpreted the gathering quite differently. Echoing the assessment from the *L.A. Weekly* in regard to the Eugene gathering, he commented, "I've been Pure before. It's pretty satisfying. But it's more important to be effective in the world." Satin believed the Greens were being held back by a "mistrust of—name one—expertise/hierarchy/efficiency/rules/power/ worldly success." Less than impressed with the keynote address by Chippewa Green activist Walt Bresette, Satin "felt another 60s syndrome coming on: the syndrome of starry-eyed whites sitting at the feet of oppressed minorities. And I had no desire to go through it again." White guilt about racism, in Satin's view, was "a sure sign that the Greens lack the maturity and self-confidence to deal with the race issue." Satin's evaluation of the Estes Park gathering concluded in his bidding farewell to the Greens, which he acknowledges as a real loss: "Whatever I may think of their internal battles and political prospects, the Greens are My People. Their life choices are my life choices; their failings mirror my own." The disillusionment and the choice to eschew further futility are hailed by Satin as a mark of his own maturity, an assessment aptly captured in the title of his report, "You Don't Have to Be a Baby to Cry."[57]

In spite of conflicts involving both ideology and personality at Estes Park, the gathering had some very positive results. The SPAKA documents were largely approved, and a seven-member platform committee was elected and empowered to hire a writer who would work the planks into a coherent draft that could be sent to the locals for ratification. The gathering was also the first to enjoy a vocal presence from men of color. Walt Bresette, a Wisconsin Chippewa who had founded the Lake Superior Greens in 1985, delivered a keynote address described the multicultural alliance building between Greens and Native Americans in Wisconsin and held out hope for similar alliances across the country.[58] African-American labor activist Kwazi Nkrumah led a workshop on alliance building that challenged many participants on the issues of white privilege and unexamined racism.[59] In these aspects, the outlook for the Greens was indeed positive.

Elkins in 1991: The Movement/Party Debate

With the platform of Green philosophy in place and the Green goals and vision articulated, the question of strategy could no longer be postponed. Those progressive writers with a continuing interest in the Greens all reported that the next step would involve addressing the relationship between movement building and electoral politics. The *Utne Reader* reported on the division of perspectives among Greens but gave favorable accounts of the electoral campaigns of Greens Jim Sykes from Alaska and Mindy Lorenz of California.[60] From a Left Green perspective, Howie Hawkins saw the next struggle to be "winning the Greens to a revolutionary strategy. As the Greens become more politicized, electoral reformism is replacing lifestyle change as the 'one true path' for many."[61] And in his essay following up on the Estes Park gathering, electoral advocate John Rensenbrink neatly touched on the most important outcomes of the event by linking the restructuring of the national GCoC, and the widespread desire to attract larger numbers of people of color to the Greens, to the relationship between movement and party. "Each has its own reason for being and each deserves its measure of autonomy within the green movement," he wrote, "including organizational autonomy as needed." Resolving the relationship between movement building and electoral politics was a question of strategy, but it became articulated as a question of structure instead. "Parallel structures that are closely interrelated seems to me a workable formula," stated Rensenbrink, reiterating his intention "to work steadily at multi-cultural and inter-movement relationships in the next several years with all others similarly committed, and to connect this organically with party building."[62] Here began a characteristically Green problem of masking the fundamental issues—in this case, questions of race and of strategy in the Greens—with other issues—in this case, structure. Once again, a Green implies that "if we build it [in this instance, a Green party], they [meaning people of color] will come." It is a classic cart-before-the-horse approach to problem solving, and not surprisingly, it creates more problems than it solves.

At one of the last IC meetings in Ann Arbor, Michigan, the June before Estes Park, a simple proposal for restructuring the national organization was drafted by Lauren Sargent, Charlie Betz, and Howie Hawkins and was forwarded to the Estes Park gathering for discussion. Perhaps because the document was seen as a Left Green creation, a ten-member restructuring committee was elected to develop a new structure by inviting democratic input from the locals. In January, midway between the summer gatherings at Estes Park and Elkins, the new restructuring proposal was mailed out to locals for a vote. The main point of contention seemed to be the composition of the Green Council, which was to be constituted equally by representatives from state Green party organizations and by regional representatives involved in movement building.[63] Since at the time Alaska was the only state in which Greens had achieved ballot status, some locals felt the new structure gave too much room to electoral activists. Other criticisms included the view that this structure gave electoral activists two votes, since many "party people" also did movement building. Finally, some felt the organizational structure concretized a disabling form of competition and reified the polarizations between party and movement.

A month after the new structure had been sent out for a vote, Rensenbrink and twenty-two other party activists convened a Green Party Organizing Committee (GPOC) meeting in Boston over the first weekend in February. Voting to exclude Left Greens Howie Hawkins and Guy Chichester from its meeting, the group proceeded to debate whether or not to remain within the Green CoC through the restructuring process. Persuaded by appeals from Greens on the restructuring committee, including Dee Berry and Charlie Betz, the GPOC ratified the new national structure proposal based on the 50 percent representation of party activists on the Green Council, a decision that was publicized to the Greens at large.[64] The new GPOC members also began their own newsletter and issued a clarifying statement saying that the restructuring proposal they endorsed included a Green Council that would "not abridge the GPOC or state parties' abilities to issue independent statements and/or endorsements." In spite of reassurances of the GPOC's commitment to movement-building activism from Charlie Betz, who had both served on the restructuring committee and attended the founding meeting of the GPOC, some locals read the statements issued by the GPOC as unequivocal rejections of accountability rather than as statements of autonomy and initiative. Other locals, largely those in California, had already moved beyond the point of debate and were spending their energies building a state Green party, registering voters, and obtaining ballot status. Out of the 135 current locals nationally, 80 signed up to participate in the restructuring process; most of the 55 that did not were California locals. By choosing not to renew their membership in the national, these locals did not receive the restructuring mailings and thus failed to participate in the restructuring vote.[65] The new structure, approved by an overwhelming 91 percent of participating locals, supported an organization integrating party and movement activists, a structure resembling the so-called Left Green Sargent/Betz proposal presented earlier at the gathering in Estes Park.

Greens in the GPOC were not pleased. Former clearinghouse coordinator, Restructuring Working Group member, and now GPOC member Dee Berry voiced her criticisms to the membership in the summer newsletter just before the gathering scheduled for August 15–21, 1991, in Elkins, West Virginia. Berry objected to the structure because it would force Greens to organize along state lines, although she conceded that state-level organizing was essential to electoral politics. She also complained that the new unified structure did not "encourage diversity" because it did not recognize "the difference between differentiation and separation." According to Berry, this drive for unity could be attributed to "some confused thinking about the difference between accountability and control," but "to assume that a unified structure will solve this problem [of accountability] is naive." Here Berry put her finger on the root of the problem: Greens had attempted to solve the deeper problems of strategy and accountability in the Green movement by addressing and temporarily resolving the more superficial problem of structure. As it turned out, the solution was only temporary. The impending rupture was aptly foreshadowed in the critique from Berry, who twice reiterated her willingness to accept the 91 percent vote in phrasing that implies otherwise: first, "The document prepared by the working group was not the one chosen in the vote of the participating locals and I am, of course, very disappointed. But the grassroots has spoken and its wishes will now be implemented"; and second, "We could have been real pioneers in the development of ecological organizations, but some of the concepts contained in the working group's proposal were probably too innovative, complex and untried for our troubled movement right now. In spite of my reservations, to believe in democratic, grassroots process is to abide by what emerges from that . . . and hope it's the best for the Greens (USA)."[66] Greens who paid attention to the undertones in Berry's critique were not surprised to hear that in late June the GPOC leadership issued a statement declaring it was premature to accept any proposed structure defining the relationship between the GPOC and the Greens. To explore the matter further, the GPOC would meet in Elkins several days before the formal opening of the gathering.

The only detailed report of these meetings is written from a Left Green perspective.[67] According to Howie Hawkins, only five members of the Left Green Network (LGN) were present during those two days (and only fifteen Left Greens attended the larger conference), but their presence was depicted as a "red menace" by members of the GPOC. Although Left Greens emphasized they had no intention of leaving the Green CoC regardless of what decisions were made, GPOC members alternately threatened to leave the GCoC themselves or charged the Left Greens with threatening to split the organization. Several women who were allied with the GPOC denounced the patriarchal behaviors of the Left Greens, claiming their own positions were ecofeminist but choosing not to elaborate on the connections between ecofeminism and national presidential politics, or ecofeminism and their preference for the autonomy of elected candidates from control by the Green membership. Others frustrated by the whole process suggested sending the "key players" (who were thereafter known as the "KPs" by those outside the struggle) to meet separately and work out their differences. Accordingly, in a meeting that ended near three in the morning, two Left Green members were coerced into a "consensus" agreement on the structure of the national organization, even though they made it clear they would offer an alternative proposal in the morning. When their proposal was offered as promised, it was assailed with charges of breaking consensus. Once the gathering was under way, however, tensions eased; people behaved more graciously to one another, avoiding personal attacks and focusing on the substantial matters at hand. By the end of the gathering, the new integrated structure was accepted.

Approximately 426 people registered for the gathering in Elkins, and in spite of a tremendous buildup of tension before the gathering, a great deal was accomplished.[68] For the first time in seven years, Greens agreed on a national action plan with three components: "Solar Power through Community Power," emphasizing the Green activism around nuclear power, renewable energy, and local sustainable economics; "500 Years of Resistance and Dignity," laying the groundwork for the 1992 actions responding to the quincentennial of Columbus's invasion of the Americas; and "Detroit Summer," which would be a campaign to work with inner-city organizations striving to rebuild devastated neighborhoods and create eco-city projects in Detroit. In a more philosophical vein, Greens at the gathering refined program statements on foreign and military policy and on economics. And while the conflicts over structure and the relationship of movement and party raged among various Euro-Green males ("KPs"), the splits in the gathering were temporarily healed by activist men of color.

First, Ron Daniels, former director of Jesse Jackson's National Rainbow Coalition, spoke about his own presidential campaign plans for 1992. Seeking to unify progressives, Daniels called for a national Progressive Convention the following August, after the two major parties had held their conventions. Daniels hoped this Progressive Convention would represent a wide spectrum of popular movements and create a "Third Force" in electoral politics that would use the electoral process to defend participatory democracy. His vision of a campaign that could support movement building, along with his endorsement of core Green values, did much to assuage Green activists' fears that electoralists would co-opt activism from the movement. African nationalist Suleiman Mahdi spoke about the African roots of ecology and his own concept of Green Justice. Meanwhile, the committee negotiating a compromise on the role of state parties within the organization reached an agreement: a Green Party U.S.A. would be created as one arm of the Green movement, and the GPOC would dissolve and be replaced with a Green Party Organizing Caucus working within the new electoral arm of the Greens. Reflecting this new structure, the national organization would be renamed The Greens/Green Party U.S.A. (G/GPUSA). Shortly after a compromise decision had been reached on the national structure, Kwazi Nkrumah, an African-American labor activist from California, took the stage and announced the formation of the Green Justice Caucus, an alliance formed from the coalition of the Women's Caucus, People of Color Caucus, Youth Caucus, and Gay/Lesbian Caucus. Nkrumah proceeded to announce the new caucus's endorsements for Greens in upcoming elections to the newly reconstructed national organization and asked those endorsed to step forward for acknowledgment. Then Nkrumah and other Green Justice Caucus members began a process of honoring many Greens who had long been active in the movement. These gestures had a unifying effect on the gathering as nothing else did. With high spirits and the fresh hope of seemingly achieving a foundation at last, Greens concluded the gathering at Elkins and returned with optimism to their locals.

In the history of the Green movement, the year 1991 and the gathering at Elkins seem to be both the high point and the end of an era of Green organizing. In the seven years since their founding in St. Paul, Greens had organized local groups around the United States, developed and ratified a national program, and restructured their national organization to accommodate new growth. After the first national gathering in Amherst, social ecologists in the Greens formed the Left Green Network as a separate but allied organization of the Green national, and Left Greens (though never populous in their membership) exerted a strong influence on both the platform process and national structure debates. At Elkins, four of the seven Greens elected to the new governing body, the Green Council, were Left Greens or Left Green sympathizers, a composition that made electorally minded Greens feel disenfranchised. Between 1991 and 1992, Left Greens repeatedly raised and finally made a de facto decision to allow their group to fold back into the Greens' national organization. The Youth Greens also dissolved during this time: mobility, lack of funds, and especially an interest in anarchist activism inspired the Youth Greens to disband or, in the case of one group, to reincarnate briefly as AWOL, a Minneapolis-based anarchist group retaining many of the original Youth Green members. As the more radical leftist factions of the Greens were dissolving or being absorbed into the national, the electoral faction was simultaneously withdrawing from the national. To those fixated on a left-right political spectrum, it would seem that the Greens began with strong tendencies on the Left and in 1991 began an informal shift to the Right. Others, preferring to import factional descriptions from the West German Greens, would describe the shift as a move from the *fundi* (politically Left but also philosophically pure, with a strong emphasis on accountability and a wariness of co-optation) to the *realo* (electorally focused and pragmatic, emphasizing autonomy and accepting the need for compromise). Of course, in West Germany, this shift preceded a real downturn in power and in popular appeal for *die Grünen*.

Though the Elkins gathering concluded with the agreement to form a single organization, many elements of structure and policy were left unresolved. Accordingly, an Ad Hoc Working Group was created to develop processes for accrediting state Green parties, representing parties in the national organization, structuring the relationship of members to the national, and making decisions about national support for state party work. But the divisions that went underground to reach unity at Elkins resurfaced on the ad hoc committee and beyond, shortly after the gathering. In the fall of 1991, letters exploring the question of their future relations with the national were circulated among electorally minded Greens, and in March 1992, the founding meeting of the Green Politics Network (GPN) was held in Kansas City. In the pages of the *Greens Bulletin* that same month, thirteen electorally minded Greens published their "Rationale for Launching a Green Politics Network." Explaining that the Greens had become "as oppressive as the patriarchal society we are committed to transforming," signatories found the movement was now tangled in replaying "the old power and control games." Because "how we do our politics and how we treat each other" are equally important, and because "the time is ripe for a national catalyst with a holistic, post-capitalist and post-socialist politics," the signatories expressed an urgency about forming a Green Politics Network. Basing their membership on individuals rather than on local groups, they professed a willingness to function "as a parallel organization with the Greens and stress[ed] the desire to be in a cooperating relationship with the Greens."[69] It was to be the last formal communication between the Greens and the GPN for three years.

Slouching toward the Millennium: The 1992–1994 Gatherings

In the three years after the Elkins gathering, a number of circumstances and events conspired to withdraw energy from the Greens' national organization. First among them was the debt. Although reports in the *Greens Bulletin* showed the national organization as having $2,716.91 in savings as of May 1990 and $4,074.03 in September 1990, by February 1993 the national organization was recording outstanding debts from 1992 of $32,438.50. Part of the deficit stemmed from the multiple transitions in the position of clearinghouse coordinator after Dee Berry's resignation. Part was simply mismanagement of funds. About $15,000 of the debt was due to costs incurred by the 1992 Minneapolis gathering. Such huge debts tend to discourage new activists from joining an organization and to dishearten even the most committed activists.

Another, more subtle circumstance was the shift in publications sent to Greens as part of their membership in the national. The publishing collective for *Green Letter/In Search of Greener Times* changed its focus from an exclusive newsletter for the Greens to a newsjournal reporting on the activities of various movements for social transformation. Claiming they wanted "to provide a newspaper in which no single movement speaks as the voice of all," the *GroundWork* collective chose the new format "to cross pollinate between movements." In effect, the new format began the process of phasing out coverage of the Greens. The spring 1992 transition issue featured *Green Letter/In Search of Greener Times* on one side, and on the reverse side the cover of the new journal, *GroundWork,* was displayed. By fall 1992, the entire journal was titled *Ground-Work,* and the Greens received coverage on 13 of the 60 pages; in the fourth issue of *GroundWork,* published in March 1994, Greens were covered on 4 of 52 pages, and by issue five, Greens received coverage on 2 of the 52 pages. Certainly, the change in coverage reflected financial difficulties with the publishing collective as well as a loss of faith or interest in the Greens nationally. Nonetheless, losing this communication vehicle increased the isolation and disconnection some locals and state activists had already felt from the national.

Another change in publications illustrated the overall political movement of the Greens during this time. *Regeneration,* a journal of Left Green thought, was launched in June 1991 by the same collective that had published *Workers' Democracy* from 1981 to 1990, thus illustrating in a tangible way the Left Greens' inheritance from the old Left. The fourth issue of *Regeneration,* published in the fall of 1992, covered the 1992 debates between party and movement activists. In the fifth issue, dated winter 1993, the editors of *Regeneration* announced the journal would incorporate the smaller publication, *Green Synthesis,* and become "the new theoretical discussion bulletin of the Greens/Green Party USA." Hence, as the Left Green Network's theoretical journal was replaced by the new *Synthesis/Regeneration,* so too the Greens national was edged out of *Green Letter* in its transformation into *GroundWork.* Possibly to counteract the loss of *Green Letter,* a national newspaper, *Green Politics,* was initiated in 1992, its production overseen by former SEAC member Eric Odell. At this same time, publication of the *Greens Bulletin* became somewhat sporadic due to a loss of funds, and Greens received more pleas for donations from the clearinghouse than any news or movement-building information. The changes in these publications mirrored the ideological and political shifts in alliances among Greens. Building good national connections requires having reliable publications for the exchange of ideas, news, and ongoing communication. As the publications changed, communications on a national level deteriorated significantly and a new period of isolationism set in. In the first part of the 1990s, Greens became much more interested in state-level organizing than in national organizing. Going into the 1992 national gathering in Minneapolis, however, it would have been difficult to foresee such changes.

The Minneapolis gathering was preceded by a three-day Green Economics Training program, yet another response to the question of national Green strategy which had somehow gone unaddressed in the movement versus electoral politics debate. In order to create a Green society, Green economics would have to be put in place, and transitional economic strategies would have to be ensured before workers would dare withdraw from exploitative or resource-intensive industries. Michael Albert, cofounder of *Z Magazine* and coauthor of *Looking Forward: Participatory Economics for the Twenty-First Century*, started off the training with a keynote address on participatory economics. Other trainers included Ellen Frank and Jim Westrich, staff economists from the Center for Popular Economics in Massachusetts; Kris Olsen and Mary Courteau, co-op organizers and managers from Minnesota; Carolyn Estes, cofounder of the intentional community Alpha Farm; Kristin Dawkins, senior fellow at the Institute for Agriculture and Trade Policy; and Terry Gips, cofounder of the International Alliance for Sustainable Agriculture. With programs such as "Basic Economics for Activists," "Transitional Economics," "The Labor and Environment Connection," and "Building a Green Society through Economic Restructuring," the Economics Training Program attracted 218 people from around the United States. Because the organizers had received grant money for the program, it had to be offered as an educational event rather than as a specifically political event; nonetheless, some people were disappointed that time was not offered to work on the economics plank of the Greens' national platform.

The Minneapolis gathering continued to address questions of national structure, the most important changes having to do with the relation of Green parties to the national movement. An Electoral Action Working Group was created and charged with accrediting state Green parties, coordinating electoral actions with issue campaigns, community organizing, and other forms of non-electoral activity. Three simple accreditation guidelines for state Green parties were developed as well: the guidelines required that "a state Green Party, Green candidate, Green elected official, or Green electoral endeavor shall (1) explicitly affirm the Ten Key Values, and (2) be willing to engage in Green conflict resolution processes, upon request of any Green local or state confederation active in the same state as the accredited electoral formation."[70] Third, state parties must not be opposed by a majority of affiliated locals within the state.

One of the most momentous outcomes of the gathering was the proposal advanced by the Women's Caucus to change one of the key values from *postpatriarchal* to *feminist*. Of course, the Women's Caucus advanced other proposals as well—formal recognition for the Women's Caucus, the establishment of a Women's Leadership Fund, two permanent seats on the Green Council, and the request that four of the seven Coordinating Committee members be women. But the change in the key value created quite a debate on the plenary floor. The proposal writers argued that "*postpatriarchal values* suggests more about the present patriarchal society we live in today than about the society we are building," and that *feminism* would "draw in more women who see that we are strongly committed to ending the oppression of women" and would convey the idea of "challenging gender socialization stereotypes that mold both women and men."[71] One opponent of the change voiced his concern the next day in *Green Tidings*, the daily grassroots publication produced at every Green gathering: "Just as females were manipulated by men to be submissive, by yielding to this term we become submissive to an ideology that oppresses us and 'feminizes' us!" In view of other objections such as this one, *feminism* was adopted by exactly the minimum required (75 percent).

At the 1992 gathering in Minneapolis, the national tripartite Green Action Plan initiated at Elkins gained renewed support. Modeled after the "Detroit Summer" component of the project, expanded plans for Green Cities projects were created for Syracuse, Los Angeles, and Detroit. For the "500 Years of Resistance and Dignity" action plan, Greens planned major anti–Columbus Day demonstrations in Denver and other cities. And the "Solar Power through Community Power" campaign to transfer reliance for energy sources from corporate-controlled nuclear power plants to community-controlled, solar-based renewables gained added visibility through the march and demonstration against Northern States Power Company (NSP). Organized by AWOL (the reincarnation of the Youth Greens) in coalition with the Prairie Island Coalition Against Nuclear Storage, the march and rally were called to protest NSP's environmental racism, evidenced not only in its operation of two nuclear power plants next to the Mdewakanton tribal reservation but in NSP's additional plans to build on-site storage casks for the radioactive waste that would soon overflow the indoor storage pools. On Friday at 4:00 P.M., the first official evening of the gathering, Greens and allied others marched from the conference site to NSP headquarters in downtown Minneapolis. The march was organized as street theater and progressed through three themes: at the front was "the dystopian nightmare created by nuclear power and general ecological ruin"; in the middle was the "social change/revolution section," featuring a multitude of green and black flags; and at the end was "utopia/the free society," featuring "windmills, the sun, and other manifestations of the potential good life."[72] Once they arrived at NSP headquarters, AWOL activists worshiped barrels of "toxic waste" and performed what was later called an "electric kool-aid toxic test," drinking colored Kool-Aid and dropping dead on the spot—an action well timed to coincide with the exodus of business executives from their offices at the end of the workday. Other Greens climbed to the top of the building and dropped a twenty-foot antinuke banner. To conclude the action, demonstrators read a list of demands to NSP.

The march energized the gathering, which was otherwised marked by the loss of two important figures. Shortly after the demonstration, AWOL spokesperson Joe Lowndes announced that AWOL was dropping out of the Greens. Many of the youth and anarchist Greens had concluded that the Greens had become a hierarchical organization, already making concessions (through electoral politics) that would allow them to fit into a system they had originally organized to transform. Greens lost another powerful figure for a very different reason. At the end of the gathering, Carolyn Estes, a prominent member of the Greens who had served as plenary facilitator at every national gathering, announced her retirement, but her closing benediction offered another upbeat ending for a national Green gathering.

Reports of the gathering appeared in local publications of the Twin Cities as well as in the progressive national publication *Z Magazine.* The weekly free paper, the *Twin Cities Reader,* ran a favorable two-page report on the gathering and the Economics Training Program, concluding that "the future may be greener than Clinton, or Bush, or anyone else suspects."[73] *Z Magazine*'s report on the gathering was written by a Green woman, Diana Spalding, who also gave an optimistic spin to the national Green Action Plan, the conference workshops, and the Women's Caucus proposals.[74] Although none of these reports commented on the similarities between the "electric kool-aid" tests of the sixties and the nineties, the *Z* article shared what was by now a common theme with the Minneapolis *Star Tribune,* which also published a brief editorial welcoming the Greens at the beginning of the gathering.[75] "At eight years of age," wrote

Diana Spalding in *Z*, "the Greens in the U.S. are maturing." In an unsigned editorial, the *Star Tribune* commented, "The Greens . . . may be growing up." And the report on the gathering published in *Groundwork* was even more emphatic: "The Greens," authors assured readers, "have grown up."[76]

After the Minneapolis gathering in 1992, the gatherings at Syracuse and Boise were anticlimactic, although their themes certainly developed the concept of Green Justice first promoted at the gathering in Estes Park. The 1993 gathering in Syracuse chose "Green Cities and Green Justice" as its theme and held good to its promise: more than one hundred Greens camped and held their congress at Earthwise Education Center, a community-supported organic farm and one of the few African-American–owned family farms in New York. The president of Earthwise, Winston Gordon, was a former Black Panther and a current member of the Syracuse Greens. Under his supervision, the farm offered apprenticeships in sustainable agriculture to homeless persons and to black youth. The educational portion of the gathering was held on an inner-city lot provided by the soul food restaurant Vera's Place, which also served food for the gathering participants. The gathering was the first to offer the "Green Sprouts" program, providing child care for the children of Greens who attended the gathering. Educational workshops on organizing locals, running campaigns, switching to sustainable agriculture, and building solidarity between Greens and indigenous people, along with numerous sessions on Green cities, made the weekend portion of the gathering go smoothly, and the event received a favorable report in the local newspaper.[77] The congress that followed the gathering, however, was consumed with matters of national organization and debt, and few new decisions were made.

For the 1994 gathering, Boise was chosen as the site since Idaho Greens were fighting legislation that, if enacted, would violate the human rights of gays and lesbians. The theme of the gathering, "Embracing Common Ground: Celebrating Human and Bio-Diversity," emphasized another important aspect of Green Justice in connecting sexual diversity with ecological diversity. Workshops addressed building solidarity with gay, lesbian, bisexual, and transgendered people, and there was a march on the capitol. Owing to the distance of Boise from most major cities and from major Green locals, the time of year, or simply the lack of publicity, the Boise gathering drew only about twenty-five activists, in comparison to the nearly three hundred participants at the Syracuse gathering.[78] It was truly the low point in national Green activity. Fortunately for the Greens, the slow grind back to visibility began that same year, when Betty Wood of Blodgett Mills, New York, applied for the position of national clearinghouse coordinator. After a year of debate while two other coordinators moved through the clearinghouse, Wood's offer was finally accepted, and the clearinghouse moved from Kansas City to Blodgett Mills in March 1995. The national gathering that year marked the beginning of a new direction for the Greens.

Albuquerque in '95: Toward National Unity

Ever since the 1991 gathering in Elkins, the electorally minded activists who shortly thereafter formed the Green Politics Network had been noticeably absent from the national gatherings of the Greens/Green Party U.S.A. Although the events in Minneapolis, Syracuse, and Boise had all been characterized by their inclusion of a direct action march and protest as part of their annual activities, along with the peaceful absence of high-level conflicts among "key players," the gatherings were also marked by a kind of national inaction. The three-part Green Action Plan first advanced at Elkins and reaffirmed at Minneapolis was diluted by the following year into a series of more manageable, locally based direct action networks.[79] Although designed to increase the level of Green activism, it was unclear how much activity actually occurred beyond the locals that sponsored these actions. One could speculate that as much as Greens despised the tension, hostilities, and personal attacks that resulted from the national-level battles between movement and party activists, it was nonetheless a conflict that propelled the Greens forward. Activists affiliated with the GPN or those who shared a GPN-leaning perspective tended to be charismatic, articulate, self-proclaimed leaders who initiated bold ventures (sometimes without the support or the knowledge of their local communities) and thus (democratically or not) kept the movement going. In contrast, the G/GPUSA Congress returned each year to the question of internal organization, picking at the topic as if it were a festering sore that wouldn't heal.

Whether because of exhaustion from the movement/party battle that culminated at Elkins or because of disenchantment with the Green movement as a whole, the numbers of participants attending national gatherings or renewing their membership in the national organization continued to fall. The GPN did not experience a corresponding rise in membership levels, either; few Greens were ready to embrace the GPN's belief that electoral activism was inherently a more succesful strategy than movement building. But although more seasoned activists had dropped out of the Greens nationally, new members had joined Green locals or state parties. These new members had no direct experience with the history of hostilities among the Greens and no interest in repeating old battles. They wanted a unified movement that would be capable of acting on Green values and electing Green candidates.[80] With several of the "key players" still active in the Greens, could that desire be realized, or would the participation of those few KPs re-create the same scenarios that had divided the Greens in the past? The 1995 gathering in Albuquerque was a first step toward exploring the possibilities.

Albuquerque was chosen as a gathering site because of the recent successes of the Greens in Santa Fe and the strong organizing network Greens had established in New Mexico. After collecting four thousand signatures to become a registered political party in 1992, Santa Fe Greens began building a reputation by working locally to improve the day-to-day lives of New Mexico citizens.[81] In Santa Fe, where property values and taxes were quite high, Greens helped organize Citizens for Property Tax Justice to protect the rights of many low-income residents whose families had lived on their land for more than four hundred years. Greens also initiated Santa Fe Hours, printing currency and creating a directory of participating individuals who wanted to barter services with other local residents on an hour-for-hour exchange. Other initiatives, such as the Living Wage Campaign and the Tenant-Landlord Counsel, added to the Greens' reputation, so when Cris Moore ran for Santa Fe City Council, he won through tremendous popular support. By 1994, just two years after founding the party, Greens won statewide credibility by running former lieutenant governor Roberto Mondragon and campaign finance reform activist Steve Schmidt for governor and lieutenant governor. As a Green stronghold and an excellent example of integrating electoral and movement strategies, New Mexico seemed the ideal setting for a reconciliation of GPN and G/GPUSA activists.

To create the possibility of realizing those dreams of Green unity, conference organizer Cris Moore publicized the gathering not as another annual gathering of the G/GPUSA but rather as a "National Green Conference," sponsored by a number of endorsers. In this way, Moore got endorsements from the GPN, the G/GPUSA, unafffiliated state Green parties, and activist groups such as various Campus Greens and the Student Environmental Action Coalition (SEAC) Southwest. The gathering drew the largest number of Greens since Elkins, with more than 230 people registering from 32 states, and international visitors from Australia, Canada, Mexico, and Niger.[82] Workshops offered a healthy balance between movement and electoral emphases, with sessions such as "How to Run for Elected Office," "Fighting Toxics," "Labor and Environment," "Fundraising," "Earth Spirituality," "Direct Action/Civil Disobedience," "Alternative Media," "Proportional Representation," and "Campaign Finance Reform." Plenary speakers were selected with a decidedly electoral focus: Pacifica Radio political commentator Saul Landau gave a speech titled "Politics and the Greens," County Council chair of Hawai'i's Big Island, Keiko Bonk gave an address called "Green Victory in Hawai'i," Green senator from Western Australia Christobel Chamarette described Green electoral strategies in her country, and Linda Martin of the GPN hosted a panel of participants from "Third Parties '96," a GPN-sponsored conference of third-party activists held earlier that year. Probably unaware that she had struck a theme, Keiko Bonk opened her plenary address and the first full day of the gathering with the statement, "It is time for the Greens to grow up."[83]

With the electorally minded activists back on the scene, the gathering was certain to face some contentious issues. These issues soon presented themselves in the Green Coordination proposal offered by the GPN and in the forty-state Green party idea presented by three electorally minded Green men—Mike Feinstein and Greg Jan of the Green Party of California and Steve Schmidt of the New Mexico Green Party. The strategic symmetry of the two proposals was barely masked by the fact that these ideas were suggested separately and by different teams of proponents. Both proposals were presented as methods of achieving greater unity on the national level. Both would effectively subordinate the movement to the party, as movement activists from the G/GPUSA were quick to point out.

The Coordination proposal offered by the GPN was circulated on the Internet about two months before the gathering. Professing a desire "to form a broad umbrella that would be a Green Coordination of many different organizations which adhere to the Green Ten Key Values," members and allies of the GPN proposed periodic meetings for engaging in "a continuing and ***nonbinding*** dialogue about Green organizing within the U.S."[84] The stated purpose of the proposal was to bring all Green activists and organizations "to the table" in a way that the G/GPUSA, ever since Elkins, had not. Movement activists reacted with suspicion. If the GPN were truly interested in maintaining a dialogue among Greens, why had their members left the G/GPUSA in the first place? The agreements made at Elkins had reshaped the GCoC into the new G/GPUSA with the expressed purpose—though, some claimed, without the result—of creating the coordination here proposed by the GPN, four years later. Finally, G/GPUSA members balked because the new Coordination would add yet another layer of bureaucracy onto the national level; there would be more meetings to attend, more administrative expenses, and conversations with no potential for decision making, enforcement, or accountability.[85] GPN members were derided as being "self-selected leaders without followers" who had returned to the G/GPUSA to claim their followers and to appropriate the name "Green Party U.S.A.," a name to which the national G/GPUSA held legal claim since the Elkins gathering.

The forty-state Green party concept was also circulated several months before the gathering, in the form of a proposal and questionnaire, the results of which would be tallied and presented at the gathering. In this proposal, the writers argued for the importance of Green participation in the 1996 national presidential race. The proposal outlined the events that would need to occur for such a campaign to be possible, offered a timeline within which those events would need to take place, and suggested that the national gathering in 1996 (which might then become an endorsing convention for a Green presidential candidate) be held at a place and time that would provide the strongest counterpoint to the conventions of the two major parties. The proposal concluded with a questionnaire asking Greens if their local or state party would participate in such a campaign and whether or not they could offer assistance in founding Green parties in other states. G/GPUSA members were shocked by the audacity of a proposal that so clearly contradicted the value of grassroots democracy and local politics, values that had been the backbone of the movement since its inception. Moreover, members roundly denounced the strategy of putting out a questionnaire on the Internet and then presenting the results as a kind of already-decided-on "Green mandate" at the gathering. In these two proposals, electorally minded activists had once again demonstrated their propensity for grand schemes, bold action, or devious machinations—depending on one's perspective. Certainly nothing of this magnitude had yet been proposed in the now eleven-year history of the U.S. Greens.

Both proposals for national unity and national action went forward in effect, without agreements being reached on either one. At the Congress of the G/GPUSA, held directly after the gathering, members passed a proposal to endorse a "Green Roundtable," replacing the word "Coordination" and its associations of decision making and action with the concept of communication only. Throughout the fall, there was much discussion and foot-dragging about the Green Roundtable, but no suggestions were put forth for holding its first meeting. Finally, the Green Council of the G/GPUSA called a meeting of the first Roundtable to be held in March 1996 in St. Louis, Missouri. Unfortunately, the call was issued unilaterally, without conferring with members of the GPN and other unaffiliated state party representatives about the date or location.

Objecting to both the process and the location, members of the GPN issued a statement that they would not attend such a meeting. Though their boycott of this specific meeting seemed justified, the GPN made no attempt to coordinate another Roundtable meeting at a different time or place.

The forty-state Green party proposal and its suggestion for a 1996 presidential campaign made quick progress in the California Green Party (GPCA). At the September statewide meeting in Northridge, the plenary passed a proposal setting up a "receptive" process whereby the Green Party of California would be able to respond to declarations from Green or Green-minded potential candidates for the presidency. In mid-October, GPCA activists found a statement by Ralph Nader in the *Chicago Tribune* saying he would consider being on the California ballot in order to pressure President Clinton to veto various pieces of legislation in the upcoming year. By November 10, GPCA activists had drafted an invitation letter to Nader and obtained the signatures of prominent leaders in the environmental and social justice movements around the state. On November 27, Nader issued a statement accepting their invitation to run for president on the ballot of the Green Party of California.

Across the United States, Greens were both excited and appalled. Who had authorized the Green Party of California to initiate a national campaign? What strategic purpose would it serve? And what was Nader's position in relation to the Ten Key Values or the platform of the California Green Party? While some activists debated these questions, others moved quickly to follow in the footsteps of California, calling meetings of electoral and movement activists in their state and proposing the idea of a Nader presidential campaign as an opportunity for new coalitions and for increased visibility for their shared messages about democracy, campaign finance reform, and corporate accountability. By May 1996, just three months before the gathering now set for Los Angeles, Nader had been placed on Green Party ballots in Maine, Virginia, Rhode Island, and California. It wasn't yet a forty-state Green party effort. But it was a national campaign that drew attention to the Greens like nothing before.

3. The U.S. Greens as a Social Movement

The parallel development of ecofeminism and Green politics in the United States can be informed by examining these movements through the lens of social movement theory. In this chapter I detail the development of the Green movement in the United States specifically as a social movement, by chronicling the history of three important groups: the Left Green Network (LGN), the Youth Greens (YG), and the Green Politics Network (GPN).

Formed in 1988, the Left Green Network reached its height of influence in 1990; by 1993 it had diminished into an association in name only (it has never entirely disbanded). Paralleling the rise and fall of the Left Green Network, the Youth Greens also formed in 1988 and made a decision to disband in 1992. In contrast, the Green Politics Network began incubating ideas in 1990 during the height of LGN influence but was not officially formed until the spring of 1992. The GPN (or ideas and strategies advocated by the GPN) has been steadily gaining in influence ever since.

The formation, popularity, and (in at least two cases) decline of these three Green groups can be seen most productively as different stages of a single movement: taken together, they outline the development of Green politics in the United States. The transition from a leftist and sometimes anarchist politics of movement building and local campaigning as advocated by the LGN and the YG, to the emphasis on statewide and national electoral politics as affirmed by the GPN, places the U.S. Green movement within the pattern of social movements around the world. To understand the importance of this comparison, I digress briefly to summarize relevant aspects of social movement theory.

Social Movement Theory and the Cycles of History

The idea that entire social systems go through cyclical change has been advanced from a variety of disciplinary perspectives. In the cultural studies perspective, scholars argue that cultural change is the main source of political and social change. Political scientists and economists detect regular cycles of political and economic change throughout history, and sociologists find that changes in states and in capitalism produce cycles of collective action. Overall, scholars of social movements have observed specific patterns and features that may be characteristic, and one of the most striking is the cyclical nature of social movements.

In social movement theory, one of the best known and most respected proponents of the concept of protest cycles is Sidney Tarrow.[1] *Power in Movement,* Tarrow's most recent text, advances his thesis by examining a variety of social movements throughout Europe and the United States over the past two centuries. Tarrow begins with an analysis of the rebellions that occurred all across Europe during the winter and spring of 1848. By counting and graphing the number of public events (marches, meetings, organized assemblies, barricades) in Germany, France, Italy, and the Hapsburg Empire, he discovered a cycle of movement events. Using these data, he developed his theory describing an internal pattern of social movements, along with the idea that such movements occur in international waves of mobilization and reform. Tarrow also uses this theory of protest cycles to examine three cycles in more recent history, comparing the Popular Front in France with the New Deal in the United States during the early 1930s, the student movements in Europe and the United States during the 1960s, and the Eastern European democratization wave of the 1980s that began in Poland and ended with the demise of the Soviet Union in 1991.

Using different periods of social movement as examples, other scholars have also discovered cycles within and among social movements. Looking primarily at U.S. history, Arthur J. Schlesinger, Jr., has observed thirty-year political-ideological cycles alternating between periods of progressive social responsibility and periods of conservative individualism.[2] In this century, Schlesinger cites the Progressives of 1910, the New Deal of the 1930s, and the movements of the 1960s as examples of the progressive arc, followed respectively by the Coolidge 1920s, the McCarthyism of the 1950s, and the Reaganomics of the 1980s, exemplifying the conservative individualistic arc of the cycle. According to Schlesinger's theory, the United States is due for another cycle of progressive social movements in the 1990s.

Drawing on both Schlesinger and Tarrow, Marta Fuentes and Andre Gunder Frank have contributed individually and collaboratively to the research and understanding of social movements. In their influential "Ten Theses on Social Movements," they argue that social movements are indeed cyclical and "related to long political, economic and, perhaps associated, ideological cycles. When the conditions that give rise to the movements change, through the action of the movements themselves and/or more usually due to changing circumstances, the movements tend to disappear."[3] Building on Tarrow's research and examining not only industrial countries but also peasant and anticolonial movements in Latin America, India, Southeast Asia, China, Japan, and Africa, Frank and Fuentes find cycles of protest occurring internationally during the same historical periods.[4] They conclude, however, that the causes of these movements— whether economic, political, or ideological—cannot yet be definitively discerned.

Tarrow's research indicates that there are exogenous and endogenous cycles of social movements: that is, just as social movements tend to peak and ebb at various historical periods, so too there is an internal cycle to each separate movement. Social movement scholars have found that organizers or leaders cannot start these movements.[5] Rather, social movements form in response to changes in what Tarrow has called the "political opportunity structure," meaning certain features of the political environment that are external to the movement (unlike money or power) and that make it easier or more difficult for people to become involved in collective action. Discontent or hardship is seldom a sufficient motivation for collective action, since the potential costs of such action—job loss, wage or benefits reductions, physical injury, punitive legislative measures, the investment of time and money, or the unlikelihood of success—are seen to outweigh the benefits. Social movements are most likely to form when political opportunities reduce the perceived or real costs of collective action, reveal potential allies, and show where elites and authorities are vulnerable.[6] The most significant political opportunity occurs when there are conflicts and cleavages among a society's elites.

Once a social movement has formed, according to Tarrow, it has a particular shape or pattern to its development.[7] When political opportunities open up, well-placed "early risers" articulate claims that resonate with the public and suggest new coalitions among previously disparate actors. When these different actors or social networks discover a convergence among their various interpretations of events—a process defined as "consensus formation"—these groups can then be mobilized for collective action.[8] By mobilizing consensus, "early risers" create or reinforce the instability of the elite, opening up further political opportunities for other actors. The early stages of protest involve a heightening of conflict, within institutions and on the streets, and a diffusion of ideas across diverse regions and sectors of the population. The diffusion of ideas spreads not only to similar groups making the same claims against similar opponents but to unrelated groups and to antagonists as well. Openings in the political opportunity structure can be used by both social movement actors and their antagonists, who organize the repression and backlash that follow closely on the social movement cycles.

As a movement gains momentum, it is characterized by experimentation, innovation, and new forms of collective action and social protest. But collective action is not invented by movement organizers; rather, each historical period has its own conventions for collective action, which Charles Tilly has called "the repertoire of contention."[9] In western Europe, before the Industrial Revolution, social protest took the form of grain seizures, field invasions, rough music, and public shaming or satirizing at festivals or major celebrations. By the middle of the nineteenth century, as Tarrow explains, social protest had shifted to include the tearing down of houses, the petition, the public meeting, the demonstration, and the barricade.[10] At present, movements tend to choose among three main forms of collective action: violence, organized public demonstrations, and disruptive direct action. Violence is the least desirable means, since it always immediately legitimates repression, polarizes or alienates the public, and relies for its continued expression on small groups of fugitive militants; moreover, the state's vastly superior capacity for repression ensures that social movements that choose violence cannot win. In contrast, organized public demonstrations have the potential to raise the uncertainty of violence, challenge the status quo, and foster solidarity among movement participants, the three goals of collective action, and this form of action has become the most conventional to date. Like public demonstrations, the power of disruptive direct action lies in its ability to challenge authorities, create uncertainty, and nourish solidarity. But even this form of action has become conventional, and as soon as a movement's repertoire becomes well known, boredom sets in: the media cease to cover collective actions, participation falls off, and movements are faced with a strategic impasse. If movement organizers choose to use violence and more emphatic rhetoric to marshal participants and attract media attention, they alienate the public, drive away potential allies, and give elites the excuse they need to initiate severe repression. If, on the other hand, movement organizers attempt to institutionalize the movement and protect their gains, this strategy transforms the movement into an interest group. The task for movement organizers, then, is not to attempt what cannot be achieved but rather to recognize the peak of the movement and try to sustain it while achieving as many gains as possible. Hence, movement leaders adapt, combine, and innovate on various forms of collective action, using spontaneity and symbolism to motivate participation and to alleviate boredom.

Any peak of social movement activity is marked by a period of increased contention: conflicts between elites are exacerbated into deep cleavages among social groups, interactions between challengers and authorities increase in frequency, and new centers of power are consolidated, leading many dissidents to believe that their movement is assured of success in reaching its goal of social transformation. But social movements cannot be sustained beyond their peak; the political opportunity structure closes, elites make concessions or take stands that co-opt the message of the movement, activist leaders are offered positions of power within the system, political actors weary of the struggle, and movements that sought fundamental social change tend to end with the achievement of surface reforms. Though frequently followed by a backlash that may destroy many of the movement's gains, social movements leave behind, in Tarrow's words, "expansions in participation, popular culture and ideology."[11]

Repeatedly, movements split apart over questions of strategy, as the more radical faction seeks continued change while the more pragmatic faction strives to institutionalize its gains. Studying European social movements of the nineteenth century, Tarrow finds a polarity between anarchism and social democracy that is replayed in the social movements of the New Left in the 1960s and 1970s: "Where the hierarchy of social democracy helped to turn a movement into a party, the anarchists' obsession with collective action and their allergy to organization transformed them into a sect"; and "where the Social Democrats attempted to internalize movement within organization . . . the anarchists foreshortened all organization into collective action."[12] Hence, the question of movement strategy can often be confused with the question of movement organization. "A key element in the decline of movements are disputes over tactics," writes Tarrow, "as some militants insist on radicalizing their strategy while others try to consolidate their organizations and deliver concrete benefits to supporters."[13] The social democrat/anarchist distinctions here aptly describe the differences between and the outcomes of these tendencies within the Greens: the Green Politics Network and the Left Green Network respectively. As the Green movement clearly illustrates, the organization of a social movement can either stifle or nourish the power of that movement.

According to Tarrow, movement organization has at least three aspects: its formal organization, the organization of collective action, and the mobilizing structures that link movement leaders with the organization of collective action. Though movement leaders are tempted to create formal organizations with mobilizing structures that take charge of collective activities, the power of centralized movements is often an illusion. The challenge for movement organizers is to create organizational structures that are sufficiently strong to resist opponents yet flexible enough to change as conditions develop and to allow enough autonomy for participants to retain and foster movement energy and participation. The most effective mobilizing structure is a network of interdependent organizations, allowing the greatest autonomy and ideological plurality among participants. Tarrow finds that such coalitions have tended to characterize social movements since the 1960s. The drawback to such networks, however, is that when the crisis for which they organized and responded to is over, there is no permanent organizational structure to continue their activism. On the other hand, decentralized movements offer a maximum of democracy and autonomy to participants but lack coordination and are easily dissolved or repressed; the decentralized structure of the Youth Greens, for example, combined with the inevitably shifting nature of student and youth populations, seems to have been a key factor in the group's demise.

In their famous study of four social movements from the mid-twentieth-century United States, *Poor People's Movements: Why They Succeed, How They Fail*, Frances Fox Piven and Richard Cloward argue that movement organizers create institutions as a means of retaining movement success, not realizing that the institutions will last only as long as the movement itself. In fact, the organization-building activities created by movement leaders have the tendency to diminish the power of the movement by directing people away from activism and into meetings. Highly critical of electoral politics, Piven and Cloward see voting as the socially defined means through which political change can and should occur, and to the degree that people believe in the efficacy of electoral politics, they participate in their own oppression. In effect, Piven and Cloward argue that involvement in electoral politics channels people away from movement politics. In capitalist societies "electoral-representative arrangements proclaim the franchise, not force and wealth, as the basis for the accumulation and use of power. Wealth is, to be sure, unequally distributed, but the franchise is widely and nearly equally distributed, and by exercising the franchise men and women presumably determine who their rulers will be, and therefore what their rulers presumably must do if they are to remain rulers."[14] In the 1990s, it is evident that the power rooted in wealth is greater than the power of electoral-representative politics. The elite maintain social control as long as lower-class groups abide by and participate in the electoral system. Piven and Cloward conclude that "it is usually when unrest among the lower classes breaks out of the confines of electoral procedures that the poor may have some influence."[15]

A decade later, Piven and Cloward augmented their findings with the publication of *Why Americans Don't Vote*, in which they argue that there is a complementarity between electoral politics and movement participation. Social movements tend to arise in response to political opportunities created by electoral volatility. When the loyalty of large voter blocs becomes uncertain, candidates emerge who articulate criticisms of the status quo as a way of gaining or retaining votes. The split among the elites named by Tarrow as the most significant political opportunity can be created and communicated through the electoral system. The fact that large numbers of Americans do not vote, however, can be attributed to structural impediments in the electoral system as well as systemic barriers in the society at large. According to Piven and Cloward, "the sharp underrepresentation of poorer and minority people in the American electorate creates an electoral environment that also weakens their ability to act politically through movements."[16] The solution to the question of social justice cannot be found by relying solely on participation in electoral politics.

How can social movement theory enhance an understanding of the Green and ecofeminist movements? In what ways does social movement theory describe—and fail to describe—these movements? After the peak of social movement activism in the sixties, some activists shifted their political focus to work on issues of nuclear power and nuclear weapons in the 1970s and 1980s, and the peace movement activists, in collaboration with bioregionalists, feminists, social ecologists, and others, birthed both the Green and ecofeminist movements. Seen exogenously, these movements are not peak social movements but rather the incubating networks and institutions that keep the ideas of social transformation alive until the next period of political opportunity. Endogenously, Tarrow's theory about the internal cycles of social movements can be best applied to the Greens, as ecofeminists have participated in creating various movements and organizations, but no single national entity that compares with

the Greens. Within the Greens, then, the shift from movement activism to electoral politics can be seen to follow the shape of social movements. The shift can
best be observed not by tracing the mainstream of national organizing, as I did
in Chapter 2, but by examining the development and demise of the Left Green
Network, the Youth Greens, and the Green Politics Network.

Within the Greens, some have compared the shift in ascendancy from the
Left Green Network/Youth Greens to the Green Politics Network to a parallel
transition within the West German Greens, from *fundi* (those who defend original Green values) to *realo* (pragmatist Greens elected to the Bundestag who
became committed to exercising parliamentary power).[17] Those disappointed by
this development have tended to describe the shift as moving from Left to
Right, a terminology that has proved offensive to members of the GPN, as well
as those Greens who support both movement activism and electoral politics.
Whereas the Left Green Network had comfortably and proudly adopted the
term "Left" to convey its stance and to emphasize connections and continuity
with the old Left and the New Left, members of the GPN never adopted and
indeed were insulted by being given the term "Right," since they see not similarities with but rather their differences from the 1990s conservative Right in
the United States. To understand the significance of this shift, it's important to
look at numbers: at its peak, the Left Green Network membership never
reached more than three hundred in a movement numbering over three thousand, though it had many more sympathizers among the Greens at large; in
1994, two years after its formation, the Green Politics Network reported a
membership of forty, though again the number of sympathizers who have not
yet joined is difficult to estimate.[18]

Overall, as the radical tendencies of the Greens shifted from a movement
emphasis to an electoral emphasis, membership in the original Greens national
organization (the G/GPUSA) has fallen consistently. Each new attempt at higher
and higher levels of electoralism, beginning with the formation of state parties
and the running of not local but statewide and later national candidates, has
been justified by the rationale that this strategy would create greater publicity,
attract more members, and invigorate the movement. Most recently, this claim
was used as justification for a presidential campaign with the candidacy of
Ralph Nader. If membership in the Greens continues to diminish, the movement will simply have followed the pattern of social movements from the last
two centuries. If, on the other hand, the Green movement is reinvigorated by
the Nader presidential campaign, the Greens may embody a shift from the
social movement cycles of the past to a new pattern of social movement, one
that ebbs and flows but does not subside.

The Left Green Network (1987–1993): "Greening the Left and Radicalizing the Greens"

At the first national Greens gathering in Amherst in 1987, all the different theoretical tendencies among the radical ecology movement were represented—namely, social ecology, deep ecology, bioregionalism, and ecofeminism—and people were introduced to the first public display of the ideological clashes that would unfold over the next several years.[19] Murray Bookchin, from the Institute for Social Ecology in Vermont, delivered a stinging attack on the theory of deep ecology and on remarks made in the pages of the *Earth First!* journal during Bill Devall's 1987 interview of Dave Foreman.[20] Bookchin and other social ecologists were critical of the New Age spirituality component among the Greens and feared it would take the movement in a direction that would be insufficiently grounded in a critique of economic and social injustices, focusing on personal transformation at the expense of public and political action. The Amherst gathering ended with a symbolic conciliatory hug between Murray Bookchin and Charlene Spretnak (who had been targeted as a representative for all spiritually oriented Greens, she was and is a cultural ecofeminist), intended to preserve peace and unity among Greens. In a forecast of the 1991 gathering at Elkins, at Amherst participants who wanted to see unity were certainly given a show, but the tensions that were politely smoothed over at the gathering's conclusion surfaced within the following year.

In 1988, the New England Regional Committees of Correspondence experienced an internal split that seemed to embody on a regional level differences regarding theory, strategy, and internal procedures that U.S. Greens would have to address at the local and national levels. Conflicts over accountability of regional representatives to the national Committees of Correspondence, along with dissatisfaction with the lack of clarity in the Ten Key Values[21] and a corresponding lack of analytic clarity among Green members, caused a number of Greens from Vermont and New Hampshire to form a Green Alliance and to present a more detailed Statement of Principles.[22] Green Alliance members were concerned about the New Age tendencies within the Greens as well as the ahistorical approach of ignoring the Green movement's position as inheritor of the old and New Left; they wanted to provide a firm foundation for future developments, particularly since the national CoC had decided shortly after the Amherst gathering to embark on a period of program writing as a way of addressing and resolving conflicts among the various perspectives within the Greens. Green Alliance members wanted to get their principles written and circulated to influence and contribute to that process.

The differences between the Ten Key Values and the twenty-one Principles of the Vermont and New Hampshire Greens truly encapsulate the most significant differences between what was the main body of Green thought between 1987 and 1991 and what by 1989 took shape as the Left Green Network. Possibly as a preliminary to the national program-writing process, Vermont and New Hampshire Greens clustered their expanded list of principles into four main categories: values, goals, strategies, and organization. Building on four Green values addressing the liberation of human and nonhuman nature (*ecological humanism, antiracism, ecofeminism, gay and lesbian liberation*), Vermont and New Hampshire Greens sought to achieve six goals of social transformation: *grassroots democracy; a cooperative commonwealth; social responsibility; ecological reconstruction; a non-nuclear, home-based, democratic defense;* and *nonaligned democratic internationalism*. The Green movement would achieve these goals through eight strategies whose combined effect characterized the Green movement: *independent politics* (not aligned with the two major parties), *direct action, movements from below, fundamental opposition* (to capitalism and hierarchical society generally), *an emphasis on programs not personalities, thinking globally and acting locally, organic grassroots growth* (i.e., community and workplace organizing), and *strategic nonviolence*. Internally, the movement would follow three simple principles of organization: *grassroots democratic confederation, democratic decentralism,* and *participatory membership*.

Considered by many outsiders (and insiders) to be the core of Green philosophy, *ecology* itself underwent various repositionings and redefinitions. The first pillar of the German Greens, *ecology* had been adopted as *ecological wisdom* in the Ten Key Values. As defined by Spretnak and Capra, *ecological wisdom* invokes the philosophy of deep ecology, a spiritual connection between humans and nature, and the necessity of shifting from an anthropocentric worldview, which places humans above nature and views all nature as existing to serve humans, to a biocentric worldview, in which humans are a part of nature.[23] But to Vermont and New Hampshire Greens, *ecological wisdom* was associated with an apolitical spirituality, a misanthropy that had come to be associated with deep ecology, and an emphasis on personal insight at the expense of social action. In their principles, *ecological wisdom* was replaced with *ecological humanism*, by which they emphasized the necessary interconnections between humans and nature: "Ecology for the Greens," they wrote, "means social ecology." To create a "nonhierarchical, nondomineering society" based on the principle of *ecological humanism*, thereby uprooting the base cause of both social and ecological crises, requires "a grassroots democracy of self-governing communities that are humanly scaled, bioregionally integrated, and cooperatively confederated."[24] The principle of *grassroots democracy* remains the same, from the German Greens, to the Ten Key Values, to the Principles of the Vermont and New Hampshire Greens, and on to the Principles of the Left Green Network, making it one of the most consistent core values of Green politics.[25]

Other important changes involved the principles of *social responsibility, nonviolence, community-based economics, respect for diversity, postpatriarchal values,* and *global responsibility.* Taken from the Four Pillars of the German Greens, *social responsibility* was changed to *personal and social responsibility* in the Ten Key Values to empower individuals by emphasizing the importance of personal changes such as lowered consumption patterns and individual political involvement. Interpreting this addition to imply a shift in responsibility, meaning that individuals were as responsible for creating social and environmental crises as were social systems of power, wealth, and force such as multinational corporations and the military, Vermont and New Hampshire Greens dropped the *personal* and kept only the *social responsibility.* In their statement, *social responsibility* shifted the emphasis of responsibility from the individual back to the society, defining this principle as the responsibility of the society to "ensure that every person's basic material needs are met"; such responsibility would include measures such as a guaranteed living wage, universal health care, and the just redistribution of wealth and work. And the German Greens' pillar of *nonviolence,* maintained in the Ten Key Values, became *strategic nonviolence* in the Vermont and New Hampshire Principles, a change that was retained in the Principles of the Left Green Network. The reasoning for this change was simply the acknowledgment that "there are circumstances that necessitate armed self-defense as a morally legitimate way to resist violent repression by domestic tyrannies or foreign invaders." Noting that the strategy of nonviolence had been elevated to a panacea, Vermont and New Hampshire (and, shortly thereafter, Left) Greens insisted that any discussion of nonviolence must include the structural and systemic violence that is institutionalized around the world. They were careful to emphasize, however, that "violence distorts the revolutionary process," giving authorities the excuse they need for further repression.[26] Because no popular revolution can succeed solely through acquiring superior force, and because nonviolent strategies tend to be participatory and democratic, nonviolence remains a central principle of Green politics.

Community-based economics seems to be incorporated and expanded into the principle of a *cooperative commonwealth,* defined as "a democratic and decentralized economic system which is fundamentally different from the centralized, exploitative economic systems of both the corporate states of the West and the bureaucratic states of the East."[27] Bringing control of the economy back to the community alone will not solve the problem of economic injustice and ecological degradation; Vermont and New Hampshire Greens emphasize that it is capitalism itself that must be replaced with enterprises owned cooperatively by the community in which they operate and managed by the workers within them. "Capitalism," according to Vermont and New Hampshire Greens, "is inherently incompatible with a humanistic, ecological society. Capitalism is not motivated by the production and exchange of commodities to meet human needs, but by the investment of capital to create more capital. Blind growth-for-growth's-sake is thus structured into capitalism, making capitalism as deadly to the planetary biosphere as cancer is to an organism. Human needs go needlessly unmet. Nature is exploited and then discarded. Social and moral bonds are degraded into amoral money relationships. Everything acquires a price."[28]

Although the original founders of the U.S. Greens had included *respect for diversity* in the Ten Key Values as a means of addressing social justice, Vermont and New Hampshire Greens believed the phrase did not communicate the central importance of social justice or the strength of their commitment to it. To clarify their meaning, *respect for diversity* was dropped and in its place more specific principles were added: *antiracism, gay and lesbian liberation,* and *ecofeminism.* Similarly, though *postpatriarchal values* had originally been chosen to convey the kind of values society would embrace once the culture had moved beyond patriarchal domination, the term was seen as too vague: moreover, it was criticized for retaining reference to a system Greens wanted to replace rather than to the kind of society Greens wanted to create. The term *ecofeminism* was chosen for its emphasis on the liberation of women (thereby expanding and specifying more clearly than *respect for diversity*) and for its recognition that the liberation of women and nature are inextricably connected projects.[29] Thus, ecofeminism was first explicitly incorporated into Green politics through the Principles of the Vermont and New Hampshire Greens, and it remained one of the fourteen Principles of the Left Green Network.

Global responsibility underwent several changes. Its core meaning was present in the strategy "thinking globally, acting locally" and it was also present in two of the Green goals: *non-nuclear, home-based, democratic defense* and *non-aligned democratic internationalism.* These points show the Green movement's inheritance from the peace movement and movements from the New Left. Finally, the principles of *independent politics* and *direct action* were added to the cluster of Green strategies, possibly to stake out a position in distinction to some tendencies within Greens for working in alliance with the Democrats or for working primarily in the arena of electoral politics to the exclusion of grass-roots activism.

These principles, the most lengthy statement of Green politics in the United States since Brian Tokar's *The Green Alternative*, were circulated and revised that summer, fall, and winter accompanied by a Call to Form the Left Green Network, which was signed by about twenty-five people. This call gave the reasons a Left Green Network was needed: to ensure that the Green movement would offer an alternative to the Democratic Party, which had continuously co-opted the energies of so many activists by promising token reforms but not making any systemic changes; to affirm the Green movement's history of social activism in the old and New Left, in response to an emerging antileftism within the larger Green movement; and to proclaim an anticapitalist stance as central to an ecological Green movement. According to the call, Left Greens were concerned by what they perceived as an "anti-intellectual irrationalism, a proselytizing religiosity, and a liberal 'tolerance' of an intolerant, mean-spirited Malthusianism." Objecting to what they saw as "a supernaturalism that promotes the separation of humanity from nature and that ultimately justifies domination and hierarchy," Left Greens affirmed their support for a "sense of experiential communion with nature" and a spirituality defined as "mutual care, respect, and a sense of community to nurture the human spirit and sustain us for political struggle." Finally, Left Greens also objected to the use of consensus decision making in the Green movement, finding it an inadequate means for resolving controversy among the multitude of often conflicting perspectives within the movement. Already in the Green movement the mandate to seek consensus on decisions was leading to organizational paralysis. Left Greens criticized consensus decision making as potentially undemocratic, for it effectively allowed a small minority to exercise veto power over the wishes of a majority. As an alternative, Left Greens proposed making decisions by first seeking consensus, but when consensus could not achieved, allowing a simple majority vote to carry out the decision in the name of the Left Greens, with dissenters remaining free to abstain from implementing the decision and free to voice their dissent publicly.

In addition to describing the LGN's differences from both the mainstream electoral activism of the Democrats and the views and procedures of the Greens, the call specified the intended relations the Left Green Network would have to the Left and to the Greens. While encouraging prospective members of the Left Green Network to remain in (or to join) the Green Committees of Correspondence, the Left Greens also welcomed unaffiliated Greens, leftists, and members of other leftist organizations. Thus, the LGN functioned both as a caucus within the GCoC and as a distinct organization, with its own principles, membership, conferences, and publications. Left Greens grew fond of saying that the purpose of the LGN was "to green the Left and radicalize the Greens," bringing an ecological perspective to the Left and bringing forward the history of the old and New Left, along with an anticapitalist critique, to the Greens. They encouraged people to join the Greens and emphasized that they did not intend to be a splinter group or to divide the movement.

By April 1989, when the First Continental Conference of the Left Green Network was held in Ames, Iowa, the twenty-one Principles of the Vermont and New Hampshire Greens had been transformed into fourteen principles that were presented for discussion and were adopted by the fifty or sixty conference participants.[30] Retaining eight principles from the Vermont and New Hampshire Greens—*ecological humanism, gay and lesbian liberation, grassroots democracy, cooperative commonwealth, independent politics, direct action, strategic non-violence, democratic decentralism*—the Left Greens amended several principles and added a few new ones. For example, *antiracism* became *racial equity; non-aligned democratic internationalism* became simply *nonaligned internationalism;* and *ecofeminism* became *social ecofeminism,* to emphasize the distinctions be-tween the West Coast branch of ecofeminism, which was more spiritually in-clined, and the East Coast branch, which was more influenced by social ecology. Finally, the principles of *human rights, radical municipalism,* and *social ecology* were added, owing to the influence of social ecologists in shaping the Left Green Network. In fact, some of these principles seem rather redundant; *social ecology* seems to include the principles of *radical municipalism, human rights, coopera-tive comonwealth, grassroots democracy, democratic decentralism,* and so forth, but activists were concerned with clarity and didn't want to leave these points open to interpretation.

At Ames the newly organized Left Greens adopted bylaws and set up a coordinating council and a clearinghouse, working groups, caucuses, and a publication vehicle (*Left Green Notes*). They agreed on three action-oriented projects: a project to radicalize Earth Day 1990, a conference on local indepen-dent politics, and a project for supporting the Diné Green Alliance in opposing uranium mining and striving to build ecological forms of development within the framework of grassroots political and economic democracy. The Left Green Network's stated relationship to the GCoC was to "work within both the Greens and the Left." Finally, LGN members agreed that Left Greens needed to bring an "anticapitalist, independent political perspective" into the working groups at the GCoC gathering at Eugene later that summer. They planned to hold regular caucus meetings at the Eugene gathering as a way of educating participants and encouraging debate.

Meanwhile, members of the GCoC were not pleased with the growth of a Green tendency that was "Left" or social ecologist, a dissatisfaction that could be traced to the founding meeting in 1984, and that had become publicly visible at the Amherst gathering in 1987. In fall 1988, before the Call to Form the LGN had been widely publicized, members of the northern California Greens issued a statement correcting what they saw as false assertions made by leftists within the Greens.[31] First, they refuted the claim that social ecology versus deep ecology was the major debate within the U.S. Greens, a misrepresentation started by Murray Bookchin in his opening address at Amherst. In his attack, Bookchin had represented Arne Naess, George Sessions, Bill Devall, Dave Foreman, and Ed Abbey as deep ecologists, when in fact whatever theory guided the statements or acts espoused by Foreman and Abbey, it was quite different from the deep ecology originating with Naess. But since Foreman, Abbey, and Naess were not present at Amherst, and had never become members of the U.S. Greens, the social ecology versus deep ecology debate had to be seen as taking place outside the GCoC. Perpetuating the idea that this debate was central to the U.S. Greens focused attention on social ecologists and took attention away from the more important debates that actually were under way: debates about strategies for the future and the evolving Green philosophy, both addressed through the process of developing the SPAKA documents. Finally, northern California Greens objected to the trend among social ecologists to emulate the West German Green Party's *fundi* faction. Attempting to recruit people by telling them that the main project of Green politics is to "overthrow capitalism" not only misrepresents Green philosophy but also alienates most people in the United States who equate capitalism with private ownership. According to northern California Greens, the Green economic vision of cooperative, community-based economics and small-scale ownership of various enterprises is much more appealing to people than the call to "overthrow capitalism"—and social ecologists should stop using that term.

Publicizing and circulating the Call to Form a Left Green Network served to emphasize the differences in viewpoint between the Left Greens and the GCoC, even before the first conference of the LGN was held. Following up on ideas expressed in that collective statement, Danny Moses and Charlene Spretnak (two northern California Greens who had signed the statement in fall 1988) coauthored an essay reviewing the development of the U.S. Green movement and charging the Left Greens with misrepresenting the differences between the two groups. According to Moses and Spretnak, Left Greens apparently presented their concern about multiracial organizing as unique to their group of Greens, when in fact the GCoC had attempted to work with people of color from the beginning in 1984. Left Greens used the term "social ecofeminism" in their principles, implying that "other ecofeminisms . . . fail to consider women 'cultural beings' as well as 'biological beings,'" a charge that was particularly offensive to Spretnak. The Left Greens portrayed the GCoC as "apolitical" based on the GCoC's emphasis on the importance of personal transformation, ecological wisdom, and spirituality to the Green movement when in fact most Greens did not believe that political activism and spirituality were mutually exclusive. In sum, Moses and Spretnak charged the Left Greens with a "vanguard mentality" and suggested that Left Greens were actually using the Green movement as a vehicle for their own preexisting agenda.[32] Their article appeared just in time for the founding conference of the Left Green Network.

Reports of the LGN founding conference, its aims and principles, appeared in both radical venues and publications of the GCoC.[33] The response from mainstream (or Ten Key Value) Greens was articulated by Lorna Salzman, who asked the question that was being raised by many GCoC Greens: "Is the Left Green Network really Green?"[34] Salzman's essay crystallized the first step in a debate between Left Greens and 10KV Greens over who would be allowed to determine the defining characteristics of "Green." In the course of the debate, one can see the central issue of the Green movement shifting, from the deep ecology/social ecology rift to the question of capitalism versus industrialism or corporatism.

First, Salzman objected to the anticapitalist stance of the Left Green Network, fearing it would be applied to small businesses and multinational corporations alike, and asked, "Is not the LGN itself proposing to socialize small businesses that play no role in the oppressive policies dictated by the corporate sector or by the Federal government?" Salzman suggested that the problem was based in their differing analyses of the root causes of oppression. From her perspective, "industrialism is the disease; capitalism and socialism are its vectors." With Moses and Spretnak, Salzman criticized the Left Greens' apparent lack of interest in nature, with ecological concerns tacked on as an afterthought to the LGN's fourteen principles. She effectively rejected the Left Green principle of *ecological humanism,* asserting that "it is *biocentrism* (whether promoted by evolutionists or spiritualists), not social ecology or humanism, that unites humanity with nature."[35] With Moses and Spretnak, Salzman rejected the deep/

social ecology debate as irrelevant to the GCoC, reminding readers that neither Foreman nor Abbey was a member of the Greens. She also rejected the criticism in the LGN's call that the GCoC Greens advocated a spirituality separating humans from nature, when all the essays on Green spirituality (most notably Charlene Spretnak's) emphasized the unique spirituality that arises from the experience of humans as embedded in nature.

But Salzman's most damaging critique repeated Moses and Spretnak's assertion that the LGN "persists in promoting an *a priori* political worldview that can then be applied across the board to all extant social problems";[36] in effect, the LGN was charged with using the Greens as a vehicle for its own leftist ideology, which included the belief that ending the domination of human by human would of necessity end the human domination of nature. In contrast, a Green critique, according to Salzman, would begin by addressing the problems inherent in the destruction of nature and thereby develop an appropriate social analysis and program for restructuring or replacing current institutions. In these exchanges, both groups wrestled over the sole definition of what it meant to be Green, rather than allowing that there might be several different versions of Green philosophy. Of course, one could charge (as Janet Biehl would do in her response) that Salzman too had an *a priori* political worldview. But bringing a certain worldview into activism is the primary way people become activists, and having an ideological motivation for one's activism is hardly cause for criticism; perhaps the error is simply in being unable to expand or adjust that worldview when one receives new information.

At the gathering in Eugene, eight or nine members of the Left Green Network submitted resolutions and raised topics they felt were being overlooked in the main Green program. Nonetheless, their presence was so compatible with the gathering that in a report published later that fall, even the SPAKA coordinators commended the LGN's participation.[37] Left Green Network members followed through on the resolutions made at their founding convention, working to educate Greens and to encourage debate by holding evening discussion sessions that ran late into the night and were attended by fifty or more people each evening. But they had not forgotten Salzman's critique.

That fall, three Left Greens responded to Salzman, specifically addressing her points on capitalism, ecology, *a priori* ideas, and ideological diversity.[38] Explaining that capitalism, not industrialism, is the base of "the edifice of domination," Tom Athanasiou deplored the fact that Salzman saw no link between small and large capitalism, when in fact the present system of multinational corporations emerged from the "human-scaled mercantile capitalism" she defended. Salzman's assault on industrialism rather than capitalism seemed naive to Carl Boggs, who argued that modern societies rely on industrial processes and that it would be elitist and racist to deny some form of industrial development to other, less-developed countries; in contrast, capitalism could be replaced and the result would be an overall improvement in human well-being, although wealthy elites would suffer from the transition.

Curiously, on the topic of ecology, both Salzman and Athanasiou cited the same lines from the Left Green Network's statement of principles: "As social ecologists, we embrace the conservation of species diversity, habitats and ecosystems and the expansion of wilderness areas. We call for ecotechnologies based on renewable, organic and non-toxic materials, energy sources and production processes that harmonize community-controlled economics with the ecology of their bioregions." Yet, because these were the only lines in the LGN principles explicitly addressing ecology, Salzman read them as a mere aside; to Athanasiou, and to most Left Greens, these two sentences encompassed the major concerns of any environmentalist. Again, the problem seemed to be the ideological orientations of the authors, which Janet Biehl was quick to point out: if the Left Green Network could truly be said to have various *a priori* ideas, Salzman would have to recognize that she had a few of her own, namely, biocentrism and a critique of industrialism (not capitalism) as the root cause of the problem.

The Left Greens backed up their charge of GCoC "incoherence" with an example from the Eugene gathering. There, according to Biehl, "a representative of the lumber industry—whose voice had the equal weight of everybody else's—succeeded in helping form the resolution on forestry—and in watering it down."[39] Greens were willing to tolerate "diversity" of antagonists such as the lumber industry, yet they were not willing to extend this tolerance to a branch of their own movement, the Left Greens. Such variances seemed inconsistent or, indeed, "incoherent" from a Left Green perspective. Finally, as Carl Boggs observed, the Greens' antileftism was effectively a form of ahistoricism, detaching Greens from nearly a century of radical activism. Boggs believed Green theory had inherited "the best elements of Marxism, social ecology, feminism, and radical democracy," developing an analysis that "denies any single basis of change" but rather emphasizes the "multiple and overlapping forms of domination."[40] In contrast, both Marxism and deep ecology appear to reduce the problem of domination to a single focus—class or nature. Acknowledging the radical history that the Green movement was heir to allowed Left Greens to avoid this singleness of focus.

The debate was continued into the following spring, when Charlene Spretnak responded primarily to the charges articulated by Carl Boggs and offered her own reading of the issues.[41] For Spretnak, the real debates in the Greens were not between social and deep ecology but rather between humanism and ecocentrism, between a Hegelian/Marxist approach and a Gandhian/ecofeminist approach, between anticapitalism and community-based economics, between strategic nonviolence and nonviolence, and between leftist politics and spirituality.[42] Her essay does much to clarify these issues. On the topic of a priori beliefs, Spretnak acknowledged that many people came into the Greens with varying assumptions and backgrounds; conflicts arose only when one group saw their original beliefs not as contributing to the evolution of Green politics but rather as the most important pre-Green position. In terms of process, Spretnak distinguished the Left Green advocacy of "a dialectical clash of opposites" as a Hegelian/Marxist approach, distinctly different from a Gandhian/ecofeminist approach to process matters. (Effectively, these differences can be seen as gendered differences between conflict and cooperation as modes of engagement.) Describing the Green vision as either "anticapitalist" or "community-based economics," Spretnak was concerned about the connotative meanings of these terms and their ability to communicate with the public. This same concern was behind her comments on the "spirituality vs. ?" debate: Spretnak argued that a rejection of spirituality would effectively alienate many activists whose religion or spirituality was the motivating force behind their activism. She cited many different religious groups and various communities of color as evidence of the power of spiritually based activism. Although Spretnak's analysis of the debates offered valuable clarification, it's doubtful that Left Greens gave her arguments much consideration. They were too busy planning, enacting, and writing about their most significant direct action event: the Wall Street Action.

Earth Day Wall Street Action: Monday, April 23, 1990

The decision to radicalize Earth Day 1990 was one of three action proposals accepted at the Left Green Network's April 1989 founding conference in Ames, Iowa. The rationale for the action was to form some active counterpoint to the corporate greenwashing that was already building up for the twentieth anniversary of Earth Day. The action drew on the history of two events: the first Earth Day and the most recent Wall Street Action. The first Earth Day in 1970, celebrated on John Muir's birthday (April 22), was the first large demonstration of public concern for the environment and has been credited with launching the wave of environmental legislation that crested during the seventies. But even that first celebration was tainted by corporate machinations: festivities were planned to coincide with and thus detract attention from antiwar demonstrations against a major spring offensive in Vietnam. Hence, the first Earth Day was seen as an attempt to gloss over the more pressing issues of the day with an ecological patina.[43] The more recent Wall Street Action—scheduled on October 29, 1979, to coincide with the fiftieth anniversary of the great stock market crash of 1929—was called by the antinuclear Clamshell Alliance to demonstrate the connections between nuclear power and corporate power and to build alliances between the antinuclear movement and the movements for peace, freedom, and social justice. For the Wall Street Action in 1979, the Clamshell formed coalitions with many grassroots groups, so that on the day of protest more than two thousand activists filled Wall Street and 1,045 arrests were made for acts of civil disobedience.[44] As inheritor of the legacy of both these events, the Earth Day Wall Street Action was intended to wrest definitional control of Earth Day from corporate polluters, whose attempts at greenwashing their own enterprises and promoting the idea that "we're all equally responsible" for environmental degradation were successfully persuading the public that it was possible to "green" capitalism. Left Greens wanted to organize an action that would effectively shift the bulk of responsibility for economic and environmental degradation away from the individual citizen to the largely unquestioned economic and political structures—in short, from the personal to the political. Not coincidentally, at the LGN's founding conference, an Earth Day action was proposed by a former member of the Clamshell Alliance and current member of the Left Green Network, Howie Hawkins.

Planning an action of this scale began shortly after the LGN's founding convention and involved building alliances within the Greens as well as with other radical activist groups. At the second national Green gathering in Eugene, Left Greens presented the idea of an action to the Greens there and invited participation. But there was a different response from grassroots Greens than from the organizational bureaucracy of the GCoC. In response to the LGN proposal voiced at Eugene, a member of the GCoC staff suggested an alternative action of "Greening Wall Street," which would involve massive participation in buying, selling, and trading shares that "reflect a shift away from conventional shares which are recognized as socially and ecologically irresponsible to shares recognized as supporting socially and ecologically responsible causes."[45] This suggestion clearly failed to understand the Left Green conviction that capitalism cannot be "greened" and indeed that attempts to "green" capitalism only serve to perpetuate the problem—and the problem, from a Left Green perspective, is capitalism. At an October meeting of the Interregional Committee (the coordinating body of the GCoC), the Earth Day Wall Street Action was again proposed for endorsement but did not achieve consensus, so the decision was brought up for final consideration at the IC meeting in March 1990. By this time, just one month before the action, the Left Greens had built up an impressive array of coalitions with more than thirty-five organizations. Not coincidentally, one member of the IC, Lorna Salzman, amended the proposal by calling for an independent GCoC action on Wall Street. The proposal failed, but those who wanted to vote in support of the Left Greens' Wall Street Action were hamstrung by the rules of consensus decision making. In the end, although two regional Green groups and fourteen Green locals endorsed the proposal, what would be one of the most significant direct actions of the Greens went forward without even the qualified endorsement of the Greens' national body.

Earth Day Wall Street Action organizers spent more than six months writing and circulating a call to participate in the action, building coalitions with like-minded groups, planning an action scenario, and compiling a handbook for the event. In November 1989, letters of invitation were sent to allied groups, along with pages explaining the rationale for the action, the principles and organizing structure for the coalition, the stipulation of nonviolence, and a timetable for planning the event. For action scenarios, organizers planned civil disobedience (groups linking arms and chaining themselves to each other or to a standing structure), mobile clusters (taking over intersections, festive marches to slow down traffic), and street theater scenes that included attaching an umbilical cord to the George Washington statue and connecting it to the stock exchange as a way to draw connections among government, corporations, and the wealthy white slave owners in "founding" the country. As a model for their handbook, organizers referred to the handbook created for the 1979 Wall Street Action, the *Up Against the Wall Street Journal.* By March 20, when the *Wall Street Action Handbook* went to press, more than forty-five organizations had endorsed the action.[46]

On April 23, events began at 6:00 A.M. when affinity groups gathered on Wall Street to position themselves for the opening of the stock exchange. Already prepared for the event, the police had arrived even earlier, dressed in riot gear, and set up rings of steel barricades and wooden sawhorses along every street leading to the exchange. As one Green activist later wrote, "While suffocating ideology and the common-sense of everyday life mask the power rela-

tions of U.S. capitalism, at least on Wall Street today the naked force that ultimately safeguards the system is on full display."[47] Throughout the morning,
demonstrators kept in motion, forcing police to shift their formations but allowing exchange workers to enter the building. At noon, people whose lives and
communities had been harmed by the corporations that traded on Wall Street
gave their testimony: victims of toxic chemical poisoning, families of people
killed in Union Carbide's explosion in Bhopal, community activists from Har-
lem, Greens from New Hampshire who would be affected by the Seabrook
nuclear power plant. In the afternoon, street theater and more protests followed. In all, nearly two thousand people participated in the action, with 204
arrested for civil disobedience.

The action received extensive coverage in the media, both within the
Greens and in the popular press, with articles and photos appearing on the
front pages or the business pages of the *New York Times,* the *Los Angeles Times,*
the *New York Post,* the *Chicago Tribune, New York Newsday, Chicago Sun-Times,*
La Prensa, the *Washington Post,* the *Pittsburgh Press,* the *Jersey Journal,* the *Tri-*
bune (Oakland, California), the *San Francisco Examiner,* the *San Francisco*
Chronicle, the *San Jose Mercury News,* and the *Contra Costa Times.*[48] After a year
of planning, a day of action, and a day of news coverage, however, the event's
deeper meaning for the Greens can be extrapolated from three articles written
by Brian Tokar, a Green who sympathized with the Left Green Network but
chose not to sign its initial call, fearing that such a group might be divisive
among the Greens.[49] In *Green Synthesis,* an internal publication of the Greens,
Tokar predicted two months beforehand that the Earth Day Wall Street Action
would be "a milestone event in the resurgence of political activism in the U.S.
for the 1990s." After the event, however, Tokar's report sounded a note of caution for readers in *Green Letter,* observing "a growing tendency for Greens to do
their work outside the structures of the Green Committees of Correspondence"
and lamenting the fact that activists "had to create a whole new coalition for the
Wall Street action."[50] Always an optimist, Tokar observed with uncharacteristic
dismay that "it is becoming increasingly difficult to be confident that there is a
well-defined Green movement in this country and that it is fully represented by
any one organizational entity." Conceding that this internal division could be a
necessary step in an evolving Green movement, Tokar speculated that "it could
also accelerate a slide toward factionalism and dissolution such as has continually plagued social movements in this country."[51] Such possibilities were named
only within the Greens. Reporting on the Wall Street Action that fall for a wider
radical readership in *Z,* Tokar bounced back, announcing that "by the end of

the day, it was clear that a new, radically ecological movement had finally come of age," a remark invoking the maturity metaphor that seemed to follow the Greens through various publications.[52] In retrospect, the Earth Day Wall Street Action can be seen as marking the high point of activism and influence for the Left Green Network.

The Left Green Network in Decline

Later that summer, Left Greens gathered to celebrate their triumph on Earth Day, to plan for the next Green gathering in Estes Park, and to address matters concerning the Network. About fifty people attended the Second Continental Congress of the Left Green Network in Plainfield, Vermont, held from June 30 to July 2, 1990.[53] In an open evaluation of the Left Green Network, members decided that the group needed "to explore and remedy the absence of a diversity of cultural representation" and to encourage "more participation of and influence by women." Members reaffirmed the purpose of the Left Green Network, which was "to articulate a radical program to raise the consciousness of the Green movement" and "to fulfill its educational role." After these initial agreements, there was a lot of contention, which might have surprised outsiders who thought Left Greens were a fundamentally united group.

The conference got off to a rocky start when Murray Bookchin criticized former Clamshell activist and Left Green member Guy Chichester for running in New Hampshire's gubernatorial race. Tensions increased as the Urban Caucus, composed largely of the New York City Left Greens, reported on the inapplicability of radical municipalism as an organizing strategy for large urban areas; rather, they perceived their first organizing efforts as needed in building solidarity among "competing ethnic groups and between disparate social and racial justice movements." Later in the gathering, Bookchin put forth a proposal explaining that gubernatorial races were incompatible with the LGN's principle of radical muncipalism. The proposal passed by a vote of 24 to 16, with six abstainers, but Bookchin was not appeased: both Bookchin and his partner, Janet Biehl, left the LGN after the gathering. In the years that followed, they rejoined and quit a few more times before their final departure.[54]

The opening night's debate was not without internal repercussions as well. Bookchin and Biehl were perceived as trying to bring the LGN in line with their own version of social ecology, or trying to protect the Western tradition while others challenged it.[55] They were opposed to attempts to incorporate identity politics (which they called "particularism") within the Left Greens and instead wanted to build a politics of the general interest. Meeting separately, the women's caucus discussed these and other matters and came out with a statement about the need for feminist process at Left Green gatherings as a way to avoid creating an aggressive, polemical atmosphere; the men's caucus explored charges of "upholding the Western tradition," the need for bringing a feminist analysis into LGN, and the problem of "confrontational and competitive debate" that foreclosed rather than invited participation.

The gathering had its positive moments of celebration and planning as well. Darryl Cherney and Mike Roselle of Earth First! gave a slide show and concert on Saturday night and carried news of developments following the May 24 car bombing of Judi Bari and Darryl Cherney.[56] To attend the LGN gathering, Cherney and Roselle took time away from their own efforts in Redwood Summer, a season of nonviolent direct actions to stop the destruction of northern California's ancient forests. Not limited to tree-sitting, road blockades, marches, and banners, Redwood Summer activities also included vegetarian potlucks, concerts by Rock Against Racism, pro-choice rallies, a Women's Equality Day celebration, war tax resistance gatherings, and vigils against U.S. intervention in Central America, against U.S. support for Israel's occupation of Palestine, and against the death penalty.[57] Left Greens affirmed their support of Redwood Summer and agreed to send a letter of solidarity to Judi Bari. Relations between Left Greens and Earth First! were visibly improved in 1990: Earth Action Network, the coalition of groups endorsing Redwood Summer, described itself as a continuation of the Earth Day Action Coalition that demonstrated at the stock exchange on April 23, 1990, and in its orientation mailings reprinted significant sections from the *Earth Day Wall Street Action Handbook* (the six coalition principles and the nonviolence agreements). The coalition principles specifically named capitalism and the military-industrial systems of both East and West as the root causes of social and ecological destruction; they affirmed that an ecological society required an end to all systems of hierarchy and domination, including racism, sexism, ageism, and homophobia; and they called for a program of social and ecological reconstruction, achieved through genuine grassroots political and economic democracy. One of the results of the deep/social ecology debates had been efforts on the part of Earth First!ers to explore their own beliefs about the root causes of the ecological crisis and to build alliances between loggers and environmentalists. This development, along with the commitment to direct action shared by Earth First! and the Left Green Network, helped ease tensions and open a path for future communication.

Other significant outcomes of the second LGN conference included plans for future developments. Left Greens agreed on the need for a Left Green program to be developed from the fourteen principles and presented for consideration at the next year's gathering, particularly in view of the massive program writing that was being conducted through the SPAKA process of the GCoC. Finally, Left Greens voted to support a "Greens for Democracy" proposal to democratize the GCoC and to advocate having structure and action proposals voted on at the GCoC gathering in Estes Park.[58]

The Greens for Democracy proposal was not created by the Left Green members who gathered at the second Continental Conference in 1990, though it was endorsed at that gathering, and nine members signed the letter that was sent to the GCoC Clearinghouse and published in the internal bulletin just days before the Estes Park gathering.[59] But the idea of a Greens for Democracy initiative was already being announced in a May 9 article Howie Hawkins had written for a progressive New York newspaper, the *Guardian*.[60] There Hawkins explained that many grassroots Greens were frustrated with the decision-making process of the GCoC, and in order to respond to events of the day, various splinter groups had formed either to organize direct action (as in the Earth Day Wall Street Action) or to build Green parties in various states. At the March IC meeting, for example, a separate Green Party Organizing Committee was formed by members who were frustrated by the GCoC's inability to act. The "movement" and the "party" tendencies were already beginning to move in different directions owing to the GCoC's inability to make decisions, given its adherence to the consensus process. To untangle the GCoC, Hawkins concluded, Greens for Democracy would suggest decision making by majority vote, with the right of minorities to dissent publicly and to abstain from implementing decisions with which they disagree; Greens for Democracy would also encourage a restructuring of the GCoC as a confederation of locally rooted independent political movements working through both direct action and the electoral arena. Hawkins advanced these ideas to the larger Left Green membership in *Left Green Notes*, where he later reported on the success of Greens for Democracy at the Estes Park gathering.[61] This gathering built on the success of the Left Green Network at Eugene, where the nine or ten Left Green and Youth Green members who attended had effectively educated large numbers of grassroots Greens about the need for an anticapitalist analysis and the history of the Left generally. At Estes Park, a small number of Left Greens present (again about ten, in a body of two hundred Green delegates and observers) succeeded in reshaping the agenda, introducing decision making by large majority votes (two-thirds for most decisions), setting aside a day for action proposals, and encouraging the formation of a restructuring committee elected out of the national body rather than being created solely from volunteers.

After much debate, Left Greens were also successful in bringing their economic vision into the SPAKA documents. When it became clear that the economics working group at the gathering was unable to solve its internal differences, delegates empowered Hawkins to draft an alternative proposal, labeled ECOnomics II. Meanwhile, the working group drafted an economics statement (ECOnomics I) that articulated a social democratic platform—that is, it was an attempt to fix the problems caused by the system rather than build an entirely new system—without a means for implementation. Most significantly, it did not cite capitalism as a root cause of ecological and economic crises. Hawkins's ECOnomics II, in contrast, presented a radical analysis of capitalism, with immediate demands for "a guaranteed job and adequate income; shorter work week; workers' superfund; progressive taxes; public banking and insurance, housing, energy, and transportation; and conversion to a peace economy." It also included plans for "public ownership and control of basic industries, worker control of production, democratic economic planning, and an expansion of public goods."[62] Green delegates voted down ECOnomics II, but since it had a large following, Hawkins was urged to revise it to include some of the main planks of ECOnomics I. The resulting draft, which passed, was marked by the differing tendencies of mainstream Greens and Left Greens: although the need for an ecological economy was emphasized, references to capitalism were eliminated and a section encouraging ecological lifestyles was added. As one observer astutely remarked, "The Greens must face the contradiction every oppositional movement has had to face in this country: if the Left Greens define the Greens' agenda, the movement will remain marginalized. If mainstream Greens retain control of the agenda, proposals and policies consistent with an ecologically based social democratic management of U.S. capitalism are likely to be appropriated by reform-minded local, State, and national governments."[63] Any social movement theorist would have agreed.

Nine months after the GCoC program had been completed at Estes Park, Left Greens received the first draft of the LGN program and were invited to submit comments to aid in its revision before their Third Continental Conference.[64] As a much smaller group than the GCoC, the 350 LGN members were able to respond to the draft through various internal publications as well as individual mailings and be reasonably sure that their ideas would be known to other Left Greens and considered in the revised program draft. The bulk of the criticisms focused on the fact that the program seemed to advocate a form of social democracy. Members of the Northern Vermont Greens specifically targeted demands for a guaranteed annual income, a $10/hour minimum wage, a thirty-hour work week, and a 95 percent reduction in the Pentagon's budget as propositions conceived from a social democratic, nationalist perspective. Murray Bookchin and Janet Biehl cited the same demands, observing that these goals could be achieved in Sweden, for example, and still perpetuate capitalism. Moreover, they voiced consternation at the draft program's suggestion under "independent politics" that Left Greens "will force the establishment parties to adopt some of our reforms," noting the demise of numerous radical movements through such mainstreaming of ideas and concluding, "It is hard to recall a genuinely revolutionary movement that stated its own willingness for its planks to be amicably co-opted by mainstream parties."[65] Of course, the Left Greens (like the GCoC) had enough internal diversity of viewpoints that the program was also criticized by a former member of the Socialist Labor Party for its failure to be sufficiently grounded in an analysis of class, reflecting a singleness of perspective that Left Greens had ostensibly transcended.

The revised program was discussed at the Third Continental Conference of the Left Green Network, held July 3–7, 1991, in Chicago. Though further revisions were suggested, the program was never completed. Instead, the conference was replete with conflicts among Left Greens about whether to pursue their independent status or simply dissolve into the main body of the Greens. Given their success in influencing the SPAKA process, many Left Greens felt more committed to the Greens. On the other side of the debate, many of the anarchists and Youth Green members of the LGN were becoming more interested in issues of racism and anarchist organizing around issues of police brutality and economic justice; at the same time, they were put off by how discussions of ecofeminism were downplayed within the LGN as if class and ecology offered a more fundamental level of analysis. An exchange on the relation of ecofeminism to the Left Greens between Laura Schere and Janet Biehl had created deep divisions among ecofeminists: in response to Schere's argument for a form of ecofeminism that embraced identity politics, Biehl argued for a more integrated stance and opposed identity politics as a form of "particularism."[66] Many Left Greens had concluded that Biehl's form of ecofeminism was untenable, and at the conference a workshop on ecofeminism was conducted by Laura Schere and Kate Sandilands to clarify its meaning and its relevance to the Left Greens. Yet, the following day, conversations resumed with an emphasis on class and ecology, as if the ecofeminist presentation had never taken place. Many ecofeminists and Youth Greens were outraged, and further debates ensued. As one former member of the Left Green Network recalled, the 1991 Chicago gathering was probably the beginning of the end for the LGN.[67]

One month later, the Left Greens achieved their biggest victory in influencing the GCoC at the national Green gathering in Elkins, West Virginia, held August 14–21, 1991. In the issue of *Left Green Notes* published just before the Elkins gathering, Howie Hawkins wrote another essay urging LGN members to get involved with the Greens.[68] According to Hawkins, many of the initial concerns that prompted the formation of the LGN had been resolved: the decision-making paralysis of the Greens had been taken care of by replacing absolute consensus with a search for consensus, backed up with a high majority vote if consensus could not be reached; fears about nonpolitical trends toward mysticism and personal lifestyle changes dominating within the Greens had largely been addressed through the clear emphasis on social and economic justice, independent politics, and anticapitalist economics. Moreover, two key constituencies that had been lacking in the Greens were beginning to participate, and Greens were counting both student activists from the Student Environmental Action Coalition (SEAC) and several activists of color as part of their membership. Hawkins also called on Left Greens to attend Elkins in order to help in shaping what would be the first nationally coordinated action agenda for the Greens and in addressing the debates between movement and party activists. As before, only a handful of Left Greens (about fifteen) showed up, but they were nonetheless able to influence the gathering to adopt a national unified structure incorporating movement and party.

As Hawkins later reported, the most pressing issue at the gathering was the question of how to structure the movement's organization and thereby shape the relationship between movement and electoral activists.[69] From a Left Green perspective, the electoral activists who constituted the Green Party Organizing Committee (GPOC) advocated a separation of party from movement so that their activities could be unencumbered by accountability to the grassroots. Claiming to represent the interests of a broader constituency that included thousands of registered voters in the statewide Green parties, GPOC activists were perceived as self-selected, charismatic leaders who effectively manipulated facts and media coverage to suit their needs. The question of separating movement and electoral activity had been raised five times in the fifteen months before the Elkins gathering—including a delegate vote at the Estes Park national conference and a restructuring referendum from the locals in April 1991—and each time the membership had voted overwhelmingly to maintain a unified structure. For a sixth time, the same decision was made at Elkins, though the process was far from amicable.

Three days before the gathering, the GPOC held a preconference meeting to address the relationship of movement and electoral activity. The meeting was attended by about sixty Greens, five of whom were Left Greens and Youth Greens. At the outset, statements by John Rensenbrink and Lorna Salzman were circulated, charging the Left Greens with seeking to take over the Greens and create a tightly controlled organization that was not truly Green (the fourteen Principles of the Left Green Network being cited as evidence, specifically the principles of ecological humanism, strategic nonviolence, and radical munici-palism). At a fishbowl session in the afternoon, according to Hawkins, speeches from the GPOC were characterized by red-baiting and gender-baiting innuen-does without a genuine attempt at understanding or reconciliation. Since the majority of Greens participating in the preconference meeting simply wanted the matter resolved, the group concluded that those with the strongest opinions (called the "key players," or "KPs") should be sent into an evening negotiation session to work out their differences. In a session that lasted until three in the morning, the two Left Greens present were charged with preventing unity by refusing to endorse a split-structure proposal of the type that had already been voted down in April. To end the meeting, Left Greens Howie Hawkins and Charlie Betz were pressed into agreeing to "stand aside" so that the group could present the split-structure proposal as a consensus proposal to the gathering the following day, even though Hawkins and Betz reiterated that the proposal was not acceptable and that they would be presenting an alternate proposal as well. The next day, both proposals were voted on, and both failed to achieve the two-thirds majority required for any proposal to be adopted.

Once the gathering began, questions of structure took a back seat to a full schedule of workshops, caucuses, and plenaries. By the time Monday's Green Congress was convened, a group spirit had been created. The new structure proposal provided by the Congress Committee described a national Green elec-toral policy to be decided by the Green Congress, not by a separate party appa-ratus. The proposal was adopted almost unanimously. To reflect the new struc-ture, the national organization was renamed The Greens/Green Party U.S.A. A new coordinating committee was elected, and a Green Justice Caucus was formed out of already existing caucuses: People of Color, Women's, Gay and Lesbian, and Youth caucuses. In many respects, the Greens created organiza-tional forms that were intended to bring people together. Left Greens were elected to several prominent positions within the new organization, and the gathering ended on a promise of unity.

It's not surprising that the Left Green Network declined in membership after the decisions at Elkins. Most of their concerns about the Greens had been resolved, and it seemed more effective to work within the larger Green organization than to keep up two separate groups. For others in the Left Greens, of course, the developments at Elkins seemed to move farther away from the actions and issues to which they were most strongly committed, and the emphasis on organization building was especially distasteful to the anarchists in the Left Greens, who saw it as a move toward bureaucracy at the expense of activism. At the LGN's Fourth Continental Conference, held in Iowa City, May 22–25, 1992, only twenty-five Left Greens attended. Once again, Lowell Nelson proposed that the Network be dissolved into the Greens and function primarily as a caucus, a proposal that had more support this time around. This shift in popular thinking within the Greens and Left Greens was both reflected in and influenced by shifts in their publications. In the following year, the primary theoretical journal of the Left Green Network, *Regeneration,* became *Synthesis/Regeneration,* adding the title of the former GCoC publication; its subtitle changed from "A Magazine of Left Green Social Thought" (Fall 1992) to "A Magazine of Green Social Thought" (Winter 1993). Meanwhile, the publication of *Left Green Notes* faltered, owing to loss of membership, income, and submissions; after 1992, it ceased publication. By May 1993, at the Fifth Continental Conference of the Left Green Network, held in Toronto, only six people attended. In the years that followed, a small group of Left Greens continued to meet at the annual national Green gathering, and a newsletter continued sporadic publication. The Network, as a whole, had ended.

The Youth Greens (1988–1992): Anarchists within the Greens, Ecologists among the Anarchists

The so-called new social movements of the sixties, as well as the various manifestations of antinuclear activism of the late seventies and eighties, were populated largely by people in their twenties and thirties. The U.S. Greens, in contrast, were formed by people in their thirties and forties, people who had been active in the earlier social movements and were acutely aware of their successes and failures. But four years after the founding of the movement, the few younger members of the Greens were becoming impatient with the slow progress of the movement. In October 1988, a Youth Caucus of the GCoC was formed at a meeting of the Interregional Committee, announcing to the IC delegates that "because we have observed a lack of participation of young people in the organized Green movement in North America, we feel there is a need for a youth caucus within the larger movement, specifically the GCoC." Showing an acute awareness of their group's composition as largely white, educated, and middle class, the Youth Caucus emphasized the need to "break through social, race, and class barriers," for "without this diversity, the Greens will be not much more than a bourgeois hobby." In the context of a shared commitment to the Ten Key Values of the Greens, the Youth Caucus distinguished itself from the GCoC by adding, "We reject capitalism, the authority of the state, and national electoral politics. We advocate the building of counter-institutions and liberated communities within a confederation of bioregions."[70] Their anticapitalist stance, their emphasis on community control, and their rejection of the state and national electoral politics showed the clear influence of anarchism and social ecology in the formation of what would become the Youth Greens.

The formation of the Youth Caucus was surely sparked by the fact that five months earlier, Janet Biehl and Murray Bookchin had spent a week at Antioch College in Ohio, speaking in several classes there as part of the conclusion to a student-initiated Green Studies Seminar.[71] The course introduced students to the history and theory of the Greens, Marx, Kropotkin, the 1930s labor and socialist movements ("the old Left"), Marcuse, and the social movements of the sixties ("the New Left"), in addition to various debates within the radical environmental movement involving ecofeminism, social ecology, deep ecology, and direct action. Many Antioch students, already members of the Greens, were inspired by this history of radical activism and by the important role youth had often played in that history. One year later, in May 1989, Antioch students eagerly hosted the first formal gathering of the Youth Greens.

The decision to form a separate organization rather than a caucus within the GCoC was the culmination of observations made at IC meetings. After the Youth Caucus statement was published in fall 1988, the Youth Caucus met again at the February IC meeting in New Orleans and drafted a longer Call to Form a Youth Caucus. At the IC meeting, however, members of the Caucus were treated coolly by some GCoC members, who had observed the names of various Youth Greens as signatories to the Call to Form a Left Green Network issued earlier that fall. Other members of the Youth Caucus felt they were treated condescendingly because of their age or gender. Nonethess, in the Call to Form a

Youth Caucus, they did not mention these observations but rather elaborated on their earlier anticapitalist, antistatist positions and emphasized the importance of youth to the vitality of social movements.[72] To increase youth participation in the Greens, they invited young people to attend a continental Youth Caucus gathering at Antioch College.

Nearly seventy people attended the five-day gathering. Plenaries in the evenings featured more seasoned activists and theorists addressing the topics of ecofeminism, critical theory, animal rights, gay and lesbian issues, and the histories of the old and New Left. Speakers included John Clark from the Delta Greens in New Orleans, author of *The Anarchist Moment* and professor of philosophy at Loyola University; Charles Allen Dews, an animal rights activist and Green from Austin, Texas; Dr. Michael Washington, from the People's Institute for Survival and Beyond in New Orleans; Howie Hawkins, clearinghouse coordinator for the Left Green Network; Chaia Heller, social ecofeminist and instructor at the Institute for Social Ecology; and Antioch faculty members James Daraja and Frank Adler.[73] During the days, workshops were conducted by conference participants, and time was set aside for working in small groups to draft and revise position papers, which were later presented to the larger gathering for discussion and possible adoption. By the end of the conference, the students had defined their identity as Youth Greens rather than a Youth Caucus, developed six key principles and drafted working papers on several other issues, created a women's caucus, and adopted three action projects. Finally, they elected two delegates to the Left Green Network, their closest ideological ally within the Greens and the Left.

Though the Youth Greens settled on only six principles in contrast to the Left Green Network's fourteen, the Youth Green principles were either ideologically attuned to or direct adoptions of the Left Green principles. Stating that "capitalism has brought us Bhopal and Love Canal, Three Mile Island and acid rain, gaps in the ozone layer and the greenhouse effect," the first principle of the Youth Greens was *anticapitalism,* a principle that was implied but not explicitly stated in the Left Green principle of a cooperative commonwealth. With the Left Greens, the Youth Greens affirmed the principles of *democratic decentralism* and *social ecofeminism,* and they augmented three other Left Green principles as well: the Left Green principle of *gay and lesbian liberation* became *gay, lesbian, and bisexual liberation;* the Left Green principle of *independent politics* became *oppositional politics* to emphasize the Youth Greens' opposition to the two-party system and to national electoral politics; and to the Left Green principle of *radical municipalism,* the Youth Greens added *revolutionary dual power,* referring to their belief that creating alternative institutions that prefigure the free society along with participation in local municipal elections would offer the most viable method of social transformation. Although they did not choose social ecology as one of their principles, the principle of *revolutionary dual power and radical municipalism* effectively articulates a central aspect of that philosophy. Working papers on concrete social practice, antiracism, radical sexuality, nonaligned internationalism, education, human rights, the mass media, exclusion of cadre groups, and the relations to other organizations were all drafted but not revised until later conferences. For action plans, the Youth Greens decided on three projects: working with the Diné in the Southwest, radicalizing the twentieth anniversary of Earth Day, and participating in the 1989 Green gathering in Eugene. All three action plans were shared commitments with the Left Green Network.

Acting on their agreement to participate in the Greens as a group, six Youth Greens (and three Left Greens) responded to an article by northern California Greens which had dismissed the deep ecology/social ecology debate as less relevant to the Greens than some had been led to believe and had also repudiated calls to "overthrow capitalism" as failing to communicate with a larger progressive audience.[74] From a Youth Green perspective, the differences between deep ecology and social ecology were crucial to the Green movement, particularly if Greens wanted to base their actions on a coherent Green philosophy. In addition, Youth Greens charged that "Greens in this country have not adequately confronted the problem of capitalism" and that refusing to use the word "capitalism" in descriptions of the problem Greens address perpetuates the insulting belief that the public is not capable of understanding political issues. From the start, Youth Greens were not slow to point out their differences with the larger Green organization.

Another difference had to do specifically with the program-writing process and the movement toward national electoral politics, which the Youth Greens observed firsthand at the Green gathering in Eugene. In a statement later adopted by the Youth Greens at their Second Continental Conference in Minneapolis that October, Youth Greens criticized the SPAKA process as undemocratic, emphasizing that "Greens will have to better include the perspectives of native people, people of color, labor, farm, youth, and the left in its program developing to genuinely claim to be a diverse and democratic majoritarian organization. The white middle class cannot comfortably write a political program in homogeneous locations such as Eugene and Boulder, and then expect others to simply join them." Instead, Youth Greens urged a process of coalition building and networking with diverse social and cultural constituencies, joining with those groups in forming a program. In addition, Youth Greens objected to the suggestion that the GCoC would hold a "Green Party U.S.A." convention in June 1992, when the Working Group on Politics had said explicitly that "we cannot sanction at this time the establishment of a National Green electoral party" and rejected suggestions of Green involvement in the 1992 and 1996 national elections as ideas needing much further discussion. Finally, Youth Greens deplored the nationalism in the title "Green Party U.S.A.," seeing it as a direct contradiction to a Green stance of anti-imperialism and internationalism.[75] That fall, beneath the Youth Greens' published statement in *Green Letter,* the journal's editor responded with the clarification that the idea of a Green Party U.S.A. convention in 1992 was not an official decision of the GCoC but simply the musings of John Rensenbrink.

Although the decision to radicalize Earth Day was made at the founding conference of the Left Green Network, it was the Youth Greens who put together the idea for an action on Wall Street. In a proposal written shortly after the Eugene gathering, Youth Greens suggested staging a series of nationally co-ordinated actions for Earth Day, to "capture the imaginations of millions of people" and thereby "put Green politics 'on the map,' establishing the Greens as a clear alternative to politics-as-usual and strongly affirming our commitment to direct action." The proposal contained four points of a political message that were later incorporated in the six coalition principles of the *Earth Day Wall Street Action Handbook,* and all six of the nonviolence agreements. At the end of the proposal, the Youth Greens described a timeline for contacting potential participants, planning the action logistics, and preparing related publications. Although the proposal was presented to the October IC meeting of the GCoC, it never gained endorsement.

But Youth Greens had also been working to build alliances on the Left, in direct action and in anarchist circles, and these allies shared more of the Youth Green perspective. In July, for example, Youth Greens attended the continental Anarchist Gathering in San Francisco and distributed their principles. The YG pamphlets inspired a Berkeley Youth Greens group to form, and it was this group that supported the Youth Green Wall Street Action with allied demonstrations in San Francisco. Nearly six hundred people showed up at the Pacific Stock Exchange at 6:00 A.M. for the demonstration, and by the end of the day forty-nine had been arrested. In Minneapolis, Youth Greens in concert with anarchist, lesbian, and women's action groups mobilized four hundred people to protest a local garbage incinerator, and twenty-six were arrested. In St. Louis,

Youth Greens joined with anarchists, Earth First! activists, and I.W.W. (Industrial Workers of the World) members to educate participants about corporate exploitation at a mainstream Earth Day event, dropping banners that read "Corporate greed kills" and "Earth Day is a corporate commercial." And at the University of Oregon in Eugene, Youth Green allies celebrated Earth Week by holding a "compost your consumer crap rally" that featured a de-roofed Cadillac filled with war toys, broken television sets, household appliances, and other nonrecyclables. The car was covered with dirt and a small garden and was later doused with gasoline and ignited.[76]

All these events had been on the agenda for the second Youth Greens gathering, held in Minneapolis in October 1989. Bylaws, working papers, strategy issues, and relations with other Left or Green organizations were all slated for discussion. But like gatherings of the larger Green movement, the Youth Green gathering in Minneapolis was marred by conflicts about membership criteria, philosophical inconsistencies, grassroots versus national organizing, and future strategies for developing the movement. Unlike the GCoC, however, Youth Greens immediately identified and addressed problems with interpersonal "process" as integral to the project of social change. "Throughout the weekend I was sickened to see us all," wrote Kate Fox, "well intentioned, dedicated young people replicating the dominant structure in our own relations."[77] "Because of social conditioning," Charlie Betz and Katie Kadwell explained, "undesirable contradictions such as racism, sexism, and elitism tend to replicate themselves within progressive groups."[78] As a group, Youth Greens were well read in the history of social movements of the old and New Left, conscious of their own role as revolutionary youth, and willing to learn from the mistakes of the past rather than replicate them. The urgency of the upcoming Earth Day Wall Street Action, along with a desire to work through communication problems, strengthened the group and kept it together.

Between the second and third Youth Green gatherings, there was plenty of planning and activity to keep people involved. After the planning meetings, phone calls, and mailings that culminated in the Wall Street Action in April 1990, many Youth Greens attended the Second Continental Conference of the Left Green Network at the end of June in Vermont, and some stayed on to attend the Institute for Social Ecology's summer classes. At the end of July, the third Youth Green gathering, at Goddard College in Vermont, drew more than seventy participants and offered a successful counterpoint to the Minneapolis gathering. Youth Greens discussed and adopted an antiracism principle, rejecting "the Old Left view that racism will automatically disappear with the destruction of capitalism." Over the five-day gathering, Youth Green women collectively drafted a statement on ecofeminism, clarifying the links between the oppressions of women and of nature and explaining how both are complicated by the functioning of capitalism. Youth Greens also supported the Left Green Network in its criticism of the upcoming GCoC gathering in Estes Park, calling the three-hundred-dollar food and lodging fee "classist," supporting the alternative camp proposed by the LGN, and affirming solidarity with the Greens for Democracy, who had organized to alter the gathering's agenda and restructure the GCoC. Finally, Youth Greens planned future actions for working with and communicating their ideas to potential allies, such as the Autonomous Anarchist Action group and the anarchist newspaper *Love and Rage*. Another of these action plans involved distributing literature, presenting workshops, and doing street theater for the October conference of the Student Environmental Action Coalition at the University of Illinois in Champaign-Urbana.[79]

Youth Greens had been watching the developments of student environmental activism over the preceding year and expected that this surge of interest would be initially mainstream but could be radicalized through education.[80] Accordingly, Youth Greens participated in the "Catalyst" conference of SEAC and were impressed by the presence of seven thousand students interested in environmental activism. In addition to distributing literature and holding workshops at the conference, one group of Youth Greens (the Minneapolis local, AWOL)[81] heckled one of the conference's featured speakers, Dave Foreman of Earth First!, for his racist and classist attitudes and then took the opportunity to educate others about its position. Youth Greens felt that the conference's dual focus on corporate environmental accountability and environmental justice was not fully communicated to participants. According to at least two reports, the SEAC conference was more successful in maintaining racial and cultural diversity in its speakers than in the students who attended: about fifty students of color formed a caucus and addressed the issues of racism and classism in the environmental movement, particularly at a conference where the majority of participants were white and middle to upper class.[82] To the Youth Greens, the need to build multiracial solidarity was becoming more apparent than ever.

During the fall of 1990, in the period leading up to the Fourth Continental Conference of the Youth Greens in Tennessee that December, a series of papers about possible strategies and future directions for development was circulated among Youth Green members.[83] Though written by diverse authors, the papers shared an awareness of the Youth Greens' place in history, their size, their potential allies, their problems, and their goals. Two writers reiterated the Youth Greens' organizational model as distinguished from the GCoC model, which sought to bring the public into the organization, internalizing the public sphere in such a way that organization building becomes an end in itself; instead, the Youth Greens sought to be a coherent group with distinct membership principles, working in solidarity with other aligned organizations. Seeking to define the relation between the Youth Greens' long-term goals and their immediate actions, writers outlined three critical areas for activism: education, organization building, and alliance building. As a result of their activism and their participation in other organizations, Youth Greens realized they needed a simple brochure describing their basic principles, a regular newsletter, and a reading list and guide to forming study groups, and they needed to develop groups of Youth Greens willing to write or speak in various fora. Several writers emphasized the desirability of a systematized membership base and dues collection process, maintained out of a well-staffed clearinghouse. And many stressed the importance of building or maintaining alliances with related groups such as Love and Rage, SEAC, the Left Green Network, and participants at the Radical Scholars and Activists Conference. Given their many difficulties, as Youth Greens Paul Glavin and Eric Jacobson pointed out, "it is fairly surprising that the Youth Greens have survived to this point, just barely avoiding the fate of what Trotsky called the 'dustbin of history.'"

Making these points and others, Jason Serota-Winston's proposal emphasized the importance of communicating effectively with different organizations and defining Youth Greens' unique position as revolutionary youth. In the first *Youth Green Newsletter,* the group had received and printed a letter from Joe Foss of the Northland College Greens, professing admiration and solidarity with the Youth Greens but deploring the level of diction that permeated their literature. "The Youth Green platforms of Revolutionary Dual Power, Radical Municipalism, and anticapitalism most often produce puzzlement and perhaps even hostility towards a group concerned with preserving and restoring the vitality of the Earth," Foss wrote. "I'd estimate two to five years of reading alternative press and being involved in alternative movements are required in order to comprehend the full meaning of those theories. How can a movement that is aiming for the profound social change of our locals, regions and world ever gain enough of a gathering if it keeps talking constantly in such a nebulous, philosophical framework?"[84] In response to this need for clearer communication, Serota-Winston proposed two strategies for creating coherent statements of the Youth Greens' aims and principles: first, writing a pamphlet to present the principles, viewpoints, and aims but without theoretical depth ("We've got to translate our social ecology rhetoric into plain English and make it relevant to people's everyday lives"); second, creating a much longer statement, which Serota-Winston compared to the Port Huron Statement of Students for a Democratic Society (SDS). Addressing potential audiences such as the Student Environmental Action Coalition, Youth Earth Action (a high school organization), the anarchist movement, and students of color, the longer statement would need to examine the role of youth in revolutionary change. "In the new left," wrote Serota-Winston, "this discussion was never fully allowed to develop, with economistic theories of the 'new working class' and concentration on labor taking precedence over discussion of the new social realities. The Youth Greens have both a responsibility and an opportunity to fully develop this discussion so that we can better understand our role as youth in social change." On the topic of working with the less radical student movement, Serota-Winston criticized the theoretical purity that had characterized the Left and was still present in the Youth Greens, reminding readers that because "we are the radical fringe of the radical fringe," by "not working with these groups, we only risk our own irrelevance." Such work would entail encouraging individuals in those organizations to question the relations between corporations and environmental destruction, between toxic waste and racism. "People aren't radicalized by being fed the right line," Serota-Winston observed. "They are radicalized by making the connections for themselves." The role of the Youth Greens would be "to promote the self-examination which leads to radicalization."[85]

At the Fourth Youth Greens Continental Conference in Knoxville, Tennessee, held in December 1990, participants discussed these proposals and presented others as well. The gathering was held in a location close to the Highlander Research and Education Center, which had been working for social and economic justice in the South for more than fifty years. Highlander had played a central role in organizing the labor movement of the thirties, the civil rights struggle, and the environmental movements of the eighties. In addition to discussing strategy and making decisions about various upcoming actions, Youth Greens spent a day at Highlander learning more about its history and current projects and participated in a Highlander workshop that helped Youth Greens identify their activist goals and address strategy questions. The group's process of self-reflection and self-assessment was fully under way.

Perhaps it was no accident that Youth Greens scheduled their Fifth Continental Conference in Oregon for the following August 14–18, on the other side of the continent from the national GCoC gathering in Elkins, West Virginia, scheduled for August 15–21, 1991. A packet mailed to all Youth Greens after the December conference in Tennessee had included the conference notes, reports from locals, and a letter from Paul Glavin of AWOL urging Youth Greens to attend the GCoC gathering in Elkins. "This is a decisive time for the Greens—ya, I know, you've been hearing that since the Summer '89 Eugene Conference," Glavin began. His letter described the escalating conflict between movement and party activists and attached the Restructuring Working Group's proposal and the membership's reaction, "Don't Divide the Greens!" According to Glavin's letter, the Youth Green Coordinating Council had not yet chosen the dates of its fifth gathering; apparently, his letter did not persuade Youth Greens of the importance of participating in the GCoC gathering.

Nonetheless, Charlie Betz of the Youth Greens attended the GCoC gathering and joined Howie Hawkins of the Left Greens through the long night of the "key players" discussion with the Green Politics Organizing Committee. Other young Greens had formed yet another Youth Caucus and were dismayed to find that a Green Justice Caucus had been formed out of all the marginalized people in the Greens, though the Youth Caucus had been "forgotten during the development of all this and brought into Green Justice after most decisions seem to have been worked through." Two members of the Youth Caucus, Jason Kirkpatrick and Eric Odell, were "notified that Green Justice had decided to give the youth caucus representation." After they had been invited over to the new group and listened to the discussion, Kirkpatrick and Odell learned that the Youth Caucus representative to the Green Justice Caucus had been chosen for them, without their participation or consent. Insulted by the entire process, Odell wrote an essay, "Ageism in the Greens," for *Green Letter,* in which he reiterated the Youth Caucus statement: "One should wonder why there are so few of us here."[86]

Meanwhile, other conflicts with Green affiliations were also taking place. Responding to the Left Green Network's draft platform, Laura Schere and Paul Glavin delivered a thoughtful critique at the Third Continental Conference of the Left Green Network, held July 1991 in Chicago. First, they objected to the overemphasis on changing social structures, which seemed to underestimate the importance of changing cultural norms as well: "The hard work of interpersonal, cultural and social innovation is subordinated to structural changes in the state and capital like the old base, superstructure model." In essence, Schere and Glavin offered a feminist understanding of the personal/political relationship, as opposed to an old leftist analysis of structure or political/public alone. They objected to the platform's analysis of identity politics movements as single-issue movements that needed to be absorbed into a movement against a common enemy, corporations and the state. "Rather than 'transcend the particularistic interest of oppressed generations, genders, ethnic groups, classes, and nationalities' we should affirm the importance of autonomy and self-determination to the development of a genuine solidarity," they wrote. In effect, the LGN draft platform's suggestion that "particularistic" movements need to be transcended by a resolution for a "general interest" echoes "the old left in asking oppressed groups to postpone their liberation until some indefinite point after the revolution." Instead, Schere and Glavin advocated "democratic forms of principled alliances and an awareness of the interrelatedness of all forms of domination" as the best way to develop "a genuinely united revolutionary movement." Finally, with other Left Greens, Schere and Glavin criticized the program's overemphasis on electoralism as a strategy for reforming municipalities, stressing that local elections should be only one strategy among many and that in some cases such elections may not even be helpful.[87] These objections, generally supported by the Youth Greens, exacerbated a growing tension between Left and Youth Greens, based on the fact that the two groups had begun moving in different directions: Left Greens were moving closer to the GCoC, while Youth Greens were moving closer to the anarchist community.

In Minneapolis, a Left Green group called the Green Union of the Twin Cities along with anarchist groups RABL and Tornado Warning, had staged a protest at the downtown incinerator in coordination with the 1990 Earth Day Wall Street Action protests. Unfortunately, not all the street tactics went as planned, police arrested many of the organizers, and confusion and a brief flurry of unauthorized rock-throwing ensued.[88] The local media played up the violence and nearly ignored the purpose of the demonstration, but the unkindest blow of all came in the form of a letter written by the Twin Cities Greens (the GCoC local) to the newspaper, citing the Green commitment to nonviolence and denouncing the action at the incinerator.[89] Although Minneapolis activists in the Green Union and the Twin Cities Greens continued to be in touch, their differences remained. Of course, these groups had to work together to some extent because the 1992 national Green gathering was to be held in Minneapolis.

But these conflicts were not the only problem YGs faced. At their Fifth Continental Conference in Oregon in August 1991, Youth Greens reviewed the challenges they faced as an organization. For the past year, the Youth Greens as an organization had seemed to lose ground: the lack of a consistent newsletter, absence of follow-through on various projects, as well as a general dissatisfaction with the name of the group were all cited as reasons for the group's decline. Issues with the name were of course related to the group's overall purpose and direction. Some members no longer wanted to be associated with the Greens, arguing that the Greens were "hopelessly middle-class and will never be more than mild-mannered reformers." Others wanted to strengthen ties with the anarchist community, and still others were annoyed with the persistent questions about how old one had to be to join the group. The two new names proposed for the group, "Ecological Anarchist Network" and "Autonomous Green Network," were sent back to the membership for discussion. Meanwhile, three Youth Greens planned a continentwide organizing tour involving speaking, meetings, and music, and the Minneapolis local took on the project of publishing a new Youth Green newsletter, *Free Society*.[90]

But the Youth Green presence and participation in the Greens was coming to an end. At the 1992 Green gathering in Minneapolis, AWOL organized a march and rally against Northern States Power as its last action with the Greens. For the preceding year, AWOL had worked with a local alliance of progressive groups called PICANS (Prairie Island Coalition Against Nuclear Storage) to fight NSP's storage of nuclear waste on the Mdewakanton Sioux reservation, where NSP already was operating a nuclear power plant.[91] The situation was a clear case of environmental racism and offered AWOL an excellent issue for demonstrating the connections between various forms of oppression and environmental degradation, as well as addressing issues of community control and renewable energy sources. But the march at the 1992 Green gathering ran into trouble, for various reasons: for example, the Greens saw the march as part of their own convention, whereas AWOL saw the march as a demonstration it had organized and to which it had invited many participating groups, including the Greens. This problem of ownership might not have presented itself except for the fact that after marching along the planned route and congregating in a rally against NSP, AWOL and other anarchists found there was a rally of the Democratic Party being held nearby, and many of them got into a shouting match with the mainstream Democrats, another action that was probably too radical for the Greens. But the dissolution had already been planned. After the march, Joe Lowndes of the Youth Greens Minneapolis local, AWOL, formally announced its break with the Greens.

The new Youth Green journal *Free Society* put out two issues, in fall 1991 and winter 1992, but by their third issue in winter 1993, the Youth Greens had dissolved. The AWOL local felt it had carried the organization for too long already, acting as a clearinghouse and supporting the journal. There seemed to be a contradiction in the fact that a small group of eco-anarchists was trying to hold together a continental network. So in true anarchist fashion, AWOL members dropped the organization when they perceived that it had outlived its usefulness. In two reflective pieces on the history of the Youth Greens, their development and dissolution were placed in historical context.[92] The difficulties Youth Greens had discussed at their last gathering in Oregon in August 1991 had proved insurmountable. To increase diversity within the organization, build alliances, and attract new members, the Youth Greens had attempted to constitute a broader network of ecological anarchists, but the project failed, mostly owing to lack of follow-through. According to former Youth Green Paul O'Bannion, "Today the Green movement is small and largely reformist, with most activity centered on electoral efforts—the very approach Youth Greens fought against. Whatever radical promise the Greens had has surely disappeared."[93] For all the Youth Green awareness of context and their relationship to social movement history, it is surprising that these articles of review and self-assessment both overlook a significant point: the trajectory of the Youth Greens from formation to dissolution closely parallels the trajectory of the Left Green Network. At the end, however, members of the two groups went in different directions: the Youth Greens went toward anarchism, and some of the Left Greens moved toward electoral activism. In retrospect, these two groups had formed the radical or revolutionary opening of the Green movement in the United States. At the height of their activism—the Earth Day Wall Street Action of 1990—the countertendency of pragmatic, electoral reform had already begun with the Electoral Action Working Group, members of which would go on to form the Green Politics Network at the same time as the Left Greens and Youth Greens were dissolving.

The Green Politics Network and the "Revolutionary Potential" of Electoral Politics

Although the Green Politics Network was not formally launched until March 1992, the roots of its formation go back to the second national Green gathering at Eugene in 1989. There, perhaps for the first time, John Rensenbrink raised the possibility of a Green presidential campaign. Though Rensenbrink's idea would have to wait another six years to come to fruition, the appeal of electoral politics as a vehicle for publicity, education, and influence was persuasive to a minority of Greens at Eugene. In October 1989, Rensenbrink and others formed an Electoral Action Working Group at the Interregional Committee meeting in Washington, "to research and share information on electoral plans and campaigns throughout the country."[94] But six months later, at the March 1990 IC meeting, the group had developed larger plans, and fifteen people signed a statement affirming their new status as the Green Party Organizing Committee (GPOC). The GPOC would be "a cooperating organization but autonomous from the IC and the GCoC," conceiving itself as "morally accountable to not only the Green Committees of Correspondence but the entire Green Movement."[95] The shift within the Green movement, from extrainstitutional movement politics to intrasystemic electoral politics, had begun.

GCoC reactions to the new GPOC were suspicious and sharply critical. The New England Green Alliance issued a unanimous resolution stating that the GPOC should be dissolved and its members reintegrated into the GCoC's Electoral Action Working Group. In their view, keeping "the electoral arm of the Green movement strictly accountable to the grassroots membership" had been the key feature distinguishing Green movements from traditional reform parties. Citing the example of European Green movements that had abandoned this "two-legged approach" (the combined efforts of movement and electoral activism) and subsequently followed the path of reformism and compromise, the New England Green Alliance questioned the kind of accountability the GPOC would have to the movement when no structures of accountability were in place.[96] But the GPOC saw these appeals for accountability as largely attempts to control, manipulate, or otherwise delay efforts already under way to build Green parties in various states. In a series of articles designed to invite middle-of-the-road Greens to consider the organizing possibilities offered through electoral politics, Rensenbrink addressed the Greens' fear of politics and power generally, emphasizing the need to build multicultural and intermovement alliances among the various progressive organizations and the importance of developing an organizational structure that allowed the maximum of flexibility and autonomy to both party and movement activists.[97] From 1989 to 1992, the debate over whether the Greens should be a movement that used electoral politics as one of many action strategies or a movement in which issue-based activism and electoral work were structurally separate grew to a boiling point.

From the viewpoint of the GPOC, the refusal to participate fully in electoral politics was tantamount to a willful desire for marginality. At the 1989 gathering in Eugene, even some international Green activists expressed frustration at the reluctance of U.S. Greens to plunge into electoral politics when the U.S. Green movement had such a good chance of being influential internationally. Wilhelm Knabe, a Green member of the West German parliament, urged the U.S. Greens to "move forward as quickly as they could—America was using up the world so fast, it had to be stopped right away," and an Australian ecofeminist denounced the consensus process as "so self-indulgent, so narcissistic. . . . Don't they see, the idea isn't to let everybody talk all they want. The point is to *get things done*."[98] Members of the GPOC agreed. The national GPOC met at the June 1990 IC meeting and twice at the September 1990 gathering in Estes Park, sharing stories of local and state party organizing and candidate races. They saw a widespread, national dissatisfaction with the two-party system that extended well beyond the Green movement and a readiness in the American public for a third-party effort. Greens would have to seize the historic moment or be swept aside.

But at the 1990 national gathering in Estes Park, Left Greens under the banner of "Greens for Democracy" succeeded in adding a leftist slant to the Greens' national program (particularly visible in the economics plank) and brought forward a proposal to restructure the national GCoC into an organization that would continue to incorporate electoral and movement activism, with the maximum of accountability to the grassroots. Because Greens at the gathering had not been empowered as representatives from their locals to make decisions apart from the SPAKA process, a Restructuring Working Group was elected from members of both Left Greens and the GPOC, charged with devising a workable national structure that would be sent back to the locals for a vote. Several GPOC members were elected to serve in the group, and they came up with a structure that would give maximum autonomy to both the movement and the electoral factions of the Greens.

The structure created by the working group met with strong popular opposition, however: in a statement signed by thirty-six Left and GCoC Greens, the Working Group's proposed structure was called "grossly undemocratic and authoritarian." According to the statement, the proposed structure instituted an organizational split between movement and party, giving half the votes on the Greens' national committee to each—a structure that was undemocratic because "these damned separate 'parties' don't exist!"[99] Critics of the working group charged it with "cav[ing] in to a small group of self-appointed 'leaders' whose party-building efforts are for the most part based on bureaucratic empire building, not grassroots organizing." The critics also objected to the high majority decision rules in the structure, citing the March 1990 IC meeting that allowed the New England Committees of Correspondence (home of the future GPOC) to be seated but did not give a seat to the New England Green Alliance (home of the Left Greens) "because only 79% instead of 80% supported keeping them on." It was a general disgust with the March IC decision that precipitated the formation of the GPOC and the subsequent calls on all sides for reorganizing the GCoC. Perpetuating high majority decision rules in the new structure and dividing movement from party in a way that practically ensured their future conflict was essentially dooming the organization to dissolve, according to the signed statement from the proposal's critics. Apparently, the critics were in the majority: by April 1991, when the Restructuring Working Group's proposal and the proposal held over from the Estes Park gathering were sent out to the membership, votes from the locals showed an overwhelming popular support (91 percent) for the integrated structure proposed by the Greens for Democracy.[100] From a GPOC perspective, the vote reflected the inability of the GCoC to allow for diversity, to recognize the difference between accountability and control, and to create a structure that would allow the organization to grow in a direction that was its logical future.[101] Meanwhile, however, the GPOC had continued to move forward with plans of its own.

On February 9–10, 1991, twenty-three members of the GPOC met in Boston to formulate some short-term goals and to begin the process of establishing an effective organization.[102] At the outset of the meeting, the group voted to exclude Howie Hawkins and Guy Chichester of the Left Green Network from attending, on the basis that their presence would force the meeting to focus on theoretical debates, when the expressed purpose of the meeting was to work with like-minded people and accomplish specific tasks. Accordingly, the twenty-three GPOC members set up various committees, including a platform/publicity committee and a committee to work with potential 1992 presidential candidates. They agreed to support Ron Daniels's possible presidential bid and to attend the Atlanta Green Justice Conference for Cultural Diversity and Progressive Movements. The group endorsed the Restructuring Working Group's proposal (which would be defeated by the larger membership two months later) and set up plans to hold another GPOC meeting at the Elkins gathering in August. Finally, they agreed to plan a GPOC conference in March 1992 to develop skills in organizing political parties and running campaigns.

By the time the GPOC arrived in Elkins, the group of electorally minded Greens had worked together for nearly two years. They had formed their own separate organization, held their own meetings, and were in the process of planning their first conference. In addition, they had experienced no lack of hostility from the GCoC and Left Greens. What is surprising is that the GPOC not only attended the Elkins gathering but actually made another attempt to negotiate a proposal for a national structure that would accommodate it—and then when its attempts were unsuccessful, it agreed to dissolve back into the

GCoC as a Green Party Organizing Caucus. A final indication of the sincerity of their desire to work with the GCoC was reflected in the new name of the organization—"The Greens/Green Party U.S.A."—which "put Green Party work and Green Party organizational capability squarely in the center of The Greens," an achievement hailed as "a major objective" by Rensenbrink.[103] Giving over the name "Green Party U.S.A." to a movement-based organization would have been a foolish move if the GPOC had intended to leave the Greens, instead of working within the organization to develop its "electoral arm." Eighteen months later, after they had given up on the GCoC entirely, former GPOC activists unveiled one of the central goals of their newly formed Green Politics Network: the Association of Autonomous State Green Parties. It was a project that could have benefited from being able to use the name Green Party U.S.A.

Suspicions about the sincerity of the GPOC in the Elkins negotiations and its commitments to the restructuring that resulted rumbled through the ranks and surfaced in a few publications. An article in the *Guardian,* a well-known leftist news weekly, portrayed Rensenbrink at the Elkins gathering as seeking "to establish the Green Party Organizing Committee as a virtually separate organization in charge of state electoral activities, unaccountable to the left-tinged, grassroots-dominated structure of the Greens." Only because the GPOC was "unable to win a sufficient majority, even within its own ranks, for a separation" did it negotiate the compromise establishing the Greens/Green Party U.S.A. Echoing a familiar phrase, the *Guardian* proclaimed that the U.S. Greens "finally came of age" at Elkins, meaning that with their new program the Greens would shed the image of a single-issue movement and build ties with diverse organizations in the progressive community.[104] But Rensenbrink's response showed a quite different interpretation. Flatly rejecting the label of "advocate for Green electoralism" and the alleged quest to establish the GPOC as a separate organization as "inaccurate portrayals," Rensenbrink called the decision at Elkins "a piece of what I consider brilliant negotiating." It wasn't that the GPOC "lost" to the leftist tendencies within the Greens; rather, "we found new ground in which the aspirations of both were met to a degree and no one had to give up their basic strategic interests." Of course, Rensenbrink emphasized that the Left Greens were still a separate organization and urged them also to become a caucus within the Greens, as the GPOC had done.[105]

Reflecting on the decision at Elkins two years later, however, Rensenbrink called it a "Left Green takeover" that "squash[ed] the GPOC" and "subordinate[d] the emerging state Green Parties, and any national association of such parties, to the will, procedures, and ideological (left anarchist) framework of

G-USA."[106] During the fall of 1991, after the Elkins decision, a series of discussions among former GPOC members eventually led to the formation of the Green Politics Network in Kansas City in March 1992. In "Rationale for Launching a Green Politics Network," a collective statement published in the March 1992 *Greens Bulletin* and thus broadcast to all G/GPUSA members, the thirteen signatories wrote: "The time is ripe for a national catalyst with a holistic, post-capitalist and post-socialist politics."[107] Yet current Green organizations were "either unsuited for the articulation of a Green politics or . . . too often overtaken by persistent counterproductive disagreement over fundamentals of philosophy, strategy, and operational style to be action-effective." They deplored the G/GPUSA's "internal demand for control," which stifled a "plurality of action strategies." Thus, they had decided to form the Green Politics Network as "a parallel organization" that would be in "a cooperating relationship with the Greens," stressing that "what we are aiming to do has to do with electoral politics in the broad sense."[108] What the group had learned, according to Rensenbrink, was that "electoral politics can be truly revolutionary."[109]

The founding meeting of the Green Politics Network was held in conjunction with its first convention, which had originally been planned by the group functioning in its earlier form as the Green Party Organizing Committee. This "Third Force" conference was the first of an annual series of GPN conferences bringing together third-party candidates and campaign managers, officeholders, and independent activists. And 1993 was a bonanza year for the GPN, with California Green Party activist Mike Feinstein organizing a "Green Parties of the West" conference in Santa Monica on February 13–14 and Rensenbrink at Bowdoin College hosting a conference called "Doing It the Grassroots Way" February 25–28 in Brunswick, Maine. In the March 1993 issue of the GPN's newsletter, Feinstein reported on the Green Parties of the West gathering, which drew more than a hundred Green Party candidates, campaign managers, and party activists from the six western states where Greens had ballot access: California, Alaska, Hawai'i, Colorado, Arizona, and New Mexico. According to Feinstein, the conference signaled a "coming of age for a movement that only a short time ago seemed paralyzed over whether to get into electoral politics at all." As a widely cited example of the movement's "maturation," Kelly Weaverling, Green Party mayor of Cordova, Alaska, pointed to his long hair and beard, explaining, "'For the next election I may cut my hair and trim my beard. Who here would not cut their hair or trim their beard to save their mother's life? When we run for elective office, we run because we are concerned for Mother Earth.'"[110] This willingness to exchange a countercultural image of the sixties for a mainstream image of the nineties became the hallmark of the GPN's strategy for moving beyond the old labels of left, right, or center and creating what the GPN's Linda Martin would call "the new mainstream."

Unlike the Left Greens, the GPN initially saw no need to rewrite the principles or platform generated by the Green movement; at the Green Parties of the West conference, however, GPN activists Tony Affigne and Greg Gerritt began circulating a draft of the "Articles of Confederation of the Green Parties of the United States." These six articles functioned as the only theoretical base of the GPN, citing succinct rules for membership, the group's principles, representation of member states, and the association's finances, newsletter, and limitations. Under "Article 2: Principles," the draft simply noted that a state Green Party or network would be eligible to affiliate if its membership voted to do so at a statewide Green convention and if the party or network "conduct[ed] its business in accordance with democratic principles and [had] at the core of its program the 10 Key Values."[111] The Association was purposely loose, as Sam Smith reported from the GPN conference on the East Coast in February 1993; it allowed enough flexibility to member organizations so that "Tony Affigne's urban focus doesn't have to do battle with the values of the Hawai'ian Greens, who, for example, gave out sweet potatoes (the gift of food in Hawai'i being a sign of friendship) as one of their more unusual campaign tactics." Smith celebrated the fact that GPN members "were not radical flakes, but ordinary Americans who had tired of the two major parties' dissin' the environment, democracy, justice, and their own constituents." At the GPN conference in Brunswick, Maine, said Smith, "there was a stunning absence of radical posturing," and mere "abstractions bit the dust as the workshops focussed on media, campaign structure and tactics."[112]

Nineteen ninety-three was also the first year of the Green Politics Network's annual retreats, held over a long weekend in spring or summer and generally designed to build community among GPN activists and provide opportunities for meeting new members and discussing future strategies. The first gathering, "Ecotreat '93," was held April 2–4 in Kansas City, where the GPN founding conference had occurred just two months before. Later retreats in June 1994, May 1995, and June 1996 were held in Chocawhatchee Bay, Florida; York, Pennsylvania; and North Bend, Pennsylvania, respectively, and addressed concerns such as the relationship of the GPN to other progressive movements, the role of spirituality in politics, and the many projects involved with the 1996 Nader presidential campaign. The central purpose of the gatherings, however, was to provide a place for relaxation and community building with political allies, a focus on fostering relationships that would sustain Green electoral activists for the work ahead.

By 1994, the GPN reported having forty members. Its annual conferences had gained in visibility and were being noted in the progressive community. "New Politics '94," held June 10–12 in Oakland, California, brought together Green Party activists from California, Hawai'i, Maine, and Rhode Island, as well as New Party activists from Oregon and representatives from *Ballot Access News*, the Center for Responsive Politics, Common Cause, Citizens for Proportional Representation, and the Fair Trade Campaign. Altogether, more than fifty independent party activists met to discuss strategies for attacking the barriers to third-party political participation. Ellen Miller, executive director of the Center for Responsive Politics, addressed the importance of campaign finance reform; Richard Winger of *Ballot Access News* gave a history of U.S. third-party participation in electoral politics during the nineteenth century; representatives from the Working Group for Electoral Democracy explained the importance of proportional representation; and the cofounder of the New Party, Danny Cantor, spoke about the strategy of fusion and how it could help third parties. Green candidates and officeholders from various states—Keiko Bonk from the Hawai'i County Council, Matt Harline of the Columbia (Missouri) City Council, and Dona Spring of the Berkeley City Council—described the challenges of running Green campaigns and working within the political system.[113] The three-day conference gave GPN activists the boost they needed to plan an even more ambitious gathering in 1995.

"Third Parties '96" was held June 1995 and January 1996 in Washington, D.C., and organized by former Hawai'i Green Party candidate for Senate, Linda Martin. The theme of the conference, "Building the New Mainstream," clearly expressed the GPN's insistence that a new populist alliance would be "neither Left nor Right" but would transcend such dichotomies to build "a broad-based, potentially majoritarian multi-party alliance." Accordingly, a wide range of third-party activists was invited, including both progressives and groups such as the Libertarian, Patriot, and Reform parties. At the June 1995 conference, more than one hundred activists from twenty-seven independent political parties and sixteen progressive organizations produced a "Common Ground Declaration" that represented full consensus on seventeen items and another dozen or so planks that achieved majorities of 80 percent or 60 percent. Though delighted with their accomplishments, conference organizers reminded participants that they could use the Common Ground Declaration in at least five different ways, which ranged from organizing communities for a local or national slate of candidates, to running a presidential campaign, to doing nothing at all with it. GPN conference organizer Linda Martin, however, chose to focus on the bright side, believing, "We have enough of a platform to actually start shopping for a candidate."[114]

At Round Two in January 1996, an ideologically diverse group of third-party activists modified the Common Ground Declaration, led workshops, and spoke on panels addressing concerns of ballot access, campaign finance reform, proportional representation, and other topics of particular interest to those committed to opening up the two-party duopoly. A panel called "Crossover Politics: Transcending the Old Labels of Left, Right, and Center" was televised on C-SPAN, and the conference received local as well as national attention in newspapers and progressive journals. As always, the GPN faced its share of criticism from Left progressives concerned about the wide divergence of political perspectives among the participants. One writer denounced the Common Ground Declaration as "a vague laundry list, developed through a manipulative process by a small group with little commitment to the outcome." Citing various planks from the declaration—"We support more open and fair access to the ballot in all elections" and "We believe that all economic activities should improve and protect the health of the earth, while promoting the happiness and prosperity of its inhabitants"—the writer scoffed at the organizers' apparent belief that "platitudes will galvanize people for a nationwide movement." The conference organizers were charged with simple window-dressing that was both "pretentious and deceptive."[115] But the most serious criticisms focused on the perceived competition between Third Parties '96 and the National Independent Politics Summit.

Ever since the GPN's formation in 1992, members had watched or participated in the development of the National Independent Politics Network, which had grown out of Ron Daniels's Project for a New Tomorrow. After its August 1992 founding at the People's Progressive Convention in Ypsilanti, Michigan, the National People's Progressive Network faltered in 1993 and 1994 because of lack of funds, but it gathered strength in August 1995 and held a National Independent Politics Summit in Pittsburgh and another summit in Atlanta the following April. Strongly rooted in communities of color, with a large number of women in leadership positions, the National Independent Politics Network showed great promise of providing a coalition vehicle for progressive political parties. In contrast, the GPN-organized gatherings of electoral activists in Third Parties '96 drew from parties across the ideological spectrum, a diversity of perspectives that critics saw as incoherence rather than as a strength. In a letter from the National Independent Politics Summit (NIPS) organizers to the GPN organizers of Third Parties '96 (TP '96), the differences between the two groups were held up for tactful scrutiny. According to the letter, NIPS organizers had rescheduled their gathering in order to avoid a conflict with TP '96, invited a GPN speaker to address their conference, and sent a NIPS spokesperson to address TP '96. In spite of these attempts to cooperate, NIPS organizers questioned the GPN's strategy of including ideologically conservative parties in its coalition, arguing that what was needed was a coalition of specifically progressive parties. In particular, NIPS organizers expressed concern over the role of the Patriot Party (Lenora Fulani's former New Alliance Party) in Third Parties '96, since Fulani's group was known for its attempted takeovers of other independent parties, its opportunism, and its disregard of both basic democratic principles and consistency in political positions. Finally, NIPS organizers reiterated their concern that "there should not be two national networks doing third party/independent politics unity-building."[116] Stressing the need for a unified, democratic network, NIPS organizers asked frankly, "Aren't the problems of discussing, deciding and coordinating unified activity in a democratic, accountable and effective manner magnified when these questions are discussed in separate networks and conferences?" From a GPN perspective, as articulated by John Rensenbrink, such concerns were "very similar to the issues that separate the Greens/Green Party U.S.A. . . . from the Green Politics Network."[117]

Both Rensenbrink and California Green Party activist Hank Chapot of the GPN responded to the NIPS letter with the same message: unity is not the appropriate goal at this historic moment. Rather, third-party activists interested in practical coalitions should emphasize "diversity, difference, [and] autonomy" as the basic paths to unity. According to Rensenbrink, the only criteria necessary "as a basis for hitherto separate groups and organizations and lone individuals to come together are nonviolence and democracy."[118] The GPN's unspoken message to NIPS was the same as its message to the Greens: the GPN had no intention of being called to "accountability" for its decisions or its actions, calls that it repeatedly perceived as attempts to control rather than to coordinate or communicate. Actually, the responses of Rensenbrink and Chapot concealed a basic discomfort on the part of the GPN with the larger progressive community, with the label "progressive," and with the leftist ideas that were at the center of progressive groups; this discomfort had been clearly articulated in early issues of the GPN's newsletter and in responses written by GPN participants at the NIPS conferences.[119]

The NIPS Presidential Candidate Task Force did not endorse any candidates for president but set up a coordinating committee to attempt to communicate and work with the GPN's Draft Nader campaign. The NIPS Presidential Search Committee had sent letters to eleven potential candidates in September 1995, including Larry Agran, Jerry Brown, Noam Chomsky, Jim Hightower, Gerald Horne, Dolores Huerta, Jesse Jackson, Frances Moore Lappé, Ralph Nader, Gwen Patton, and Joni Whitmore. Thus, the potential for coordinating a national presidential campaign between the two networks was present. When Ralph Nader was chosen as the Green presidential candidate, however, many NIPS participants expressed concern over his lack of consistent history in dealing with issues specific to communities of color, as well as his unwillingness to speak to issues of social justice during his campaign, and the two groups remained at odds. While NIPS activists turned their attention to internal restructuring, emerging as the Independent Progressive Politics Network (IPPN) in the spring of 1996, the GPN activists focused energies on spreading the Nader campaign from state to state. With the 1996 presidential campaign—the first Green presidential campaign—the GPN was at the peak of its power.

4. Ecofeminists in the Greens

From Petra Kelly in West Germany, to Ariel Salleh in Australia and Charlene Spretnak in the United States, ecofeminists have been central to the founding of the Green movement internationally. In the United States, the book written primarily by ecofeminist Charlene Spretnak, *Green Politics,* sparked the founding meeting of the Committees of Correspondence. Moreover, the history of the U.S. Green movement bears the influence of numerous ecofeminists: Charlene Spretnak's organization of the founding committee and her contributions in drafting the Ten Key Values, Ynestra King's participation in the 1987 Amherst gathering, Marti Kheel's inclusion of animal rights in the life forms plank of the national Green platform, the statements from WomanEarth Feminist Peace Institute to the Greens' national program process at the 1989 Eugene gathering, Margo Adair's opening of many national gatherings with a guided meditation, Sharon (Shea) Howell's leadership in the "eco-city" project called Detroit Summer, Chaia Heller's efforts in the founding and Laura Schere's in the development of the Youth Greens, the many ecofeminists who contributed to the development of the Left Greens (Janet Biehl, Stephanie Lahar, Cora Roelofs, Joan Roelofs, Catriona Sandilands), Dee Berry's years of service as Greens' clearinghouse coordinator, Annie Goeke's efforts in founding the Gylany Greens, among many others. The work of ecofeminists in the Greens has involved not only ecofeminist projects but also the more fundamental projects of feminism itself: achieving equal rights and representation for women (a liberal feminist goal), revaluing many characteristics and behaviors traditionally devalued as "feminine" (a radical feminist goal), and working to eliminate racism and classism within the organization as well as within the larger society (a socialist feminist goal).

Not surprisingly, ecofeminists have often predicted that the success of the Green movement would depend on the ability of Greens to uproot sexism and patriarchal behaviors within the movement. "The liberation of women," Ynestra King observed, reflecting on the 1987 Green gathering in Amherst, "must be central to Green politics if [the Greens] are to survive and grow."[1] In her appraisal of the West German Greens' first four years, Charlene Spretnak observed, "One problem all wings of the party have in common is sexism," a problem that had already caused several Green women to "keep some distance from the patriarchal style of politics" in the Bundestag or to identify themselves first with other movements. Yet the problem of sexism was "not taken seriously by most Green men," a shortcoming Spretnak found "ironic because no other problem is so damaging that it costs votes, keeps people from joining the party, keeps many Green members from actively working within the party, and keeps certain party officials—even at very high levels—from giving their best effort to party work." Part of the problem had to do with the Greens' sudden success: taking office just two weeks after winning the election in a long and extremely hectic campaign, the West German Greens had little time to plan or to practice postpatriarchal ways of interacting. Hence, "with no concrete, comprehensive plans for an alternative mode of operating, they slipped into the familiar, patriarchal patterns."[2] After the Greens were voted out of the Bundestag in December 1990, Petra Kelly openly lamented the "permanent state of ideological warfare" between *fundi* and *realo* factions, a battle that Charlene Spretnak called "macho 'hardball politics.'"[3] Drawing from the experiences of the West German Greens to guide a potential U.S. Green movement, Spretnak concluded that postpatriarchal politics in the Greens would work best at the local, grassroots level. The history of the U.S. Green movement, however, reveals a shift in focus from the local, grassroots level to the levels of state and presidential politics, and it is my thesis that this shift corresponds directly to—and may even be the result of—an attenuation of ecofeminist and feminist presence and perspectives within the movement. To trace this shift, I begin with the foundations of the movement: the Ten Key Values.

Spiritual/Cultural Ecofeminism and the Ten Key Values

At the founding meeting of the Committees of Correspondence in August 1984, sixty-two people convened to set the direction for a Green movement in the United States. Over the course of a weekend together, they decided what type of organization to set up, what to name it, and where to locate an informational clearinghouse. But the most important decision they made involved articulating a Green philosophy and political vision. As with the founding of the Greens, there are at least two different "origin stories" for the Ten Key Values.

According to Charlene Spretnak, there was "general agreement" among those present at the founding meeting that "more than the four pillars [from the West German Greens] was needed; people felt those concepts needed to be expanded, made more specific, and fine tuned."[4] During a brainstorming session, numerous suggestions were recorded on a flip chart and copied down on paper, and a scribe committee was charged with combining these suggestions into a statement of key values and circulating it among the participants. The scribe committee consisted of Eleanor LeCain and Charlene Spretnak in Berkeley, and Mark Satin in Washington, D.C. As Spretnak recalls, "The only major addition our committee made to all the suggestions was the idea of presenting the sub-topics under each key value as a question for discussion, in order to invite participation in our grassroots organizing. That idea and others came from Mark Satin; Eleanor and I agreed, and so did everyone who had been at the founding conference and then received our draft in the mail." Founding participants suggested "fine tunings" that were incorporated into the draft before it was printed in grassroots publications around the country.

A somewhat different story is told by Howie Hawkins, who also attended the founding meeting and later withdrew his support from the draft of the Ten Key Values. He explains,

> Political philosophy was discussed indirectly in the acceptance of a draft of Ten Key Values as an initial discussion paper that would generally indicate the political direction of the CoC. Charlene Spretnak and Mark Satin were the principal writers who ran their drafts past the meeting periodically over the weekend. It was basically an expansion of what had been the West German Greens' initial basis of unity, the "four pillars" of Green politics—*ecology, nonviolence, social responsibility,* and *grassroots democracy.* Ecology was changed to "ecological wisdom," reflecting the spiritual and mystical bent of many present. Social responsibility was changed to "personal and social responsibility" to reflect the New Age emphasis on personal transformation. Added were decentralization, community-based economics, postpatriarchal values, respect for diversity, global responsibility, and future focus. Postpatriarchal values was a euphemism for feminism and respect for diversity for racial equality.[5]

What difference would it make whether the Ten Key Values emerged from brainstorming sessions with sixty-two participants, with LeCain, Spretnak, and Satin serving as scribes, or whether Spretnak and Satin brought to the meeting a Ten Key Values draft for commentary, incorporating the comments they received and circulating the new draft by mail for approval? Why were the terms *community-based economics, postpatriarchal values,* and *respect for diversity* chosen rather than the terms *anticapitalism, feminism,* and *antiracism?* In both Ten Key Value narratives, Spretnak and Satin played a significant role in facilitating the articulation of Green political thought, and the philosophies they represented have left their influence on the Greens' ideological foundation.

The Ten Key Values were shaped in the context of cultural feminist and New Age thought, perspectives that were prominently represented by at least two of the three scribes/authors. Spretnak had edited *The Politics of Women's Spirituality* and would soon author *The Spiritual Dimension of Green Politics,* and Satin was the author of *New Age Politics* and would become publisher of the New Age newsletter *New Options.*[6] Spretnak's position as a spiritual/cultural ecofeminist is revealed not only in her important work on goddesses and women's and Green spiritualities but also in the following words: "Ecofeminism grew out of radical, or cultural, feminism (rather than from liberal feminism or socialist feminism), which holds that identifying the dynamics—largely fear and resentment—behind the dominance of male over female is the key to comprehending every expression of patriarchal culture with its hierarchical, militaristic, mechanistic, industrialist forms."[7] Although Spretnak's and Satin's books developed their sources in different ways, both authors drew upon radical and cultural feminist critiques of women's oppression. These critiques, which had emerged from women's disillusionment and subsequent separation from the New Left of the sixties, argued that men's domination of women under patriarchy was the root cause of all other oppressions.

The sixty-two founding Greens may have chosen the term *community-based economics* over *anticapitalism* because cultural feminism and New Age thought are both antileftist. Both Spretnak and Satin rejected leftist critiques, preferring instead the West German Greens slogan that had graced the cover of Spretnak and Capra's book, *Green Politics:* "We are neither Left nor Right; we are in front." Spretnak's antileftism is expressed in *Green Politics* through various comments about the "Marxist-oriented Greens who seem to thrive on 'conflict politics'" (p. 148) and who reject "a holistic/feminist analysis of technology and economics" (p. 149). Also revealing is the book's portrayal of big labor unions "who seldom look beyond the immediate issues of wages and growth" as an obstacle to Green politics, rather than distinguishing between the union bosses and labor's rank and file and seeking ways to build coalitions between labor and the Green movement. Satin's antileftism permeates his *New Age Politics*, whose title concept he defines as moving "beyond liberalism," "beyond Marxism," and "beyond the Anarchist alternative."[8] The association of cultural ecofeminism and New Age thought with antileftist politics is significant in that both cultural ecofeminism and antileftism mark the founding of the U.S. Green movement and its period of presidential politics over a decade later.

Postpatriarchal values may have been chosen over *feminism* for at least two reasons. First, the conservative backlash against feminism was already underway at the time the Greens were founded, and many Greens then and now want to avoid any negative associations that the term *feminism* might invoke. But the term *postpatriarchal values* is also more closely tied to ideas about a paradigm shift, a concept that was very popular in the early eighties. New Age writers and intellectuals observed that behaviors and traits of an old paradigm were falling from favor and a new paradigm was being discovered. At the same time, radical and cultural feminists discussed many of these same concepts in terms of patriarchal versus matrifocal or woman-centered cultures. In either case, the behaviors to be discarded, and those to be embraced, were remarkably similar:

old paradigm (patriarchy)	new paradigm (women's culture)
• hierarchy	• networks
• center vs. margins	• decentralization
• conflict	• unity
• competition	• cooperation
• militarism	• nonviolence
• autonomy	• accountability
• separation	• interconnection
• individual	• community
• singularity	• diversity, multiplicity
• public (where the men work) as the only political sphere	• personal/private (where the women work) as a political sphere as well
• short-term, self-centered	• long-term, child-centered
• human-centered	• ecocentric
• emphasis on outcome ("the ends justify the means")	• emphasis on process ("the means embody the ends")
• top-down or "majority rules" decision making (distant government controlling local communities; Robert's Rules within the community)	• bottom-up or empowerment (grassroots democracy for local communities; consensus decision making within the community)

- exclusive, concern for self
- separation of church and state

- inclusive, concern for others
- recognition of the relationship between spirituality and politics

Each one of the Ten Key Values reflects the constellation of values on the right.[9]

The most salient problem with the Ten Key Values is that they do not offer a critique of the way that race and class have influenced the development of technologies, economies, or social and political systems that are ecologically destructive—and they do not specify the need to eliminate capitalism or racism as integral to an ecological agenda. Significantly, neither New Age thought nor cultural feminism offers an analysis of capitalism or racism. For New Age thought, this absence is explained by its emphasis on the primary importance of personal transformation. For cultural feminism, the absence is explained by its radical feminist origins. From a radical feminist perspective, the oppression of women and the associated devaluation of the "feminine" under patriarchy is the root cause of all other oppressions; thus going to the root, by ending women's oppression and valuing all those things associated with the "feminine," would of necessity end all other oppressions as well.[10] But as Janet Biehl has argued, "Dropping capitalism and statism from direct consideration in feminist theory renders feminism nonrevolutionary" and subject to co-optation; to avoid this problem, she has urged, "it is high time that ecofeminists challenged the notion of 'primary oppression' and thereby rekindled discussion of the relationship of feminism to the left."[11] Hence, while the analytical strength of cultural feminism, cultural ecofeminism, and the Ten Key Values lies in their emphasis on the relevance of personal and cultural transformation to achieving social and ecological justice, this strength is also their limitation. By excluding specific critiques of other systems of oppression such as capitalism and racism, the Ten Key Values set up a Green movement that was ripe for takeover by a more conservative interpretation.

Social Ecofeminism and Deep Ecology: Resisting the Embrace

At the first national Green gathering in Amherst in 1987, the social ecology/ deep ecology debate received much attention, virtually overwhelming any opportunity to observe the connections being made between cultural ecofeminism and deep ecology or the distinctions between social ecofeminism and deep ecology, not to mention social ecofeminism and social ecology.[12] But in the two years between the Amherst and Eugene gatherings, while academic ecofeminists were debating deep ecologists in the pages of *Environmental Ethics,* social ecofeminists in the Green movement were resisting overtures from deep ecologists and bioregionalists as well.

In 1987, following debates advanced at the Green gathering in Amherst and the Ecofeminist Perspectives conference at the University of Southern California, Ynestra King, in response to Kirkpatrick Sale in the pages of the *Nation,* explained the differences between social ecofeminism and other branches of the radical environmental movement—namely, cultural ecofeminism, deep ecology, and bioregionalism.[13] In his essay, Sale describes ecofeminism as a "hybrid" of feminism and ecological politics (free of influence from leftist politics), an "amalgam" that articulates women's new understanding, based on experiences of working for political transformation in the environmental and Green movements, that "the problems are of culture and values more than politics and laws."[14] He portrays ecofeminism as combining "that 'scientific' thought so often the province of men and the intuitive experience of subjugation and exploitation known to women" and suggests four "hallmarks of present ecofeminist thought": goddess cultures, earth-based spirituality, bioregionalism, and deep ecology. In sum, Sale did not describe the ecofeminism advanced by King.

Nevertheless, in his presentation of ecofeminism, Sale provides a fairly accurate description of cultural ecofeminism: he cites approvingly the strategy of combining gendered attributes to create a holistic analysis, a strategy used by both cultural ecofeminists and deep ecologists (in contrast to challenging as essentialist the association of gender with behavior, as social ecofeminists and other feminists tend to do). In effect, cultural ecofeminists and deep ecologists share a strategy of reversing valuations in the classic culture(man)/nature(woman) dualism in which culture is valued over nature: deep ecologists urge humans to subordinate themselves to nature (biocentrism), and cultural ecofeminists celebrate women's connections to nature and many traditionally feminine characteristics. Sale correctly perceives cultural ecofeminism's emphasis on personal and cultural transformation as more significant than—or, at least, of necessity prior to—political, legislative, and economic transformation. Moreover, his focus on goddess cultures and earth-based spirituality as the salient features of ecofeminism accurately portrays cultural ecofeminism, though this branch has many other political tendencies as well; cultural ecofeminism is distinguished by its emphasis on spirituality not because that is its only emphasis but because no other branch of ecofeminism has so fully recognized the importance of spirituality. Finally, the fact that Sale cites bioregionalism and deep ecology as features of ecofeminism can be attributed to Judith Plant's involvement in the bioregional movement and Charlene Spretnak's frequent references to "ecofeminists and deep ecologists" in a way that suggests this is a coherent and comfortable grouping.[15] But in 1987, the various branches of ecofeminism had not yet been named or developed, leaving Sale and King each with a firm grasp of the leaf or stem, convinced that he or she alone had the whole ecofeminist tree.

Ynestra King's response to Kirkpatrick Sale offers a clear articulation of social ecofeminism's significant differences from cultural ecofeminism, bioregionalism, and deep ecology. Flatly rejecting the suggestion that goddess cultures and earth-based spirituality provide any basis for ecofeminism, King explictly defines the roots and principles of what would later be known as social ecofeminism:

> Although most of us come from the left and maintain a commitment to the leftist projects of human liberation, historical analysis and an opposition to capitalism, we share the social anarchist critique of the economism, workerism and authoritarianism of a myopic socialism that has not challenged the domination of nonhuman nature or taken ecology seriously. We both extend and critique the socialist tradition, sharing with socialist feminist theory an analysis of patriarchy as independent of capitalism, and with cultural feminism an appreciation of traditional women's life and work. Also, taking ecology seriously has meant that we can't opt for a piece of a rotten, carcinogenic pie (like liberal feminists) or set up the woman/nature connection as the enemy of feminism. Connecting women to nature need not acquiesce to biological determinism (the legitimate fear of socialist feminists) if nature is understood as a realm of potential freedom for human beings—both women and men—who act in human history as part of the natural history of the planet, in which human intentionality and potentiality are an affirmed part of nature.[16]

King's affirmation of the leftist, anarchist, and feminist contributions to ecofeminism stands in clear contrast to the cultural ecofeminism described by Sale. In addition, King rejects bioregionalism for its failure to provide an analysis of human oppression: small, ecologically sensitive communities can still foster racism, sexism, and homophobia, all of which are unacceptable from an ecofeminist perspective. Like bioregionalism, deep ecology also ignores entrenched structures of human oppression, focusing exclusively on the "laws of nature"—as defined by deep ecologists.

King's critique of deep ecology is extensive, addressing deep ecology's positions not only on hunting but on human identity, hierarchy, and population. First, King draws on Marti Kheel's critique of "the pro-hunting stance of the deep ecologists" and the defense of "privileged white males of the developed Western countries . . . [going out to] kill something *to realize their identities* as natural beings" as an example of deep ecology's inherently masculinist bias. She describes deep ecology's rejection of distinct human selves as fundamentally antithetical to the feminist project of reconstituting women's identities and perspectives. Moreover, she finds deep ecology's rejection of anthropocentrism for biocentrism as a simple "inversion" (what social ecofeminist Laura Schere would later describe as "replacing one centrism for another") and cites the commitment to ecological humanism as the crucial difference between ecofeminism and deep ecology.[17] In this, King's analysis provides a lens on the cultural feminism of the Ten Key Values—particularly in the value of *ecological wisdom* and the curious contradiction between its emphasis on biocentrism and the Green value of *decentralization*—and the social ecofeminism of the Left Green Network, whose first principle was *ecological humanism*. Finally, King rejects the Malthusian wing of deep ecology as deeply misogynist, racist, and homophobic, "with no analysis of U.S. imperialism, corporate capitalism, the debt of the Third World to the First and the enforced growing of cash crops to pay our banks as the causes of famine in the Third World and enormous suffering in Central America." Population will not be controlled until women have economic and social power and the radical "social, racial, and economic inequities around the world" are addressed. King's conclusion that social movements must strive first "to end the domination of human over human in order to end the domination of people over nonhuman nature" is a succinct articulation of social ecology's core principle,[18] and it stands in direct opposition to both deep ecology and cultural ecofeminism.

Sale's description of ecofeminism can be seen as one example of a larger phenomenon within the Green movement throughout its history: the perspective that ecofeminism is a subsidiary of the Green movement rather than a distinct movement of its own. Although neither King nor Sale explicitly remarks on this phenomenon, Sale's definition—and King's emphatic redefinition—articulate this struggle between merger and autonomy for ecofeminism.

As Janet Biehl observed, "Women know from long experience that when they are asked to become 'one' with a man, as in marriage, that 'one' is usually the man. Ecofeminists should be equally suspicious of this 'ecological' oneness."[19] The invitation to merge was coming from men in the arena of ecological politics and philosophy, and in both cases it meant erasure of ecofeminist identities, philosophies, and perspectives.

In 1988, a cofounder of the Left Green Network and committed social ecofeminist, Janet Biehl, pointedly critiqued the sexism in deep ecology's "advances" toward ecofeminism, concluding that "ecofeminists have nothing to gain in such an embrace."[20] Biehl's critique focuses on four specific areas in which deep ecology puts women in a double bind. Although some of her observations have since been developed more thoroughly by ecofeminist philosophers, Biehl's unique emphasis on the double bind has not been repeated. Since feminist philosopher Marilyn Frye has identified the double bind as a central characteristic of systems of oppression, the significance of Biehl's work should not be underestimated.[21] As a social ecologist and leading theorist in the Left Green Network, Biehl offers a development of social ecofeminism that is particularly relevant.

Deep ecology's identification of anthropocentrism as the central problem of modern Western industrialized culture treats humans as an undifferentiated whole, Biehl observes. At the same time, however, deep ecologists affirmed and even sought to emulate women's position as "closer to nature," a celebration they shared with cultural feminists and cultural ecofeminists. But as Biehl points out, by holding women equally responsible with men for an anthropocentric position that has devalued and destroyed nature, and simultaneously perceiving women as "closer to nature," deep ecology leaves women with nowhere to stand.

The deep ecological self, based on a connectedness that erases difference, is both celebrated and sought after; moreover, this connected self is portrayed as a preexisting feature of women's psychological makeup, one that is to be emulated by men. Biehl cites feminist psychological research showing how women's "soft" or "permeable" ego boundaries have prevented women from pursuing their own rights and interests. But women's search for selfhood is "the revolutionary heart of the feminist and ecofeminist movements," Biehl explains. Being told to "think like a mountain" when we are now beginning to find our own consciousness as women is "a slap in the face." And this is deep ecology's second double bind for women: deep ecology seeks to deny difference at the same time it seeks to appropriate an aspect of feminine psychology.

Deep ecology's fetishization of wilderness perpetuates a culture/nature dualism that is deeply ethnocentric. As Biehl explains, most Native American cultures have no word for "wilderness" because there is no hyperseparation between humans and nature in preindustrial, ecologically sustainable cultures. For ecofeminists, deep ecology's conception of wilderness as a "sacred space" in which to heal from the alienation of mechanized society becomes particularly relevant in a context where women and nature are portrayed as wild and chaotic, a portrayal that has been used to justify the domination of both women and wilderness. Thus conceptualized as "healers," women and nature are supposed to play the nurse to wounded male deep ecologists, a role that leaves little nurturance left over for women or for nature. Here is one of Biehl's most radical assertions, and one that ecofeminists are only beginning to pick up on ten years later: "Women are not 'chaotic' but rational," Biehl argues, "and nature, too, is not 'chaotic' but rather follows a logic of development toward increasing complexity and subjectivity, replete with differences, individual variations, and the slow formation of selfhood."[22] Although it would be unlike a social ecologist to argue that nature has *reason* (the defining characteristic of humans, according to social ecologists), Biehl comes fairly close to it by arguing for nature's "logic." Deep ecology thus denies reason to women and logic to wilderness at the same time it requires women and wilderness to provide the space for healing so men can restore their own wholeness. It is clear that the wholeness of deep ecological men depends on the denial of wholeness to women and wilderness.

Finally, deep ecology's focus on the problem of overpopulation and its solution of fertility programs contains an inherent contradiction: on the one hand, deep ecologists deplore the progress of industrial society; on the other hand, they demand fertility programs, which have been made possible largely through the progress of industrial society. Moreover, their solution overlooks the real solution to population, which is feminism itself. But this solution would blow apart all the other features of deep ecology, with women thinking like mountains, being wild and chaotic, and being closer to nature. In sum, Biehl urges ecofeminists to resist "deep ecological self-oblivion."[23]

The warning was an important one. Some male deep ecologists, critical of ecofeminism, were fond of saying that deep ecology had already articulated the most valuable insights of ecofeminism: a sense of self as interconnected with nature, earth-based spirituality, and a rejection of Western culture's overrationalization, mechanization, and isolation. To the extent that ecofeminism wasn't repeating deep ecology—in social ecofeminist critiques of hierarchy, capitalism, and the state and in arguments for social justice as the necessary foundation for ecological health—ecofeminism was "anthropocentric" and could safely be ignored. Thus, in these debates with deep ecologists and with Greens, social ecofeminists struggled on two different fronts to retain a distinct perspective and a distinct movement. At the same time, other ecofeminists were working to bring an ecofeminist perspective into the Green movement through their participation in building Green locals, attending national gatherings, and developing the national Green platform.

Building the Movement: Ecofeminists in the Green Committees of Correspondence, 1989–1991

The years of the annual national Green gatherings at Eugene, Estes Park, and Elkins arguably marked the height of ecofeminist involvement in the GCoC, as well as the nearly sacrosanct status of liberal and cultural feminisms in influencing certain ways of proceeding. For example, liberal feminism could be seen in the fact that gender balance was required in all administrative bodies and in the processes of every meeting: regions had to send two representatives, a man and a woman, to any administrative meeting, and discussions were frequently organized by placing potential speakers in a "stack" and alternating speakers between men and women. Cultural feminism's influence could be found in the fact that decisions were made not by voting but by consensus, a process that was seen as much more feminist. Gatherings were often opened with a guided meditation, and "women's ways of knowing"—that is, intuition, feelings, relationships, spirituality—were given special recognition (in theory, if not always in actuality). Moreover, collaborative writing, the process whereby the national Green platform was developed, has frequently been claimed as a feminist process for its inclusivity and its reliance on frequent and effective communications among participants.[24] Yet, in spite of these attempts to bring a feminist perspective into the Greens, ecofeminists were never able to gain much of a standing within the movement. In this section, I examine several instances wherein feminist and ecofeminist ideas were made available but failed to generate support: consensus decision making, the proposed statements for the Green national platform submitted by WomanEarth and by the Life Forms Working Group, and the antiracism trainings and projects.

"Voting is violence," as one Green became famous for remarking, based on the observation that traditional voting excludes and disempowers the minority for the sake of the majority. In contrast, consensus decision making gives each person power equal to the sum of everyone else. To facilitate consensus decision making at the national Green gatherings, organizers called on Caroline Estes, a feminist bioregionalist and cofounder of the intentional community Alpha Farm. As Estes explains, Robert's Rules of Order were crafted by Colonel Robert during the gold rush frenzy of San Francisco in 1867.[25] Surely, this procedure for decision making retains the militaristic, competitive, and acquisitive mentality of the context in which it was crafted. Consensus decision making, on the other hand, came out of the Quaker tradition and was designed to build community through cooperation, attentive listening, and the belief that although every person has a part of the truth, no single individual has it all; widely used in the nonviolent direct action movement, consensus soon became synonymous with feminist process. Apparently taking "feminine" to be the equivalent of "feminist" (a hallmark of cultural feminism), Estes believes consensus is indeed a feminist process because "it's more inclusive, more compassionate; it requires paying attention to everybody, and it brings about the same kind of caring as women do in mothering."[26] Many Greens had been active in the antinuclear movements of the eighties and thus were already familiar with the process of consensus decision making. These were some of the many reasons people believed this "nonviolent" process of decision making would be well suited to the Greens.

Unfortunately, it wasn't, and the consensus process itself was blamed for the near paralysis and inefficacy of the Interregional Committee, the national coordinating body of the Green movement. Left Greens and Youth Greens alike were consistently critical of the consensus process, because, when one person was capable of "blocking" a decision that the majority was ready to carry out, consensus effectively allowed minority rule. One Youth Green attributed the Greens' reliance on consensus, despite its proven failure to assist them toward a decision, to an inability to accept the simple fact of conflict.[27] One Left Green pointed out that "to insist that nothing happens in the name of the Greens until all agree is, in practice, to insist that nothing happens."[28] In fact, consensus decision making had not been effective for the Clamshell Alliance, an antinuclear direct action movement that was formed in 1976: as Clamshell activists discovered, consensus process was not suited to a group of individuals whose primary interest lay not in achieving consensus but rather in moving the organization toward their own point of view or in gaining power for themselves.[29] And this was the problem with the Greens. Several years after she retired from facilitating the national gatherings, Caroline Estes reflected on the reasons that consensus had failed in the Greens. "They weren't trained in consensus," said

Estes, "and the political agendas were too strong. If you come in with your mind made up, consensus won't work."[30] For consensus to be an effective process, all participants need to agree on a common purpose. In sum, the Greens made the error of mistaking a feminine or cultural feminist process (in that its avoidance of conflict, its inclusivity, and its emphasis on individual empowerment and community building are all characteristics associated with women) as a one-size-fits-all feminist process. But feminism is characterized by its attention to context, not its rigid adherence to rules or methods. A genuinely feminist process would have involved Greens in assessing the movement as it really was (not how they wished it might be) and then adopting or developing a process that suited their unique needs. Instead, a misguided adherence to feminine (not feminist) process hindered their effectiveness and was eventually replaced by falling back to a simple majority vote when consensus could not be achieved.

In other instances, Greens could not be moved to accept ecofeminist insights, particularly when it came to the platform itself. At the 1989 national gathering in Eugene, for example, six statements were submitted to the platform process on behalf of the WomanEarth Feminist Peace Institute. What is curious about this presentation is that it came at a point when WomanEarth was nearly defunct: according to Noël Sturgeon, after the coordination of WomanEarth was relocated to the Bay area, it became inactive after August 1989.[31] The six statements from WomanEarth were written largely by ecofeminists who were eager to participate in building the institute but who had not been part of the project up to that point; only Ynestra King and Starhawk, the two ecofeminists who originally conceived of the ecofeminist peace institute, were involved in the past projects of WomanEarth. The statements submitted to the Green gathering at Eugene included a statement on ecofeminism written by Ynestra King, Irene Diamond, and Charlene Spretnak; a statement on spirituality written by Spretnak and Starhawk; a statement on racism titled "Toward Diversity" (possibly in keeping with one of the Ten Key Values, "respect for diversity") written by Margo Adair; a statement on bearing and caring for children written by Irene Diamond; an animal rights proposal written by Marti Kheel; and a statement on nonviolence by Spretnak.[32] Of these writers, Diamond, Kheel, and Adair were already working with the Greens. Spretnak had stopped attending national gatherings after Amherst but remained active in local and statewide Green politics. King had stepped back from the Green movement after the Amherst gathering, though she was later temporarily involved in building a Green local in New York City, and Starhawk was never a participant in the Greens.

What they had in common was a desire to influence Green politics by bringing an ecofeminist perspective to the platform process.

Each of the statements articulates a feminist understanding of the personal/political connection, a perspective that distinguishes ecofeminism from both social ecology (which critiques social structures rather than cultural values) and deep ecology (which emphasizes personal transformation but does not critique social or economic structures other than to defend wilderness from their operation). In the statement defining ecofeminism, Ynestra King explains that the ecological crisis is inseparable from the many social crises, and Irene Diamond discusses ecofeminism's critique of dualisms, positioning women as part of both nature and culture. Charlene Spretnak describes the ecofeminist contributions to the Green movement as including "not only analysis, theory-building, and policy recommendations, but also an emphasis on feminist process, without which we feel the Green movement will never reach its potential." They conclude by emphasizing an ethic of care. In a single page, three ecofeminists offer a straightforward and coherent explanation of ecofeminism's relevance to Green politics.

In the statement on spirituality, Spretnak and Starhawk explain the necessity for personal as well as political transformation: "We value all spiritual practices that help cleanse the mind of ill will so that love and compassion can flourish. Dominance and exploitation will not end," they write, "as long as hatred, cruelty, and indifference drive so much of human action." Margo Adair makes the same personal/political connection in the statement on diversity, which she begins by observing, "Racist socialization is the glue that keeps institutional racism in place." In the statement on bearing and caring for children, Irene Diamond connects the private with the public in her criticism of reproductive technologies, her defense of women's right to choice as a necessary component of women's participation in the politics of the public sphere, and her incisive analysis of Western culture's fear of death. Marti Kheel's twelve-point plank on animal liberation positions nonhuman animals within the Green values of nonviolence and ecological wisdom and cites a claim from the GCoC brochure: "There is no solution to the ecological crisis that fails to uproot human domination in all its forms." And in the statement on nonviolence, Spretnak connects militarism and poverty, domestic violence and cruelty to animals, the economic enslavement of third world nations and racism in the United States. All the WomanEarth statements emphasize the theme of interconnection.

None of the statements survived in the final version of the Greens' na-

tional platform. At Eugene, many of the platform working groups were ill prepared or confused or simply did not attend. Confronted with the disarray, organizers shifted the conference from a decision-making body to a gathering focused on learning and discussion, with the understanding that working groups
would develop specific statements through a clearly explained process over the
next year and would present those statements for a vote at the 1990 gathering in
Estes Park. It was shortly after the Eugene gathering that John Rensenbrink
recruited political science professor Christa Slaton to oversee the collaborative
writing process and persuaded Margo Adair, editor of *Green Letter,* to assist in
the effort by publicizing regular activity reports and platform drafts. Possibly
unknown to Rensenbrink, Adair was positioned to become the next co-coordinator of WomanEarth, but when Rachel Sierra resigned because of personal
obligations, the organization folded for lack of racial parity.[33] Of course, Adair
would not have used her position as coordinator of the platform process to
push through the WomanEarth statements. The point here is that even with a
feminist writing process, along with feminist (Slaton) and ecofeminist (Adair)
coordinators, the Green national platform still did not put forward the Woman-
Earth statements. Perhaps this omission had more to do with process than
substance. In the Autumn 1989 issue of *Green Letter,* an ecofeminism plank was
published which explicitly requested that the gathering in Estes Park "provide a
plenary session for the ecofeminist analysis and allocate daily workshops to
articulate the various facets of the position," arguing that "it is not sufficient at
this stage to subsume ecofeminism within other working groups as has happened at the Oregon meeting."[34] Moreover, in that same issue of *Green Letter,*
the Eco-Philosophy Working Group stated that "the *post-patriarchal value* has
been changed to *eco-feminism* for additional clarity and completeness." Even
with these assertions, distinct ecofeminist statements and perspectives were directed to other issues or platform planks, where they were later subsumed or
voted down.

The Life Forms Working Group members faced their own set of challenges
in getting their plank adopted by the larger Green movement, although the
group was ably facilitated by a number of experienced activists. Marti Kheel, an
ecofeminist who contributed the statement on animal liberation to the WomanEarth statements and whose work on animal ecofeminism was becoming
widely known, was the spokesperson for the group. A Green who had written
widely about the need for the animal liberation and Green movements to work
in coalition, Charles Dews served as co-coordinator. And a woman who might
well be known as the "mother" of the animal liberation/feminist connection,

Connie Salamone, also worked on the planks while participating in a New York City Greens local.[35] Together they crafted statements using each one of the Ten Key Values to demonstrate that speciesism was antithetical to a Green vision. Then they put forth a plank addressing the retainment of origins in natural gene pools (addressing plant and animal concerns as well as genetic engineering), the preservation and sustainability of ecosystems, and the quality of life for animals and plants alike.

In April 1990, just months before the gathering in Estes Park, the Life Forms Working Group received a critique of its statements from the Rocky Mountain Greens. Instead of taking issue with some of the recommendations made for animal liberation—vegetarianism, the reintroduction of native predators, and an end to sport hunting, trapping, livestock grazing on public lands, and the breeding of companion animals—the Rocky Mountain Greens opposed the language used in applying the Ten Key Values to an analysis of animal oppression. In each case their objections turned on the use of arguments invoking an ecofeminist perspective. The value of *nonviolence* may not be extended to nonhuman animals, they argued, not because of any inferiority of other species but because "life on the planet Earth is by nature violent." The Rocky Mountain Greens also objected to the application of *postpatriarchal values* to other species, claiming that the attribution of all oppression, including speciesism, to "patriarchal social and economic structures" was a form of "male-bashing." On applying the value of *community-based economics* to nonhuman species, Rocky Mountain Greens rejected the analysis that human and nonhuman species were exploited by multinational corporations, arguing that "this statement ignores individual responsibility." And unless the Life Forms Working Group chose to rewrite its statements, the Rocky Mountain Greens vowed to block consensus. Refusing to analyze the structures of oppression or to consider that humans could live nonviolently with other species, the statement from the Rocky Mountain Greens reveals a basic resistance to an ecofeminist perspective. In spite of these objections, most of the recommendations from the Life Forms Working Group survived the platform ratification process at Estes Park and were included in the Green national platform; nevertheless, the application of the Ten Key Values to nonhuman species did not go forward, nor did the people working in the Life Forms Group. Marti Kheel, for example, was exhausted by the process of battling with people unwilling to listen to alternative viewpoints.

Finally, Shea Howell and Margo Adair were two ecofeminists whose work within the Greens was largely underappreciated. As ecofeminists, both women had attended the West Coast meetings of WomanEarth II in 1989, and as white women they were also among those who volunteered to leave the meeting in order to allow those who remained to achieve racial parity. Not only had Adair been selected to co-coordinate WomanEarth had it survived; she also cofacilitated the Greens' platform writing process during 1989–90, edited *Green Letter*, and brought an ecofeminist perspective to the Green gatherings through her guided meditation exercises that opened many meetings and her frequent workshops on unlearning racism. Together Howell and Adair operated Tools for Change, offering training programs to groups and organizations on uprooting relations of domination and on alliance building, with a particular focus on race and class.[36] Their double-sided leaflet "Toward Healing All Our Relations," abstracted from their pamphlet *The Subjective Side of Politics*, was often the only and always the most-cited resource in the Green movement for understanding racism, sexism, classism, and other forms of domination. Moreover, "Detroit Summer," part of the Green Action Plan initiated in 1991, was actively coordinated by Shea Howell.

The idea for Detroit Summer was first created by Detroit urban activists James and Grace Lee Boggs as a way to address community problems through direct grassroots activism. Sharon Howell, Roberto Mendoza, and the Detroit Greens immediately became part of the effort, planning projects and contacting community activists. Before the project was introduced to the Greens in 1991, the people of Detroit had already formed "112 neighborhood organizations, 30 neighborhood small business associations, 300 cooperatives in housing, food, day-care and worker collectives."[37] Recognizing the efforts of Detroit activists as a model of Green theory in action, Greens adopted a Detroit Summer project as part of a tripartite Green Action Plan for 1992, with the idea of sending students and other Green volunteers to Detroit to assist in the efforts that were already under way. But as Howell recalls, the Greens' national membership never followed through on this project, which was intended to build multicultural, intergenerational alliances. In spite of the good efforts made by Howell and Adair, a particular style of politics continued to dominate the Greens, and the project of unlearning sexism and racism—much less building multicultural alliances—went largely undone.

Social Ecofeminists and the Left Greens/Youth Greens

Although the term "ecofeminism" was never articulated in the Ten Key Values of the Greens, social ecofeminism was from the start a principle shared by the

Left Greens and the Youth Greens. According to Chaia Heller, Murray Bookchin first began using the term "eco-feminism" in 1976 as he mapped out the curriculum for the Institute for Social Ecology (ISE).[38] In 1980, Ynestra King and other feminist activists organized the Conference on Women and Life on Earth: Ecofeminism in the '80s, a gathering inspired by King's study and teaching at ISE as well as her commitment to developing a feminist peace politics. But the organizers of the Women and Life on Earth conference and the Women's Pentagon Actions of 1980 and 1981 thought of their work in terms of ecofeminism or feminist peace politics. It was not until the mid-eighties that Chaia Heller, who had also been studying and teaching at the ISE, began using the term "social ecofeminism" as·a way of acknowledging the influence of social ecology as well as distinguishing this particular version of ecofeminism. Although she frequently lectured on social ecofeminism, and thus her ideas were widely available among Left Greens, Youth Greens, and others at the ISE, Heller did not write up her notes in essay form until 1990.[39] Published in the winter of 1987, Janet Biehl's ecofeminist critique of deep ecology does not use the phrase "social ecofeminism," nor does Ynestra King's rebuttal of Kirkpatrick Sale, though her clarifying definition of ecofeminism effectively articulates a social ecofeminism. Not until October 1988 in Janet Biehl's essay "What Is Social Ecofeminism?" did the term become explicit. It was adopted as a founding principle of both the Left Greens and the Youth Greens less than a year later.

In April 1989, at their founding conference in Ames, Iowa, members of the Left Green Network offered a succinct definition of social ecofeminism as one of fourteen founding principles:

> Left Greens are committed to the liberation of women, to their basic reproductive rights as well as their full participation in all realms of social life. We believe in a social ecofeminism that seeks to understand and uproot the social origins of patricentric structures of domination. Unlike other ecofeminisms that accept patriarchal myths and cultural definitions of women as more "natural" than men and as existing outside culture, social ecofeminism regards women as cultural beings, as well as biological beings, and seeks to understand and change the social *realities* of the relationships between women, men, the political realm, the domestic realm, and all of these to nature.

Inspired by presentations and discussions with Chaia Heller, John Clark, and Howie Hawkins during their weekend conference on Green politics, students at

Antioch College formed the Youth Greens in May 1989. Writing position papers on each of six core principles, the Youth Greens were perhaps even more explicit than the Left Greens in their analysis of women's economic, individual, and cultural oppression: "Social Eco-feminism in the Youth Greens recognizes capitalism's inherent oppression of women and others. We critically analyze the relationships between power, gender, and social structure, and the relationships among all forms of oppression. We actively pursue egalitarian principles through affinity groups, active dialogues between men and women, and corrective measures on a personal and group level."[40] At their third national gathering in July 1990, Youth Greens developed a two-page ecofeminist statement defining ecofeminism as an analysis of the interconnection of all forms of domination. From the perspective of social ecofeminism, Youth Greens explicitly identify the role of capitalism in perpetuating women's oppression and the applications for an ecofeminist critique of motherhood, sexuality, health care, direct action, antiracism, and an "erotic body politic." Both the Left Greens and the Youth Greens were careful to define social ecofeminism as a theory that "recognizes the historical connections between the domination of women and the degradation of 'nature'" but that rejects the dualism of woman/nature as opposed to man/culture. According to the Youth Green statement, "Ecofeminists are laying the myth of biological determinism to rest."

From the beginning, social ecofeminism was not uncritically accepted in either the Youth Greens or the Left Greens, and feminists in both groups had to struggle with sexism. At the founding of the Youth Greens at Antioch, for example, Chaia Heller was "met with a fair amount of animosity" from young men who felt her speeches were "aggressively lesbian" and accused her of "recruiting for the eco-feminist movement."[41] Women who formed a separate women's caucus as a space to discuss Green theory issued a statement to other conference participants, asserting "it is obvious that the prevailing social oppressions of our society have not been transcended by the youth green movement" and emphasizing that "the values and contributions of [a feminist] caucus are necessary for the success of the youth green movement and we expect full support." Of course, it wasn't only the Youth Greens who experienced this problem: as Antioch college reporter April Cope observed, when Left Green Howie Hawkins was asked what he thought the connection was between ecofeminism and the Greens, he merely said, "I don't know. What do you think?" The student asking the question reported being "surprised that there was such a serious lack of understanding about ecofeminism. He basically didn't know anything about ecofeminism, and didn't appear to be interested in knowing more."[42]

In spite of these early difficulties, several ecofeminists described both the Left Greens and the Youth Greens as some of the most politically astute activists they had ever worked with.

In terms of direct action, the clearest example of the convergence of eco-feminism and Green politics was manifested in the Earth Day Wall Street Action. As models for their action, members of the organizing committee drew on the examples of two previous demonstrations: the Wall Street Action of October 29, 1979, organized by the antinuclear Clamshell Alliance on the fiftieth anniversary of the great Stock Market crash, and the Women's Pentagon Actions of November 1980 and 1981. In creating the *Earth Day Wall Street Action Handbook,* organizers referred to the handbook from the Clamshell Alliance's Wall Street Action, adding explicitly ecofeminist essays such as Chaia Heller's "Take Back the Earth," Margo Adair and Sharon Howell's "Embracing Diversity: Building Multi-Cultural Alliances," Judi Bari's "Timber Wars," Ynestra King's "The Ecology of Feminism and the Feminism of Ecology," and perhaps most important, a full reprint of the Unity Statement from the Women's Pentagon Actions. Finally, organizers modeled the day's events on the scenario developed for the Women's Pentagon Action, which had four stages: mourning, rage, empowerment, and defiance.[43] For the Earth Day Wall Street Action, organizers sent mass mailings to all two hundred fifity Green locals, all locals and contact persons of the National Anti-Toxics Campaign, and hundreds of student groups, inviting them to submit two-hundred-word statements describing how their communities had suffered from out-of-control corporations. Like the Women's Pentagon Action ribbon of life, this Scroll of Anger and Mourning was intended for prominent display during the noon speak-out, when coalition members addressed demonstrators, stock exchange workers, and passers-by. In theory and in practice, the Earth Day Wall Street Action of the Left Greens and the Youth Greens articulated an ecofeminist perspective.

Of course, ecofeminists within these groups still had to combat sexism. At the Second Continental Conference of the Left Green Network in July 1990, the women's caucus discussed the need to develop a feminist agenda for the LGN. Such an agenda would include changing the communication format of the conferences, which was characterized by a "polemical, repetitive oratorical style" and large-group plenaries "dominated by the rhetorically 'strongest' men in the room." As an alternative, the women's caucus suggested small-group discussions, circulating drafts of articles for discussion before the conferences, and assigning a "process watcher" to assist the facilitator in ensuring that everyone had a chance to participate.[44] Later that year at the Youth Green gathering, women confronted a similar problem in their gender caucuses. While the men's caucus finished early and waited nearly an hour without notifying the women, the women's caucus ran overtime discussing issues and ideas, noting an improved level for women's participation in the group's discussions yet observing that "the gendered poles of passivity and assertiveness" had not disappeared. When the women returned to the plenary, a confrontation ensued. According to Youth Green and social ecofeminist Laura Schere, the phenomenon of "guilt politics" was preventing men from effectively examining the problem of gender socialization, a task she urged them to engage in. "In order to improve on the rocky history of gender relations among Youth Greens, and keep women from being so alienated that they turn their energies elsewhere," Schere emphasized, "we must engage in this difficult work both locally and as an organization. Only then can we hope to take on the characteristics of a true counterinstitution, enjoy each other as rational beings, and work harmoniously together in pursuit of the same goals."[45] In both the Left Greens and the Youth Greens, ecofeminists recognized the value of working in coalition with a broader movement but emphasized the importance of keeping women's caucuses to maintain their identities as distinct from the group. Though feminism was implicit in an anarchist agenda—and social ecofeminism was explicit in the principles of Left and Youth Greens—"as long as there continue to be remnants of sexism in any organization," one Left Green woman explained, "feminists need the strength, clarity and definition that autonomous women's groups provide."[46]

It came as a surprise to many social ecofeminists, then, when Janet Biehl's new book, *Rethinking Ecofeminist Politics,* advocated abandoning ecofeminism in favor of social ecology, a theory she believed would assuredly address the concerns of women. Though the Left Green organizing bulletin published a wholly uncritical review of Biehl in an issue just before Third Continental Conference, at the conference itself Laura Schere and Kate Sandilands offered workshops on feminism which took Biehl's work in two different directions.[47] Using Biehl's conclusions as a departure point, Schere warned against the Left Green tendency to collapse individual identities in the desire to create a unified Left. From Schere's perspective, ecofeminists were making crucial contributions to the understanding of domination; rejecting their insights would mean creating a "prematurely unified theory and practice that obscures real historical differences." With Schere, Sandilands affirmed women's subjectivity, but with a different strategy. Criticizing the Left Green principle of social ecofeminism for its divisiveness, its "double-distancing from feminism," and its obsession with "defining what is wrong with all hitherto existing attempts to combine feminism and ecology," Sandilands advocated discarding the principle entirely and replacing it with "women's liberation." Apparently, a number of the women at the conference agreed with her, and the principle of social ecofeminism—along with any references to ecology—was dropped. In 1991, with the publication of Biehl's book and the Chicago conference of the Left Green Network, the brief popularity of social ecofeminism in the Greens was nearly over.

Almost too late to have any effect, the editors of the Left Green Network's discussion bulletin, *Regeneration,* sent out a call for papers to be submitted for a special issue on feminism. The call was circulated in fall 1991, after the fifth (and final) conference of the Youth Greens and the contentious national Green gathering in Elkins, which reorganized the Greens' national into the Greens/ Green Party U.S.A., subordinating the party to the movement in such a way that members of the Green Party Organizing Committee left the organization altogether and formed the Green Politics Network just six months later. The Left Green Network would have one more continental conference, in May 1992, before its membership numbers dropped. In short, the "movement" aspect of the Greens was waning. Nonetheless, the call attracted at least two articles on "Green/feminist process," repeating arguments for less combative communication styles, defending the value of women's caucuses, and suggesting that "little can substitute for men and women taking a hard look at how they perpetuate (and tolerate) sexism, oppressive gender roles, and heterosexism in their relations with friends, lovers, relatives, comrades, children, co-workers, etc."[48] Although the issue contained a new essay from Chaia Heller titled "Eco-cide in Women's Bodies" and a report on the World Women's Congress for a Healthy Planet from Stephanie Lahar, overall the editors could only reflect, not resuscitate, the views and the presence of social ecofeminists.

From *Postpatriarchal Values* to *Feminism* in the G/GPUSA

In August 1991, a month after the Left Green Network's conference in Chicago, the Green Committees of Correspondence held their fourth national gathering in Elkins, West Virginia. The gathering has been discussed as a turning point in the Greens' national organization (see Chapter 3), marking as it did the last time party and movement activists worked together in a single national organization. Ecofeminism—or rather, the rhetoric of liberal and cultural feminisms, and cultural ecofeminism—played a significant role in the division of Green activists into two separate national organizations. According to the activists who formed the Green Politics Network, the blatant sexism of the Greens in the GCoC (combined with their own desire to form an electoral organization) motivated the Green Party Organizing Committee activists to withdraw from the organization. According to the women who remained in the newly reorganized Greens/Green Party U.S.A., the sexism they faced in the movement was no more and no less than women face in the larger society, and they charged the GPN activists with using the rhetoric of feminism to cloak a very patriarchal drive for political power. Many of these same women, at the 1992 gathering that followed Elkins, introduced a resolution to change one of the Ten Key Values from *postpatriarchal values* to *feminism.* Thus, within the period of a year, the central articulations of the Green movement had been revised to emphasize *women's liberation* (LGN) or *feminism* (G/GPUSA), and during this time the Green electoral activists withdrew from the movement, in part because of its inability to transcend patriarchal behaviors. It is my thesis that, as with *Regeneration*'s special issue on feminism, the changes in core values came too late and offered little more than lip service to solving a fundamental problem with sexism and patriarchal behaviors; I see a correlation between the disappearance of social ecofeminism and the unrestrained growth of patriarchal "politics-as-usual" in the Greens. Moreover, I find a disturbing compatibility between patriarchal politics and cultural ecofeminism.

Criticisms about patriarchal behaviors in the Greens' national organization began surfacing in 1991 and 1992. At the 1991 national gathering in Elkins, the preconference meetings of the Green Party Organizing Committee, called to address the vexing relationship of movement and party and how that relationship should be structured, included the presence of ecofeminists speaking on behalf of the GPOC. For example, John Rensenbrink yielded a third of his allotted speaking time to Terri Williams of St. Louis, an ecofeminist who had split off from the Gateway Green Alliance in St. Louis because the "male-oriented, patriarchal Left Greens had taken over."[49] Later, former national clearinghouse coordinator Dee Berry received extra time to express her ecofeminist analysis of the problem, which she described as a conflict "between garden variety Greens and Left Greens." According to Berry, the party/movement debates were exacerbated by "this patriarchal Left Green behavior," at which point another GPOC leader, Barbara Ann Rodgers-Hendricks of Florida, burst into tears. With three women objecting to sexism, it seems there was surely some foundation to their claims.

Nor were they alone in their charges. Christa Slaton, the political scientist who had coordinated the national platform writing process from 1989 to 1990, left the national gathering at Estes Park, and the entire Green movement, after being publicly "trashed" there by members of the Left Greens' ad hoc group, Greens for Democracy. In her review of the U.S. Green movement, Slaton cites several women who express frustration with "the dominance of males practicing politics as usual." Although many local and statewide Green groups had attempted to implement the value of *postpatriarchy* through liberal feminist strategies—such as seeking gender balance on all their committees, instituting procedures to ensure more participation from women, pairing male-female teams to facilitate meetings, and rotating speakers so that no one person dominates—still, "males tended to dominate the process." According to Slaton, the problems reached a peak at the gathering in Elkins, after which "many members and former leaders—particularly women—broke away and formed a parallel organization called the Green Politics Network (GPN)."[50] Although she could not be induced to continue her participation in the Greens, no matter what the form, Slaton agreed to be one of thirteen signatories to the "Rationale for Launching a Green Politics Network."

There was a buildup to that statement, of course, involving first the resignations of Barbara Ann Rodgers-Hendricks and Dee Berry from the Green Council, along with various private communications among GPOC members. After her initial letter of resignation, Berry followed up publicly in December 1991 with another letter to the Green Council and members of the G/GPUSA. In this letter, Berry specifically attributed her resignation to her discovery of "new homes in two strong movements that are gaining strength and are beginning to come together": ecofeminism and "the idea of a third force political party." Berry defines ecofeminism as "a strong female force that is realizing that if the planet is to be healed it will be up to us women to lead the way," for women have always been the healers and the caregivers: "There is a creative female energy in both men and women at the very depths of our beings that is a strong force for life. This force, like life itself, is sexual, spiritual, messy, ecstatic, unpredictable and represents death as well as life. Patriarchy has always been afraid of this energy because it cannot control it or reduce it to fit its neat intellectual theories. So the reaction has been to violently oppress it." Women have withdrawn from patriarchal battles and have yielded political power in the process, she writes. But in view of the current environmental crisis, women must step forward and reclaim their own power, redefining politics as "a creative force for life." To defend women from being overwhelmed in the struggle with patriarchal forces, Berry invokes the strength of the Green warrior:

We must integrate our female energy with the power of the Green warrior, the positive male force of both women and men. Unlike the soldiers of patriarchy who get their power by destroying or putting down others, Green warriors get their strength from being who they are. Thus, to use the positive male force is to define ourselves by what we are, not by whom we oppose. To use the positive male force is to understand the need for fair and open rules and to take responsibility for upholding them. It is to have the courage to make tough choices and accept responsibility for the results of our actions. It is to act boldly, forthrightly, and do what needs to be done, to leap boldly into the future.

In brief, Berry's resignation letter offers an eloquent articulation of many key characteristics of cultural ecofeminism. From a cultural ecofeminist perspective, behavioral traits are inherently gendered; liberation comes from achieving a kind of psychological androgyny, containing a balance of "good" masculine and feminine traits ("the positive male force" and the "creative female energy") available to both men and women. Committed to the Ten Key Values and the value of *nonviolence*, Berry has explained that her idea of the "Green warrior" is not intended to invoke associations with militarism.[51] Yet this version of cultural ecofeminism is open to exploitation from other forces: in its celebration of traditional gender roles for women (i.e., healers and caregivers) and men (warriors), it does nothing to challenge these dualisms or to make other, nontraditional roles available to women. The female/eros and male/thanatos associations lurk just beneath the surface of Berry's ecofeminism. As socialist feminists first argued, these associations are a product of social construction in the context of an oppressive patriarchal culture; the liberation of women and other oppressed people will come not from reversing the valuation of devalued gender roles but from challenging the very construction of gender itself.

Portions of Berry's letter were repeated verbatim in the "Rationale for Launching a Green Politics Network," published in the March 1992 edition of the *Greens Bulletin*. There the GPN founders explain that they have launched a new organization because the original movement "seems unable to come to terms with the oppression of women, and with the positive female and male in all of us." In their experience, women have "found the Greens as oppressive as the patriarchal society we are committed to transforming," and men "who have stood up for the positive female . . . have been put down and/or crowded into the old power and control games." In an effort to leave these behaviors behind, GPN founders propose creating a new organization that values women's leadership and is capable of providing an alternative to patriarchal politics:

> We must take back our political system from the forces of patriarchy that have defined the nature of politics for the past four thousand years. There is a creative female energy in both men and women at the very depths of our beings that is a strong force for life. This force, like life itself, is sexual, spiritual, messy, ecstatic, joyful, unpredictable, and represents death as well as life. Because patriarchal men fear and distrust this energy in women, in some men (particularly gay men), and in nature itself, they have violently oppressed and dominated this creative energy to the point where all life is now threatened. It is vitally important that all of us, the oppressed and the oppressor alike, liberate ourselves and nature from these patterns of dominance and oppression. This will not be easy. Therefore, because women have almost universally been victims of the oppression and because they embody the life force, they can and must take the lead toward liberation.

Not every woman shared these sentiments, of course. Women in the Greens/ Green Party U.S.A. felt quite capable of taking the lead right where they were.

At least three separate statements were written by G/GPUSA women, both individually and collectively, responding in protest to what they perceived as a divisive tactic on the part of the Green Politics Network founders. In a statement titled "Gender and Splits in the Greens," one woman exclaimed, "I resent being placed in the ironic position where I must muffle my opposition to the dynamic being created by the GPOC Steering Council letter signators, or appear to be a traitor to my sex." All the women writers believed the GPN statement used the rhetoric of feminism to conceal the GPN's real purpose for leaving the Greens: creating a separate organization for Green Party organizing. Women defending the Greens charged GPN founders with continuing "to organize in a manner that is essentially competitive, antagonistic, and unprincipled." It is significant that none of the women writers challenged the critique of sexism in the Greens. Two writers referred to the Mediation Council and the Women's Caucus as appropriate resources for addressing sexism in the Greens. One woman cited her years of activism as a basis for assessing the GPN's claims: "I have worked in leadership positions with several social change organizations," she wrote, "and The Greens are by far the most sophisticated, fair, and serious about changing power dynamics within the organization." But the process of transforming gender relations would be a slow one, women agreed. According to the collective "Women's Statement on Sexism and Division in the Greens," signed by twelve women, "sexism is pervasive in our society, and it is indeed present in our organization, as in every organization we know of." Stating their commitment to support women and women's leadership in the Greens, the writers asked, "If we abandon hope here, where openness to feminist values is widespread, how can we hope to create change in the larger society?"[52]

With these events in recent memory, women attending the 1992 national Green gathering in Minneapolis put forth a motion to change the key value from *postpatriarchal values* to *feminism*. Arguing that *postpatriarchal* is "difficult to understand" and "implies that our values are coming out of values based on patriarchy," the women's caucus proposal writers asserted that *feminism* is both "straightforward and recognizes the rich contributions of feminist theory to the Green movement."[53] The motion did not go forward without considerable opposition. One man protested, "If males submit to being identified as 'feminists' or supporting 'feminism,' they submit themselves to 'reverse sexism.'"[54] Others feared the new term would be "divisive and polarizing." A large majority of Greens, however, were ready to acknowledge that sexism was a serious problem within the Greens: "Women are chronically under-represented except where gender balance is mandated," wrote one man. "More profoundly, women have to continually struggle against masculinist styles of work, debate and leadership." In the end, the proposal was adopted by exactly the minimum required (75 percent). Greens hoped its adoption would signal a shift toward "validating and supporting a feminist transformation of The Greens."[55]

Possibly responding to the exodus of several women to the Green Politics Network, members of the Women's Caucus spent a significant portion of their time addressing the importance of women's leadership. One of the ideas to come out of the caucus, along with the key value change to *feminism*, was the proposal to implement a Women's Leadership Fund. In spite of efforts to mandate gender balance on key committees, in spokespeople, and in working groups, caucus members noted, "it is men who dominate our national meetings and publications, and more often than not initiate new Green actions and thought (or at least take the credit for it)."[56] The Women's Leadership Fund would make funds available to women, who traditionally have reduced access to funds needed for travel and other expenses related to holding leadership positions. Other proposals for increasing women's leadership included a request to institutionalize women's space at the gatherings and to adjust gender balance on the Greens Coordinating Committee, so that four of the seven seats would be held by women. Unfortunately, none of these proposals addressed the problem of transforming patriarchal behaviors among the Greens, and the problem continued to grow.

The majority of that task had to be resolved by the men themselves, of course, and many men at the conference challenged other men on patriarchal behaviors. The new key value received tremendous support from the Men's Caucus, "M.E.N." (Men Evolving Naturally), which issued a statement that "feminism is also for men in that it challenges gender stereotypes which impoverish us as well as subordinate women." Resolving to challenge those stereotypes and to act as feminist allies, the Men's Caucus initiated a "Green Sprouts" program to provide child care at national Green gatherings. The caucus resolution specified that "at least one half of the volunteer shifts assisting with the program shall be filled by men, and at least one half by non-parents."[57] Unlike the Women's Caucus proposal, the Men's Caucus proposal received unanimous support. At the end of the gathering, Caroline Estes, who had facilitated consensus decision making at four of the five national Green gatherings, announced her retirement. Saying that in the early days of the Green movement there had been too much mistrust, egotism, and competitiveness, "now," she concluded, "you have love, trust, and unity, and with these three things you can do anything."[58] From Estes's perspective, the shift from stereotypically masculine to stereotypically feminine behaviors was a positive sign of the Greens' potential success. But liberal and cultural feminist strategies had a way of letting women down in the Greens.

Four years after *postpatriarchal values* was changed to *feminism,* the former 1994 California Green Party candidate for secretary of state, Margaret Garcia, lamented, "Whatever happened to Green feminism?" Although naming issues and problems specific to the California Green Party, her descriptions echoed earlier assessments from women about the Green movement generally. According to Garcia, women were present at the local level, where work focused on local elections and movement-building issues such as meeting with other organizations, building coalitions, and addressing local problems. But higher up in the organization, men predominated, and "state party meetings and decisions often reflect the opinions of men who no Green Party locals ever see." The problems came not just from the location of men and women in the organization but from the fact that women's views were continually discounted. In a state that began its Green Party "with roughly one man to every three women,"

Garcia reported, the California Green Party was "lucky if it sees one woman to every seven men." Originally, the California Green Party was known not only for its high numbers but for the strength of its women's caucus: "It was there that such physical remedies to male indifference, such as standing on tables, barking, and other behaviors, were born." But women grew tired of making the same points over and over again. "We are accused of bickering when we voice dissent," said one woman. "If you are taking time away from your personal life and children," said another, "you want it to be for a worthwhile project with tangible goals. Spending meeting after meeting keeping egos in check is not a productive or healthy way for me to spend my time."[59]

In 1996, women in the Green Party of California faced a dilemma they never expected: the presidential campaign of Ralph Nader, initiated by several men in the California Greens. "Our very first chance to run a candidate for president," wrote Garcia, "and we are running a straight, white male who lives three thousand miles from California. So much for growing our own candidates." In Garcia's view, the Nader campaign directly violated "founding promises of introducing only gender-balanced, multi-racial tickets with a woman as head of the ticket." But the thirst for a "happy ending" had always followed writers who assessed the Green movement. Like Green women before her, Garcia concluded that such disappointments would only make Green women stronger, more organized, and more determined. "We are becoming more assertive among the men in the party," she concluded, "because we realize the Green Party of California is not the safe space we thought it would be—for feminism." Garcia's more frank assessment remained embedded within her essay: "Do we really think we can have a positive effect on society when we haven't yet adequately dealt with our own sexism and racism?"[60] As Garcia confided a few months after her essay appeared, she was giving the California Green Party until the end of the year; then, if conditions for women had not improved, she, like the other strong women before her, was leaving.[61]

"Power" Feminism, Spiritual/Cultural Ecofeminism, and the Green Politics Network

Was the situation for women any different in the Green Politics Network? Surely, the declaration that had founded the organization made it seem that women's views would be respected and that women would be encouraged to take leadership roles. In fact, although its manner of operating was considered patriarchal by some, the GPN featured many women in leadership positions. Ranging in perspectives from "power" feminism (Keiko Bonk) and liberal feminism (Linda Martin) to spiritual/cultural ecofeminism (Dee Berry, Anne Goeke), women in the GPN enjoyed support from their male colleagues and a freedom from the debilitating assaults on women's leadership which they felt had characterized the Greens overall.

One cluster of women's leadership in the GPN came from the Hawai'i Green Party, which had nurtured the work of Christa Slaton, Keiko Bonk, Toni Wurst, and Linda Martin. In 1992, Keiko Bonk won a seat on the County Council of the Big Island of Hawai'i. But Bonk did not attribute her success to feminism: "Feminism is for my mother's generation," she said.[62] To questions about sexism and racism as potential obstacles during her campaign, Bonk has simply responded, "The only instances of sexism were with people instructing me about appropriate attire and makeup. I just told them, 'don't worry about it; my generation can wear lipstick and think at the same time.'" To other women seeking leadership and possibly running for office with the Greens, Bonk counsels, "Be strong and do it. . . . Use your confidence from what you've been given, from what's been won for you in the women's movement. Be bold, be assertive, and do what needs to be done. When people don't feel women can do this or that, it's their problem. Now, we've got to take the power into our own hands."[63] Clearly, Bonk's version of feminism is what is popularly called "power feminism," a version of liberal feminism that suggests that if women don't jump into the white male world and take power, it's our own fault.

Nowhere was this position more clear than in Bonk's keynote address to the 1995 Green gathering in Albuquerque. Reelected to her position on the Hawai'i County Council, Bonk had become chair after struggling against both Democrats and Republicans. At the Albuquerque gathering, Bonk made it clear that "politics is simply the struggle to use power for specific ends." With statements such as "we are not all equal, and we never will be," and "much of the status-quo is both beautiful and admirable," Bonk succeeded in thrilling some of her listeners and alienating many others.[64] From a feminist perspective, one of Bonk's most questionable assertions came in her metaphoric description of politics and the Green official:

> Every Green who gets into office or into a government position supporting someone in office, has to learn one very difficult lesson. They must learn to be polite and civilized while they watch rape. Everyday the powerless and the land are raped by people who do not care, people who enjoy it. And you must watch and smile, because it is your job to

get into the middle of the gang rape and look for that one participant that is not real enthusiastic, the one you might be able to influence. You take all the allies you can get, in whatever form they come to you.[65]

From her experience in leadership as an elected Green official, Bonk had learned that "becoming a leader means growing up faster than others," and in her opinion, "it is time for the Greens to grow up."[66] Bonk's use of the proto-typically Green maturity metaphor meant a willingness to embrace electoral politics and to work within the system. To those critical of Bonk, the maturity metaphor implied a loss of Green values, particularly the value of the means as embodying the ends, and a transition within the Greens and the GPN to sheer political opportunism.

In 1992, Linda Martin ran for U.S. Senate against thirty-year Democratic incumbent Daniel Inouye, just months after the Hawai'i Green Party qualified for ballot status. Though a first-time candidate, Martin received nearly fifty thousand votes (about 14 percent), more than any other third-party congressional candidate in 1992. But Martin was no novice: from her years of work in advertising and marketing, she had garnered certain transferable skills. With a background in modeling and a few years as a self-described "corporate wife," Martin knew how to present herself to the public with poise and ease. Add to that her leadership in a countywide initiative to limit growth in San Diego County, her work to create affordable housing in San Diego and in Hawai'i, and her work with grassroots organizations such as Common Cause/Hawai'i, and Martin was prepared for the challenge. Moreover, her experience writing and producing family-planning films for such groups as Planned Parenthood made her uniquely qualified to use the opportunity when serious sexual assault and harassment allegations against Senator Inouye were revealed in the final weeks of the campaign. Promising to keep the issue alive even after the campaign, Martin was instrumental in forming a community-based coalition of more than fifty activists called Code of Silence/Broken. Though Martin's liberal feminism seemed more woman-friendly than Bonk's, both Green women hailed from the school of "power feminism."

In an interview with a local Hawai'ian paper, Martin took care to present herself as particularly "normal": "I guess when people hear Green Party, they expect someone really radical or something," Martin told Oahu's *Midweek Magazine*. Her carefully crafted self-presentation was part of a larger project of what she saw as "mainstreaming" the Greens: "We are the mainstream of the future," she said.[67] As organizer of the GPN's "Third Parties '96: Building the New Mainstream," Martin was right in place. But what was her philosophy? As she told the Oahu reporter, "I wasn't so much attracted to the Greens as I was disgusted with the Democrats."[68] For some Greens, Martin's definition of "mainstream" translated into a kind of reformist politics rather than the more revolutionary politics embraced by grassroots Greens.

Toni Wurst was Martin's campaign co-chair and later took her place as co-chair of the Hawai'i Green Party when Martin moved to Virginia. In 1995, Wurst ran for the Hawai'i House of Representatives, and in an act of genuine solidarity, Martin returned to Hawai'i to spend a month assisting Wurst's campaign. Though Wurst was not elected, she received 41 percent of the vote, an excellent showing for a third-party candidate by any standard. Ideologically, Wurst professed an attraction to the views articulated through ecofeminism but felt it was "too idealistic to be practical"; Green politics, on the other hand, was geared for the real world.[69]

Former GCoC clearinghouse coordinator Dee Berry clearly articulated spiritual/cultural ecofeminism, with her approval of "positive" gender traits, her metaphor of the "Green warrior," and her perspectives on Green spirituality. According to Berry, "If we Greens ignore or deny the spiritual basis of our movement, we will not survive."[70] From her perspective, the popularity of Green politics reveals a shift from an old-paradigm politics to a new worldview, from the viewpoint of rational Western Man to a new Planetary Person:

Western Man sees his world as
1. materialistic—reality composed of separate, discrete objects. Competition is the norm.
2. patriarchy organizes and distributes power through dualism and hierarchy
3. nation states—dividing the world locked in militarized conflict
4. driven by progress
5. machine as metaphor

The Planetary Person sees the world as
1. connected—everything is interrelated. There is no enemy on which to project our "dark" side.
2. holistic—each life form is a unique manifestation of evolution
3. dynamic—all of reality is energy in motion
4. organized by ecological principles
5. the nation state is eroding
6. hologram as the new model of reality
7. social justice replaces progress as the goal of social and economic activity[71]

Interpreting and redefining the Ten Key Values, Berry articulates her own Green vision, based on seven values: the politics of empowerment (which relies on *grassroots democracy* and *community-based economics*), the politics of satyagraha (or *nonviolence*, in which she argues for using consensus decision-making processes and opposing militarism), the politics of compassion (meaning *social justice* and *personal and social responsibility*), the politics of liberation (or *post-patriarchal values*), the politics of ecology (or *ecological wisdom*), the politics of the Green warrior, the politics of joy and celebration ("to have fun and laugh with each other"), and the "acceptance of spirituality as an integral part of all we do, including our politics."[72] In her reformulation of the Ten Key Values, Berry omits specific references to *decentralization, respect for diversity,* and *future focus*, though she might argue that these points were implied in "the politics of compassion" or "the politics of empowerment." Unique to Berry's reformulation are her last three points about the Green warrior, the politics of joy (i.e., building and valuing community among Green activists), and the emphasis on spirituality in politics, which she says is the defining feature of Green politics. All three points characterize spiritual/cultural ecofeminism. Berry defines the Green warrior as "part of the emergence of the positive male that has been so long suppressed by the phoney masculinity of patriarchy. We desperately need the good hearts of good men and good women. We need bold warriors who can act decisively to save the planet."[73]

Like Berry, Anne Goeke emphasizes embracing "positive" gender traits of the feminine, as explained in her founding pamphlet for the Gylany Greens. On the cover page, a circle is drawn floating on waves; inside it, a list of characteristics floats in the lower half; the upper half is filled in with semicircles and is titled "A Way of Being Gylany Green"; in the center is the black-and-white image of the Tau. Filling the lower half of the circle, the words or characteristics of a Gylany Green are identical to what are traditionally considered "feminine" traits:

freeing	share	coalescence	song	kind
holistic	lateral	soul	consensual	balance
gentle	connecting	encouraging	heart	
peaceful	softness	enhance	nurturing	forgiving
embracing	meditation	courtesies	sensual	ecological
reverence	empowering	warmth	vulnerable	
nature	peace	encompassing	emotion	
flexible	spiritual	permissive	lovingness	empathic

spherical	respect	spontaneity	wholistic	flowing
futurist	indigenous	third world	participation	
cooperation	supportive	harmony	wisdom	

"Gylany" is a word taken from Riane Eisler's *The Chalice and the Blade;* Goeke writes that "gyne" means "woman, and "andro" means "man"; the "l" between the two means "linking" rather than "ranking." "In this sense," Goeke explains, "the 'l' stands for the resolution of our problems through the freeing of both halves of humanity from stultifying and distorting rigidity of roles imposed by the dominating hierarchies inherent in androcratic systems."[74] What is also significant about these sheets defining the Gylany Greens is that Goeke offers almost two pages of questions. Like Spretnak's original articulation of the Ten Key Values, this list of questions—while admittedly avoiding a rigorous philosophical statement of political beliefs—functions as a way of inviting others to participate in the shaping of answers. Unlike some other ecofeminists, spiritual/cultural ecofeminists seem willing to leave room for different answers.

Spirituality was also the link between Green politics and ecofeminism for Goeke, who belonged to both the G/GPUSA and the GPN because she saw her role as a bridge builder. At the 1993 Greens gathering in Syracuse, Goeke and others proposed the Earth Spirituality Caucus as an ongoing project of the G/GPUSA; by 1995, she had also proposed and received endorsement of an Earth Spirituality Network from the GPN. Goeke explained that the purpose of the Earth Spirituality Caucus/Network was to provide an opportunity at the opening and closing of Green gatherings for activists to come together as a community, on a spiritual and feeling level, to complement and clarify their coming together as political activists. "What we are doing as Greens," Goeke explained, "is more than what happens in our lifetime. If we can just recognize that common bond, take that moment to think about our relationships to each other and to the earth, we can draw on a strength that will carry us through some very difficult moments. If you believe in the interconnectedness of all life—if you have a consciousness of this universal home—then you are believing in a very spiritual aspect of things."[75] Goeke's version of earth-based spirituality articulates an ecofeminist redefinition of the self as interconnected with human and nonhuman life on earth. From that interconnected sense of self comes a redefinition of self-esteem, a way of valuing self and others based on relationships of care and of survival, which transcends the stereotypically feminine valuing of other more than self (codependency) and the stereotypically masculine valuing of self more than others. It is also quite different from the deep ecological expansion of the male self to include (i.e., erase, annihilate) all others. In fact, building community and healing the wounds of patriarchy/the dominant culture is a crucial task for any effective group of activists. Spiritual/cultural ecofeminists have emphasized the importance of these tasks, and activists in the GPN have joined in acknowledging this as well. As the Earth Spirituality Caucus of the G/GPUSA, Goeke, and others believe, one of the characteristics of "earth spirituality" is that it promises to "heal the previous antagonism between religion and nature, mind and matter, into one of complementarity and balanced harmony."[76] Spiritual ecofeminists Elizabeth Dodson Gray, Riane Eisler, and Charlene Spretnak have all described how patriarchal religion has explicitly authorized the subordination of nature. The Earth Spirituality Caucus's recognition of this antagonism, and its goal of rejecting this false dualism, captures a core characteristic of cultural ecofeminism.

Another fairly startling characteristic of spiritual/cultural ecofeminism is its critique of reason. Charlene Spretnak has criticized the "value-free pure 'reason'" of Enlightenment humanism as a patriarchal political construction defined in ways that further the domination of women, nature, and all "others": "To reject the cult of rationalism places thought, feelings, value, ethics, and meaning in the larger context of the Earth community, which is certainly a basis for a coherent politics."[77] Of course, this critique is not the sole property of cultural ecofeminism: as Val Plumwood, an ecofeminist philosopher, has thoroughly explained in *Feminism and the Mastery of Nature*, the "master model" has relied on the definition of reason as the distinguishing characteristic of the master, against which all "others" are defined; lack of "reason" is sufficient justification for subordination. Along similar lines, the Earth Spirituality Caucus members wrote, "Earth Spirituality directs us to collaborate with those in the social activist movements, encouraging them to turn from reason alone as the source of their activities (if this should be the case) to a 'Soul of the Whole.'"[78] As Goeke commented, "Shifting our relationship to the earth, how we perceive the future, how we perceive the past," is the goal of Earth Spirituality, and "that shift is more of an internal shift than an intellectual shift."[79]

For the G/GPUSA, Goeke has served as a representative for the Women's Caucus, the International Working Group, and the Green Global Network. In her community of Lancaster, Pennsylvania, she cofounded a Women in Black group that met weekly on the steps of the county courthouse, holding a silent vigil as a reminder of the Serbian, Muslim, and Croat women who were being raped and beaten in the name of war; she also cofounded the Lancaster Greens in 1990 and organized local events for Earth Day 1995. A board member of the

Voice for Choice Coalition, as well as a longstanding member of NOW (National Organization for Women), the Women's Environment and Development Organization (WEDO), and Co-op America, Goeke has shown her commitment to both Green politics and feminism. Goeke's particular philosophy of ecofeminism can be seen in her belief in the power of individual tranformation, in her emphasis on spirituality, and in her projects, such as the Gylany Greens. According to Goeke, "We as individuals can make these changes. It just depends where you feel you'd like to start."[80] And the best place to start, she believes, is with oneself: "If we are going to be effective, the area of change we need to focus on is getting to people's inner self, so they can too see the whole picture and bring the best decisions out of themselves. The whole picture view enables us to know how to make decisions about our life. There is a sense of peace that exists when we give up the ego and let our oneness take its place. Less of a struggle and more effective our activism becomes."[81] As a true spiritual/cultural ecofeminist, Goeke suggests "implementing consensus into the formula," because "each of us has a piece to this puzzle and events will evolve." Though deeply involved in activism in her community and nationally, Goeke affirms, "Being Green is personal," and "we must always begin our green work inside to the outside."[82] What spiritual/cultural ecofeminism offers, then, is a quintessentially feminist understanding of the linkage between personal and political; an understanding of the importance of personal, cultural, and institutional transformation; a valuing of the traditionally feminine realm, which includes a valuing of women's and earth-based spirituality; and a sense of interconnectedness that is characteristic of all ecofeminisms.

In 1996, the women leaders of the GPN gained additional prominence, as Linda Martin established a Draft Nader Clearinghouse to rival the one in California, and Anne Goeke was chosen as Nader's stand-in vice-presidential running mate on the ballots in fourteen states. But the Nader campaign showed the limits of liberal feminism, "power feminism," and spiritual/cultural ecofeminism in addressing the root causes of oppression—and in maintaining a distinct ecofeminist voice or presence in the Greens.

5. Divisions among the Greens

The cover of the March 1990 issue of *Green Synthesis* depicts an elephant surrounded by six men with their eyes closed, their hands touching various parts of the animal. On the elephant's back, one man feels the ear; on the ground, two men touch either the trunk or the tusks, while two others grip the leg or the tail, and the sixth man stands with his palm flat on the elephant's side. Of course, the drawing is intended as a visual representation of the poem printed inside the cover, "The Blind Men and the Elephant," by John Godfrey Saxe. The poem's message is that although each blind man has a firm grasp of one portion of the elephant, none of them can see the whole. Because of this lack of "vision," the men "disputed loud and long / . . . each was partly in the right, / And all were in the wrong!" One can understand the editors' point for using this poem and image to describe the internal debates of the Greens. Although in every debate each side had certain merits, each also had certain oversights. Taking the best of these various perspectives could have created a coherent movement for social justice and environmental health. Instead, each faction focused excessively on differences, ignored commonalities, and failed to listen to well-founded criticisms. Moreover—as implied in the selection of "The Blind Men and the Elephant"—sexism and racism contributed to these divisions. As a result of these internal conflicts, many activists left the Greens.

The contentious debates that characterized the Green movement, particularly from 1987 to 1991, were not unique to the Green movement per se: rather, these debates had been ongoing battles within the New Left, the radical ecology movement, and the various movements for social justice. The Green movement was simply an attempt to bring these several preexisting movements together on the basis of shared principles. The evolution of that attempt can be seen in the Greens' journal, *Synthesis:* originally subtitled "A Newsletter and Journal for Social Ecology, Deep Ecology, Bioregionalism, Ecofeminism, and the Green Movement," the journal became *Green Synthesis* in September 1988 and dropped the specifying subtitle. Explaining that *Green Synthesis* had been adopted as the official Green Committees of Correspondence journal, the editors chose the new name "to show that the issues that tend to divide the Green movement are less important than those that unite us." The journal's editors (and the activists within the movement) were unable to demonstrate such unity, however: between 1987 and 1992, the Left Greens strongly influenced the GCoC in structure and in philosophy, making the Left Green organizations (the Left Green Network and the Youth Greens) seem superfluous, while members of the Green Party Organizing Committee left the GCoC entirely to form the Green Politics Network by 1992. The "synthesis" had failed. Not surprisingly, then, with the winter 1993 issue, *Green Synthesis* was adopted by the Left Green discussion journal, *Regeneration: A Magazine of Left Green Social Thought,* and the journal that emerged, *Synthesis/Regeneration,* was subtitled "A Magazine of Green Social Thought" (no longer exclusively "Left"). That the Green movement could not tolerate internal differences but rather approached them as a problem to be overcome says less about the Greens than it does about the fragmented state of the Left in post-sixties America.

Of course, activists within the movement were deeply disturbed by the conflicts and worked to mend internal relations, most notably by addressing the process of the debates. In 1988, for example, just as *Synthesis* was affirming the commonalities within the Greens by becoming *Green Synthesis,* two articles appeared in Green publications concerning the importance of communication style, respect, and community building within the Green movement.[1] "If we remember that everyone has been damaged by the sick society in which we live," urged Margo Adair, "we will have a more generous spirit when confronted with the myriad of frustrating interactions that are commonplace." Adair cites "competition" and "individualism" as the main problems interfering with effective communications and the exchange of ideas.[2] David Perry offered a similar diagnosis: "We come to this effort with all the scars, fears, and emotional baggage that we have inherited. We are all wounded, women and men alike." Like Adair, Perry suggests various strategies for de-escalating conflict and for communicating with respect, asking the question that would be asked again by Green women facing the problem of sexism in the Greens: "If we cannot learn to love, work, and struggle with one another, how can we expect to reach the rest of humankind?" And Perry's conclusion articulates a perspective shared by many cultural feminists and ecofeminists: "Ours is a revolution first within ourselves, and its face will show first in the fabric of our relationships."[3] Not everyone within the Greens agreed to the importance of this "revolution from within" for social movement activists, however, and the outcome speaks for itself.[4] My experience within the Green movement has convinced me that lasting social change occurs on many levels, transcending distinctions between "public" and "private" or "inside versus outside" the system: social transformation of the kind envisioned by Green and ecofeminist theories alike must involve structural transformation of economics and government, but these changes can be brought about only on the crest of a deeper cultural transformation that of necessity affects interpersonal relations and intrapsychic processes as well.

In this chapter, I address the central conflicts within the Green movement. They can be grouped into three general areas: conflicts dealing with philosophy, conflicts regarding the representation of various constituencies, and conflicts over strategy for developing the movement. It's important to note that in many cases the conflicts were fought out among the "stars" of the movement; many grassroots activists were impatient with the conflicts, not understanding or not caring about the various points of contention. In every case, the conflicts were between men, and the term "cockfights" was frequently heard among activists. This is not to say that there weren't differences among the women feminists and ecofeminists in the Greens—there *were* differences, and it would have been helpful to articulate them more fully. Although some women in the Green movement were comfortable in addressing differences, the majority tended to be more focused on building the movement than on engaging one another in philosophical debates. As a result, the differences articulated by Green men framed the debates and structured the factions.

Philosophical Divisions among the Greens

Although there have been a number of philosophical divisions among the Greens, the conflict that received most attention was the debate between social ecology and deep ecology, a debate that received so much notoriety it was eventually mediated by the Learning Alliance, and the dialogues that resulted were published by South End Press.[5] Most Greens weren't even aware of the differences between social ecology and deep ecology until Murray Bookchin's keynote address at the first national Green gathering in Amherst in 1987. Bookchin, the founding father of social ecology, had been writing social treatises since the 1950s; the Norwegian philosopher Arne Naess, the founding father of deep ecology, published his landmark essay on deep ecology in 1973.[6] From 1973 until 1987, Bookchin's work had been well regarded by deep ecologists: many of his ideas had inspired central tenets of deep ecology, one of his essays appeared in the first anthology on deep ecology in the United States, and his work on social ecology received favorable remarks from Bill Devall and George Sessions in the bibliography of their pioneering text *Deep Ecology.*[7] But the theory and practice of deep ecology were slightly different: academics such as Arne Naess, Warwick Fox, Bill Devall, and George Sessions articulated the philosophy, whereas wilderness activists in Earth First!—people such as Ed Abbey, Dave Foreman, and Chris Manes—acted on the theory of deep ecology as they interpreted it. Bookchin's critique of deep ecology was not directed specifically at Naess but rather was inspired by a particularly inept comment Devall elicited from Foreman during an interview for the Australian periodical *Simply Living:* "When I tell people how the worst thing we could do in Ethiopia is to give aid—the best thing would be to just let nature seek its own balance, to let the people there just starve—they think this is monstrous. . . . Likewise, letting the USA be an overflow valve for problems in Latin America is not solving a thing. It's just putting more pressure on the resources we have in the USA."[8] When these statements were compounded with the racist, sexist, and heterosexist remarks in "Population and AIDS," published in the *Earth First!* journal in a column authored by the pseudonymous "Miss Ann Thropy,"[9] along with Devall and Sessions's advocacy of an ecological holism that erases human differences, Bookchin had a well-founded critique.

As some Greens would later protest, Foreman, Abbey, and Manes were not actively involved with the Green movement, and hence the alternative media were mistaken in portraying Bookchin's criticisms—and the responses from Arne Naess, Warwick Fox, George Sessions, Bill Devall, and Joanna Macy in the pages of *Green Synthesis*—as the largest debate *inside* the Greens. Other Greens felt the debates were entirely relevant, particularly as activists began working together on the national platform: it became clear that ideas drawn from deep ecology, social ecology, ecofeminism, bioregionalism, animal liberation theory, and several other radical ideologies were influencing people's theory and activism within the Greens and should therefore be more fully articulated and debated. Years later, even some deep ecologists would argue that the criticisms leveled against deep ecology were in fact directed against statements from Earth First! activists rather than from philosophers of deep ecology. For this reason, it is important to review the eight principles of deep ecology, formulated by Arne Naess and George Sessions in April 1984, while camping in Death Valley, California:

THE BASIC PRINCIPLES OF DEEP ECOLOGY
1. The well-being and flourishing of human and nonhuman Life on Earth have value in themselves (synonyms: intrinsic value, inherent value). These values are independent of the usefulness of the nonhuman world for human purposes.
2. Richness and diversity of life forms contribute to the realization of these values and are also values in themselves.
3. Humans have no right to reduce this richness and diversity except to satisfy *vital* needs.
4. The flourishing of human life and cultures is compatible with a substantial decrease of the human population. The flourishing of nonhuman life requires such a decrease.
5. Present human interference with the nonhuman world is excessive, and the situation is rapidly worsening.
6. Policies must therefore be changed. These policies affect basic economic, technological, and ideological structures. The resulting state of affairs will be deeply different from the present.
7. The ideological change is mainly that of appreciating *life quality* (dwelling in situations of inherent value) rather than adhering to an increasingly higher standard of living. There will be a profound awareness of the difference between big and great.
8. Those who subscribe to the foregoing points have an obligation directly or indirectly to try to implement the necessary changes.[10]

Many of these points were part of a common Green philosophy already articulated in the Ten Key Values through such phrases as "ecological wisdom," "personal and social responsibility," and "future focus." Salient aspects of Bookchin's critique of deep ecology focused on points four and five above: according to social ecology, terms such as "population" and "humanity" erased human differences of race, class, gender, sexuality, and nationality, directing the discussion to individuals instead of examining social and economic structures, and thereby obscuring the root causes of social injustices as well as environmental ills. In the theory of social ecology, the domination of human by human (men dominating women, and men dominating men) had led to the human domination of nature; therefore, deep ecologists' efforts to end the domination of nature would enjoy only partial or short-lived success because deep ecologists remained focused on a symptom of the problem rather than the root cause of the problem. Moreover, deep ecology's emphasis on biocentrism, earth-based spirituality, and the redefinition of the self as Self (interconnected with all life) seemed to take the place of a serious analysis of the economic and political structures that rely on, require, and perpetuate the oppression of both the majority of humans and vast areas of "nature" to serve a minority of earth's wealthy elite. Because the analysis of the problem would shape the strategies developed for solving that problem, Bookchin and others in the Greens believed it was essential to come to some agreement about the root causes of social and environmental crises.

Once Bookchin had launched his critique, the deep ecology/social ecology debate was carried out in the pages of *Green Synthesis* for more than three years.[11] Of course, the debate spilled over into the pages of alternative journals as well, but in *Environmental Ethics,* one of the more academic and philosophical journals of the environmental movement, it left out social ecologists and took place largely between ecofeminists and deep ecologists.[12] In articles by ecofeminists such as Marti Kheel and Ariel Salleh, ecofeminism was defined through its critique of deep ecology, which primarily focused on observations that deep ecology erased human differences and offered no analysis of the ways that patriarchal structures and beliefs had contributed to (or even caused) ecological crises. In alternative or progressive journals (which were more widely read by Green activists), social ecofeminists such as Ynestra King and Janet Biehl advanced critiques of deep ecology based on its inattentiveness to human differences of race, class, and sexuality, its lack of an economic analysis, and its heavy reliance on individual, personal transformation and earth-based spirituality as the primary methods for addressing environmental crises.[13] Though quick to criticize deep ecology, social ecofeminists did not articulate their differences with social ecology; they were less reluctant, however, to distinguish their views from cultural ecofeminism, particularly in its emphasis on spirituality.

Another perspective on the deep ecology/social ecology debate is its reformulation as a debate between spirituality and politics. For although Bookchin's attack at the 1987 Green gathering was directed in part against deep ecologists, the conflict also manifested itself as an assault by social ecology against cultural

ecofeminism through the strained relations between Bookchin and Charlene
Spretnak, whose recently published *The Spiritual Dimension of Green Politics*
(1986) was used to position her as the stand-in for all the apolitical aspects of
New Age spiritual "eco-la-la" (a term coined by Chaia Heller and quoted approvingly by Bookchin). Certainly, earth-based spirituality was a common
ground for cultural ecofeminism and deep ecology, and this compatibility had
been cited by Spretnak, though for the time being she remained silent on other
areas of disagreement. But claims that spirituality had replaced political activism
for all cultural ecofeminists merely advanced a straw woman argument, particularly in the case of Spretnak, whose active involvement in the Green movement
as well as the women's spirituality movement amply proved.[14] Interestingly
enough, Bookchin was not always opposed to spirituality or to a spiritual component in political activism; but once he saw in deep ecology and in goddess
spirituality the ways that spirituality was being elevated while economic and
political analyses were seemingly deemphasized, he lost hope for the possibility
of a liberatory ecological spirituality. Social ecology's ultimate resistance to spirituality was not shared by all social ecofeminists, however. In her response to
Kirkpatrick Sale in the *Nation,* for example, Ynestra King explained that although "'goddess cultures' and 'earth-based spirituality' are not the basis for
ecofeminism," there are still "many women who have been prominent in the
feminist spirituality movement [and who] have come to identify with ecofeminism (and many of them, like Susan Griffin and Starhawk, are politically active,
left-identified social anarchists)."[15] Similarly, for Chaia Heller,

> an ecological spirituality represents a celebration of the interconnected-
> ness of all life and also the distinctiveness in each life form. . . . An au-
> thentic ecological spirituality goes beyond a spirituality informed by a
> "deep" ecology by celebrating the qualities which distinguish human
> nature from non-human nature as well as celebrating that which makes
> women different from men. An ecological spirituality informed by so-
> cial ecology transcends a hierarchical view of nature, revealing the ab-
> surdity of espousing a greater reverence for non-human life.[16]

For Janet Biehl, however, spirituality (and especially goddess spirituality) had
vitiated ecofeminism to such a degree that she finally disclaimed any association
with ecofeminism and favored social ecology.[17]

Earth-based spirituality provided a common ground for cultural ecofeminists and activists in the Green Politics Network. "Society needs spirituality,"
wrote John Rensenbrink, explaining that "spirituality means the recovery of

intrinsic values, the return to love and being and the 'unbought grace of life.' "
"Spirituality is thus a fundamental political question," Rensenbrink explained,
"just as political life is a fundamental spiritual question."[18] Cultural ecofeminists
such as Dee Berry and Anne Goeke agreed. "The big lie of patriarchy," wrote
Berry, "is that spirituality is separate and above our everyday lives." Instead,
Berry believed that "transforming our religions may be necessary to transform
our politics."[19] For Goeke, earth spirituality was simply the understanding that
"we know how we are interconnected. . . . Recognizing earth spirituality in the
green movement . . . strengthens the bonds between us, helping us to trust one
another . . . creat[ing] a new way to interact."[20] Spiritual Greens recognized that
spirituality could be a strong force for social change and that the spiritual beliefs and needs of many people were not being addressed by the spokespersons
and agendas of the two major political parties. Meanwhile, those parties were in
direct opposition to many Green values. In Spretnak's view, feminists were endangered by the advances of patriarchal religions, "the largest mobilized force
trying to defeat" feminists.[21] For this reason, Spretnak argued it was politically
crucial to "make most church-based activist Christians, Jews, and Muslims feel
welcome and wanted" in the Greens, and she hoped that "the Judeo-Christian
focus of *The Spiritual Dimension of Green Politics* was a small step in this direction."[22] Thus, spirituality became a dividing line between social ecologists and
social ecofeminists on the one hand, and cultural ecofeminists, deep ecologists,
and activists in the Green Politics Network on the other hand.

Within the Greens, the social ecology/deep ecology debate manifested itself
in the formation of various factions. Social ecology was the philosophy that
powered both the Left Greens and the Youth Greens, and social ecofeminists
were present in both groups; deep ecology, cultural ecofeminism, and particularly earth-based spirituality informed a loose-knit faction known as the "neither Left nor Right" Greens, some of whom later formed the Green Politics
Network. But these are only generalities; it would be inexact to say that all
members in each group shared a particular viewpoint or that Left Greens and
"neither Left nor Right" Greens were always at loggerheads. For example, one
topic on which members in all these groups were more closely aligned was
population. In the 1991–92 draft of the national platform finalized at Elkins,
there are just two sentences on population: "We advocate family planning and
birth control and support agencies that provide these. . . . We endorse ongoing
dialogue about the implications of population policies to guard against racist,
sexist, or economic bias." Contrary to the deep ecological view that overpopulation was a primary cause of environmental degradation, cultural ecofeminists,
social ecofeminists, social ecologists, and many Greens alike agreed that popula-

tion was a symptom of deeper problems and could be approached only by examining those root problems.[23]

From my readings, the most comprehensive critique of population would have to include at least seven components. First, the question of population cannot be addressed without examining the overconsumption of the first world nations in relation to the third and fourth world nations; smaller numbers of people consuming three hundred times what the majority consumes—and consuming goods imported from other bioregions, in addition to those produced in their own bioregion—must provide the context for any discussion of the environmental impact of human populations. Second, one must consider the problem of poverty, which often requires families to have many children to stabilize the family income and to provide economic and food security for the parents in their old age. Third, the role of sexism in confining women's social worth to the single role of childbearing must be challenged. Fourth, the quality of infant and maternal health care needs to be raised: women whose infants seldom live past their first birthdays are not likely to have fewer children until they can be assured that those children will survive. Fifth, the definition of masculinity, which includes the ability to "father" (though not necessarily support) many children, needs to be revised. Sixth, colonial relations between nations and the problem of militarism needs to be resolved, so that women in colonized nations will not be pressured to bear many children and thus provide more future soldiers to defend their nation. Finally, the topic of sexuality itself needs to be less of a taboo: free and safe contraception needs to be made widely available, and the assumption of heterosexuality and childbearing as women's only and proper fulfillment needs to be challenged.

After making some or most of these points, however, opinion within the Greens diverged. Those on the Left—social ecologists, social ecofeminists, and Left Greens—would not carry the discussion any further, content that if these social injustices were addressed, there would be no problem with population. Those in the "neither Left nor Right" camp, however, acknowledged that human population would have to be a consideration in any ecological program. "There can be no doubt," wrote John Rensenbrink, "that if there are limits prescribed by nature, then there is also a limit to the number of people a bioregion, or a planet, can or should support."[24] Contextualizing her remarks with qualifications about the need to address the institutionalization of patriarchal attitudes and to support women's self-determination, cultural ecofeminist Charlene Spretnak asserted that "the health of the biosphere demands that the rate of population growth level off *everywhere* and then decline (with the exception of tribal peoples in danger of extinction)."[25] These views were more compatible with the viewpoint of deep ecology in regard to population. Among other Greens, however, population reduction was advocated without any awareness of social justice concerns; these views were in the minority, as the 1991–92 national platform statement makes clear.

In sum, the so-called deep ecology/social ecology debate could have been a four-way discussion of differences and commonalities among social ecologists, social ecofeminists, deep ecologists, and cultural ecofeminists, but gender dynamics constricted popular perceptions of the debate to a battle between male philosophers. The fundamental differences between the two philosophies—vastly simplified for the purposes of summary—along with their related theories and the groups within the Greens who identified with these philosophies, can be seen in Table 1.

Table 1: Social Ecology/Deep Ecology

	Social Ecology	Deep Ecology
sees the problem as	hierarchy, capitalism	anthropocentrism, overpopulation, industrialism, consumerism
sees the root cause as	humans dominating humans, leads to humans dominating nature	anthropocentrism
sees the solution as	ecological humanism democratic decentralism	biocentrism the deep ecological Self
takes as its goal	radical municipalism social justice	wilderness protection population reduction
strategy advocated within the Greens	local electoral politics local movement	earth-based spirituality electoral politics (esp. statewide) personal/individual transformation
manifest in Green groups	Left Greens Youth Greens social ecofeminists	Green Politics Network "neither Left nor Right" Greens cultural ecofeminists
views	humans as part of nature sees nature in culture	nature outside culture (i.e., "wilderness")
originates in	New England	West Coast

In two often overlooked essays, bioregionalist and social ecologist Brian Tokar describes the differences between social ecology and deep ecology, examining their relationships to the land and the cultural history of the land where each theory originated.[26] In the western United States, land ethics were shaped by a frontier mentality of rugged individualism, often "personified in the figure of the lone frontier scout" whose personal connection to the land involved seeing it both as "a source of spiritual nourishment and as a powerful force to be tamed." In the late twentieth century, well after the closing of the frontier, most people in the West live in dense population centers surrounded by huge mountains beyond which are vast expanses of undeveloped land; in such a context, argues Tokar, nature is "just a place to be visited on weekends and enjoyed in one's leisure time." Moreover, the impact of civilization on the land is intensified in the West by the suddenness and the scale of development, leading many people to conclude that the real threat to ecological sustainability is overpopulation instead of overdevelopment. In contrast, Tokar observes, "a pastoral rather than a frontier ethic shaped settlement patterns in the East," and with early agricultural land uses often "decided on a communal basis," a cooperative relationship with the land followed from cooperative relationships between people. People in the East, as in most of Europe, thus tend to see human relationships to the land in more social terms. These historical differences in people's relationship with the land have influenced the philosophies that evolved on each coast: "Social ecologists in New England have inherited an affirmative vision of human communities sharing a cooperative relationship with the land," writes Tokar, "while many deep ecologists in the West have embraced a more isolationist frontier ethic, with its harsher, more rugged view of both wild nature and human nature."

Neither philosophy represents the full range of human experience, Tokar concludes. And though it has not yet been fully developed, a comparable analysis could be used to describe at least two branches of ecofeminism: social ecofeminism, which originated in New England, and cultural ecofeminism, which originated on the West Coast (particularly the Bay area of northern California). Social ecofeminism is influenced by the legacy of the Left, whereas cultural ecofeminism has been able to thrive in a cultural context that affirms many spiritualities; however, both of these branches of ecofeminism share an inheritance from the direct action, nonviolent antinuclear movement.[27] Neither branch of ecofeminism offers a full view of ecofeminist philosophy; for example, neither social nor cultural ecofeminism addresses the important place of animals in ecofeminist theory.

Animal Liberationists and "Animal" Ecofeminists

Although the political platforms of Green parties in Germany, England, and Australia include clear statements of advocacy for animal liberation, attempts to place animal liberation within the central framework of the Green movement in the United States have generally met with mixed success.[28] Animal liberation concerns (along with "biological diversity") were included as one of nineteen planks in the Greens' national platform when it was first approved in 1991–92, and animal liberation has been a key component in the platforms of many state Green parties, from California to Minnesota. But the actual dietary practices, purchasing decisions, and activism of individual Greens has varied widely from the beginning. Many Greens' inability to interrogate their own speciesism, and the speciesism of Western industrialized culture, has led most animal liberation activists to stop believing in the efficacy of the Green movement altogether. As one animal liberation activist Green explained, "If we can't communicate these ideas to people in the Green movement—people we work closely with over months and even years, and whose values we share—how can we expect the Green movement to educate the wider society?"[29] It was the same question feminists in the Greens had asked themselves.

The issue of animal liberation did not figure in the debates among social ecology, deep ecology, social ecofeminism, and cultural ecofeminism, nor did it produce a faction within the Greens in the same way that the preceding philosophies inspired the Left Green Network, the Youth Greens, or the Green Politics Network. One reason for this omission stems from the philosophies of deep ecology and social ecology. According to deep ecologists, the very topic of animal liberation is a form of anthropocentrism, since animal liberationists usually advance arguments for extending to nonhumans the rights currently accorded humans. The deep ecological vision of biocentrism usually involves large wilderness areas full of plants, minerals, and soil; if animals are mentioned in those wilderness areas at all, they are often described as predator and prey, heavily engaged in competing for survival; the (usually male) human act of killing wild animals, and subsequently consuming and/or wearing their bodies, is conceived of only from the human standpoint, as an act of spiritual reconnection with the wild. (Being hunted, killed, skinned, and eaten is not explored from the perspective of the "prey," though one would expect it is less than a "spiritual" experience.)[30] Deep ecologists have not addressed the "wild nature" of animals in dairy production, fur ranches, factory farms, laboratory experiments, zoos, rodeos, or aquariums. For social ecologists, at first glance animal liberation seems to be included in the liberation of nature: that is, because they believe the human oppression of nature stems from the human oppression of other humans, social ecologists focus on strategies for advancing social justice as a way of achieving ecological goals. But for many social ecologists, as for many leftists, animals fall in the space between "humans" and "nature" (or in the case of social ecology, "second nature" and "first nature"), and consequently the topic of animal rights is never addressed.[31] This silence is a notable failure of social ecology, given its otherwise inclusive critique of hierarchy and its inheritance from anarchism (many anarchists recognize speciesism as a form of hierarchy and choose vegan lifestyles). It seems neither a biocentric ("deep") nor an anthropocentric ("social") ecological perspective is capable of including nonhuman animals as subjects rather than objects; indeed, to date, ecofeminism is the only radical environmental theory to address and incorporate the concerns of animal liberationists.

Without a philosophical home in either social ecology or deep ecology, animal liberationist Greens formed their own caucus to advance their ideas within the Green movement and to influence the content of the national Green platform. By 1991, most of these activists had left the Greens, disillusioned by the hostility directed toward animal liberation. Since 1991, many individual animal liberation activists have passed through the Green movement, initially attracted by the Green philosophy but later disappointed by the manifest indifference to animal liberation concerns. Activists who support animal liberation and who continue to work within the Green movement may be remaining in part because they believe they can influence the beliefs and behaviors of their local Green group; or they may see their own views as a personal choice, and one not requiring their departure from the Greens; or finally, they may see animal liberation as a political issue of less importance than, say, grassroots democracy or sustainable economics.

In 1987, animal liberation activists attended the first national Green gathering in Amherst with high hopes, believing they would join other progressives who would readily sympathize with their concerns. But Kim Bartlett, an editor for the *Animals' Agenda*, recalls that "despite Green declarations about the need to 'uproot human domination in all its forms,' and much genuflection at the altar of ecological harmony, the perspective of a large portion of conference attendees was decidedly anthropocentric." Animal liberation concerns were "cavalierly dismissed" as a "fringe issue," Bartlett reports, though these same activists seemed unable to note the incongruity of "discussing nonviolence with great passion over plates of animal flesh."[32] It was almost too much for animal liberationists when barbecued chicken parts were served at the July 4 picnic, and they responded by leafleting and picketing the food line, holding huge photographs of poultry farms.[33] Their actions garnered a mixed reception: some Greens met in a circle to discuss the concerns of animal liberation but could not achieve consensus, while others actually tried to shout down the demonstrators. For Charles Allen Dews, a Green activist from Austin, Texas, the message of animal liberation and its relevance to the Green movement became clear when "a brave and beautiful woman" took the speakers' podium and introduced herself to the fifteen hundred people present as a "radical feminist Jewish lesbian vegetarian Green animal liberationist." The speaker was Batya Bauman, an indefatigable activist who served as the East Coast coordinator for Feminists for Animal Rights from 1987 through 1996. As Dews recalled, "Her nominative string of labels slapped me into the awareness that all oppressions of any one group by another are inseparable issues. Oppression is the rank fruit of the hierarchical vine."[34]

Feminists for Animal Rights cofounder Marti Kheel was present at both the Amherst gathering and the 1988 Greening the West gathering. For this gathering, with the food provided primarily by the anarchist group Food Not Bombs, the issue of dietary ethics caused much less of a stir, since the meals were entirely vegetarian and mostly vegan. Kheel offered a workshop on the connection between ecofeminism and animal liberation, and activists from both FAR and the Animal Rights Connection staffed information tables and leafleted the food lines with information about the Green/vegan connection. At these first gatherings of the U.S. Greens, animal liberationists were motivated by the potential for informing the Green movement, and the words of Charles Dews captures their views: "The animal liberation movement and the Green movement represent one and the same impulse. We are heirs to the tradition that has worked indefatigably to free black people from slavery, women from male domination, homosexuals from heterosexist intolerance, people of color from racism, and on and on."[35]

It helped that the motivation of the animal liberationists was reinforced by a high level of organization: at a midnight meeting during the Amherst gathering, the steering committee of the Animal Liberation Caucus worked overtime to draft a twelve-point animal liberation plank for inclusion in a possible national Green platform. The efforts of Green animal liberationists and "animal" ecofeminists were manifestly linked when an abbreviated version of these same twelve points was presented by Marti Kheel in the WomanEarth Feminist Peace

Institute's package of statements delivered to the 1989 national Green gathering in Eugene. Together, Kheel and Dews co-chaired the Life Forms Working Group and developed the animal liberation planks that were later approved for the national platform.

Between 1987 and 1991, animal liberationists in the Greens made a concerted effort to educate Greens on the importance of animal liberation. In the summer of 1988, Connie Salamone gave a workshop titled "Green Women and Animal Rights" at a New England Green Women's Weekend. Many activists had already read Sharon Seidenstein's report, "Cattle Grazing on Public Lands," published earlier that spring in *Green Letter,* and were making the connections between a meat-based diet and environmental degradation in the West.[36] In fall 1988, *Green Letter* published two articles exploring the place of animals within an ecological, liberatory worldview. The lead story, by John Mohawk, explained the relationship between animals and humans in traditional native cultures, suggesting that "when the West adopts the practice of seeing the animal world through Indian eyes we will surely have the ideological and emotional tools to struggle for a better world."[37] The article (reprinted from *Daybreak,* a journal of Native American concerns) clearly did not advocate vegetarianism but rather described a cultural context in which the human relationship with animals and nature would preclude such practices as vivisection, factory farming, fur ranching, and modern cattle grazing. The same issue of *Green Letter* also carried a review of Marjorie Spiegel's *The Dreaded Comparison: Race and Animal Slavery* by Billy Ray Boyd, a noted vegetarian author and Green.[38] Pointing to the Left Green principles of *ecological humanism* ("to free ourselves from all forms of hierarchy and domination") and *ecofeminism* ("to replace cultural patterns of hierarchy and domination"), as well as the key values of *nonviolence* ("ahimsa or dynamic harmlessness") and *respect for diversity* (unnecessarily limited "only to those 'isms' that divide the human race against itself"), Boyd argued that animal liberation was central to the Green vision whether one was a Left Green or a "neither Left nor Right" Green. Quite suggestively, he rejected deep ecology as a framing philosophy for animal liberation, for its "pseudo-spiritual talk about such things as animals 'offering' themselves for human food."[39] As "animal" ecofeminists soon suggested, the "spiritual" tradition of animal sacrifice either was anthropocentric (if it assumed animals themselves chose to die to benefit humans) or, if the animals were killed by humans, functioned as a plea-bargaining device for guilty humans who believed that if animals were killed, humans would be allowed to live.[40] For the carnivorous Greens, Boyd's review could not go unchallenged.

Two issues later, Mark Linenthal—"a Green who hunts"—defended his position as both hunter and Green by invoking selections from Paul Shepard's *Nature and Madness* and various texts from the Spanish philosopher Ortega y Gasset, who observed "one does not hunt in order to kill—one kills in order to have hunted." Linenthal professed he had "no quarrel with vegetarians" but only with "people who can happily eat the meat they bring cut and wrapped from the supermarket and who object to hunting because it is wrong to enjoy the process whereby animal flesh becomes meat." That "process"—hunting—was for Linenthal a process of reconnecting with "the Other which human language cannot name, which we honor as the source of our being, and with which we wrestle if we are to see beyond the limits of an artificial world."[41]

Though he agreed with Linenthal on the topic of carnivorous humans who refuse to hunt, Boyd was quick to respond to what he saw as the absurdity of Linenthal's argument. Suggesting that "one of the principles of social change requires that when we seek to get rid of a particular social practice or institution, we must identify the positive social and psychological functions it serves, then seek alternative ways to perform them," Boyd was able to find alternatives for all the possible needs that hunting fulfills—food, release of anger, human bonding, reconnection with nature, excitement—except one, asking, "Where else but on the hunt can one play God with such impunity?" From this perspective, Boyd noted, "the pleasure of playing God may not find its equivalent in a Green world," and he suggested Linenthal and others reconsider the differences between "power over" and "empowerment" in a Green (and ecofeminist) vision. Anticipating possible arguments attempting to justify hunting by appealing to its integral place in early hunter-gatherer societies or, more recently, indigenous cultures, Boyd explained, "While hunting is not *inherently* inappropriate, unecological, or cruel, *in our current situation it is all three.*"[42]

In the same issue of *Green Letter* as Boyd's response, the feature article was an interview with John Robbins.[43] Robbins, whose father had founded the Baskin-Robbins Ice Cream empire, turned away from the meat and dairy industries and the related agribusiness, chemical, and pharmaceutical industries that supported them. In his book *Diet for a New America*, Robbins exposed the interconnections between Western dietary practices and the degradation of the environment, world hunger, poor human health, and of course limitless animal suffering. The interview offered numerous facts and examples to persuade even the most reluctant reader. That same summer at Eugene, the WomanEarth proposals containing the twelve-point animal liberation plank were presented to the Green gathering at Eugene, and the Life Forms Working Group headed by Kheel and Dews took on the task of platform writing. Although their plank was prefaced with a point-by-point discussion of how animal liberation was integral to each of the Ten Key Values, resistance to animal liberation persisted among some Green groups. At some point during 1989–90, popular sentiment about animal liberation shifted in the Greens, from potential agreement to actual opposition, and along with it went the optimism animal activists had felt about the Green movement.

Just before the 1990 national Green gathering at Estes Park, where the Greens' national platform would be voted on by the delegates, Rick Whaley of the Milwaukee Greens published an essay in *Green Letter* titled "Food and Politics," in which he focused on the question "whether to serve meat at gatherings." As predicted by the subtitle—"Ideological Purity . . . or Respect for Cultural Diversity?"—Whaley's argument advanced the belief that if Greens embraced animal liberation, people of color would be alienated. Arguing that "a successful movement can't be built without an anti-racist perspective and involvement of people of color," Whaley felt the choice for the Green movement was fairly simple: "Do we ban meat or do we offer options for individuals and different cultural groups?"[44] To his credit, Whaley's perspective was grounded in his experience organizing Wisconsin's small farmers, animals rights activists, consumer groups, and Greens to oppose Bovine Growth Hormone, as well as his principled stance with other Wisconsin and Minnesota Greens in defense of Chippewa spearfishing rights.[45] By framing the issue as a mutually exclusive choice between supporting the liberation of animals or the liberation of people of color, however, Whaley fell into the same logical trap as those who believe that society must choose between "jobs versus environment." As "animal" ecofeminists and other animal liberationists had observed, arguments defending the option of carnivorism for everyone in a group by appealing to the culinary history of a single group (i.e., African-American "soul food" or Native American hunting practices) function as attempts to manipulate "white guilt" and to justify the continued oppression of nonhuman animals simply because they have been used as food by oppressed humans. Women have also been oppressed in the past, and everything from clitoridectomy to slavery and colonialism is part of someone's cultural heritage. Modern struggles for social justice rely on the belief that it is not only possible but necessary to criticize the systems we have inherited, taking history and culture into our own hands and improving on it. The cultural traditions of many ethnic groups contain a meat-based diet, and arguments for vegetarianism today have more to do with modern lifestyles and modern contexts, particularly the context of intensive animal agriculture (a practice included in no culture's history before today).

Whaley's essay advocating a carnivorous option at national Green gatherings must have been particularly disappointing to Marti Kheel, the Feminists for Animal Rights activist who not only co-chaired the Life Forms Working Group for the Greens but also coauthored the Ecofeminist Task Force proposal for cruelty-free conferences at the National Women's Studies Association in June 1990. Drafted primarily by Batya Bauman and Marti Kheel, with assistance from Stephanie Lahar and Greta Gaard, the Ecofeminist Task Force proposal recommended that "in keeping with the feminist tenets of nonviolence and the concept that the personal is political," the Coordinating Council should "make NWSA a model of ecological and humane behavior by adopting a policy that no animal products—i.e., the flesh of cows, pigs, chickens, and fish, as well as all dairy and eggs—be served at the 1991 conference, or at any future conferences, and that every effort be made to provide meals which satisfy the health, conscience, and palate of NWSA participants." Unfortunately, the 1990 NWSA conference was marred by the racism inherent in the organization's structure and administrative practices, and after numerous attempts at negotiation, the Women of Color Caucus walked out of the conference and the organization; in such a context, the Ecofeminist Task Force proposal (like almost everything else) received little attention or discussion, and the writers were not surprised to learn that it was later refused adoption by the Coordinating Council.[46] It is interesting that NWSA in 1990 was an organization institutionalizing racism and speciesism, linking the oppression of people of color and animals in a way that Rick Whaley could not conceive. As it turned out, the national Green organization suffered a similar fate, as after numerous debates and struggles for inclusion, the interests or presence of both people of color and animals still did not figure significantly in the composition of the Greens.

On the back page of the *Green Letter* issue that carried Whaley's article, the editors reprinted Chrystos's "Poem for Lettuce," in which the poet defends lettuce against "the vicious vegetarians." A number of disappointed readers wrote to protest the prominence, the ridicule, or the implied ignorance of the editorial staff in publishing such a poem and received two responses from the editors. One editor explained that she was the only vegetarian on the editorial staff and that the issue had gone to press while she was out of the country. The other editor apologized only for "neglecting to note that the author of 'Poem for

Lettuce,' Chrystos, is a Native American woman, and . . . [for] failing to connect the poem with the article inside, 'Food and Politics,' by Rick Whaley." According to this editor, the poem's real meaning is not an "attack on vegetarians" but rather an understanding that "no life form wishes to be eaten"—not even lettuce—and that "all life, even the plants, exists through the consumption of other beings." Ignoring the difference between the pain and suffering experienced by animals as compared to vegetables, the editor concludes, in implicit agreement with Whaley, that supporting the liberation of animals will effectively alienate people of color and "that a powerful and effective Green Movement can only develop through alliances and coalitions with other social forces, who are not likely to agree with us on every point. Self-righteousness and intolerance will get us nowhere."[47] By the winter of 1990, it was already clear that the Green movement was not going to be a suitable location for animal liberation activism.

Oddly enough, the majority of the Life Forms Working Group's suggestions made it into the national Green platform that was voted on at Estes Park and finally approved at Elkins in 1991, under the plank "Biological Diversity and Animal Liberation." Nevertheless, the compromised quality of many of the statements was apparent: Greens would oppose factory farming but not small-scale livestock operations; Greens would advocate that vegetarian meals be made available in the schools but would not support a wholly vegetarian diet at Green gatherings; and Greens had "not yet answered the question of whether animal experimentation is ever a necessary or appropriate tool." Many animal liberationists left the Greens at this juncture, and those who came later were disappointed when they discovered this lack of commitment to animal issues. In the March/April 1996 issue of the *Greens Bulletin,* for example, a Green woman's letter of resignation from the Green Council, the Editorial Board, and the *Green Times* staff explained:

> While any Green meeting serves meat or dairy products, while any
> Green excuses abuse of non-human sentient life as a valid expression of
> culture, while we court dairy farmers and see the enemy as rBST and
> not the entire dairy industry, the meaning of what it really means to be
> Green is lost. . . . I am a descendant of the indigenous peoples of Ireland, who incidentally practiced human sacrifice. Will any Green who
> supports a Native American's right to hunt also support my right to
> roast my human neighbors? Respect for diversity does not include the
> right to murder non-human sentient life and call it culture.[48]

Of course, individual Greens may have continued to support animal liberation, just as individual animal liberationists have been eloquent in advocating the coalition of animal liberation efforts with the Left or with the Green movement.[49] In practice, however, the two movements, after a temporary attempt at coalition, have remained at odds.

Divisive Issues, Marginalized Constituencies

To be effective, a broad-based transformative movement for social and environmental justice must be inclusive in both its analysis and its composition: that is, it must have an analysis of the ways the "isms of domination" (i.e., racism, sexism, classism, heterosexism, ageism, ableism, speciesism, anthropocentrism) are mutually reinforcing and conceptually as well as structurally interconnected; and that analysis must be manifest in the physical bodies of movement activists. From both a Green and an ecofeminist perspective, the best opportunity for achieving fundamental social change is through building an active coalition of many constituencies: farmers, workers, Native Americans, African-Americans, Asian-Americans, Hispanic Americans, Pacific Islanders, feminists, GLBT activists, youth groups, seniors, animal liberationists, environmentalists, peace activists, disability rights activists, and so on. Although Green theory showed varying degrees of inclusivity in its analyses, in practice the U.S. Green movement has not extended much beyond the constituency where it originated—the white middle class.[50] Certainly, part of the problem may have been in the statements of philosophy themselves: in the Greens/Green Party U.S.A., for example, the key values of *respect for diversity, social justice,* and *postpatriarchal values* are not explicit in articulating a commitment to addressing the concerns of people of color, GLBT activists, and women. Even though *postpatriarchal values* was changed to *feminism* in 1992, the meaning and use of the new term have been in dispute ever since, and some Green groups purposely do not use it at all (on sexism in the Greens, see Chapter 4). In contrast, the Left Greens explicitly named *racial equality, social ecofeminism, gay and lesbian liberation,* and *human rights* in the first draft of their principles, and the Youth Greens named *gay, lesbian, and bisexual liberation* and *social ecofeminism* in their first list of principles, adding *antiracism* in 1991. Founding principles notwithstanding, all branches of the U.S. Green movement have been predominantly white, male, heterosexual, and middle class.[51] In this section, I examine various efforts to diversify the Greens in terms of race, sexuality, and class.

Antiracism and People of Color

From the beginning, the Greens have sought to build a multiracial and multicultural movement. For the founding meeting of the U.S. Green movement, held in St. Paul in August 1984, the five-member inviting committee (Harry Boyte, Catherine Burton, Gloria Goldberg, David Haenke, Charlene Spretnak) planned to build a multiracial Green movement by collaborating with people of color from the ground up. To this end, Catherine Burton raised nearly ten thousand dollars to pay for airfares for activists from communities of color. Gloria Goldberg, acting coordinator for the Institute for Social Ecology, volunteered to organize the event and administer the funds using the office equipment already at her disposal. More than two hundred activists from a wide range of constituencies and issue areas were invited, but ultimately only sixty-two attended. None of the activists of color (and few of the white activists) responded to the initial letter of invitation, and Goldberg, overwhelmed with the tasks of organizing, did not follow up, nor did she ask for help from the other organizers. In the end, with no people of color as applicants, Goldberg used the funds to support travel for six of her colleagues from the Institute for Social Ecology (one of whom did happen to be the Chicano community activist Chino Garcia). None of the ISE instructors knew the money had been earmarked for people of color or that only two representatives from each organization were invited, and they did not offer to repay the funds when they learned of the error. Understandably, their innocence was of little solace to Catherine Burton, who quit the Greens shortly after the founding meeting, saying she felt "ripped off" by the way her fundraising efforts had been misappropriated.[52] Hence, the founding meeting of the U.S. Greens was attended by white, middle-class intellectuals and activists, an imbalance that immediately put movement activists in the questionable position of having to do "outreach" to people of color, on the basis of Ten Key Values and a movement agenda that, although loose, had already been drafted. The difficulty was compounded by the process of naming the new movement: some activists at the meeting argued that the name "green" would alienate people of color, connoting "environmentalism as a middle-class concern that carries no commitment to social justice," and the group chose instead the name "Committees of Correspondence" in tribute to the "network of grassroots political groups during the American Revolutionary Era."[53] A Left Green later pointed out that naming the Greens after a group from the American Revolution was at the very least questionable from a Native American perspective.[54] In sum, the founding meeting of the U.S. Greens exemplifies the first of several methods Greens have used in the attempt to bring in people of color: based on the assumption that people of color have less money than white people (i.e., conflating race and class), white Greens have attempted to raise funds to pay expenses for people of color to attend Green gatherings.

At the next three Green gatherings, each of which was foundational to the movement, people of color were noticeably absent. At the first national Green gathering in Amherst in 1987, "the predominance of white participation was a disappointment."[55] In fall 1988, at the Greening the West regional gathering in northern California, "the proportion of people of color among the total partici-pants was as disappointing as it [was] at past Green gatherings around the country."[56] And at the founding conference of the Left Green Network in April 1989, "most conference participants were white, middle-class, and male."[57] To remedy the situation, some participants suggested a second strategy for increas-ing multiracial participation, arguing that "Greens must reach out to minor-ities."[58] Ecofeminist and Green activist Margo Adair was quick to point out the drawbacks to "outreach," which "only duplicates the problem, because people of color were not involved in the setting of the agenda and therefore must participate on white terms." In her position paper "Toward Diversity," submit-ted with the WomanEarth Feminist Peace Institute statements at the 1989 gath-ering in Eugene, Adair gave the best advice available for building multiracial coalitions: "We need to seek out situations in which the parameters are being set by people of color," she urged. "Successful alliances will be built when whites support the various struggles that people of color have initiated in their own communities to reclaim self-reliance and healthful ways of life."[59] Though it took a long time for Greens to use this strategy—and only a few Green groups did—this method was the most effective one to be tried.

Other Greens offered their own solutions, both personal and philosophi-cal. According to one woman participant in an ecofeminist workshop held at the Greening the West conference, the problem with racial imbalance was the fault not so much of the organizers as it was of the people who attended. She suggested that every white person could have brought along one or two per-sonal friends who were people of color, then added, "If you people don't each have two or three friends who are people of color, then this group really is in trouble."[60] This third strategy of increasing multiracial participation in the movement by building or increasing interracial friendships in people's personal lives was never addressed again, though it would have exposed the inherent racist segregation that characterizes much of U.S. society.

Another Green, Richard Grow, felt that the Greening the West gathering

"systematically excluded people of color" based on various practical and philosophical issues. First, the conference did not foreground the topic of racism by
scheduling it as a plenary with no competing sessions; instead, antiracist trainings were presented as just another workshop, competing with two dozen other
workshops offered at the same time. To Grow, this scheduling signified that the
problem of racism had not yet been recognized as central to the main agenda of
Green philosophy. The scheduling reflected the second problem, which was that
"the agenda of the conference, and of the green movement itself, is quite liter-
ally set by white people and therefore reflects mainly the concerns of white
people." Greens could not expect to see increased involvement from people of
color, since "an agenda addressing the needs of people of color cannot be set by
white people alone, no matter how 'sensitive' or sympathetic." A third problem
with the gathering was the level of abstraction and philosophical discussion,
which would not appeal to people in specific situations of ecological degradation needing to develop specific actions to survive. Finally, Grow criticized the
Greens' refusal to recognize the history of the Green movement in previous
social change movements or in relationship to histories and cultures other than
their own European predecessors (i.e., the West German Greens). "White privilege lies at the core of the green movement's ahistoric character," Grow wrote,
"since it is mainly white people who have the luxury, and perhaps the need, to
deny and ignore their own role in history."[61]

At the second national Green gathering in Eugene, Bharat Patankar, a visi-
tor from India, reported on what he termed a "monochromatic green gathering."[62] Criticizing the location of the conference as too "far from the factory-
polluted neighbourhoods where some of the most important U.S. environmental
struggles are going on," Patankar lamented that of the five hundred or so delegates "only about one-fifth were women and there was scarcely a black face
to be seen." From Patankar's perspective, the problem for the Greens was a
matter of both constituencies and philosophies. Patankar was "surprised" that
there was no group within the Greens which was also involved directly in "a
farmers' or workers' movement based on an ecological perspective"—instead,
"nearly all seemed to be university based." Patankar saw Greens "fighting for
the maintenance of the old forests in Oregon" and in the process coming into
opposition with both the logging companies and the loggers themselves. "This
seems to be a dangerous situation for the Greens," he observed. "Unless and
until" the U.S. Green movement becomes "organically connected to the struggles of workers, farmers, minorities and women," he emphasized, "it will not be
possible for the movement to go very much ahead." The absence of diverse

constituencies was based in part on gaps in a newly emerging Green theory. For example, in their debates over whether to use the term "anti-industrialism" or "anti-capitalism," Greens failed to recognize that both industrialism and capitalism were responsible for economic injustice and would need to be transformed. In supporting cooperatives, Greens assumed these would "naturally" become "democratic and decentralised institutions" and did not want to consider the fact that in other countries (i.e., India), a broad-based cooperative network is controlled by a very small group of elites. Patankar objected to the mention of "Gandhian nonviolence" in discussions of the Greens' commitment to nonviolence, explaining that Gandhi "never had any idea which came near a true ecological perspective" but instead was "patriarchal and supported maintaining the caste system minus untouchability": as Patankar put it, "No low-caste person in India would ever join a green movement that took Gandhi as its exemplar." Finally, while recognizing the importance of spirituality in the Green movement, Patankar found that the discussions on Green spirituality proceeded "as if humans as a whole have done wrong to the earth but have not done any wrong to the vast majority of the exploited population," a view that was leading Greens toward "an abstract and dangerous spirituality that ends in justifying concrete forms of exploitation." In each of these philosophical points, Patankar explained, Green analyses were leading the movement away from a potential foundation for solidarity with farmers, workers, women, and people of color.

One way to develop this needed change in analysis was to educate the membership. The *Green Letter* editorial collective, of which Margo Adair was a prominent member, committed itself to this challenge by actively seeking writers who were not white and articles that would address issues of social and environmental justice. Given the composition of the Greens' membership, however, this commitment led the *Green Letter* collective to seek out relevant essays by people of color published in other journals. This method reached an all-time peak in the spring of 1989, just before the Eugene conference, when five out of seven articles on environmental justice had to be reprinted from other journals to achieve the kind of racial balance the editors sought.[63] The effectiveness of "cross-publication" (reprinting articles by people of color outside the Greens in order to educate white people within the Greens) is difficult to gauge. It was the fourth method Greens used in the attempt to include more people of color, and it is commendable in that it recognized the problem as a need to transform the current membership rather than a need simply to add people of color.

Greens tried harder. The next method for achieving multiracial representation involved bringing in "star" people of color into positions of prominence within the Greens, in the hope that their perspective would influence Green policies and actions and inspire other people of color to follow their lead and join the Greens as well. This strategy seemed to reach a peak in 1991 at the national Green gathering at Elkins. There the Greens had the highest number of people of color in leadership or positions of prominence: Kwazi Nkrumah, Sulaiman Mahdi, Ron Daniels (all three African-Americans), and two Native Americans, Roberto Mendoza from Maine and Walter Bresette from Wisconsin (Bresette did not attend Elkins but has been a member of the Greens since 1985). Although Sulaiman Mahdi and Ron Daniels were both brought into the movement by Green Party electoralists, their allegiance shifted to the larger Green movement as they learned more about the internal politics of the Greens. Ron Daniels, former executive director of Jesse Jackson's Rainbow Coalition, spoke to Greens about his upcoming presidential campaign as a movement-based campaign aimed at establishing a permanent new political party. California Green activist Kwazi Nkrumah began working with the Greens at Estes Park, and at Elkins he was a vocal participant in the movement/party debates, criticizing the California Green Party as a "white political vehicle" whose haste to get on the ballot had harmed alliance-building efforts. Suleiman Mahdi was an African nationalist activist from Atlanta. Originally calling for a black homeland in the American South as a way of making good on the promise of "forty acres and a mule" after the Civil War, Mahdi merged this idea with a bioregional ethic, "a synthesis that is helping introduce a fuller ecological awareness into southern Black communities that are facing the worst ravages of industrialism."[64] It was Mahdi who came up with the term "Green Justice" in a dream, and thanks to these African-American men, the most divisive gathering in U.S. Green history was pulled together at the end through Nkrumah's announcement of the newly formed Green Justice Caucus, their nominations for various leadership positions, and the honoring of Greens who had played important roles in the events of the conference.

But how successful was this strategy of bringing in people of color "stars"? The Green Justice Caucus was formed out of several preexisting caucuses: people of color, women, gays and lesbians, and youth. Although this new caucus was greeted with applause by those outside it, some of its member constituencies felt a certain unease with the new grouping. For example, members of the Queer Caucus and the Youth Caucus felt they were added as an afterthought. Reporting on the gathering at Elkins, Johann Moore asked, "Were Queer people added to the Green Justice Caucus as an afterthought? Maybe so, but we were added, I believe, because of my personal outspoken pressure at the Gathering."[65]

Eric Odell of the Youth Caucus reported, "We were forgotten in the development of [the Green Justice Caucus] and brought into Green Justice after most decisions seemed to have been worked through." Both Odell and Jason Kirkpatrick of the Youth Caucus were "notified" that Green Justice had picked the Youth representative for them—a woman who hadn't been part of the Youth Caucus at the gathering—and both were annoyed by the paternalism of this strategy. Odell concluded, "Our caucus must be allowed to make its decisions for itself, and further must be involved in the Green Justice group's decision-making process from the beginning."[66] It seems that the problem of setting the agenda before inviting the participants was not simply a white problem but a male problem as well. It is notable that all five "star" people of color were men. This doesn't mean there weren't women of color in the Greens—Yanique Joseph of New York City and Lydia Herbert from Syracuse were notable exceptions—but they weren't invited into leadership positions the way the men were.[67]

Also at the Elkins gathering, Euro-American Greens decided Greens didn't have many people of color because they didn't yet have anything to "offer" them. Consequently, the sixth method for bringing people of color into the Greens was developed—the Green Action Plan of 1991, which included three projects addressing social and ecological justice: Detroit Summer, Solar Power through Community Power, and 500 Years of Resistance. Roberto Mendoza, a Native American who was one of the five men of color in prominent positions at Elkins, had actually been working with the Greens for some time, beginning with the Left Green Network in 1989. There he had agreed to coordinate the Diné Green Alliance Support Project, one of three action proposals endorsed at the first Left Green Network gathering. Originally proposed by Anna Rondon and Howie Hawkins, the Diné Green Alliance Support Project involved on-site support and nonviolent defense for the Diné eco-community, organizing an ecological development conference, developing educational materials for grass-roots education, supporting pilot projects in social and ecological alternatives, and mobilizing around specific campaigns. Unfortunately, there was little follow-through on the project, which may have been the reason Mendoza, along with James and Grace Lee Boggs (African-American activists) and Sharon Howell (a white ecofeminist and Green activist in Detroit), proposed the Detroit Summer project.

Like the Diné Green Alliance Project, Detroit Summer was originally conceived of by activist communities in Detroit, who realized that their city would have to be rebuilt by themselves. Greens simply proposed supporting a project that was already planned by a local community. In the tradition of Mississippi

Freedom Summer (1964) and Redwood Summer (1990), Detroit Summer was proposed as a way of inviting large numbers of youth to travel to Detroit and work to rehabilitate the city during a two-week period from July 12 to August 2, 1992. Approximately two hundred youths from around the U.S. joined four hundred youth from Detroit in projects led by local community groups. Plans included rebuilding homes, marching on crack houses, planting urban gardens, preparing workshops, and attending cultural events. Ecofeminist and Green Sharon Howell participated in coordinating the project.[68]

The second part of the Green Action Plan, "Solar Power through Community Power," involved organizing "Sun Day" activities around Earth Day 1992. The theme itself was planned to call attention to the environmental racism involved in such projects as the James Bay hydroelectric project in Québec and the Northern States Power nuclear power plant located on the Prairie Island Indian Reservation in Minnesota. The goal of this action plan was to call for a move away from environmentally destructive energy practices (which relied on racist assumptions about suitable sites for waste storage) and toward environmentally sustainable energy sources, shifting ownership from the oil and electric utility industries to local communities. One outcome of this action plan was organized by AWOL, the Minneapolis Youth Green Local, which had been working with the Prairie Island Coalition Against Nuclear Storage and arranged a march and rally with PICANS against NSP in conjunction with the 1992 Green gathering in Minneapolis.

The third component of the Green Action Plan, "500 Years of Resistance and Dignity," involved Greens in national protests organized to transform the quincentennial celebration of Columbus Day from a glorification of colonialism into an opportunity for multicultural education. In Philadelphia, Greens fought to keep the name of Delaware Avenue (named after the indigenous tribe) from being changed to "Christopher Columbus Boulevard."[69] In Colorado, Greens worked in coalition with the American Indian Movement to shut down the Columbus Day parade. The first Columbus Day parade in the United States was held in Denver in 1906, so Denver seemed the logical place to concentrate the protests. On October 12, the many efforts to educate and organize paid off in Denver, as an estimated three thousand people showed up to protest Columbus Day, while only one float and twenty-five people came to the parade route, thereby canceling the parade.[70] When we look at the Green movement nationally in 1992, it would appear that all these efforts in the Green Action Plan were successful. Hence, it came as a surprise that at the 1992 national gathering in Minneapolis, after the march on NSP for Prairie Island and the first report on the success of Detroit Summer, the proposition for renewing endorsement of the Green Action Plan was rejected in favor of establishing local direct action networks. Sadly, these networks never functioned, and the Green Action Plan of 1991–92 can be seen in retrospect as the high point of the movement-based Greens.

The method that worked best for the Greens in building coalitions with people of color involved coming on board a project for social and environmental justice that had been initiated by communities of color. This strategy was the basis for the Boulder Green Alliance in their work with AIM activists to oppose Columbus Day; it was used by Detroit Greens in organizing Detroit Summer '92; and it was followed by the AWOL Youth Greens and other groups in their support of the Prairie Island Mdewakanton Indian community in Minnesota. In some cases, Euro-American Greens were unable to resist taking the lead in these coalitions, and when they did assume too much leadership and visibility, tensions within the coalition escalated. In Cleveland, for example, the Northeast Ohio Greens ran into difficulties while participating in a coalition of Native Americans and community activists to plan events in opposition to the Columbus Day celebration. As one Green activist reported, minutes for the coalition meetings were published bearing the Greens' return address on Northeast Ohio Greens letterhead; distinctions among the participating organizations were not always clear, thereby giving undue prominence to the Greens; finances were poorly recorded; and finally, when the United Church of Christ sought endorsement for an already planned protest, it approached the coalition leaders rather than the American Indian community. To resolve these problems, the coalition was brought in line by an American Indian activist, who declared that all matters of the Quincentennial belonged to the indigenous community, which would make all decisions for the group. As a result, the coalition was restricted to implementing the decisions of the Native American leadership. For many Greens, this loss of control and leadership was a difficult yet important step toward building solidarity with the native community in Ohio.[71]

Probably the most successful and long-lasting multiracial coalition for the Greens occurred in northern Wisconsin from 1987 to 1991, as Greens and other community groups formed a Witness for Nonviolence in support of native treaty rights. The idea was proposed by Walt Bresette, a Chippewa who had founded the Lake Superior Greens in 1985 as a way of celebrating his own birthday on July 4. As both a native person and a Green, Bresette was ideally positioned to call for coalition work in defense of Chippewa treaty rights. At a

January 1988 gathering of the Upper Great Lakes Green Network, Bresette described numerous racist assaults on Chippewa spearfishers which had escalated during the 1987 spearfishing season. These rights had been enumerated in the treaties of 1837, 1842, and 1854, in which the native people ceded their land to the United States but maintained their rights to hunt, fish, and gather wild rice on the ceded territories. After these rights were reasserted in 1987, white hunters in northern Wisconsin responded with virulent racism: such slogans as "Spear an Indian, Save a Walleye," "Save Two Walleyes, Spear a Pregnant Squaw," "Welfare or Walleye: You Choose" and "Timber Niggers" began to appear on road signs, car bumpers, and building walls. Whites in rural Wisconsin organized a group called Protect American Rights and Resources (PARR) to harass the spearfishers and their families at the boat landings, and some anti-treaty protesters used motorboats to create wakes that would swamp canoes or dragged anchors through spawning beds to scare away the fish. Bresette's description of the problem provided the context for his request: come to the spring boat landings and stand with the native people in a Witness for Non-violence. Wisconsin Greens responded in force.

What followed was a five-year battle in defense of the Chippewa of northern Wisconsin. Throughout the struggle, the racist charges of PARR defied logic and yet went unchallenged by Wisconsin government: to the charge of depleting the fish, Chippewa allies showed that spearfishing took only 2 percent of the walleye total catch in Wisconsin; to the charge of destroying tourism, Greens and others pointed out the deleterious impacts of racism and the threats of potential violence on tourism. As Rick Whaley explained, "Chippewa treaty rights has been the most dramatic and galvanizing of all the Green gathering issues. There is a deeply felt intersection of Native American earth philosophy and traditional practice, on the one hand, with the Green values of ecological wisdom, eco-feminism, and social justice, on the other."[72] In 1990, four years into the spearfishing battle, Walt Bresette delivered the keynote address at the national Green gathering in Estes Park, describing the struggles and the coalitions being made in northern Wisconsin. From Bresette's perspective, the struggles had been exacerbated through increased pressure on rural culture—the loss of small farms to real estate speculation, agribusiness, and urban sprawl. The deeper problem was a loss of culture. And the solution was building a sustainable local economy and working in coalition across differences. Bresette's speech eloquently explained the uselessness of white guilt and the importance of active solidarity with native people:

We need everyone; the question is, what gift do you bring and what is our political goal? What is your gift? And you must believe me on this, there is no medicine man waiting for your phone call to tell you! There's no shaman out there—to guide you! You are the shaman; you are the power. You must trust me on this. I know that! You must stand up now, and lead yourself, and your family, and your community. You must trust yourself; and if you trust yourself and if you know your-self—and you must be proud of that! Get rid of this guilt! Leave it out-side the doors! Come in strong, and tall, and proud, because I want to link arms with you. We have a war to fight, and we need warriors.[73]

After the 1991 spring spearfishing season, a permanent injunction was issued against the physical interference by white protesters, on lakes or at landings, with native spearfishing, and the (overt) battles against the Chippewa finally ended. The Wisconsin Greens attempted to shift the activist networks that had been built around spearfishing to address ongoing battles against mining on native lands, but this issue did not draw as much widespread support. Nonetheless, the feelings of goodwill between Native Americans and Greens in Wisconsin continue to this day.

After events such as Bresette's keynote address at the 1990 national Green gathering, the formation of the Green Justice Caucus in 1991, and the march and rally for the Prairie Island Mdewakanton community in 1992, organizers for the national Green gathering in 1993 attempted to build on these lessons. For the Syracuse gathering, Greens were invited to camp on the grounds of Earthwise Education Center, an African-American sustainable farm run by Syracuse Greens member Winston Gordon. The sessions for the gathering were held in Syracuse, on an empty lot next to Vera's Place, a soul food restaurant that catered the conference. The only real trouble at the gathering occurred when AIM activist Vernon Bellecourt urged Greens to join an impromptu pro-test of a performance that involved a reenactment of colonial conquest and was an insult to the local native people. Without much discussion, many Greens boarded buses (which magically appeared without prior discussion or arrange-ment, it seemed) and traveled an hour to the other side of town to support Bellecourt. It was with no small amount of dismay that Greens then found themselves embroiled in a battle between two local native tribes: the group they had intended to support and the Onondaga who were performing leading roles in the theatrical reenactment.

There have been other such mishaps at national Green gatherings, due in part to the ineptitude or racial guilt of white organizers. At the Albuquerque gathering in 1995, for example, a press conference was arranged at noon on one day so that elected Greens from around the United States and other countries could speak about Green politics for the New Mexico media. Organizers unwisely allowed one late-arriving native man to participate in the press conference although it was widely known that he had several private grievances with the Greens: not only had he failed to obtain widespread popular support for his cross-country Caravan for Justice; he had also failed to receive full funding for his family to be housed and fed at the gathering because he bypassed the procedures for requesting aid and simply arrived on the first day with several family members, expecting funding for the entire group. Not surprisingly, then, when he took the microphone at the press conference, this man denounced the Greens as a group of racists and hypocrites, taking at least fifteen minutes to develop his case and refusing to yield the stage. Little by little, Greens left the platform, and finally one of the organizers succeeded in persuading the man to step down. Although Greens familiar with the history of this man's activism were aware that there was more than one side to his criticisms, there was no way of communicating that perspective to the media.

Thus, despite efforts of varying success, Greens as a whole have not been able to build lasting coalitions with or maintain a significant constituency among people of color. Just one year after the exhilarating formation of the Green Justice Caucus, the "persistent whiteness" of the Greens' national community was again manifest at the 1992 gathering in Minneapolis. "We still have an overwhelmingly Euro-American membership alongside a tenuously multicultural national leadership," lamented Joseph Boland.[74] Three years later, at the 1995 national gathering in Albuquerque, the situation was unchanged. "Only 10 percent of the attendees were people of color," reported New Mexico Green Party member and gathering organizer Cris Moore.[75] After a decade of dealing with the same problem, some Greens began showing signs of resignation or complacency, arguing that it was better to work with the people who showed up than to lament over the people who stayed home. Yet the Green movement could build local, bioregional, or even national coalitions with groups such as the Indigenous Environmental Network, the Indigenous Women's Network, the Southwest Network for Environmental and Economic Justice, the Citizens' Clearinghouse for Hazardous Waste, Great Lakes United, or any number of grassroots activist groups cognizant of the need to address social justice and environmental health simultaneously.[76] But the national trend in the Green movement has turned way from local issue-based organizing to focus on electoral politics, a shift that may foreclose any further opportunities for multiracial coalition building at the grassroots.

Heterosexism and the Lavender Greens

While Greens spent years agonizing over the low numbers of people of color in the movement, few noticed or remarked on the near invisibility of gays, lesbians, bisexuals, and transgendered persons (GLBT). For the first seven years of the movement, GLBTs attempted to organize a caucus at various gatherings, but there was little followup. Part of the reason for this indifference may have been the fact that organizing around sexual identity was not the first priority of those GLBTs drawn to the Greens. Ecofeminists such as Ynestra King and Sharon Howell focused their activism on multiracial coalition building. Social ecofeminists Chaia Heller and Cora Roelofs put their energy into building the Left Green Network. Other GLBTs, such as Charles Dews, Marti Kheel, and Batya Bauman, came into the Greens expressly to develop a focus on animal liberation. Still others, including Hugh Esco and Bill Bradley, stepped forward from the Men's Caucus to create the Green Sprouts program for providing child care at national gatherings. Of course, GLBT rights were written into the Greens' national platform in 1991 and in every state platform from Hawai'i and California to New Mexico, Minnesota, Wisconsin, Rhode Island, and Virginia. Hence, although the Greens were rarely homophobic, they were frequently heterocentric, a distinction that would become more relevant during the 1996 presidential campaign.

Although Greens on the Left declared commitments to GLBT issues from the start, a GLBT caucus of the national Greens took much longer to form. The difference may be due in part to the principles or key values that articulated the core philosophy of each group: for the GCoC (later G/GPUSA), key values such as *personal and social responsibility,* which later became *social justice,* or *respect for diversity* didn't offer an immediately identifiable articulation of support for GLBT rights and concerns. In contrast, at the April 1989 founding conference of the Left Green Network, the fifth of fourteen principles of the Left Greens was an unequivocal statement on *gay and lesbian liberation:*

> Left Greens demand the sexual and social emancipation of people of all sexual preferences. We support every effort by lesbians and gay men to achieve substantive equality and civil rights in all areas, such as jobs,

housing, and child custody, as well as anti-AIDS funding. We recognize that lesbians and gay men are demanding not only their own freedom and dignity but that of all people, for as long as sexuality is not free, people are doomed to thwart their most basic desires for love, pleasure, and creativity.

Similarly, in May 1989, the Youth Greens included *gay, lesbian, and bisexual liberation* as one of their six central principles and later wrote a working paper, "Radical Sexuality," that analyzed the relationship between the oppression of human sexuality and the hegemony of the patriarchal state:

> In our society there is an ongoing war against sexuality. This attack by the State and right wing religious forces is tantamount to attempted State control over every conceivable aspect of our existence—including our pleasure! Faced with the danger that unrestricted sexual freedom might lead people to seek after freedom in all areas of our lives, the State has declared certain sexual acts illegal and supports efforts of religious zealots to reduce sex to restricted, militarily organized "duty." . . . The patriarchal system controls and manipulates sexuality in order to perpetuate and solidify itself. In Western culture this tradition can be traced back to the Christian tradition, but more importantly to feudal times, when the monogamous heterosexual institution of marriage was introduced . . . [and] the necessity of the transfer of property from father to son made it imperative that the son knew for sure who his father was. Since a matrilineal descent system did not allow for this, the male power figure had to make sure that the woman remained monogamous. . . . We feel that the Left (in the U.S. and worldwide) has often failed to deal with sexuality as an integral part of the movement for world social justice. Sexuality cannot be an "add on" issue.

True to their word, the Youth Greens continued to offer the most articulate statements on GLBT liberation. When their journal *Free Society* was finally published in fall 1991, it included a "lesbian and gay caucus statement" and an article on combating heterosexism. The following (and final) issue of their journal in winter 1992 carried responses to the lesbian and gay caucus statement, along with a "Queer Feminist Insert" describing activism in the Lesbian Avengers and discussing the definition of "queer."[77]

Creating a GLBT presence in the national Green organization, by contrast, was much slower. At the 1987 national gathering in Amherst, a mailing list for a Bisexual, Gay, and Lesbian Caucus was created, and thirty-three people signed up, but there is no record of any follow-up. The next manifestation of a GLBT presence appears in the Autumn 1989 issue of *Green Letter*, which published the evolving SPAKA statements that would become the Greens' national program in 1991. There an "Intimacy and Partnership" caucus of seven people "met for the first time . . . at the national Green gathering in Eugene." The group listed some concerns for addressing heterosexism and supporting GLBT liberation and concluded their statement with the words, "As long as sexuality is not free, people are doomed to thwart their most basic desires for love, affection, pleasure, creativity, and relationship."[78] This wording, taken directly from one of the Principles of the Left Green Network, shows a Left Green influence on the formation of a GLBT group in the national Greens; but the linguistic obscurity of the name, "Intimacy and Partnership," seems more characteristic of the national Greens than it does the Left Greens or Youth Greens. Although "Intimacy and Partnership" reportedly requested "time and place for a working group" to meet at the 1990 gathering in Estes Park, there is no record of their meeting or their work.

In 1991, a tenuous GLBT presence in the Greens was finally affirmed as part of the newly formed Green Justice Caucus. As the founding representative of the (then) Queer Caucus, Johann Moore recalled that queer people were added as an afterthought.[79] At the Minneapolis gathering in 1992, Moore proposed that each constituent caucus of Green Justice receive two seats on the Green Council, an idea that was upsetting to some—in particular, to Suleiman Mahdi, the African-American activist from Atlanta who had conceived of the Green Justice Caucus. After a long conversation in the early hours of the morning with Mahdi, Hugh Esco, and Kwazi Nkrumah, "some common ground seemed to be reached" and Moore was allowed to take a seat on the Green Council.[80] While the GLBT presence was facing slow acceptance on the national level, the Lavender Greens subgroup of the San Francisco Green Party was developing a working platform outline with statements on civil rights, health and aging, education, youth, violence, and culture, and sending out information to Greens across California and around the nation.[81]

In 1993, when right-wing homophobia became visible on a national level, Greens responded on a national level. In Colorado, Greens worked to oppose the passage of Amendment 2, which would prohibit statutory protection of gays and lesbians at all levels of government in the state and void all legal claims of discrimination on the basis of sexual preference. The Green Council endorsed both the national boycott of Colorado and the national 1993 March on Washington for Lesbian, Gay and Bi Equal Rights and Liberation. The GLBT Caucus hosted a reception and organizing meeting on the eve of the march, and the following day, heterosexual and GLBT Greens marched together.[82] With the help of straight Greens such as Eric Odell, Johann Moore designed a brochure for the GLBT Greens shortly after the march, and the GLBT Caucus identity seemed more secure.

Unfortunately, what would have been the high point for the GLBT Caucus coincided with the low point for the Greens nationally, when in 1994, the national Green gathering was held in Boise, Idaho, to demonstrate support for the queer community there. In Idaho, as in Colorado and Oregon, a vicious right-wing campaign to pass antigay legislation had been formed. Under the name of Idaho Citizens Alliance, the group attempted to advance an agenda that was antichoice, antienvironment, and antigay, with gay rights as the first target. To affirm solidarity with GLBT people and to emphasize a recognition of the interconnectedness of all oppressions, the Greens/Green Party U.S.A. declared that the theme of its 1994 gathering in Boise would be "Embracing Common Ground: An International Celebration of Human and Bio-Diversity." Working with the local group, Idaho for Human Dignity (IHD), Greens planned a six-day gathering featuring weekend workshops by IHD and a Sunday march and rally at the state capitol; on the days preceding and following the weekend, Green workshops and the Green Council meetings would be held. Unfortunately, a mere twenty-five or thirty Greens showed up for the gathering.

The following year in Albuquerque, however, the GLBT Caucus reconvened with renewed strength, growing to a membership of about twenty people, equally divided between men and women, though with only two people of color. A lesbian representative from the caucus, Patti Myers, was finally chosen to sit on the Green Council, and Myers shortly thereafter contributed an essay to *Green Politics* explaining the civil rights needs of gays and lesbians.[83] Thanks largely to the efforts of Johann Moore, the GLBT Caucus also organized Queer Caucus meetings at related conferences such as the National Independent Politics Summit in April 1996. As Moore sees it, the basis for the slow growth of the GLBT Caucus in the Greens has been twofold: GLBT activists have not yet left the two major parties and created a vocal presence in third parties such as the Greens, nor has the national GLBT community developed itself as a serious voting bloc to be reckoned with; as a result, perhaps, Greens and other progressives have not taken seriously the need for GLBT liberation. "I find there is a lack of the same degree of active solidarity and rhetorical support for Queer liberation," Moore observes, "as there is for the liberation of communities of color. Prioritizing the liberation of one community over the liberation of another is not the politics of radical solidarity which I believe in, and which I think most Greens believe in." To exemplify his point, Moore recalls a conversation with one of the key organizers for the Independent Progressive Politics Network on the topic of queer liberation, in which the organizer had asked Moore, "Don't you think the liberation of people of color is more important?"[84] This attitude is not likely to build solidarity among identity groups and progressives on the Left. Yet, because popular media images portray gays and lesbians as economically privileged, the actual human rights violations of queers can be made to seem less significant.[85] In the Nader presidential campaign, Green organizers seemed indifferent to Nader's refusal to defend gay rights on the basis that he didn't take a stand on "gonadal politics." Only when gay and lesbian activists began making open declarations of leaving the Democratic Party for the Greens did some of the leaders express a Green commitment to queer rights, making open assurances that Nader had been persuaded not to repeat such homophobic remarks (for more information on the Nader campaign, see Chapter 6).

Green Economics and Labor

Left Greens, Youth Greens, and the "neither Left nor Right" Greens diverged dramatically in their analyses of economics, and the debate on Green economics reached its crescendo during the years devoted to national program writing (1989–91). For Left Greens and Youth Greens, a Green economic program had to build on analyses inherited from the "old Left" (i.e., Marxist analyses of capitalism and class relations, along with socialist and communitarian ideas of worker control and ownership), the "new Left" (i.e., critiques of social and economic structures on the basis of race, gender, sexual orientation, age, nationality), and the environmental movement (i.e., assessing the environmental costs of production, consumption, and waste). These perspectives were articulated through the Left Green principle of *cooperative commonwealth* and the Youth Green principle of *anticapitalism*. For the "neither Left nor Right" Greens, a Green economic program could be developed by relying on the key values of *community-based economics, ecological wisdom,* and *grassroots democracy:* these Greens believed that small businesses were preferable to large corporations, that wealth and free enterprise were not inherently antiecological, that local economies were most likely to be democratic and ecological, and that talk of opposing capitalism would only alienate potential allies and deter people from joining the Greens. In their view, the overriding problem to be confronted was not capitalism but industrialism.

From the diversity of viewpoints at Amherst, these two distinct perspectives on economics took shape by the time of the 1989 gathering in Eugene. There the Left Green Network gave nightly sessions on economics and social ecology, and Greens hotly debated whether the fundamental economic (and ecological) problem was capitalism or industrialism. "Neither Left nor Right" Greens were wary of leftist critiques of capitalism, observing that past efforts to replace capitalism had created a new class of bureaucrats while overlooking the environmentally damaging processes of industrial societies. Moreover, the legacy of American individualism, the residual effects of McCarthyism and the cold war, and an eagerness to disassociate the Green movement from the New Left made it unlikely that mainstream Greens or the wider American public would respond favorably to ecological economics that included any language about "workers," much less naming "capitalism," "socialism," or "communism." But with these words off limits, "neither Left nor Right" Greens weren't able to develop their economic vision much beyond the key value of *community-based economics;* instead, their solutions relied on individual transformation (i.e., reduced consumption, recycling, etc.) and later turned to legislative and electoral reforms. In contrast, Left Greens generated reams of analysis and proposals for redistributing wealth, redirecting funds from the military to social programs, and restructuring the workplace on the basis of ecological and democratic values. Hence, when members of the economics working group reached an impasse on fundamental ideological questions in ECOnomics I, they asked Left Green Howie Hawkins to draft ECOnomics II. Of course, Hawkins's draft did not pass until the plenary deleted references to "capitalism" and added language from the preconference draft advocating consumer boycotts of socially or ecologically irresponsible businesses and favoring "ecologically sound personal lifestyles."[86] With these changes, Hawkins's proposal was carried through the platform-writing process and later became part of the Greens' national platform final draft in 1991.

As a follow-up to the discussions at Eugene, *Green Letter* devoted a special issue to ecological economics in the winter of 1990, and a series of articles provided a straightforward overview of Green perspectives on economics, though lacking a leftist critique. The lead essay offered an explanation of the relation between economics and ecology for noneconomists: thinking of the earth's resources as a form of wealth, the writer explained that a sustainable economy would require humans to live on the "interest" from nature's "capital" and to leave the "principal" untouched. The current affluent lifestyles of many first world inhabitants as well as third world elites were a result of an economy based on using up the earth's "principal"; these practices were simply unsustainable and would lead to global bankruptcy if allowed to continue unchecked. Other articles in the issue looked at economics from a bioregional perspective, explaining the functions of community currency and the importance of local banking and investing. Green economic strategies based on the ideas of bioregionalism and community-based economics had been part of the earliest foundations of the Green movement: Lois Arkin's work in the Eco-Village of Los Angeles, along with Carolyn Estes's exemplary participation in the intentional communities movement, had provided inspirational models for many Green locals. In addition, Greens had advocated ecotechnologies such as solar, wind, and cogeneration and alternative transportation such as bicycling, light rail, and other forms of mass transit, along with transforming small businesses into worker and consumer cooperatives. All these strategies were part of a Green economic vision that was indeed "neither Left nor Right" but shared by both. It was in the formulation of transitional economic strategies that Greens ran into philosophical troubles.

If economics was a crucial and divisive issue for Greens in theory, the practical aspects of economics involving coalitions with labor (i.e., loggers, oil rig workers, factory workers, farmworkers, garment workers, and so on) proved equally difficult, and many diverse constituencies never became a part of the Green movement. For example, sustainable organic farmers and labor activists would have composed a crucial constituency, but few joined (Winston Gordon being a notable exception). Moreover, the labor movement in the United States was essentially inert following a decline in membership that began after World War II.[87] Efforts to revive a labor movement began in 1995 with Tony Mazzochi's Labor Party Advocates, though this third-party effort had no immediate plans for running candidates; similarly, a union-organizing institute prepared to train union organizers in the spring and summer of 1996. As David Croteau's research on social activism and working-class culture has shown, it is not possible for middle-class social movement activists to organize the working class.[88] Hence, the Greens' best hope seemed to be forming coalitions with a labor movement once it was under way. Without such a movement, Greens were left to their own devices.

One attempt to create a labor-environment coalition was led by Judi Bari in northern California.[89] With her background in carpentry and union activism, Bari was more attuned than other environmentalists to the needs and concerns of the loggers. Bari not only encouraged Earth First! activists to distinguish between loggers and management but attempted to assist loggers by organizing a local of the I.W.W. in northern California. This attempt failed because it brought urban armchair history buffs from the cities to organize loggers. As Bari realized, any labor movement in northern California would have to come from the workers themselves and from the local situation. As a result, the loggers remained unorganized, working at ecologically destructive and personally hazardous jobs during the logging season and going on welfare during the winter, a situation most conducive to the profits of the timber companies that exploit both the land and the people of the land. Until the Greens develop an economic program detailing tangible strategies for workers interested in making an economic transition from capitalist employment to sustainable economic practices and worker-owned cooperatives, there will be little hope of resolving the false dualism of environment versus employment.

Recognizing this need, as soon as the national platform-writing project had been completed, Greens planned a three-day economics workshop to precede the next national gathering in Minneapolis in 1992. Diana Spalding, a Green from the Women's Caucus, coordinated a series of workshops and presentations, selecting progressive economists from around the nation. Most notably, Michael Albert of *Z Magazine* offered presentations and workshops based on his book *Looking Forward: Participatory Economics for the Twenty-First Century,* which explained the differences between capitalism, "coordinatorism," and economic democracy.[90] Other advocates of ecological economics were invited but were unable to attend at the last minute: Susan Meeker-Lowry, whose work has focused on socially responsible investing and strategies for implementing community-based economics, and Roy Morrison, who has studied the origins and present functioning of a system of cooperatives in Mondragon, Spain.[91] Unfortunately, the Mondragon cooperatives developed democracy among humans without reference to ecological criteria, and their system of production relied heavily on the manufacture and sale of conventional stoves and refrigerators. Nonetheless, Greens looked to Mondragon as a recent model of cooperative economics that could provide guidelines for developing economic structures that were both socially just and ecologically sustainable.

Noticeably absent from all discussions of Green economics was the perspective of ecofeminists: that is, what would an ecofeminist economic theory look like? Would it differ from theories of sustainable, cooperative economics, and if so, in what ways? Feminist economist Marilyn Waring has come the closest to providing a starting point for an ecofeminist economics with her critique of the United Nations System of National Accounts (UNSNA) and gross national product (GNP) accounting and the way women's work and the work of nature goes unrecorded in masculinist economic accounts; yet her analysis fails to account for differences of race and class among women.[92] In contrast, ecofeminists Maria Mies and Vandana Shiva have provided ecofeminist critiques of development, an international system of economics that transfers wealth and resources from third world to first world nations, and they have also commented on GATT.[93] Although their critiques do not attempt to analyze the internal economics of the United States, they address the importance of changing all unsustainable production- and consumer-oriented economies to local, sustainable subsistence economies.

The economic question whether to direct Green efforts toward reforming existing economic institutions or toward building alternative community-based institutions became, in the strategy debates, the question whether to focus on electoral politics or movement building. By 1996, with the Green presidential campaign of Ralph Nader, the question seemed to have been answered by the practices of the Greens themselves.

Green Strategies for Social Transformation

Differences in philosophy among Greens, along with members' varying identities and backgrounds in other activist groups, inevitably led to debates about which strategies of social change would be most effective and efficient. In the early years of the movement (1984–89), Greens seemed to take a holistic approach to organizing, agreeing that the central task of the Green movement was to establish local groups of activists who would work on specific issues within their communities, building coalitions among preexisting single-issue progressive organizations and encouraging those activists to make the connections among the various forms of domination. Some Green locals had already begun running candidates for local elections, and the strategy of participating in local electoral politics, particularly as an educational vehicle, was seen as one aspect of a multifaceted Green movement for social transformation. Accordingly, bioregionalism was also a strong force within the Greens, especially since the Green movement had been launched at the first North American Bioregional Congress in 1984. Green theory emphasized the importance of cultural transformation to any genuine and lasting social transformation: alternative journals and alternative media, education, earth-based spirituality, unlearning racism/sexism work-shops, renewable energy sources, youth groups, and Green study groups were all means of transforming the culture as well as transforming the individual activ-ists, thus strengthening the movement. Originally, Greens believed that creating a strong grassroots base was the first step toward social transformation.

Building community—socially, economically, geographically—was a cen-tral focus of the U.S. Green movement in the early years. The facilitator for the Greens' national conferences, Caroline Estes, immediately introduced Greens to the ideas of the intentional community movement based on her own participa-tion in founding Alpha Farm in Oregon and in building the Fellowship for Intentional Communities nationally. In Los Angeles, Green ecofeminists Lois Arkin and Julia Russell established Eco-Home and began work on Eco-Village in the heart of the inner city. Together with Bob Walter, they organized the First Los Angeles Ecological Cities Conference in 1991, geared toward "greening" Los Angeles.[94] Believing community to be the antidote to the alienation experienced by so many first world inhabitants, Arkin and Russell laid plans for an Eco-Village based on ecological, social, and economic community and began build-ing the groundwork to make it happen. Ecologically, inhabitants of Eco-Village would foster community with other humans and the earth through organic community gardens, water reclamation, alternative energy, nontoxic building materials, and sustainable transportation methods. Socially, Eco-Village would build community among residents through the physical construction of co-housing clusters and community centers and through consensus decision mak-ing. Economically, residents of Eco-Village would have the opportunity to par-ticipate in a Local Exchange Trading System (LETS), socially responsible investing, and barter. While working on building community locally, Arkin and Russell hosted meetings for the newly formed Los Angeles Greens at Eco-Home.

Other Green bioregionalists such as Kirkpatrick Sale and Brian Tokar kept Greens informed of the values and the progress of the bioregional movement.[95] The popular bioregional quiz "Where you at?" was widely circulated among Greens as a way of encouraging activists to become aware of indigenous people, animals, and plants in their bioregion, building a stronger connection to place as a crucial step to laying a foundation for a Green movement.[96] Bioregionalism was itself seen as an effective grassroots strategy for social change, progressing from an awareness of one's own bioregion and building local community, to establishing worker-owned cooperatives and training others to do the same.[97] By working locally, Greens proclaimed, a movement could eventually gain control of the bioregional commons.

In the larger ecofeminist movement, connections between ecofeminism and bioregionalism were made primarily through the work of Judith Plant, a Canadian bioregionalist and ecofeminist living in British Columbia. Plant's edited anthology, *Healing the Wounds: The Promise of Ecofeminism* (1989), was the first ecofeminist anthology in North America. Many of the contributors to Plant's coedited anthology *Home! A Bioregional Reader*—Murray Bookchin, David Haenke, Sue Nelson, Kirkpatrick Sale, Brian Tokar—had been or continued to be active in the Greens. In her essay from that volume, Plant argues that bioregionalism leads to a revaluing of "home" and thus a revaluing of what has been traditionally considered women's realm.[98] But although Plant and others have emphasized the connections between ecofeminism and bioregionalism, they have remained silent on some of the potential problems: for example, racial, cultural, and sexual diversity and tolerance within bioregions and how human rights would be guaranteed; economic or ecological differences of wealth or poverty among bioregions and how these inequities might be balanced.[99] As Ynestra King observed in her response to Kirkpatrick Sale years earlier in the *Nation,* "There are no social ethics in bioregionalism, so there is no *a priori* commitment to the liberation of women, or to opposing racism or to any other particular program." Commenting on the "underlying anti-intellectualism and antiurbanism (and occasional anticommunism)" in bioregional movements, King concluded, "From an ecofeminist perspective, one needs an ecological, social ethic that asserts that some practices are right and others wrong, even if practiced in your own bioregion with agreement among the people there."[100] If bioregionalists could resolve these questions, which are of concern not only to ecofeminists but to any activist striving for ecological and social justice, then bioregionalism could provide a suitable movement strategy for ecofeminists and Greens alike.

From the start, Greens prided themselves on their movement's "two-legged" approach: combining the strengths of issue-based activism and electoral politics, Greens envisioned not just a movement for the campaign season or the single issue but a year-round movement of locals capable of building alternative institutions as well as correcting existing ones. This dual strategy would help the Green movement go forward well beyond the ability of those who focused exclusively on either electoral politics or issue-based activism. It was an "inside/outside" approach, a "movement party," and it fit well with the Green commitment to postpatriarchal values. Electoral politics and the administration of government had a long history—in the United States and elsewhere in the West—of being the domain of the dominant class. Wealthy, white, heterosexual (or gay but closeted) men had a two-hundred-year history in U.S. electoral politics. In contrast, women's participation in politics began in nineteenth-century social movements: the antislavery movement, the temperance movement, the anti-vivisection movement, the social housekeeping movement, and later the suffrage movement. In the twentieth century, women's participation in electoral politics (as individuals, rather than through their husbands or their race or class identity groups) has been a very recent phenomenon, and the history of the occasional white woman and even more rarely the woman of color in elected office has just begun. What Greens didn't recognize was that although a Green movement offered a location for activism for Greens of diverse genders, races, classes, and sexual orientations, a move into Green electoral politics would require a conscious commitment to diversity if the movement were not to conform to the historically produced structure of electoral politics and become a movement of wealthy, white, heterosexual males. Moreover, the structure of electoral politics in the United States was particularly hostile to third-party organizing: to ensure equitable participation, Greens would have to address the need for proportional representation (versus the present "winner take all" system), campaign finance reform (versus the present campaigning by the wealthy), changes in ballot access regulations (whereby third parties need to collect thousands of signatures just to qualify for each election), and equitable media coverage. And finally, Greens would need to consider the experiences of other third parties in U.S. history, as well as other Green parties around the world; the power of the structure itself to reshape and co-opt activists could not be underestimated. But these considerations were swept aside.

Despite early successes and amazing turnouts (up to one hundred or two hundred activists) at founding meetings, Green locals experienced slow growth. Local groups seemed to thrive under the right circumstances—which included the size of the city or town, the presence or absence of other activist groups, and the participation of experienced grassroots organizers—but for many Greens, the movement wasn't growing quickly enough. To support the growth of Green locals, more experienced Greens put together an organizing manual that was distributed through the national clearinghouse and ran a series of essays in *Green Letter* offering advice on the basics of organizing: recruiting membership, fundraising, running meetings, sharing leadership, choosing issues, and maintaining healthy group dynamics.[101] These essays were necessary because the majority of people drawn to the Greens were attracted by the Green philosophy, not by Green activism; many of these people had never been activists before. As a result, many Green locals needed to focus on issues of internal process, structure, and decision making, with activism coming only after these issues were addressed. From the beginning, there were some salient characteristics of building locals which Greens ignored at their peril. Though some of the most durable Green locals have been in major cities such as Cleveland, San Francisco, New Orleans, and St. Louis, Green locals tend to be most effective in smaller towns and cities, such as Santa Fe, New Mexico; Duluth, Minnesota; Superior, Wisconsin; and Burlington, Vermont. It is sometimes harder to build community in areas with larger populations, as many large cities are already served by a variety of single-issue activist organizations. Those Green locals that did not succeed followed a predictable decline: after a year or two of what appeared to be successful organizing, the local retreated from scattered attempts at activism and focused on building publications, networking with other organizations, and forming study groups. Though these strategies were usually chosen as responses to real needs, they also functioned to keep the group out of the fray. The local then got a reputation for being an irrelevant study group, and the action-oriented organizers left to join more active single-issue groups. A downward spiral of interest then led to the group's dissolution.[102]

Another, more serious problem for Green locals involved translating the holistic Green vision into activism: that is, for any single issue of concern to Greens, there were already single-issue activist organizations in many communities. A Green strategy for activism meant choosing issues that could most easily be used to demonstrate the connections among various forms of oppression. The most successful Green activist campaigns addressed multifocus issues such as sustainable development, which had the capacity to involve activists concerned about forests, clean water, residential taxes, hazardous waste, living wages, and job security; food quality, as in the campaign against recombinant Bovine Growth Hormone (rBGH), which involved activists interested in animal liberation, sustainable farming, consumer health, and environmental quality; sustainable economics, as in the campaign against the North American Free Trade Agreement (NAFTA), which garnered support from animal liberationists, labor activists, consumer advocates, environmentalists, feminists, and civil rights activists. But in the absence of such multi-issue campaigns, Green locals faltered.

In contrast, electoral politics seemed to be an arena in which the multi-issue focus of the Greens could be used to an advantage. Thus, the emphasis on movement building was challenged in 1989 at the national gathering in Eugene. There John Rensenbrink introduced the idea of a Green presidential candidate, and though the majority of Greens dismissed the idea as premature, Rensenbrink's suggestion sparked the imagination and aspirations of a few Green activists. In October 1989, at the next Interregional Committee meeting, Rensenbrink and a few others formed an Electoral Action Working Group to develop avenues for participating in electoral politics, and by March 1990 the group had become the Green Party Organizing Committee. Meanwhile, Greens in California were experiencing similar growth. Through a series of statewide meetings in January, February, and March 1990, electoral activists in California decided to form a state Green Party, despite vocal opposition from grassroots men, women, and the few people of color within the movement. Together these events led up to the formation in 1992 of a separate national group to focus on Green electoral politics, the Green Politics Network, and the 1995 decision to run a Green Party presidential candidate—a decision and candidate selection made by a small group of electoral activists within the California Green Party. At each of these turning points, the debate about strategy for the U.S. Greens developed in a fairly linear progression from an advocacy of a Green movement with many strategies, of which electoral politics would be only one, used by and accountable to movement activists, to an emphasis on Green electoral politics as the most efficient and effective method of bringing the Green vision to the larger public. At each level, what became known as the "movement/party" debate developed greater urgency, as the disparity between local movement activists and more polished electoral activists grew.

All along the way, party activists professed a commitment to the idea that the party would also engage in movement and issue-based activism to build the party, and to a large extent this was true. In Maine, for example, where John Rensenbrink lived, the campaign to elect Jonathan Carter for governor easily shifted gears when Carter lost the first election in 1994 with only 6.4 percent of the vote and went on to become a local and national hero as an advocate for a clearcutting ban. By the fall of 1995, Carter was spearheading the Ban Clearcutting Campaign in Maine, which collected fifty-five thousand signatures in support of a referendum calling for a public vote on clearcutting. The referendum was accompanied by a six-point initiative developed in consultation with environmentalists, foresters, loggers, forest products manufacturers, and concerned residents.[103] In New Mexico, which by 1995 had become a showcase model of Green activism and electoral politics, the Santa Fe local had effectively led the way to organizing the state. After collecting four thousand signatures to become a registered political party in 1992, Santa Fe Greens responded to local issues by founding Citizens for Property Tax Justice to assist local residents who faced rapidly escalating property values, and by forming a Living Wage Campaign to help people who work in Santa Fe earn enough to live there. In 1994, former lieutenant governor Roberto Mondragon won instant credibility for the Greens by shifting his party allegiance from the Democrats to the Greens and running with campaign finance reform activist Steve Schmidt for governor and lieutenant governor, respectively. Their campaign received about 25 percent of the vote in Santa Fe County and over 11 percent statewide, effectively establishing the Greens as a reputable third party in New Mexico.[104]

In Minnesota and Wisconsin, two Green groups at the southwestern tip of Lake Superior provided excellent models of Green locals in action. The Lake Superior Greens (LSG) sponsor an annual "Living Green" conference each January, complete with workshops for integrating Green values into lifestyle changes as well as strategies for lobbying, direct action, and issue-based activism. The LSG has also placed a number of elected local officials on the Douglas County Board of Supervisors and the Superior City Council. Across the harbor, the Duluth Area Green Party (DAGP) was created in the spring of 1995 to provide a vehicle for Twin Ports Green activists who wanted to address issues specific to Duluth. The group got its first opportunity for activism in the 1996 mall sprawl referendum, which brought together seasoned environmentalists and labor activists in a common goal. In the face of massive retail chain development on the banks of Miller Creek, DAGP organizers were careful to set the terms of the issue as "mall sprawl" rather than "environmental degradation" or "no growth" politics. They focused their rhetoric on issues of downtown and neighborhood business, living wages, potential traffic congestion, and costs to taxpayers. With ties to the labor newspaper in Duluth and to the environmental community, DAGP activists were able to bridge the gap among a variety of constituencies—seniors, labor, environmentalists, small business owners—and to win the referendum.[105] These examples of effective locals prove that even as the movement/party debates were shifting the U.S. Green movement nationally from a movement to an electoral focus, there continued to be effective Green locals that persisted in combining issue-based activism, education, and other strategies of social transformation along with local or state-level electoral politics with great success.

In the national shift from movement-based locals to state electoral activism, the California Green Party led the way. In 1990—the same year the Left Greens and Youth Greens were enjoying what would be the height of their activism in the Earth Day Wall Street Action—the California secretary of state registered the Green Party as a political body intent on qualifying for the California state ballot in 1992. Possibly as a response to the rhythm of the California Green Party registration and qualifying schedule, the movement/party debates peaked twice, first in the summer of 1990, through a series of published viewpoint essays in *Green Letter,* and again in 1992, in a series of essays published in *Regeneration.* After 1992, the movement/party debate was effectively ended through the victory of the electoral activists, not because they had answered to anyone's satisfaction but their own any of the questions or objections raised by the movement activists, but simply because they persisted in building the party in spite of those objections. To their credit, the electoralists in the Greens tended to be visionary and charismatic, effective speakers and good media managers; of course, they took these characteristics to be not only necessary but sufficient earmarks of leadership, a topic of further debate among Green activists.

The movement/party debate in California came to the attention of Greens nationally through Carl Boggs's essay "Why the California Greens Should Wait to Have a Party," first published in the *Greens Bulletin* in May 1990 and reissued in the summer 1990 volume of *Green Letter.*[106] Boggs was a well-respected theorist among Greens, both as an author of the book *Social Movements and Political Power* and for his participation in the Westside Greens local and at various California local and state meetings as well as at national gatherings. For these reasons, Boggs's numerous objections should have merited some concern. From his perspective, the process of forming the party was antidemocratic: at all three statewide meetings, there had been little discussion of the idea, attendance had been low, and members were not notified that the idea of a state party was being placed on the agenda for discussion and decision making. Because the process had been antidemocratic, important questions that should have been addressed were swept aside—questions about the advantages and disadvantages of starting a statewide party, the relationship between party and movement, available resources for starting and maintaining such a party, and the relevant histories of other Green parties internationally as well as third parties in the United States. Then, even though vocal opposition to the formation of a state party was raised at the third statewide meeting, Green electoralists vowed to push ahead with the idea and held a press conference the following day. Their position was that the movement and the party should be separate organizations, a position that neatly paralleled the formation of the Green Politics Network that same month on the opposite coast. With separate organizations, Green electoralists would be free to pursue their goals, unencumbered by calls for "accountability" from movement activists.

In addition to the problem of undemocratic process, Boggs pointed out, the California Greens were not ready to form a statewide party because the grassroots base had not yet been established. Greens were still largely white, middle-class environmentalists who needed to build strong, active coalitions with organizations in communities of color, with labor activists, and with other social movements. Greens could run effective local campaigns based on their activism in local issues and, after establishing a strong community base, could seek to connect those communities in a statewide party. Without that preparation, Boggs predicted, the California Green Party would have no hope of winning against the well-funded candidates of the two-party system. Moreover, their credibility in communities of color, with labor, and with women's groups would be hopelessly destroyed. Finally, as Greens lost election after election, activists would become disheartened and the movement itself would falter. From Boggs's perspective, forming a state party at that stage in the movement was tantamount to a death wish. His conclusion was prophetic:

> We in the United States have a pronounced tendency to view politics as the search for a quick fix, immediate electoral victories, and as much media exposure as possible. The Greens, of course, stand for a completely different model of social change. Yet in California the Greens are in danger of falling into the same strategic trap that has foiled so many third parties in the past. The establishment of a statewide party now will, sooner or later, undermine our grassroots vitality, take us down the path of electoral failure, and destroy the very essence of Green politics.[107]

His concerns were echoed by other grassroots Green activists, who saw in the party a movement toward co-optation, careerism, and reformism. As clearinghouse coordinator Charlie Betz had commented, the premature formation of the California Green Party meant that "an all-white organization now has the notorious problem of asking people of color to come on board."[108]

Green electoral activists such as Kent Smith, Mike Feinstein, and Bob Long listened to these objections with impatience. As Smith observed, "There has been a dramatic jump in interest from the news media since the formation of the Green Party." Long took a laissez-faire attitude, arguing, "There is absolutely nothing wrong with any individual or group of individuals initiating a particular Green activity or approach. If there are those who disagree with a particular action, there are plenty of other worthwhile activities that they can pursue." Apparently, the process of consensus decision making was irrelevant in the case of electoral politics, and the question of electoralists' accountability to the movement was not to be answered. According to Long, while those who "feel that a state party is unwise . . . have every right to try to convince others by reasoned argument . . . they cannot mandate that others follow their recommendations." Both Long and Feinstein emphasized that the party would be accountable to the eighty thousand registrants whose signatures would be gathered in order to qualify the party; this view is quite different from seeing the party as a function of the movement. To justify their haste (only three months) in making the decision to form a party, Long and Feinstein pointed to the threat of takeover of the Green Party name by a group of discredited activists called the Siloists, The Community, or Green Future. Apparently, this group had disrupted "legitimate" Green groups in several countries already, and there was some evidence they might have targeted California as well.

These debates were developed further in the two years it took the California Green Party to qualify for state ballot access. By the fall of 1992, when the special issue of *Regeneration* devoted to Green electoral politics finally appeared, positions had become fairly entrenched. Electoral activists (who were often, but not always, members of the Green Politics Network) argued that a Green party was needed for the simple reason that movement building wasn't working. As Bob Long explained, "The movement building approach in Southern California had reached a plateau and perhaps was withering. People are attracted to the movement and when immediate results are not forthcoming, lose interest and motivation." Others pointed to the fact that the Green philosophy did not easily translate into activism, since most activism tended to focus on single issues. Moreover, as Tom Stafford wrote, by the time Greens were formed and began their activism, they found themselves competing with single-issue activist groups, and "there wasn't much that the Greens could do that the other groups were not already doing, and doing it quite effectively." David Spero, another Green Party of California advocate, agreed: "There is no reason for people to join the Greens to work on any particular issue. Other folks are already doing it, and no single issue makes much of a difference anyway." But Greg Gerritt, a member of the Green Politics Network, put it most succinctly in his Darwinian survival-of-the-fittest metaphor for social-change activists:

The natural world is a place of competition. Better-adapted organisms survive. Only organisms adapted to the niches available to them survive. . . . [Because activism is single-issue, and most issues are already being addressed by single-issue organizations, these niches are filled.

Hence,] the niche available to the Greens is political party organizing,
and the activists most attracted to the Greens' holism need a political
party in order to have an effective vehicle for directly confronting the
power of the ruling class, and having an opportunity to overthrow that
power.[109]

Of course, as both eco-anarchists who draw their philosophies from Kropotkin's
Mutual Aid and feminists who have challenged the male biases inherent in the
biological sciences have discovered, the natural world is largely a place of cooperation, and mutual aid within species is requisite to survival. Competition is
the exception, not the rule.[110] The "naturalness" of competition is one of the
foundational beliefs of a liberal worldview, and thus Gerritt's metaphor reveals
the root of the difference between the electoral advocates and the movement
advocates.

As movement advocate and Left Green Eric Chester argued, the liberal
worldview conceives of social change "as the result of the cumulative effect of a
series of small, incremental reforms. Within this process, electoral victories constitute an instrumental means of achieving change." But this viewpoint is antithetical to a revolutionary perspective, which sees social change as occurring
primarily through direct challenges to the established order, not by participating in that system, and definitely "not through the electoral process."[111] The
problem with establishing a Green party, according to movement advocate Diana Frank, is that it "perpetuates the myth that the system works." In the
context of the United States, electoral politics diverts activists away from "working to make real, fundamental change" and into spending "time and money
working within a system that cannot work for us," maintaining the "depen-
dence of the people on individual leaders, rather than empowering them
through their own community action."[112] In the history of the United States, Ed
Jahn argued, "going into mainstream politics has been the kiss of death for
movements like the Greens."[113] The problem is that if a third party articulates a
radical agenda that becomes popular, the two major parties have only to repeat
the same message and thereby co-opt the more radical agenda of the outsiders
by persuading voters that these concerns can be addressed within the two-party
system. Then, after the voters have returned their loyalties to the major parties
and the progressive movement has been destroyed, the elected candidates can
decide whether to fulfill any of their promises. This sequence of events is exemplified in the downfall of the Populist movement, the most successful coalition
of farmers and workers in the history of the United States.[114] At the most, this

strategy has revealed the major flaw in the so-called democratic system—a failure of accountability—and it has yielded merely incremental reforms, not holistic transformation. Moreover, this incremental approach has not been responsible for the major achievements for social justice in the twentieth century: as Howie Hawkins pointed out, "Everything we have won we have imposed on the establishment by direct action from below—from the social programs and labor union rights won by the sit-down strikes of the 1930s, to the civil rights, anti-war, and anti-nuclear victories won by the sit-ins of the 1960s and 1970s."[115] Instead of building a third party, movement activists maintained, effecting specific reforms in the processes of electoral politics would go a long way toward opening avenues for actualizing a Green vision. Specifically, movement activists argued for the importance of campaign finance reform, term limits, proportional representation, and the possible uses of initiative, referendum, and recall.

The differences of the debate involved the choice between a "movement party" and a "party movement," as Howie Hawkins and Suleiman Mahdi explained. A "party movement," according to Hawkins, was "a movement of many organizations toward an independent party," and this should not be the goal of the Greens. If anything, it should be a transitional stage toward the real goal of a "movement party," by which Hawkins and others meant "a united organization that is active in movement building and issue work as well as elections."[116] As Mahdi explained, the movement party would be "accountable to the movement and direct participatory democracy," whereas the party movement would be accountable only to "the party and representative democracy."[117] Without the movement, the electoral activists in the Greens "will either sell out to the system at the first successes or crumble at the first disappointments," Hawkins predicted. Moreover, the movement was needed "because most of the existing power structure is not up for election. The monopolistic giants of the 'private sector' (the corporations, banks, foundations, universities, and mass media conglomerates) as well as the 'permanent state' (the bureaucracies, police, and military) will be there the day after the election even if Greens win every office in the country. And the extra-parliamentary actions of this power structure—disinvestment, propaganda, violence—will severely circumscribe what a Green government might do."[118] As one activist who had come to the Greens after working for years in the Socialist Labor Party observed, most Green Party advocates "suffer from the delusion that they can use capitalism's political system to change capitalism. They fail to realize that political democracy exists to prevent and to contain popular dissent."[119]

These views were supported by scholars ranging from Frances Fox Piven and Richard Cloward in *Poor People's Movements* to Audre Lorde in "The Master's Tools."[120] But the electoralists simply could not be stopped by arguments based on the historical record or by calls for accountability. With appeals to "trust" and gestures to the failing numbers of movement activists, electoralists moved to put the party apparatus in place. Hence, the shift from movement building to electoral politics, originally intended (at least in part) to gain greater momentum for a faltering movement, repeated the same dynamic of the larger society: that is, instead of examining why the movement was faltering and seeking to go to the root of that problem, activists chose to start building upward from a faulty foundation. Then, when state party activism had reached a plateau, activists in the California Green Party decided it was time to initiate a national electoral campaign. In this way, instead of providing an alternative to the status quo, Greens followed a pattern of addictive behavior that characterized U.S. society at large:[121] by seeking solutions at higher and higher levels of political activity, Greens failed to make good on their original vision of *grassroots democracy, decentralism,* and *postpatriarchal values.*

Some activists realized this failure earlier than others. For example, a year of experience coordinating the national program-writing process had led Christa Slaton to conclude that "Greens have a wonderful ideology" but have been unable to "integrate the major green values in a new politics among themselves."[122] Once again, the process did not go unnoticed by movement activists, though what is surprising is that they continued to participate in a movement that was already drifting away from its founding vision. As one editor of *Regeneration* noted, "Greens agree that we should repudiate the Siloist 'Green Future' and Randy Toler's 'National Green Party' as dishonest attempts to capitalize on the Green name without being chosen by the Green membership. But, when individuals who have been part of our movement act the same way, should we make exceptions for them, or respond to them in the same way as we respond to Green Future and the National Green Party?"[123] The problem for the Green movement as a whole was that movement activists never resolved this question of accountability. As a result, electoral activists were able to take whatever actions they chose under the banner of The Greens, alienating grassroots members with their apparent disregard for dissenting views and their willingness to compromise on key values. With the Nader presidential campaign of 1996, these fissures within the movement became visible on a national level.

6. Democracy, Ecofeminism, and the Nader Presidential Campaign

Insofar as democracy is concerned with relationships, with equality and power, feminism is a requisite component of any truly democratic theory. Although the link between feminism and democracy now seems self-evident to most feminists, the two theories did not develop in tandem: according to accounts from patriarchal history, democracy has been around since the time of ancient Greece, but feminism is a more recent phenomenon.[1] If we look only at the Western tradition, feminism can be traced from its origins in seventeenth-century Europe, through the Enlightenment and the development of liberalism, to the "first wave" of liberal feminism and on to feminism's "second wave" of the 1960s, which developed the branches of radical, cultural, Marxist, socialist, and womanist feminisms, influencing the development of lesbian and queer feminisms, and later the varieties of ecofeminism as well. In the United States, feminism's first wave was brought about through the experiences of privileged women who were nonetheless excluded from democracy; indeed, in the course of their development, both feminism and democracy have been characterized by movements for greater and greater inclusiveness. But although democracies have not been particularly inclusive of feminism, the feminist movement (especially the second wave) has both developed and been characterized by structures and strategies of participatory democracy.[2] Like the feminist movement, the Green movement in the United States has taken democracy—and specifically, grassroots participatory democracy—as one of its central principles, a value inherited from the West German Greens and one that has remained consistent across the various factions of Greens in the United States (see Chapter 3). But the 1996 Green presidential campaign of Ralph Nader challenged the meaning of grassroots democracy for the Greens, at the same time that it ostensibly used political (electoral) democracy and economic democracy (in the critique of corporations) as its central campaign messages.

My purpose here is to use the Nader campaign as an entry point for a discussion of Green, grassroots democracy and for developing some preliminary considerations for an ecofeminist theory of democracy. To accomplish this, I examine some of the characteristics of Green democracy in theory, along with the successes and shortcomings of its first national application as praxis—the collaborative process of writing the Greens' national platform. After summarizing the history and developments in the Nader campaign, I discuss the campaign as the second national application of Green democracy, showing how the practice of national electoral politics rearticulates (and restricts) Green democracy within the framework of liberalism. To examine that framework more fully, I then turn to feminist critiques of liberal democracy to show that the Green theory of grassroots democracy includes the goals of liberal feminism but fails to consider more transformative feminist critiques (i.e., Marxist and maternalist) of democracy, an omission that in part explains (but does not justify) the impasse of Green electoral politics in the United States. With these discussions as a foundation, I then turn to ecofeminist critiques of liberal democracy and conclude with some suggestions for an ecofeminist reformulation of democracy.

The Theory of Green Democracy

From the beginning of the Green movement in the United States, the concept of democracy has been defined in conjunction with the term "grassroots" and with the key values of *decentralization* and *community-based economics* or *radical municipalism*.[3] For the Greens, democracy has been defined as a participatory process whereby people have direct control in making the decisions that affect their lives; for this process to be effective and inclusive, it must occur at the local level, and thus Greens envision a restructured society that returns decision-making power to the base (grassroots). In every discussion of Green democracy, Greens refer to both political processes and economic structures: that is, Greens recognize that power is both political and economic and that simply addressing the processes of government will not suffice in reconstituting grassroots democracy. Greens advocate building local economies and technologies that work with (rather than against) the local ecology, and businesses that are worker-owned and worker-managed. Finally, Greens imagine a restructuring of society in terms of housing, business, and industry which reduces the ecological impact of human transportation needs at the same time that it brings people together, creating a sense of community, in which democracy is most likely to be practiced. Cohousing, intentional communities, eco-villages, and neighborhood organizations are all potential vehicles for the practice of Green political and economic democracy, the latter through local economies, local currencies, and barter.

In the organization of Green groups, from the local level to the networks and associations, Greens have been careful to emphasize that "the means embody the ends" and that the structure of the Green organization must prefigure the society Greens hope to create. Even in the state platforms and local campaigns of Green candidates, Greens have emphasized various components of democracy that have remained consistent during the first decade of the Green movement in the United States. For example, linking the key values of *social justice* and *democracy,* Greens have insisted on parity whenever possible: in their elected representatives to state or national organizations, in their candidates for local or statewide office, Greens have sought gender balance and, where possible, racial balance as well. In choosing their leaders, Greens have been concerned with issues of accountability and representation; they have emphasized the importance of sharing leadership and training new members to lead; they have considered, and in many groups practiced, the process of rotating leaders so that no single individual is continually the spokesperson for the group. In decision making, Greens have tended to seek consensus first, with a fall back to supermajority (60 or 75 percent), and groups have only reluctantly resorted to majority rule when decision making seemed otherwise impossible. From a Green perspective, simple majority rule is unacceptable, since too many voices are excluded and majority votes can lead to undemocratic policies. "Whether we intend it or not, our gatherings do become a model for social change," Gateway Greens member Don Fitz has explained. "Every Green gathering is a rehearsal for changing power relationships at work, in neighborhoods, and throughout society."[4]

Externally, in their campaigns for public office and in their political work, Greens have sought to transform the processes of electoral politics to increase the practice of democracy. Recognizing the role that wealth plays in the selection of candidates and in the tremendous costs of publicity during the campaign, Greens have supported campaign finance reform (i.e., campaign spending limits, guaranteed and limited media coverage). Because the two-party system in the United States effectively restricts the terms of political debate and as a result has been charged with discouraging political participation, Greens have advocated replacing the current "winner take all" dualistic electoral system and its associated financial rewards for the two major parties with a system of proportional representation (sometimes including preferential voting) that equalizes campaign funding, media coverage, and elections. In many states, Greens have successfully used the processes of initiative and referendum to challenge corporate welfare (i.e., the Corporate Welfare Responsibility Act of California) and ecologically unsound business practices (i.e., the Maine logging referendum). Finally, Greens have researched strategies for revoking corporate charters when corporations fail to behave as "good citizens."[5]

The Green commitment to grassroots, participatory democracy was first implemented on a national level through the process of writing the Greens' national platform. This project of national collaborative writing was co-coordinated by political science professor Christa Slaton, retired political science professor John Rensenbrink, and *Green Letter* editor Margo Adair. Slaton, who was primarily responsible for coordinating the platform-writing process, described the process itself as an example of "greenroots politics, a decentralized network of grassroots democratic organizations" working together. As Slaton stressed, for Greens "the process of developing our program is of equal importance to the final product." She admitted that "to be truly democratic requires time, commitment, responsibility, and—above all—patience and mutual respect," yet the outcome is "a process of working together through difficulties to produce a unity and clarity of purpose that forms a solid foundation for future development."[6] Co-coordinators Margo Adair and John Rensenbrink were even more emphatic in their definition: "Democracy is not about deciding if you support this or that person to do politics for you. True democracy is creating policy collectively."[7]

Yet for a variety of reasons, this first national attempt to practice Green democracy did not achieve the full participation Greens had hoped for. In her summer 1990 assessment of the platform process, midway between its inception at Eugene in 1989 and its ratification at Estes Park in 1991, Slaton described some of the impediments to the process of democracy. After the national platform had been divided into nineteen key areas through a process of grassroots decision making, working groups were formed to develop strategy and policy in each of these areas. Working-group coordinators were volunteers who were also participants in their working groups: "Some were more responsible, some less responsible," reported Slaton, "and some disappeared into thin air." Requiring teamwork from these inexperienced coordinators produced additional problems, as did the requirement that coordinators maintain regular contact with working-group members, a responsibility that entailed a financial burden that Greens had no means of compensating. The requirement of gender parity among coordinators often meant that people were coerced into working on issues in which they had no interest, and as soon as the Eugene gathering ended, these co-coordinators disappeared. Because many of the issues addressed at Eugene were then reopened by working-group members who had not attended, coordinators sometimes felt they knew where these discussions would lead and prematurely closed debate or dismissed input, leaving working-group members feeling shut out. Finally, the working-group coordinators had been given no standardized format to follow in writing their statements; of all the difficulties, this one was the most easily remedied.

These impediments can be compared with the impediments many women's organizations experienced in their practice of participatory democracy. According to Anne Phillips, women active in the women's liberation movement faced several identifiable obstacles.[8] The emphasis on equality—which meant that women rotated through positions of leadership and organizational support, regardless of some women's unique skills and abilities for performing certain functions—hampered movement effectiveness by failing to use the expertise of its members. The emphasis on face-to-face meetings not only sent conflict underground by producing false consensus but also meant that attendance was limited and unrepresentative, since few could attend so many meetings on a regular basis. As Jo Freeman's famous essay, "The Tyranny of Structurelessness," explains, the refusal to create structures for decision making and leadership meant that groups were open to manipulation by de facto leaders and charismatic spokespersons.[9] Finally, because the movement lacked specific procedures for certifying membership, spokespersons, or representatives, activists could not claim to represent a specific constituency other than themselves. Thus, in both the women's liberation movement and the Green movement that came after it, the limits of participatory democracy became evident: first, only a small group of zealous activists is willing to attend countless meetings to ensure full participation; the majority of activists, while genuinely concerned about the issues of their movement, are nonetheless consumed with the duties of their personal lives. Moreover, movement activists bring with them their unique socialization,

which affects participation in meetings: engagement with or avoidance of conflict, effective speaking or silence, and introducing or rejecting new ideas or
topics are all socialized behaviors that affect participation. Next, even with democratic structures in place, accountability—whether in terms of following
through on commitments or tasks or faithfully representing the movement and
adhering to movement principles—will always be a topic of concern.

As Margo Adair and John Rensenbrink explained, "SPAKA [writing the
document that would become the platform] was to create a participatory process to formulate a Green platform for the U.S.—to create an identity."[10] As
Green organizers realized, participating in the process of democracy forms relationships among individuals previously unknown to one another, and the formation of these relationships creates a collectively articulated identity. This
identity is a central concept of radical democracy. Many of the new social
movements—the women's movement, the American Indian Movement, the
Black Panther movement, the queer movement—have been formulated around
the idea of identity politics. Activists wondering how to reinvigorate and build
coalitions among the various movements for social change have yearned for a
vehicle that would offer the organizing force of identity politics but have been
unable to imagine an identity broad enough to affirm difference yet coherent
enough to provide the means of articulating a shared agenda.[11] Chantal Mouffe
suggests that vehicle may be found in the concept of citizenship, an identity
formed through the practice of direct, participatory democracy.[12] But what
identity is constructed when social movements participate in the practice of
liberal democracy? While Greens hoped that principles articulated in the Ten
Key Values would guide and govern Green participation in electoral politics,
some feared that the present political structure would overpower any Greens
campaigning for or elected to public office beyond the local level. In 1996, the
Ralph Nader presidential campaign exemplified many of these hopes and fears.

The Ralph Nader Presidential Campaign

How could a movement founded on such values as "decentralization" and
"grassroots, participatory democracy" come to support a man who would neither join the Green Party nor run on its state or national platforms in his
candidacy for the highest elected office in the United States? If such a campaign
were to be launched in the 1996 presidential election, this question had to be
raised and resolved at least two years in advance.[13] In January 1995, the former

New Mexico Green candidate for lieutenant governor, Steve Schmidt, approached two California Greens to discuss the possibility of using the successful New Mexico platform as a model to bring electoral and direct action Greens together. As it stood, the national platform provided no guidance for nominating or endorsing a national candidate, much less for implementing policies drawn from the Ten Key Values on a national level, omissions that might even be interpreted as a mandate against such a campaign. As the primary author of the New Mexico platform, Schmidt was able to obtain private funding to support his work for several months while he adapted his platform to a national context. Meanwhile, the two California Greens—Mike Feinstein of Santa Monica and Greg Jan from Oakland—agreed to develop a proposal for a forty-state Green party in 1996. By June 1995, just a month before the national Green gathering in Albuquerque, Feinstein and Jan had distributed their proposal to Greens via e-mail, enclosing a survey that would be tallied and used to facilitate discussion at the Albuquerque gathering.

According to the proposal, the reasons to form a forty-state Green party were many (Feinstein and Jan were reluctant to call it a "national Green party" just yet). A recent Times Mirror poll had shown that 57 percent of the public supported the idea of a third party; moreover, other possible contenders for that role, the New Party and Labor Party Advocates, hadn't tried to organize nationally and, organizationally speaking, were relatively recent efforts. In contrast, the Greens had a ten-year history of activism, and many Greens had already gained experience running candidates at the local, county, and state levels. If any political organization on the progressive Left was going to step in to the vacuum created by the rightward swing of the Democrats, the Greens were most prepared to make that move. And the historical context indicated that such a move could be well received: the passage of both NAFTA and GATT under the Clinton administration, Clinton's failure to deliver on campaign promises such as universal health care, and the unresponsiveness of the Democrats to their traditional constituencies had created a situation in which only 37 percent of the public was participating in electoral politics (a statistic representing voter participation in the November 1994 congressional elections). Invoking the Greens' recent success in New Mexico, where a prominent Democrat (Roberto Mondragon) defected to join the Greens and ran a gubernatorial campaign that prompted a dramatic increase in Green activism across the state, Feinstein and Jan argued that a "name" candidate in a Green presidential campaign could have the same "coattails effect," obtaining national publicity for Green ideas and ultimately building the membership into a national alternative party. At the end of their proposal was a timeline, suggesting the deadlines for making progress toward such a visionary goal: if the survey were approved at Albuquerque, the ideas could be more widely discussed in the fall, possibly leading to a decision by November 22, the first state party qualification deadline. The survey solicited feedback on both the forty-state proposal and the idea of a presidential campaign in 1996 and invited suggestions for possible presidential and vice-presidential candidates.

At the Albuquerque national gathering, Feinstein, Jan, and Schmidt held a session on the forty-state Green party proposal and the survey concerning Greens' receptivity to the idea of a Green presidential candidate in 1996. Although little over 20 percent of those receiving the survey had responded to it, the responses were 90 percent in favor of both proposals. To Green movement activists, it appeared that only those who favored such a campaign had responded to the survey, making it statistically unsound to conclude that there was widespread support for a presidential campaign. Moreover, serious dissent regarding the possibility of fielding a presidential candidate was aired in the session, with movement activists voicing the same objections John Rensenbrink had heard when he proposed the idea at the 1989 Eugene gathering six years before: the Greens weren't ready, there weren't yet parties in all the states, there wasn't the multicultural alliance building Greens had wanted to see, and there simply wasn't the grassroots base to support such a campaign. Nonetheless, Feinstein and Jan went ahead, and at the Green Party of California statewide meeting on September 16–17, they advanced and obtained approval for a proposal regarding the presidential primary. In the absence of any other guidelines, the proposal set up a "receptive" process, so that if a suitable national candidate appeared, the Green Party of California would have a process for responding.

In mid-October, Ralph Nader told Rogers Worthington of the *Chicago Tribune* that he was considering being on the California ballot because of Clinton's vacillation on deregulatory measures covering securities fraud, telecommunications, legal services, and welfare. And when Clinton approved legislation abolishing the fifty-five-mile-per-hour speed limit, Nader became even more emphatic.[14] It was exactly the opportunity Feinstein and Jan had wanted. Drafting an invitation letter to Nader, they were able to obtain signatures from more than forty progressive activists in California—among them Robert Benson from Loyola Law School, Medea Benjamin of Global Exchange, David Brower from Earth Island Institute, Randy Hayes from the Rainforest Action Network, Michael Parenti, Ramona Ripston, Ernest Callenbach, Peter Camejo, Claire Greensfelder, and Ted Hayes—offering persuasive evidence that the invitation was a popular one. Once Nader responded in the affirmative, the California Green Party activated its formal "receptive" process, obtaining approval from the Campaigns and Candidates Working Group, the Statewide Coordinating Committee, and then the county representatives. With one or two representatives from every active county voicing their approval, the secretary of state was notified, and Nader's acceptance statement was released on November 27.

What did Nader's candidacy mean for Greens in other states? Initially, Nader agreed only to run on the March 1996 California primary ballot, but his acceptance statement noted that his campaign "will be just as serious as citizens choose to make it." Green electoralists were very serious. For those in states that had already obtained ballot access, the process was as simple as obtaining approval from state party members and drafting a letter of invitation to Nader. Within a month, John Rensenbrink had approached Nader about running on the Maine ballot and Tony Affigne had followed suit in Rhode Island. By the time of the endorsing convention in August, Nader was on the ballot in twelve states that held a potential 127 electoral votes: Alaska (3), California (54), Colorado (8), Hawaii (4), Iowa (7), Maine (4), Nevada (4), New Jersey (15), New Mexico (5), Oregon (7), Utah (5), and Washington (11). Nader was listed as a Green Party candidate in all but two of these states: Oregon, where the Pacific Party was planning to change its name to Green, and Washington, where he was listed as an Independent. Since there are 538 electoral college votes, a presidential candidate must garner a minimum of 270 to win the election—or have the potential to win that many votes. If Nader could be placed on the ballot in enough states by the start of the fall presidential debates, he would have a greater chance of polling more than 5 percent of the popular vote (roughly 5,230,000 votes, based on the 1992 presidential election), thereby qualifying the Greens to receive approximately $3.8 million in federal funds to organize their next presidential campaign, in the year 2000. To receive those funds, however, Greens needed to show a history of organizing from previous years, a history of being a national party with a national office. Though the electoralists held the limelight, the movement base—as organized through the Greens/Green Party U.S.A.—held the history. The Green Politics Network, the G/GPUSA, and all unaffiliated state Green parties would have to come together under the G/GPUSA name in order to be eligible for the federal campaign funds.

These were the concerns and motivations of Green electoralists going in to the August 1996 Green national gathering at UCLA. Given their recent successes, they were practically jubilant. But all was not rosy in Green-land; many grassroots Greens had objections that surfaced early on in California, where just over twenty thousand out of eighty thousand registered California Greens (only one in four) had bothered to vote in the March primary. In the year preceding the Nader campaign, California Greens were barely able to get a quorum of fifty at a state party meeting. If the Nader campaign was going to resuscitate and dramatically increase a faltering Green presence as the Nader campaigners predicted, why were only one in four Greens voting in the primary? According to Greens at the grassroots, nonparticipation was one way Greens could voice their dissent from the electoralists and the processes behind the Nader campaign, which many Green movement activists perceived as fundamentally undemocratic.

Green dissenters were concerned about running a national campaign before developing a national grassroots base, but they had other objections as well. First, some Greens opposed Nader's candidacy on the basis of Nader himself: if Greens were genuinely committed to candidate accountability, they argued, why choose for our first presidential candidate a man who not only did not belong to the Green Party but refused to run on our platform? By what means would such a candidate be held accountable? Although Nader's history of activism and political involvement seemed impeccable, some Greens were dismayed to see the holistic Green vision reduced to the two issues Nader articulated in his "Concord Principles" and which formed the basis of his own platform: corporate accountability and the tools of democracy.[15] Moreover, many Greens found that Nader had been strangely silent on issues of identity politics: activists in the gay and lesbian movement, the civil rights movement, the American Indian Movement, the women's movement, and the animal rights movement could find little in Nader's history which addressed their concerns. These Greens pointed out that a Green commitment to gender balance and multicultural diversity indicated that in a precedent-setting national campaign, Greens would be most internally consistent with their values if they selected a woman and/or a person of color from within the Green movement as their first national candidate. Green dissenters were also concerned about Nader's running mate and hoped the person selected would meet the qualifications that Nader did not, thereby giving the Green ticket the kind of gender balance, racial balance, and accountability that the Greens had long advocated (albeit in the subordinate position of vice-presidential candidate).

Other concerns focused on the undemocratic process of the Nader campaigners and the way a presidential campaign had been "decided on" by a small group of self-selected leaders within the Greens and offered to the majority of Greens merely for their approval. Many California Greens were not notified that a "receptive" process for a presidential candidate was going to be submitted for approval at their statewide gathering in September 1995; later, after Nader had already been invited to run, the "receptive" process was activated, and each county got one vote—not a vote by consensus, or by delegates, but a winner-take-all vote, which seemed fundamentally opposed to Green values. As a consequence of this "receptive" process of polling counties individually, most California Greens were never offered the opportunity to participate in the decision whereby a specific candidate was invited to be on the ballot for the presidential primary. On a larger scale, owing to California's numerous votes in the electoral college, any decision made in California was likely to have national implications; yet the self-selected leadership in California did not consult with Greens in other states in a way that made room for voicing, acknowledging, and considering dissent. Instead, at every step, the actions of the electoralists were made known to the membership, the grassroots were given time to voice their objections and their concerns—and then the de facto leadership proceeded as planned. Nowhere was this process of replacing grassroots democracy with an oligarchic rule of the elite more evident than in the national platform-writing process that accompanied the presidential campaign: inviting the participation of Greens through e-mail (hardly a democratic medium, even in 1996), a four-member "ad-hoc Green Platform Committee" with Steve Schmidt in the lead produced a national platform that was distributed at the August 1996 national gathering, ostensibly replacing the previous national platform, which had been written with widespread grassroots participation in a three-year process. Early in 1996, the situation grew even more tense as Green electoralists competed for leadership among themselves. In Washington D.C., Linda Martin of the Green Politics Network set up a Draft Nader Clearinghouse, which competed directly with the California campaign efforts as well as the G/GPUSA national clearinghouse in upstate New York. By dominating media coverage of the campaign, offering legal advice designed to support the electoralists' activities, and sending paid and unpaid organizers into states that had explicitly chosen not to organize a Nader campaign, the Draft Nader Clearinghouse eventually prevailed.[16] Ironically, in their haste to make history as the party that opened up democracy, Green electoralists were losing sight of a key Green value about the inevitable linkage between the means and the ends.

The process of selecting Nader's vice-presidential candidate serves as a case in point. As the objections of some Greens to the Nader campaign were made known, it became evident that the vice-presidential position could be used as a vehicle to assuage those concerns. By mid-April, a set of criteria had been formulated: ideally, the candidate would be a woman, a person of color, a member of the Greens, a grassroots activist, a well-known figure—and someone whose campaigning would not compete with that of Nader, who had vowed to spend no more than five thousand dollars on his campaign and thereby avoid all federal regulations about campaign expenditures. Since no national decision was forthcoming, and electoralists in various states needed to gather signatures to place Nader on the November ballot, states began selecting "favorite daughters" to stand in as vice-presidential candidates, with the understanding that they might be asked to step down once Nader's chosen running mate was made known. Through this process, seven vice-presidential candidates were in the running at the time of the Greens' nominating convention in August: Anne Goeke, a Euro-American Green from Pennsylvania, who was on the ballot in at least nine states; Deborah Howes, a Euro-American from Oregon, who was on the Pacific Party ballot there; Muriel Tillinghast, an African-American member of the Greens and the Independent Progressive Politics Network, who had been active with the Student Non-violent Coordinating Committee and the civil rights movement and was on the ballot in New York; Krista Paradise, a Euro-American Green running on the ballot in Colorado; Madelyn Hoffman, a Euro-American environmental activist and founder of the Grass Roots Environmental Organization, who was on the ballot in New Jersey; Bill Boteler, a Euro-American environmentalist who was on the ballot in the District of Columbia; and Winona LaDuke, a Chippewa activist and founder of the White Earth Land Recovery Project and the Indigenous Women's Network, who was being considered for the ballot in Connecticut and Texas. Although LaDuke was not a member of the Greens and had previously refused invitations to run for elected office with the Green Party in Minnesota, her record of activism was internationally respected, and popular sentiment among Green electoralists was that LaDuke would be the candidate most acceptable to Nader. But this sentiment was not universally shared among Green women.

At the 1996 Green national gathering, the Women's Caucus met daily to develop a unified position on the vice-presidential candidacy: some women were concerned that only Green women be considered for the position; others challenged the president/vice-president relationship as a heterosexist model, in which the vice-president was feminized into powerlessness, and critiqued any cooperation with the vice-presidential selection process as a strategy for co-opting feminist concerns; and still others saw the Nader campaign simply as an opportunity to publicize the Green Party and urged others to support this effort. After lengthy debate, the Women's Caucus reached an agreement and presented its decision to the nominating convention, where the caucus was warmly received: with Goeke, Hoffman, Howes, Paradise, and Tillinghast present, and with a videotape of LaDuke, the Women's Caucus announced its decision that the vice-presidential position must be filled by a slate of candidates who would act as a "cabinet" of advisers. In this way, the Women's Caucus explicitly rejected the winner-take-all, celebrity-seeking framework of electoral politics and affirmed the contributions of each woman involved. Their victory was short-lived, however: two days after the nominating convention, the Draft Nader Clearinghouse announced that Nader would choose his own running mate from the slate of candidates and urged Greens to "maintain unity [i.e., silence any objections] throughout this process."

Other events of the so-called nominating convention on August 19, 1996, at UCLA brought the paradoxes of a Green presidential campaign into focus. The first panel presented an overview of the Nader campaign, featuring the speakers who had made it happen. These seven speakers (six men and one woman, all white) told the Green gathering that "this is a whole new model of electoral politics." As one speaker conceded, "There's mostly men on this panel, but we realize that women constitute 70 percent of the movement in this country." In the sessions throughout the afternoon, no request was made and no vote was taken to nominate or endorse a Green presidential candidate. When Ralph Nader took the podium at 6:00 P.M. (and held it until 8:15), asking for or accepting the Greens' nomination was no part of his erudite speech on the history and importance of democracy. As he mounted his scathing critique of corporate control, electoralists in the Green audience could not restrain themselves and began chanting, "Go, Ralph, go! Go, Ralph, go!" To his credit, Nader appeared extremely uncomfortable with this outburst and gestured for silence. "The intonation should be, 'Go, *we* go!'" Nader corrected them. Obediently, the audience took up the change and chanted "Go, we go!" at this juncture and at several other points in Nader's speech. The chant became part of the signature of the Draft Nader Clearinghouse, which appended "GOWEGO!" to the end of all its messages throughout the rest of the campaign. The fusion of these several words into one symbolized the transformation of the Green movement within the structure of national electoral politics and the effects of top-down decision making on the creativity and authority of the grassroots. Resistance, critical thought, plurality of voices, dialogue—all were subsumed as never before through the processes of this national campaign.

Thus, the Nader presidential campaign exposed significant differences in the way Greens viewed the role of leadership in a democracy. Certainly, almost every Green was familiar with Freeman's "Tyranny of Structurelessness," which argues that a structure for leadership and for accountability must be established early if a group is to function democratically. During the collaborative writing process for the original national platform, the Seattle local warned, "Persons who have leadership capability should be aware constantly of the seduction of becoming a hero or charismatic personality" and urged Green groups to pay careful attention to participation and accountability in decision making.[17] John Rensenbrink, founder of the Green Politics Network and author of *The Greens and the Politics of Transformation,* emphasized that "in no area of life is the problem of means and ends more critical than in questions of leadership." Four years before his endorsement of the Nader campaign, he argued persuasively against the leadership style exemplified in the dominant culture: "The charismatic personality, so assiduously promoted and embellished by established media, and so much emulated by rising politicians of the oligarchy, is regarded by the Greens as a big part of the problem of politics today. The packaging of persons into 'Hollywood'-type stars intensifies the artificiality of politics. It estranges the person who 'leads' from the people who are 'led,' and robs the person who is packaged in this manner of an authentic life."[18] Greens seemed to agree that the dominant style of leadership was a patriarchal one that focused power and decision-making authority at the top of a pyramid, leaving little room for flexibility or input from the grassroots. Margo Adair, an ecofeminist who facilitated the national platform-writing process and led many workshops on combating racism, had both written and spoken on the importance of moving from leadership to empowerment through collaboration within and among Green communities.[19] The radical feminist distinction between old-style leadership forms that dominate ("power over") and feminist leadership that empowers the community ("power to") was well known in the first decade of the Green movement.

As the Greens moved into electoral politics, however, the definition of leadership shifted as well. At the 1995 national Green gathering in Albuquerque, Keiko Bonk, chair of the County Council on the Big Island of Hawai'i, described a different kind of Green leadership in her keynote address:

Twenty years [sic] of Green politics should have taught us a few things about ourselves as Greens. We are not all equal, and we never will be. . . . Every Green must ask, "Can I lead, can I learn to lead, or should I accept that my sacrifice will come as support for others?" No

one is always a leader. Good leaders get to be good leaders by supporting good leaders and those who know more than they do. There is
nothing shameful in serving someone who knows more than you, or in
serving someone who has faults.[20]

Some Greens perceived Bonk's interpretation of leadership as a *realo* perspective, developed from her own struggles and achievements in office. In Bonk's
view, leadership meant not only gaining access to elected office but, once
elected, "using power to serve justice" and fighting "to gain majority control of
democratic institutions." This liberal or "power feminist" perspective was more
closely aligned with traditional leadership models and was the form articulated
through the practice of the Nader campaigners. As Kwazi Nkrumah, a labor
organizer who had been with the Greens since 1990, explained, the Nader campaign brought out the fact that the Greens were experiencing an internal class
war: the electoralists spearheading the campaign were organizing in a way that
fit with their class background, and because no similarly placed leadership had
emerged from the grassroots Greens, the electoralists easily stepped into what
they perceived as a vacuum of leadership.[21] This shift in leadership—from a
feminist, participatory model of collaboration and empowerment to a traditional model of decision making from the top and support (but not input)
from the bottom—served as one indicator that the Green movement had
changed its focus, from its radical beginnings in social and cultural transformation to a liberal movement for obtaining power and making changes within the
present system.

The move from radical to liberal could also be seen in Nader's own conception of democracy, a populist version of liberal democracy that foreclosed
the possibility of building genuine coalitions across differences of race, gender,
and sexual preference and with communities that had traditionally been regarded as potential allies for the Greens. The de facto leadership of the Greens
had chosen Nader not only for his popular appeal and his history of civic
activism but for his willingness to confront the corporate control of government. Instead of the United States being a government "of, by, and for the
people," Nader was fond of saying, it had become a government "of the Exxons,
by the General Motors, and for the Duponts."[22] Reclaiming democracy, according to Nader, would require implementing fundamental changes in the political
system, replacing the current winner-take-all system with a form of proportional representation, placing limits on candidates' campaign expenditures,

guaranteeing free media coverage to all candidates, instituting term limits with a maximum of twelve years in office, and placing "none of the above" on the ballot—all changes the Greens had also advocated. Nader also supported initiative, referendum, and recall, a system that allows citizens to place measures directly on the ballot without going through their elected representatives and that Greens in several states had used effectively.[23] Greens largely agreed with Nader's position that "significant, enduring change will require an institutionalized shift of power from corporations and government to ordinary Americans."[24] The method for achieving that shift was articulated in Nader's Concord Principles, which spelled out the components of his "new democracy tool box."

According to Nader, the roles for citizens in a democracy could be divided into the public and private spheres. "We all know that as private citizens we have to take care of our families and personal well-being," he explained. "But, if we live in a democracy, we also have to be public citizens. We have to work on problems of the community—making our government responsive, making the economy more beneficial to more people."[25] Consistently, Nader identified six roles that citizens play in a democracy: voter, taxpayer, consumer, worker, shareholder, student. Under the current system of corporate control, he argued, citizens were virtually powerless in each of these roles, and hence the first task of any social reformer must be the reconstruction of democracy: "Without this reconstruction of our democracy . . . even the most well-intentioned politicians campaigning for your vote cannot deliver, if elected. Nor can your worries about poverty, discrimination, joblessness, the troubled conditions of education, environment, street and suite crime, budget deficits, costly and inadequate health care, and energy boondoggles, to list a few, be addressed constructively and enduringly."[26]

Though Nader's dual messages of corporate accountability and democratic renewal were particularly crucial in a presidential campaign whose issues were largely defined by Democratic incumbent Bill Clinton and Republican challenger Bob Dole (Tweedledum and Tweedledee, as Nader would say), from an ecofeminist perspective there were significant gaps in Nader's conception of democracy. For example, the division of democracy and citizenship into the realms of public and private meant that Nader could avoid taking a position on women's right to reproductive choice or on same-sex marriages, declaring both to be "private" issues that he would not address.[27] Moreover, Nader's six-fold conception of citizenship offers no room for emphasizing cultural or racial diversity, gender equity, or ecological economics and protections. In effect, the rhetoric of citizenship invoked by Nader serves to conflate human differences of race, class, gender, and sexuality into a unitary identity of "citizen," which can then be (and has been) manipulated by the dominant class to serve its exclusive interests, all the while excusing this manipulation as a service to "the common good." Because Greens had not scrutinized the concept of democracy or developed a Green definition of "the common good," most Greens were persuaded that expanding democracy would benefit every citizen group equally.

Nowhere were the limitations of Nader's democracy more evident than in his refusal to take a stand on Proposition 209, the so-called California Civil Rights Initiative, designed to restrict state affirmative action programs. On Pacifica Radio's "Democracy Now" program, Nader told cohost Larry Bensky, "I'm not going to take positions for or against [CCRI]. . . . We have to build democracy. We have to turn it into a political issue." Bensky, convinced that CCRI was already "a political issue," pressed his question again, explaining that he had spoken to "many communicy activists—Latinos and African-Americans—who intend to do a lot of organizing" against CCRI. "If you're going to build a political movement in a multiethnic state like California," Bensky concluded, "how can you afford to ignore an issue that is at the top of the agenda of so many potential voters on your side?" But Nader held firm. "People know where I stand on these issues," he asserted, "I just have to focus on the democracy issue."[28] With these words, Nader offered a paradoxical definition of democracy as something both separable from and larger than the issues of social justice. By demanding that activists focus on his version of democracy as the primary issue and a necessary prerequisite to any other goals of social justice, Nader employed the same "one liberation fits all" rhetoric that had been used to unify progressives in the past: in the thirties, the issue was class; in the eighties, it was nuclear power. In each case, this rhetoric functioned to subordinate the aims and interests of marginalized groups to the single issue of concern to the movement leadership. It was a strategy that ultimately failed to build coalitions, by failing to demonstrate a genuine interest in and commitment to the concerns of diverse others.

A few Greens suspected that, just like trickle-down economics, "trickle-down democracy" would never reach those who needed it most. What the Greens needed was a vision of radical democracy, which was already implied in the Green movement at its founding. To understand the difference between liberal democracy and radical democracy, Greens would have to understand the critiques of democracy posed by the New Left and by feminists and consider the findings of ecofeminism.

Feminist Critiques of Liberal Democracy

Whereas the first wave of feminism in the United States focused primarily on issues of exclusion and participation in social and political processes, the second wave has been characterized by its interrogation of those structures. Then and now, liberal feminism shares many of the assumptions of liberalism which inhere in the structures of liberal democracy. These assumptions have more recently been exposed and challenged by feminists of the second wave—radical, Marxist, and socialist feminists who have found a masculinist, elitist bias in the fundamental assumptions of liberalism. Because a thorough discussion of feminism and democracy is beyond the scope of this book, I summarize only those feminist critiques of liberal democracy which have been most influential in shaping ecofeminist democratic thought. If ecofeminists are to develop a democratic theory that adequately accounts for the needs, concerns, and perspectives of not just women but all those disenfranchised others, both human and nonhuman, that theory will have to address certain problematic assumptions of liberalism.

As feminists and political scientists have explained, liberal democracy is based on a specific notion of the individual, with the assumption that human beings are fundamentally rational creatures whose existence is ontologically prior to society ("atomistic, a priori individualism").[29] The rational individuals of liberalism have specific rights that must be protected in the formation of any relationships among them; hence, the social contract is particularly concerned with protecting individuals from society. The most fundamental motivation of these rational individuals is the pursuit of self-interest, called "freedom," which will most likely be in conflict with the self-interest of other rational individuals, especially given liberalism's assumption that there is a scarcity of resources; hence, the relationship among these rational individuals will be competitive. From a liberal perspective, all individuals are equal, and social justice should entail the opportunity for equal participation among individuals. The function of society, then, is to ensure the freedom of all its members to pursue their own self-interest, to receive a fair start in the "race" for material goods, and to act as much as possible without interference from others ("negative liberty"). Liberalism is emphatic in restricting its influence to that realm in which rational individuals compete for material gain (the public) and protecting (but not regulating) individual freedoms or rights outside the public realm (the private). As many feminists have observed, liberalism is based on a conception of the individual as male, as heterosexual, and as the owner of women, children, animals, and nature, whose bodies he may use as he deems suitable or necessary.[30] This liberal notion of the individual provides the defining basis for citizenship in liberal democracy. Hence, one task for feminist and ecofeminist theories of democracy involves redefining not only democracy but citizenship itself.

Mary Dietz has identified two distinct approaches among feminists critiquing liberal democracy: Marxism and maternalism. Marxist feminists have argued that the liberation of women is possible only through the termination of the liberal nation-state, the end of patriarchy, and the transformation of capitalism. Marxist feminists tend to focus on the transformation of structures rather than the philosophical critique of concepts: their vision of a just and democratic society requires transforming capitalist patriarchy into an economy of worker-owned cooperatives based on liberatory egalitarian relationships among workers, along with collective ownership of public services and utilities. Although this transformation would surely offer an improvement over the current oppressive structures, Marxist feminism does not offer an explicit critique of such central political concepts as citizenship, community, freedom, participation, and democracy.[31] In contrast, maternalist feminists have recognized the masculinist bias inhering through all realms (not just production or economics) of the public sphere and have argued for replacing masculinist individualism with the ethics of care and maternalism currently relegated to the private sphere. Drawing on Nancy Chodorow's object-relations theory and Carol Gilligan's moral development theory to distinguish between the masculinist ethic of justice and the feminine ethic of care, maternalist feminists would redefine the democratic citizen in terms of her/his relational capacities, love, and care for others. But as Dietz observes, the maternalist argument is flawed just like any other argument that upholds one side of a dualism against the other.[32] As socialist feminists and ecofeminists have noted, upholding what patriarchal thought has defined as "women's sphere" as morally, ethically, or politically superior to the male sphere leaves intact, and indeed perpetuates, this dualized view of reality, which is the central characteristic of patriarchal thought.

In the end, Dietz argues for a form of democracy that "brings people together as citizens," a practice that transforms the individual "into a special sort of political being, a citizen among other citizens."[33] In short, one could argue that the practice of participatory democracy creates the context for a different kind of identity politics, by expressing the always-shifting identity of the citizen. For feminism, it is crucial to emphasize that the citizens who are constructed through the practice of participatory democracy are not homogeneous; indeed, feminists have criticized civic republicanism for conflating its definition of universal citizenship with homogeneity, an erasure of difference which ultimately functions to secure the dominance of privileged groups that present their interests as "universal" and "the common good." Instead, concerned with protecting difference in such a way that the definition of "citizenship" becomes multiple rather than singular, feminists and ecofeminists have been influenced by the theories of Chantal Mouffe, who defines citizenship in a radical democracy as "an articulating principle that affects the different subject positions of the social agent while allowing for a plurality of specific allegiances and for the respect of individual liberty."[34] Influenced by both postmodernism and feminism, Mouffe is careful to emphasize the numerous and diverse identities of individuals and to observe the limitations of identity politics when based on the assumption of a shared unitary identity that overrides all others. Mouffe's conception of radical democratic citizenship has contributed to an ecofeminist rethinking of democracy.

Ecofeminist Critiques of Democracy

It should come as no surprise that in North America, the ecofeminists who have given the most consideration to the project of democracy have been social ecofeminists whose primary involvement with the Green movement has been through the Left Greens: Ynestra King, Janet Biehl, and Catriona Sandilands. While other ecofeminisms have distanced themselves from the Left (possibly inheriting radical feminism's response to the New Left's exclusion of feminist concerns), ecofeminists trained in social ecology found a more hospitable framework for developing a critique of not only patriarchy but hierarchy and domination as well. At the same time that Left Greens and social ecofeminists were discussing social ecology's theories of radical municipalism, democratic decentralism, and grassroots democracy, social ecofeminists began developing their own critiques of democracy. Reflecting on the first national Green gathering at Amherst, Ynestra King—probably the first ecofeminist to address the connections among ecofeminism, democracy, and the Green movement—emphasized the important contributions ecofeminism had to offer the larger Green movement:

One reason that ecofeminism is essential to the green project is that, in drawing on the Western democratic tradition, the greens are still working with a political legacy that is founded on the repudiation of the organic, the female, the tribal and particular ties between people. Even as greens are resuscitating (and reinventing) the democratic tradition, I am mindful that the original citizen in that tradition is male, propertied, and xenophobic. He has separated himself from the slime and ooze of the earth as a condition for political life.[35]

From King's perspective, the success of the Green movement depended on its responsiveness to the insights of ecofeminism, along with many of the central principles of social ecology. But though her ecofeminism was developed in the context of social ecology, King has repeatedly refused the designation of "social ecofeminist," arguing that ecofeminism should offer a comprehensive critique that need not be divided into various factions. And although King did not develop her remarks about ecofeminism and democracy any further, it is clear that her perspective would have differed considerably from Janet Biehl's.

Biehl's version of social ecofeminism is more closely aligned with social ecology than with the ecofeminism articulated by King or Sandilands. As such, Biehl's social ecofeminist critique of democracy reveals some of the strengths and weaknesses not of ecofeminism per se but of social ecology. As strengths, I would cite its refusal to embrace the dualistic and essentialist equations of cultural feminism (i.e., women/feminism/liberatory and men/patriarchy/oppressive) and its readiness to investigate each topic or circumstance in terms of hierarchy and domination; its clear status as a descendent of the Left; and its acceptance and celebration of the lessons and the experiences of "the Left that was."[36] Its weaknesses include a willingness to salvage the best features of the Western intellectual tradition by excusing or overlooking oppressive features or circumstances that others have considered salient; its insistent anthropocentrism, often articulated in the "first nature/second nature" distinction; and finally, its celebration of reason. Biehl's investigation into the origins of democracy in ancient Greece bears many of these features.[37]

Because many feminists and ecofeminists would find her analysis of ancient democracy too forgiving of Athenian sexism and classism, most relevant to this study is Biehl's nearly unqualified celebration of citizenship as defined through Athenian democracy. "The notion of a common humanity or *humanitas* eventually replaced the blood tie as the basis for political life," writes Biehl, arguing that this definition of citizenship offered greater inclusivity and freedom than the earlier kinship systems, where "the boundaries of exclusion and inclusion are fixed by birth into a tribe." But Biehl contradicts herself here: arguing first that "the attributes that . . . made citizens political equals . . . the human capacities for rationality and ethics . . . are basically universal," she later concedes that "the Athenian *polis* did not actualize the potentiality of its own innovation. All human beings were not in fact admitted to the Athenian *polis*."[38] And why was this? Precisely because "the human capacities for rationality and ethics" which defined citizenship were not recognized as universal attributes after all; the very construction of rationality and ethics was based on an exclusionary strategy requiring that certain humans be denied citizenship.[39] Here, it seems, Biehl's argument would have been altered by considering feminist and postmodernist critiques of false universalism and appeals to the "common good" which end up reinforcing the hegemony of the ruling class. Again, the difficulty can be traced back to social ecology (and, to be fair, this viewpoint is generally shared among the Left) and its rejection of identity politics as "an uncritical assortment of narrow interests," according to Murray Bookchin, writing about movements comprising the New Left: "Their aims should be sought within a *human-oriented* framework, not within an *exclusionary* or *parochial* folk-oriented one."[40] Social ecology conceives of a movement based on the recognition of human differences as fundamentally hostile to the solidarity that is requisite to a truly revolutionary Left. Biehl too has rejected identity politics as a suitable vehicle for organizing, calling it "particularistic" and observing that it may not even be leftist: "There is no reason to believe that an identity group's struggle for its positive ends will necessarily mean that it is committed to ideas such as freedom and face-to-face democracy, or that it will be antistatist and anticapitalist." Instead, Biehl calls for reconceiving a "broad human community" as more potentially liberatory than the "particularism" of identity politics.[41] Here she seems to be trapped in the paradox of liberal democracy, forced to choose between recognizing and defending individual interests, on the one hand, and a politics that transcends individualism and upholds the common good, on the other. But ecofeminists have argued that the interests of both entities must be preserved, for each is connected to the other, and the assumption that these interests are in conflict is itself a characteristic of an oppressive patriarchal system and thus an unsuitable component of a liberatory theory.[42] Chantal Mouffe's conception of the social agent as "constituted by an ensemble of 'subject positions' that can never be totally fixed," and its implications for a radical and plural democracy based on a "chain of equivalences" linking various liberatory struggles, offers a possible resolution to this paradox by allowing for the interests of both individual citizens and society.[43]

The radical democratic theory of Ernesto Laclau and Chantal Mouffe,[44] particularly its application to questions involving ecology and social justice, has been explored at greater length by Catriona Sandilands, a Canadian social ecofeminist. Sandilands has been a participant in Left Green gatherings in the United States (to date, no Left Green Network has developed in Canada), has contributed to Green journals, and has worked to develop the Toronto Greens.[45] At the 1991 Left Green gathering in Chicago, Sandilands led the move to change the Left Green principle of "social ecofeminism" to "women's liberation," ostensibly to make the concept more understandable and inviting to newcomers. But most recently, her work has focused on the relationship between ecofeminism and democracy.[46] According to Sandilands, ecological democratic theories must move beyond the unitary subjects of identity politics and embrace a movement of postmodern selves in relationship. Such is the current political practice already, Sandilands observes; "it's the theory that's catching up."[47]

Sandilands's applications of Laclau and Mouffe's theory of radical democracy to movements of radical environmentalism, and particularly to ecofeminism, make an important contribution toward advancing a dialogue on ecofeminism and democracy. In her essay "From Natural Identity to Radical Democracy," Sandilands explores recent attempts to reconceive nature as a subject rather than an object. Influenced by feminist critiques of dualism and the separation of self and other inherent in Western thought, those who reconceive nature as a subject inadvertently create another problem, that of "speaking nature," "speaking for nature," or "speaking as nature." Although Sandilands agrees that "constructing nature as a subject is the task of environmentalism, in some form or another," and that "the move toward an identity for nature is . . . a deeply democratic one," the problem it creates involves "the impossibility of finding a nature to be spoken democratically, unmediated by processes of subjectivation."[48] In effect, "nature defies representation as discourse," Sandilands notes. "The moment where nature emerges into discourse is always already a moment of its social construction, a moment where it becomes something else."[49] Moreover, the "identity" of nature is not unitary but multiple. Constituting nature as a subject in accordance with the rhetorical strategy of identity politics is not the best technique for developing an ecofeminist theory of democracy, for the very reason that, from an ecofeminist perspective, identity is not unitary and fixed, nor is it constituted in isolation, as liberal theory would have us believe: rather, identity is constructed through relationships. As Sandilands explains, "Politics do not emerge from identity, but identity, incomplete, partial, and transient, emerges from politics."[50] Sandilands's critique exposes the limitations of identity politics as a vehicle for developing a theory of radical ecological democracy.

The alternative Sandilands suggests is based on Laclau and Mouffe's conception of a "chain of equivalences among democratic struggles," emphasizing "the relatedness of a variety of forms of oppression and liberation." This "chain of equivalences" seems very close to the perspective advanced by ecofeminists: the idea that the oppression of women, people of color, the poor, queers, nonhuman animals, nature itself "exist as equivalences, as occupying the same space in relation to the antifeminist, antiecological Other."[51] As Mouffe is careful to underline, this "relation of *equivalence* does not eliminate *difference*—that would be simple identity. It is only insofar as democratic differences are opposed to forces or discourses which negate all of them that these differences are substitutible for each other."[52] Exploring the relationship between ecofeminism and democracy, Sandilands effectively shifts the focus of investigation from the particular *identities* of various oppressed groups to the *relationships* between those groups and the oppressive structure, arguing that democracy consists not in the identities of specific individuals but in the relationships among social actors. Making connections among the various movements for social and ecological justice, ecofeminism (and other radical democratic theories) establishes a "chain of equivalences" that includes nature in the struggles for social transformation and that is itself an articulation of the unfolding logic of democracy: "Coalition is not simply useful; it defines the potential of each element in the chain. The creation of coalition rests upon the strengthening of a chain of struggles constructed not through the recognition of a privileged, revolutionary subject, but through the solidification of equivalences between struggles." For Sandilands, ecology requires democracy, just as democracy, according to its own internal logic, must include ecology: "Struggles for nature must be, ultimately, radically democratic because there is no other way of struggling 'as nature'; instead, we produce nature through the process of articulation itself."[53] Certainly, from an ecofeminist perspective, the political "individual" is fundamentally interconnected, constructed through relationships with both human and nonhuman nature. Democracy without ecology is not just anthropocentric but acontextual, offering an incomplete and thus inaccurate description of the social and political community.

There are two potential problems with Sandilands's theory. First, the chain of equivalences is constructed in opposition to the "antiecological Other," a construction that perpetuates the structure of dualism that many have argued is a characteristic feature of oppression. This problem may be a feature of Mouffe's thinking rather than of Sandilands's: indeed, Mouffe has argued, "To construct a 'we' it must be distinguished from the 'them' and that means establishing a frontier, defining an 'enemy.'"[54] Second, the chain of equivalences links all oppressed struggles but offers no explicit means of linking with those who may experience few of the costs of oppression and perhaps even some of the benefits (i.e., white heterosexual men who are neither poor nor working class) and yet who share a commitment to liberatory struggles nonetheless. Obviously, these problems are conceptually related. One task of an ecofeminist theory of democracy might be to explore the paths for linking white men of privilege to work in solidarity with the oppressed, empowered by the recognition that these struggles are inherently interconnected to their own lives whether or not they experience oppression directly. One way to foreground this interconnection is through an ecofeminist reconception of human identity as fundamentally relational, born out of and developed through relationships with other humans, animals, and nonhuman nature itself. These criticisms notwithstanding, the shift Sandilands has provided from liberal democracy's individualistic definitions of identity to radical democracy's relational chain of equivalences offers the groundwork for developing a new concept of citizenship compatible with the ecological democracy she imagines.[55]

Already, outlines for an ecofeminist reconception of citizenship have been drawn in the work of ecofeminist philosopher Val Plumwood, who has been actively involved with the Australian Greens. In "Has Democracy Failed Ecology? An Ecofeminist Perspective," Plumwood provides a critique of liberal democracy and several departure points for developing an ecofeminist conception of citizenship.[56] According to Plumwood, the defining feature and the superiority of democracy (as contrasted to other political systems) lies, ostensibly, in the ability to detect, respond to, and correct problems within the system. But the form of democracy currently in practice, liberal democracy—a form that combines representative democracy with liberal market economics, or liberal capitalism—is responsive primarily to the concerns of the elite, ignoring the problems, needs, and concerns of society's least privileged. Because those most oppressed (by race, gender, economics, nationality, or an intersection of these) are also those seen as "closest to nature," they are the ones to feel the first and the worst effects of liberal capitalism's assault on nature.[57] By failing to detect and respond to the concerns of the least privileged, then, liberal democracy effectively ignores an important source of ecological information and correction. Positing both social justice and ecological responsiveness as criteria of "adequacy for democracy," Plumwood argues that liberal democracy has failed both democracy and ecology.

Sadly, mainstream environmental movements and many movements for social justice continue to seek resolution of their concerns within the framework of liberal democracy. Seduced by a liberal definition of success as achieving reforms within the existing system, and enticed by the (elusive) promise of quick results, these movements become stuck in a series of repetitive and largely ineffectual strategies that exhaust activists and lead to disillusionment and loss of vision.[58] Within the framework of liberalism, moreover, democracy's failure to respond to the efforts of such activists is blamed on the individual citizen, whose voter participation record has not been consistent, whose purchases have included items wrapped with excessive packaging, whose aluminum cans have been carelessly discarded rather than filling the curbside recycling sacks, and whose efforts to seek justice through the channels of representative democracy have just not been persistent enough. By blaming the individual, of course, the system is spared, and because liberal democracy is presented as the only form of democracy and the best political system available, activists are induced to believe there is no alternative but to "try harder" within the system. But liberal democracy is not interchangeable with democracy per se; rather, it is only one form of democracy, and a partial form in that it responds primarily to the privileged elite. By failing to be ecologically responsive—by failing to respond to the needs and concerns of the least privileged—liberal democracy reveals itself as a political system that is incapable of providing social and ecological justice.

Liberal democracy's pretense of social equality and responsiveness, Plumwood argues, rests on liberalism's dualized notion of political and economic citizenship. Individuals are offered participation in the processes of liberal democracy via political citizenship, an identity enacted in the public realm through the role of "voter." Meanwhile, larger and larger areas of economic activity are being reconceived as events occurring in the private realm, where the freedom of the economic citizen to pursue his own self-interest is protected from public control (i.e., international trade agreements such as NAFTA and GATT protect corporate profits against regulations that would address the health and concerns of individuals or the environment). The public realm, considered the proper arena for democratic control, is offered up to political citizens through the process of voting. Yet political citizens in a liberal democracy are largely prevented from affecting the shape and distribution of power. Why? Since the majority of power in liberal democracy is not political but economic, and since economics are increasingly privatized and therefore exempt from democratic control, genuine transformations of power are not accessible through the electoral system. Resolving the dualism of citizenship by showing that radical democracy reconceives the public and the private as equally political realms, Plumwood holds, is the best alternative for achieving social and ecological justice.

Plumwood's critique of liberal democracy reveals that the gendered separation of public and private is an aspect of the "liberal recognition of political but not economic and ecological citizenship [which] rests on a form of mind/body dualism."[59] Here Plumwood suggests not one but three different forms of citizenship in an ecological democracy: political, economic, and ecological. In liberal democracy, these several forms of citizenship have been reduced to one— the political, ostensibly one who votes—and that one is not inclusive. But Plumwood's fragmentation of citizenship sidesteps the possibility of elite appropriation by foregrounding those aspects of citizenship containing roles and responsibilities the elite would deny. A trifold conception of citizenship fits well with Sandilands's concept of radical democracy and its chain of equivalences: in short, the citizenship logically compatible with an ecofeminist theory of radical democracy will have to be multiple, not singular. Moreover, these multiple forms of citizenship cannot be retrieved without addressing other forms of exclusion and denial that underlie their conception.

Plumwood's theory of the master model (an intersection of race, class, gender, and species domination which usefully complicates earlier arguments addressing the "male" domination of women and nature) explains the ways that liberal dualisms such as mind/body, male/female, public/private, reason/emotion, and culture/nature underlie the structure of Western thought and are characterized by a valuation of one side of the dualism (the male/mind/reason/culture aspect) and a corresponding devaluation of the other (the female/body/emotion/nature aspect).[60] For liberal democracy, the separation of the public and the political from the private realm, and the corresponding associations of the public/political realm with the rational, the human, and the male, is itself a dualism that can be seen as part of the master model, a conceptual structure that includes but is not limited to dualisms such as

public   private
male   female

reason	emotion
*order	chaos
*commonalities	difference
universal	particular
*civic	domestic
*rights	responsibilities
culture	nature
realm of freedom	realm of necessity
*first world	two-thirds world
*production	consumption
production	reproduction
*politics	ethics

The dualisms marked with an asterisk (*) are not directly named as part of Plumwood's original framework but have been addressed elsewhere in her work or developed by other ecofeminists; because these dualisms function in the same way as the others, they appear to be additional aspects of Plumwood's master model.

Although they do not refer to Plumwood's framework of the master model, ecofeminists Maria Mies and Vandana Shiva have written extensively on the operations of colonialism that involve a dualized separation of the first world from the two-thirds world, the realm of freedom from the realm of necessity, the realm of production from the realm of reproduction and consumption, culture from nature, white from nonwhite, and of course masculine from feminine.[61] They explain how the logic of colonialism has reversed perceptions of the actual flow of goods and resources, so that the first world is perceived as the realm of freedom and production, while the colonized two-thirds world is perceived as the realm of mindless and valueless reproduction; moreover, the colonized are depicted as needy and dependent on handouts from the first world, when in fact it is the colonial practices and overconsumption of the first world which have created real material poverty in the two-thirds world. In the conclusion of their book *Ecofeminism*, Mies and Shiva explain that there can be no genuine freedom for everyone until we find freedom within the realm of necessity, the realm of nature and subsistence, rather than industrial capitalism's realm of limitless production.

Although liberal democracy's central dualism has seemed to be the gendered division between public and private, other associated dualisms have required that politics be defined as opposed to ethics, and rights as contrasted with responsibilities. In the public realm of politics, all value is instrumentalized, as any activist knows: it is virtually impossible to be taken seriously in a public hearing on wetlands preservation, for example, if an activist articulates any of the ethical values that may form the primary grounds of her activism. To purchase credibility, activists have been restricted to using the language of the public sphere: the linguistic currency of rights, production, freedom, cost/benefit, and so forth. Why are we so surprised when our efforts fail, achieve minimal improvements, or succeed only to be reversed a few years later? Nature's value cannot be articulated or maintained in the public realm of liberal democracy. As Marilyn Waring's work has shown, the problem is hardly limited to the United States: international accounting systems—which tally up activities in the realm of production—are based on an anthropocentric denial of nature's productivity, the labor of people in colonized or less industrialized nations, and much of women's work as well.[62] Although the production profits are made in the public sphere, the role of economic citizenship is denied in liberal democracies: in this way, the political citizen can enjoy the *rights* of profit while avoiding the *responsibilities* of its associated costs—which are borne largely by women, the colonized, the animals, and the earth itself.

Ecofeminists have criticized the gendered dualism that divides ethical language into rights and responsibilities and have tended to avoid this language altogether in developing theory.[63] The problem with rights-based language, as feminists have noted, is the fact that it is grounded in a notion of autonomous individualism, which is (not coincidentally) central to liberalism. Using the rhetoric of rights, one would have to accept the idea of a central individual whose rights-worthy characteristics might be recognized in marginalized others, and based on their similarities to that rights-bearing individual, these others might also be extended certain rights. The rhetoric of rights is incapable of extending value to different others. As a theory that opposes hierarchy and values diversity, ecofeminism is unlikely to find much use for rights-based ethics. But the rhetoric of responsibilities has not been popular with ecofeminists either, for the simple reason that this language often subordinates the needs and interests of the "responsible" individual. In effect, rights and responsibilities, like the gendered dualisms of masculinity and femininity, are defined in such a way as to benefit the master: the masculine rights-bearer is allowed to retain an exclusive focus on self, pursuing self-interest above all else. As Plumwood has explained, in this framework egoism is perceived as both normal and rational, whereas altruism is a problem to be explained. Not so for the feminine ethic of responsibilities, which tends to focus on relationships and carries the potential of subordinating the interests of the feminine self. Neither rights nor responsibilities provides the language suitable for an ecofeminist ethical theory.

The reason for this unsuitability has to do with the associated conceptions of the self: whereas rights-based ethics assumes an autonomous individual self, responsibilities-based ethics assumes a self-in-relationship to such a degree that the individuality of the self may be obscured. As a way of transcending this dualism, ecofeminists have conceived of an ecological self-in-relationship that both preserves individual identities and emphasizes the way human and nonhuman relationships shape the identities of all those involved.[64] Unlike the ecofeminist ecological self, the autonomous rights-bearing individual of liberal theory—by failing to recognize relationships and responsibilities—is capable only of instrumentalizing relationships with others. "Instrumentalism is a way of relating to the world which corresponds to a certain model of selfhood," Plumwood explains, "the selfhood conceived as that of the individual who stands apart from an alien other and denies his own relationship to and dependency on this other."[65] Ecofeminists have consistently rejected instrumentalism as a suitable method for determining value in an environmental or feminist ethic, and some ecofeminists have also challenged the notion of intrinsic value, arguing that it is the other side of a dualized notion of value: the concepts of both instrumental and intrinsic value follow a logic of assessing value based on the isolated identity of the individual. But if ecofeminist arguments for the interconnectedness of all life and the necessity of making ethical decisions in specific contexts have validity, then neither the identity nor the value of any individual can be defined in isolation. Ecofeminism suggests an ecological understanding of value, a means of determining the sustainability of specific relationships in terms of the individuals involved, their connection to one another as well as to the contexts in which they function.[66] These relationships and contexts alter and shape participants' identities, and because these ecological systems are not static but fluid and shifting, identities will also be shifting in response to each relational context, each historical moment. Rejecting the autonomous individual of liberal democracy, ecofeminism restores a self-in-relationship to human and nonhuman others which is well suited to both radical democracy and the multiple contextual roles of citizenship. Restoring these connections to democracy means transforming the dualisms of liberalism.

A central goal of both Green politics and ecofeminism is to reconnect politics and ethics, culture and nature, economics and ecological sustainability, democracy and global social justice. This reconnection will not take place as a singular event; for a lasting reconnection of politics and ethics, the very structure of liberal democracy and the dualisms of Western thought will need to be reconceived on the basis of continuity, interconnection, and relationships rather than separation, autonomy, and individualism. Human identity must be reconceived as fundamentally interconnected with nature. As Carol Adams has said in regard to animal ecofeminism or vegetarianism, we must restore the "absent referent,"[67] which in this case means recognizing that the "political" element of democracy includes not only ethics but the realm of nature, which is the only place where freedom—and survival—is possible for all.

Toward an Ecofeminist Theory of Radical Democratic Citizenship

A PLEDGE OF ALLEGIANCE TO THE FAMILY OF EARTH

I pledge allegiance to the Earth, and to the flora, fauna and human life that it supports, one planet, indivisible, with safe air, water and soil, economic justice, equal rights and peace for all.

—Women's Environment and Development Organization

The "I" who speaks this pledge of allegiance is an ecological citizen of the earth, not a citizen of the nation-state; her loyalties are based on her relationships with not only humans but plants, animals, and ecosystems. Her economic citizenship is alluded to in her commitment to economic justice; her political citizenship is expressed in her commitment to equality and her opposition to militarism. Though ecofeminists have privately debated how best to characterize the philosophy and strategy of the Women's Environment and Development Organization, this pledge of allegiance reconceives some of the fundamental elements of liberal democracy: the limits of society in the nation-state, the limits of community in humans with specific properties, the separation of human community from other human communities and from nature, the concept of liberty as social noninterference in the autonomous individual's free pursuit of personal gain, and the implication that an inclusive form of justice can exist in contexts characterized by environmental degradation, overconsumption, militarism, the religious justification of privilege, and the concentration of global wealth in the hands of an elite minority.[68] Of course, there are certain concerns with WEDO's pledge: how does it ensure a commitment to racial justice, gender justice, and human diversity? Why does it continue to use the language of rights and in doing so perpetuate liberalism's notion of the rational individual? Does the WEDO pledge adequately articulate the interconnections between economic and ecological citizenship? What does "equal rights" have to do with transforming gender roles, rather than simply including them and thereby reinforcing the oppressive culture that supports liberal democracy? and so forth. Nonetheless, WEDO's pledge reveals a recognition that achieving the goals of social and ecological justice requires reconceiving assumptions about democracy and citizenship. Here I explore a few of those central concepts and how they might be transformed through an ecofeminist approach.

Plumwood defines ecological citizenship as "the recognition of others in nature, acknowledgement of the political character of relationships with nature, . . . ecologically responsible production and development behaviour as well as . . . consumption and household behaviour."[69] Citizenship does not occur in a vacuum, and ecological citizenship shifts the context of "belonging" from the hierarchical nation-state to the ecological community, which includes human and nonhuman animals, plants, nature, and the promise of future generations. Recognizing the interconnectedness within and among ecological communities, ecological citizenship involves taking responsibility for the ecological impacts of production, consumption, and waste, both in industry and in the household. It encourages citizens to live sustainably within the limits of the ecological community, voluntarily limiting the size and the impacts of human communities in a way that maximizes freedom for ecological citizens of all species. Implicit in the concept of ecological citizenship is the recognition of diversity—biodiversity, species diversity, human diversity—as crucial to a healthy and functioning ecosystem. It is fundamentally connected to economic and political citizenship as well.

Connecting economic and ecological citizenship, for example, means that the so-called externalities of accounting in liberal capitalism would be internalized: in other words, the labor of women in the home, in child care and elder care, along with the labor they do in support of other wage earners, would now be accounted for; similarly, the value of nonhuman nature itself would be recognized. Economic citizenship would remove economic operations from the realm of the "private" and recognize these as subject to democratic control, with the greatest decision-making power given to those most directly and most adversely affected by these processes. Of course, economic citizenship would require the restructuring of work in such a way that everyone is given the opportunity to do both mental and manual work; everyone is able to enjoy the experience of agency in the workplace; the quantity of work is equalized, solving the imbalances of an overworked few and an unemployed many; leisure time for family, community, and civic activity is valued and guaranteed; work in the home and work in industry is recognized as having equal social and therefore equal economic value; and all forms of employment offer a living wage.[70] With economic citizens living sustainably in their production, consumption, and waste, there will be ample resources for everyone (thereby disproving liberalism's belief in a scarcity of resources and the correlated need for competition). Indeed, as Mies and Shiva observe, a subsistence lifestyle is the only guarantee of freedom and provisions for everyone.

Value itself would be redefined along these three axes of citizenship. Disrupting the liberal dualism of mind as defined over and against the body, ecological citizens would recognize the life-sustaining importance of "bodies of matter" and expose the masquerade of corporations-as-(living)-bodies. Economic value would be defined in direct correlation to sustainability. Nature's own processes would be recognized not as production but as generation, and the generativity of nature would be respected, not controlled or managed into overproduction (i.e., the Green Revolution and rBGH as methods of demanding more than nature generates). Similarly, humans would not be required to produce more than is sustainable; self-worth would not be measured by one's production output. Women's worth would not be measured in terms of reproduction.

Political citizenship would revise certain liberal notions about society: for example, the "social contract" would be based on the understanding that every human is born into a social and ecological community that existed before that individual's birth; hence, the "social contract" would involve a commitment to respect social and ecological relationships and to live sustainably within the relationships on which all life depends. An ecofeminist assessment of democracy builds on and advances the anthropocentric feminist critiques: just as feminism has foregrounded the multiple exclusions of liberal democracy in its notions of participation and decision making and its definition of citizenship, ecofeminism foregrounds the exclusions of feminist critiques, challenging the consistently marginalized status of both animals and nature. A nonanthropocentric conception of political citizenship must find some way of voicing the concerns of animals, nature, and future generations in any democratic process of decision making.[71] Radical democracy cannot occur in the context of an oppressive culture, and for this reason transforming liberal democracy and the lifeless passivity of the consumer/voter will require transforming the culture as well. One aspect of that transformation surely involves disrupting the dualism of reason and the erotic, a dualism that underlies and has authorized colonialism, sexism, speciesism, racism, heterosexism, and the domination of nature itself.[72]

In practice, at least one example of a radical democracy compatible with ecofeminism is already under way in the United States. Fittingly, in 1992, the same year the Green Politics Network was established, the National Independent Politics Summit was formed at the People's Progressive Convention in Ypsilanti, one of the achievements of the Ron Daniels 1992 presidential campaign.[73] This convention brought together groups such as the National Committee for Independent Political Action, the Greens/Green Party U.S.A., Campaign for a New Tomorrow, independent state parties such as California's Peace and Freedom Party and Pennsylvania's Consumer Party, as well as dozens of social movement organizations. Although the network languished in 1993 and 1994 owing to resource limitations, in 1995 the steering committee began making phone calls to organize a National Independent Politics Summit in April 1996. The express purpose of this group, now renamed the Independent Progressive Politics Network, is to form coalitions among electoral and activist efforts of the independent Left. Membership in the IPPN is open to organizations committed to progressive independent politics; individuals who wish to join must do so as representatives of a particular progressive community. Thus, the organizational structure safeguards identities at the same time that it fosters coalitions. The steering committee consists of twenty-five people, of whom at least 40 percent must be people of color and at least 50 percent must be women; the twenty-five elected members then appoint five more to "diversity seats" to round out the composition of the committee in terms of geographic, organizational, or any other type of representation needed. Currently, the network includes organizations such as Black Workers for Justice, California Peace and Freedom Party, Campaign for a New Tomorrow, Highlander Center, the Greens/Green Party U.S.A., National Black Rank and File Exchange, National Committee for Independent Political Action, Progressive Dane/New Progressive Party, Project South, Socialist Party USA, and Southern Organizing Committee for Economic and Social Justice.

The model for the Independent Progressive Politics Network is the New Zealand Alliance, a group formed by the Green Party, the New Labor Party, and the Maori Party, which successfully spearheaded a campaign that in 1994 succeeded in switching New Zealand's electoral system from a winner-take-all plurality (as in the United States) to a mixed-member system of proportional representation. In the United States, an independent progressive party movement would benefit from a similar alliance, since each of the strongest progressive efforts still has a specific but limited constituency: for example, the Greens originated from the peace, environmental, and feminist movements; the Labor Party is based in the organized labor movement; Campaign for a New Tomorrow is rooted in communities of color; and the New Party is strongest in universities and communities where ACORN is already organized. With each constituency bringing its own perspectives and programs to the table, a network alliance rather than a unitary party offers the best opportunity for the practice of radical democracy.

What are the implications for ecofeminism? Though its adherents strive to create a wholly inclusive theory, ecofeminism can never be—nor should any group aspire to be—the single umbrella for a progressive movement, simply because, time and again, movements that have attempted to internalize social diversity within a single organization have devolved into a rule of the movement elite. Nor should ecofeminists join wholeheartedly in other organizations that simply include our concerns and perspectives on a laundry list of values or principles. So long as women and nature are oppressed in the larger society, these tendencies will be manifest in progressive movements as well, and hence an autonomous ecofeminist presence, organization, and community will be necessary.[74] In sum, the theories of radical democracy and the ecofeminist commitment to diversity and plurality indicate that the most effective way to structure a progressive movement is through an inclusive network alliance of diverse groups based on solidarity rather than unity, using both electoral and issue-based activism, working together for social and ecological justice.

Conclusion

In a 1988 article written for *Z Magazine,* Ynestra King, one of the principal organizers of the first ecofeminist conference and one of four keynote speakers at the Greens' first national gathering, voiced a cautious optimism about the potential future of the Greens. If they could create "a theory, culture, and strategy that embodies the legacy of the new left come of age," she wrote, "the lefts, both old and new, should note that the best chance for the historic continuation of the red and the black is in the green."[1] Less than a decade later, ecofeminism had become more of a perspective than a movement, and divisions within the U.S. Greens deepened (particularly the division between theory and practice) as the national focus shifted from issue-based politics to party building. Why had these movements faltered?

In 1996, as various Green locals and even some statewide organizations continue to flourish, the practice of democracy and the commitment to feminism has tended to recede at the higher levels. Nationally, Greens remain divided and diminished by differences that have gone unacknowledged or unresolved and by commitments that have been too quickly broken. In Amherst, the Green movement seemed positioned to avoid old-style coalition attempts that combined energies in "a lowest-common-denominator effort which is frustrating, partial to all concerned, and agenda bound," and to promise "a different kind of coming together, where the deepest truths of participants are listened to and honored."[2] During the six years that followed Amherst, however, constituency after constituency left the Greens as their central concerns went unheeded.

The turning point for the movement came when the Greens' national organization became the Greens/Green Party U.S.A. in 1991. Ostensibly an agreement that would accommodate the concerns of every faction within the Greens, this decision marked a shift for the Greens nationally.

Although it wasn't apparent at first, the decision to transform the Greens into the G/GPUSA benefited the electoralists most of all. Still dissatisfied with the new G/GPUSA's inability to give state parties a voice, electoralists in the Greens formed the Green Politics Network in 1992. And although the path of building transformative social movements has never been particularly clear, the path to building a political party has been fairly well traveled. GPN activists lost no time in developing movements into electoral parties in the states where their views were best represented, and three years after the founding of the GPN, electoralists were ready to launch the Greens' first presidential campaign. Meanwhile, weakened by the loss of their most vocal (albeit warring) constituencies, while accumulating debts and suffering a series of personnel turnovers in the national clearinghouse, activists in the G/GPUSA struggled to maintain local groups but failed to enact a national strategy or to achieve national visibility. Inevitably, they repeated past mistakes of other social movements.

The difficulties of the New Left, according to King, included "sexism, anti-intellectualism, a dearth of political experience, and a lack of critical historical perspective," and these difficulties carried over into the Greens.[3] For ecofeminists, the most immediate and ultimately most destructive problem was sexism, as Greens continually wrestled with overcoming patriarchal patterns of thought and behavior. *Postpatriarchal values* was initially named one of the Green movement's Ten Key Values and was defined as moving beyond sexism in terms of gender parity as well as eschewing masculinist styles of leadership, communication, and organizing. At the 1992 national gathering, urged on by the Women's Caucus, the Greens replaced *postpatriarchal* with *feminist* amid much controversy. Paradoxically, as the word "feminist" progressed to the foreground, the transformative meaning of feminism receded and was increasingly replaced by liberal feminist notions of gender parity in representation within the GPUSA or an even weaker commitment to equal pay or child-care services. As the Greens moved closer to electoral campaigns and farther from grassroots community organizing—a move they made without a clear recognition that the transition involved a shift from "women's" traditional sphere for organizing to "men's" traditional sphere of politics—the numbers of women also dropped, and with them went many of the feminist voices. But the final blow to feminism in the Greens was the 1996 campaign to run Ralph Nader for president, initiated by the California Green Party and later supported by Greens in Maine, Virginia, and Rhode Island and various Greens throughout the United States. Not only were the Greens proposing a national-level campaign, in direct opposition to their promises of grassroots politics, but they had selected a white heterosexual male to represent them.[4] Discomfort grew as Nader revealed, first, that he was not, nor did he intend to become, a member of the Green Party, and second, that he was not running on the Green platform. Green commitments to candidate accountability were thrust aside in the race for fame, and Nader's later refusals to take a position on women's right to reproductive choice, domestic partnerships, civil rights (as in the California Civil Rights Initiative), or animal rights (commitments made in the California Green Party platform) were superfluous affirmations of what was already painfully evident: the practices of national electoral politics and national electoralists were not consistent with the theory and the values of Green politics.

For ecofeminists, insufficient attention to the political implications of the differences among ecofeminisms, the backlash against all forms of feminism, the lack of a consistent and diverse movement constituency, and the failure to maintain an autonomous ecofeminist organization or network all served to impede the growth of ecofeminism as a movement. As political developments within the Greens made clear, feminists and ecofeminists working within mixed-gender organizations without connections to an autonomous feminist or ecofeminist movement could be easily ignored or overruled, as neither liberal feminism nor cultural ecofeminism (separately or in combination) offers a critique comprehensive enough to withstand patriarchal politics. By 1996, most feminists and ecofeminists in the Greens realized they were operating within a movement that did not fully understand feminism. But feminisms and ecofeminisms within the Greens were silenced not because of spirituality or essentialism (as some critics of cultural ecofeminism had maintained) but because they lacked an informed critique of capitalist economics, race and class oppressions, and the differences among various forms of democracy. For these, ecofeminism would need to recognize and reclaim its position as heir to more than a century of social movement activism on the Left.

In the 1980s and 1990s, social-change activists have become increasingly aware of the fact that an effective movement for social and ecological justice will have to be a grassroots, populist movement, embodying the full range of differences of identity and articulating the fundamental interconnections of all oppressions. Building such a movement depends on fostering a widespread recognition that all these movements are potential allies in a larger struggle for freedom, ecological health, and economic and technological sustainability. The fits and starts of attempting to build grassroots, democratic movements have not been wasted, particularly if we can learn from them. For the Greens, or for any future movement seeking to join identity-based and issues-based constituencies in a populist framework, perhaps the biggest lesson is the importance of practicing participatory democracy and dialogical politics—voicing and listening to difference, and building a comprehensive critique in which everyone's vision is represented. Genuine, lasting coalitions cannot be built on a lowest common denominator or single-issue foundation; rather, new transformative coalitions for social and ecological justice will have to be shaped with a genuine awareness of and commitment to the concerns of each member constituency. In their formulation of the Ten Key Values, the Greens voiced this recognition, but in the years that followed, the movement drifted away from that commitment, as more and more constituencies were told the familiar line, "Wait until we achieve this more important goal—then we'll address your issues." It is to the credit of the original Green vision that so many constituencies stayed with the Greens as long as they did. And there is still the potential that grassroots activists in the Greens will be able to reclaim their voice within the movement and create a national democratic structure for joining Green movement and party activists.

Beyond listening to difference, Greens and other activists could use a variety of strategies to build on the lessons learned. For example, many new activists have joined the Greens as a result of the visibility Greens achieved through Nader. These new members are largely unaware of the internal inconsistencies of the Nader campaign and have been drawn in by the Green philosophy and by the shared recognition that U.S. politics needs a Green alternative. To bring these people into Green activism and to focus their efforts in a direction that will not repeat past mistakes, Greens need to establish or at least make available in all groups a consistent method for welcoming and educating newcomers in Green philosophy, feminisms and ecofeminisms, social movement history, and the practices of participatory democracy. Without this continual education in place, the result is a loss of historical and movement memory, and with it comes the potential of repeating old mistakes and relearning old lessons. Moreover, as the more experienced people burn out or move on, there will be fewer and fewer experienced activists to take their place unless this continual education is made available. Next, Greens need to pay renewed attention to feminist models of leadership as an extended dialogue among participants, rather than following patriarchal models wherein an individual leader's monologue focuses on seeking supporters for his prepackaged ideas. Effective democratic leadership needs to be reconceived as more than the individual traits of charisma, vision, and the ability to "think big"; democratic leadership must be understood as the process of empowering others and carrying out projects initiated, developed with, and supported by the grassroots. Without this commitment, movements have the potential to become "dumbed down" from a radical, transformative movement to a movement for incorporation or mainstreaming.

From cultural ecofeminists, Greens can learn the importance of personal healing, self-esteem, and the practice of mutual respect among movement participants. Activists who use their activism as a vehicle for articulating their identity rather than for acting on ethical, political, and/or spiritual commitments leave themselves ripe for exploitation, manipulation, and power struggles. Men secure in their own identities are not threatened by feminism; white people who have reconnected with their own cultural heritage and worked to unlearn their inherited racism make better allies in the struggle against racism; heterosexuals who have explored and are secure in their own sexual identities are not threatened by queers. Although a political movement hardly need devolve into a narcissistic self-help group, it is also true that liberatory movements are more effective when they are composed of healthy, liberated individuals, particularly in positions of leadership. (Note that this is not the case for fascist movements—in fact, the more dysfunctional the individuals, the more powerful the movement. Contemporary and historical examples abound.)

Greens and ecofeminists alike need to develop a more thoroughgoing critique of technology and to address the central importance of economics and the role that capitalism plays in degrading ecological systems and diminishing conditions for workers around the world. Social movements of the nineties and beyond would benefit from providing ongoing education for activists on the practical connections between economy and ecology, with a variety of sustainable economic alternatives available or in the works. Community-based economics, community-supported agriculture, worker-owned and worker-managed businesses, and movements against biotechnology all have tremendous mobilizing appeal, because people have been led to believe alternatives to capitalist economies and technologies do not exist. Strategies for creating local, sustainable economies and technologies will be at the root of any transformative political, environmental movements in the future.

In addition, it is crucial that Greens and ecofeminists build alliances and support movements not affiliated with or underrepresented in their own constituencies. In 1996 alone, the Labor Party has come into existence, possibly signaling that the forty years of labor's declining potency as a movement have finally ended. Not only the labor movement, but the environmental justice movement, the queer movement, and the antitoxics movement have all been overlooked as progressive constituencies whose participation is essential for building a radically democratic movement. Greens and ecofeminists need to look directly at who is in their movements, whose views are represented, and which groups they have been most able to mobilize. It is neither necessary nor possible for any single movement to internalize the diversity of the society, although at various points both Greens and ecofeminists have thought their movements might become the "umbrella" under which other movements would gather. Understandably so: the United States was founded on the cult of the individual and has been influenced by monotheism. There is a strong socialization to create "one out of many" (*e pluribus unum*). Unfortunately, as ecofeminists working within the Greens have found, when the many become one, that one tends to reflect the characteristics and the concerns of the dominant group. Instead of a single, comprehensive movement, we can create a radically democratic movement by developing a deeper understanding of the interconnections among the many forms of oppression, articulated as a commitment to build coalitions with those groups not represented in our own constituencies. To protect and to strengthen the many voices for social justice, the many must remain *many*.

Ecofeminists can learn from the Greens and from the work of ecofeminists in the Greens. A radically democratic movement for social and ecological justice will be larger than ecofeminism and larger than the Greens. Yet we can only bring about that movement by working with and through our communities— and our communities will always be partial, unrepresentative, incomplete. Only the coalition of a variety of progressive communities will bring about the transformations needed to articulate a radical democracy, and in that coalition, an ecofeminist vision will find expression.

Appendixes

Appendix A: Chronology of Ecofeminism

1974   François d'Eaubonne, *Le féminisme ou la mort*
        Women and the Environment Conference, University of California,
        Berkeley

1978   Susan Griffin, *Woman and Nature: The Roaring Inside Her*
        Mary Daly, *Gyn/Ecology: The Metaethics of Radical Feminism*
        Ynestra King teaches ecofeminism at the Institute for Social Ecology

1979   Elizabeth Dodson Gray, *Green Paradise Lost*

1980   *April*
        Carolyn Merchant, *The Death of Nature: Women, Ecology, and the
        Scientific Revolution*
        Women and Life on Earth: Eco-Feminism in the '80s, University of
        Massachusetts, Amherst; more than 800 women attend
        November
        Women's Pentagon Action

1981   *April*
        First West Coast Ecofeminist Conference, Sonoma State University

November
Second Women's Pentagon Action

1982   Feminists for Animal Rights (FAR) founded by Marti Kheel and others

1983   Léonie Caldecott and Stephanie Leland, eds., *Reclaim the Earth: Women Speak Out for Life On Earth*

1986   WomanEarth Feminist Peace Institute is formed (March) and holds a conference (August) at Hampshire College, Amherst, Mass.

1987   *March*
USC Ecofeminist Conference (papers to be collected in *Reweaving the World,* ed. Diamond & Orenstein)

1988   Vandana Shiva, *Staying Alive: Women, Ecology, and Development*

1989   Judith Plant, ed., *Healing the Wounds: The Promise of Ecofeminism*
Andrée Collard with Joyce Contrucci, *Rape of the Wild: Man's Violence against Animals and the Earth*
Women's Environment and Development Organization (WEDO) established by Women USA Fund, Inc.
June
Ecofeminist Caucus formed at the National Women's Studies Assn. annual conference in Baltimore
August
Last communication from WomanEarth Feminist Peace Institute

1990   Irene Diamond and Gloria Feman Orenstein, eds., *Reweaving the World: The Emergence of Ecofeminism*

1991   Janet Biehl, *Rethinking Ecofeminist Politics*
February
Ecofeminist Visions Emerging (EVE) forms in New York City
November
WEDO sponsors World Women's Congress for a Healthy Planet, where the Women's Action Agenda 21 is created in preparation for

the UN Conference on Environment and Development in Brazil in 1992

1992 *March*
Midwest Environmental Ethics conference, Ames, Iowa

1993 Carol Adams, ed., *Ecofeminism and the Sacred*
Greta Gaard, ed., *Ecofeminism: Women, Animals, Nature*
Maria Mies and Vandana Shiva, *Ecofeminism*
Val Plumwood, *Feminism and the Mastery of Nature*
December
EVE ends

1994 Karen Warren, ed., *Ecological Feminism*
March
"EcoVisions: A Conference about the Important Connections between Women, the Animals, the Earth, the Future," sponsored by Friends of Animals and held in Alexandria, Virginia

1995 *March*
"Ecofeminist Perspectives" colloquium, sponsored by the departments of philosophy and religion at the University of Dayton, Ohio

Appendix B: Chronology of the U.S. Greens

1984 *May*
First North American Bioregional Congress, Ozark Mountains
August
Founding meeting of 62 people, St. Paul, Minn., at Macalester College. The name "Committees of Correspondence" is chosen. Four Pillars of the West German Greens are expanded into the Ten Key Values, the foundation of the movement

1985 *December*
CoC Clearinghouse moved to Kansas City

1987 *July*
First national Green gathering, Amherst, Mass. Rensenbrink proposes

drafting a national Green Program for the '90s, shortly thereafter titled the SPAKA document for Strategy and Policy Approaches in Key Areas

1988   Call for a Left Green Network issued
October
Youth Greens formed as a caucus within the [Green] Committees of Correspondence

1989   *April*
First Continental Conference of the Left Green Network, Ames, Iowa
May
First Youth Green gathering, Antioch College, Ohio. More than 70 young people attend
June
Second national Green gathering, Eugene, Ore. 190 SPAKA documents produced by the grassroots reclassified into 19 Key Areas for Issue Working Groups around which the gathering is structured. Name changed to Green Committees of Correspondence (GCoC)
October
Electoral Action Working Group created at the Washington, D.C., meeting of the Interregional Committee of the GCoC
Second Youth Green Conference, Minneapolis

1990   *April 23*
LGN and Youth Greens participate in the Wall Street Action, in coalition with 70 other groups and approximately 1,500 people
June
Third Youth Green Conference, Plainfield, Vt., at Goddard College
July
Second Continental Conference of the Left Green Network, Plainfield, Vt.
September
Third national CoC gathering, Estes Park, Colo. SPAKAS ratified and sent to membership for a vote
December
Fourth Youth Green Continental Conference, Knoxville, Tenn.

1991   *February*
     First Autonomous National meeting of the Green Party Organizing
     Committee (GPOC), formed from the Electoral Action Working
     Group
     July
     Third Continental Conference of the Left Green Network, Chicago
     August
     Fifth Youth Green Continental Conference, Dexter, Ore.
     Fourth national GCoC gathering, Elkins, W.V. Greens renamed The
     Greens/Green Party U.S.A. (G/GPUSA) to reflect resolution between
     movement and electoral activists. GPOC dissolves

1992   *Winter*
     AWOL forms from the ashes of the Minneapolis Youth Greens. Youth
     Greens dissolve
     March
     Founding meeting of the Green Politics Network (GPN), Kansas City,
     Mo.
     May
     Fourth Continental Conference of Left Green Network, Iowa City,
     Iowa
     August
     Fifth national G/GPUSA gathering, Minneapolis. National Action Plan:
     Detroit Summer, 500 Years of Resistance, Solar Power through
     Community Power

1993   *February*
     GPN hosts "Doing It the Grassroots Way," Bowdoin College, Maine,
     first in a series of coalition meetings of third-party electoralists
     May
     Fifth Continental Conference of Left Green Network, Toronto
     August
     Sixth national G/GPUSA gathering, Syracuse, N.Y., at Earthwise Edu-
     cation Center, an African-American organic farm. More than 300
     attend. Theme: Green Justice and Green Cities

1994   *June*
     GPN hosts "New Politics '94: Nuts and Bolts for State and Local

Victory," San Francisco, second of the series of coalition meetings

August

Seventh national G/GPUSA gathering, Boise, Idaho. Theme: Embracing Common Ground: Celebrating Human and Bio-Diversity. Daunted by massive debt and infighting, only 25 activists show up

1995   *June*

GPN hosts "Third Parties '96: Building the New Mainstream," Washington, D.C., at George Washington University, third of the coalition meetings. Common Ground Declaration produced

July

Eighth national Green gathering, Albuquerque, N.M., at the University of New Mexico. GPN members, GPUSA members, and unaffiliated Greens gather for the first time since Elkins in 1991. GPN proposes the Green Roundtable/Coordination

1996   *March*

First Roundtable Meeting, St. Louis, called by G/GPUSA and boycotted by GPN

August

Ninth national Green gathering, Los Angeles, at UCLA. Ralph Nader runs for president on the Green Party of California ticket

Appendix C: The Original Ten Key Values of the U.S. Greens

1. *Ecological Wisdom*

How can we operate human societies with the understanding that we are *part* of nature, not on top of it?

How can we live within the ecological and resource limits of the planet, applying our technological knowledge to the challenge of an energy-efficient economy?

How can we build a better relationship between cities and countryside?

How can we guarantee the rights of nonhuman species?

How can we promote sustainable agriculture and respect for self-regulating natural systems?

How can we further biocentric wisdom in all spheres of life?

2. *Grassroots Democracy*

How can we develop systems that allow and encourage us to control the decisions that affect our lives?

How can we ensure that representatives will be fully accountable to the people who elected them?

How can we develop planning mechanisms that would allow citizens to develop and implement their own preferences for policies and spending priorities?

How can we encourage and assist the "mediating institutions"—family, neighborhood organization, church group, voluntary association, ethnic club—recover some of the functions now performed by the government?

How can we relearn the best insights from American traditions of civic vitality, voluntary action, and community responsibility?

3. *Personal and Social Responsibility*

How can we respond to human suffering in ways that promote dignity?

How can we encourage people to commit themselves to lifestyles that promote their own health?

How can we have a community-controlled education system that effectively teaches our children academic skills, ecological wisdom, social responsibility, and personal growth?

How can we resolve interpersonal and intergroup conflicts without just turning them over to lawyers and judges?

How can we take responsibility for reducing the crime rate in our neighborhoods?

How can we encourage such values as simplicity and moderation?

4. *Nonviolence*

How can we, as a society, develop effective alternatives to our current patterns of violence, at all levels, from the family and the street to nations and the world?

How can we eliminate nuclear weapons from the face of the Earth without being naive about the intentions of other governments?

How can we most constructively use nonviolent methods to oppose practices and policies with which we disagree and in the process reduce the atmosphere of polarization and selfishness that is itself a source of violence?

5. *Decentralization*

How can we restore power and responsibility to individuals, institutions, communities, and regions?

How can we encourage the flourishing of regionally based culture, rather than a dominant monoculture?

How can we have a decentralized, democratic society with our political, economic, and social institutions locating power on the smallest scale (closest to home) that is efficient and practical?

How can we redesign our institutions so that fewer decisions and less regulation over money are granted as one moves from the community toward the national level?

How can we reconcile the need for community and regional self-determination with the need for appropriate centralized regulation in certain matters?

6. *Community-based Economics*

How can we redesign our work structures to encourage employee ownership and workplace democracy?

How can we develop new economic activities and institutions that will allow us to use our new technologies in ways that are humane, freeing, ecological, and accountable and responsive to communities?

How can we establish some form of basic economic security, open to all?

How can we move beyond the narrow "job ethic" to new definitions of "work," "jobs," and "income" that reflect the changing economy?

How can we restructure our patterns of income distribution to reflect the wealth created by those outside the formal, monetary economy: those who take responsibility for parenting, housekeeping, home gardens, community volunteer work, etc.?

How can we restrict the size and concentrated power of corporations without discouraging superior efficiency or technological innovation?

7. *Postpatriarchal Values*

How can we replace the cultural ethics of dominance and control with more cooperative ways of interacting?

How can we encourage people to care about persons outside their own group?

How can we promote the building of respectful, positive, and responsible relationships across the lines of gender and other divisions?

How can we encourage a rich, diverse political culture that respects feelings as well as rationalist approaches?

How can we proceed with as much respect for the means as the end (the process as much as the products of our efforts)?

How can we learn to respect the contemplative, inner part of life as much as the outer activities?

8. *Respect for Diversity*

How can we honor cultural, ethnic, racial, sexual, religious, and spiritual diversity within the context of individual responsibility to all beings?

While honoring diversity, how can we reclaim our country's finest shared ideals: the dignity of the individual, democratic participation, and liberty and justice for all?

9. *Global Responsibility*

How can we be of genuine assistance to grassroots groups in the Third World?

What can we learn from such groups?

How can we help other countries make the transition to self-sufficiency in food and other basic necessities?

How can we cut our defense budget while maintaining an adequate defense?

How can we promote these ten Green values in the reshaping of global order?

How can we reshape world order without creating just another enormous nation-state?

10. *Future focus*

How can we induce people and institutions to think in terms of the long-range future, and not just in terms of their short-range selfish interest?

How can we encourage people to develop their own visions of the future and move more effectively toward them?

How can we judge whether new technologies are socially useful—and use those judgments to shape our society?

How can we induce our government and other institutions to practice fiscal responsibility?

How can we make the quality of life, rather than open-ended economic growth, the focus of future thinking?

Principles of the Vermont and New Hampshire Greens
(1988)

Ecological Humanism
Antiracism
Ecofeminism
Gay and Lesbian Liberation
Grassroots *Democracy*
Cooperative Commonwealth
Social Responsibility
Ecological Reconstruction
Non-nuclear, Home-based, *Democratic* Defense
Nonaligned *Democratic* Internationalism
Independent Politics
Direct Action
Movements from Below
Fundamental Opposition
Programs, Not Personalities
Thinking Globally, Acting Locally
Organic Grassroots Growth
Strategic Nonviolence
Grassroots *Democratic* Confederation
Democratic Decentralism
Participatory Membership

Across the various articulations of the Green movement, only one value remained consistant: *democracy*. The meaning of this term was strongly contested during the 1996 Nader presidential campaign.

Ten Key Values of the U.S. Greens
(1984)

Ecological Wisdom
Grassroots *Democracy*
Personal and Social Responsibility
[Social Justice, 1991]
Nonviolence
Decentralization
Community-based Economics
Postpatriarchal Values [Feminism, 1992]
Respect for Diversity
Global Responsibility [Personal and Global Responsibility, 1991]
Future Focus

Principles of the Left Green Network
(1989)

Ecological Humanism
Social Ecology
Racial Equality [Antiracism]
Social Ecofeminism
Gay and Lesbian Liberation
Grassroots *Democracy*
Cooperative Commonwealth
Human Rights
Nonaligned Internationalism
Independent Politics
Direct Action
Radical Municipalism
Strategic Nonviolence
Democratic Decentralism

Four Pillars of the German Greens
(1982)

Ecology
Grassroots *Democracy*
Social Responsibility
Nonviolence

Political Principles of the Youth Greens
(1989)

Anticapitalism
Democratic Decentralism
Gay, Lesbian, and Bisexual Liberation
Oppositional Politics
Revolutionary Dual Power and Radical Municipalism
Social Ecofeminism
Antiracism [1990]

Appendix D: The Pillars, Values, and Principles of the Greens

Appendix E: Interviews

Margo Adair. Groundwork Collective; Greens Mediation Council. June 5, 1993. San Francisco.

Carol Adams. Feminist-vegetarian and ecofeminist author and activist. July 9, 1994. Louisville, Ky.

Lourdes Arguëlles. Ecofeminist educator and activist. October 26, 1995. Claremont, Calif.

Lois Arkin. Coordinator, Los Angeles Eco-Village. June 6, 1993. Santa Monica, Calif.

Judi Bari. EarthFirst! activist. February 25, 1995. Willits, Calif.

Amy Belanger. Greens National Clearinghouse coordinator. August 15, 1993. Syracuse, N.Y.

Dee Berry. Green Politics Network. Telephone interview, June 11, 1996.

Keiko Bonk. Green member, Big Island of Hawai'i County Council. May 23, 1993. Volcano, Hawai'i.

Walt Bresette. Lake Superior Greens. July 31, 1993. Fond du Lac, Wis.

David Conley. Douglas County Board of Supervisors. July 31, 1993. Superior, Wis.

Jan Conley. Lake Superior Greens. August 6, 1993. Superior, Wis.

Deane Curtin. Ecofeminist philosopher. July 16, 1993. St. Peter, Minn.

Debbie Domal. Animal Liberation activist and member, Green Party of Minnesota. April 13, 1995. Minneapolis.

Josephine Donovan. Feminist theorist. August 21, 1993. Portsmouth, N.H.

Riane Eisler. Feminist author. June 24, 1993. St. Paul, Minn.

Regina Endrizzi. California Green Party State Coordinating Committee. June 2, 1993. San Francisco.

Hugh Esco. Green Sprouts coordinator. August 10, 1993. Syracuse, N.Y.

Carolyn Estes. Cofounder, Alpha Farm. Telephone interview. June 26, 1996.

Mike Feinstein. Green activist. June 1, 1993. Santa Monica, Calif.

Margaret Garcia. Green Party of California. Telephone interview, May 1996.

Anne Goeke. Greens/Green Party Network. August 13, 1993. Syracuse, N.Y. Telephone interview, July 8, 1996.

Winston Gordon. Green activist and cofounder, Earthwise Education Center. August 14, 1993. Syracuse, N.Y.

Elizabeth Dodson Gray. Feminist theologian. August 18, 1993. Wellesley, Mass.

Lori Gruen. Ecofeminist philosopher. April 1, 1995. Dayton, Ohio.

JoAnn Haberman. Cofounder, Green Party of Minnesota. July 23, 1993. Minneapolis.

Chaia Heller. Social ecofeminist; Left Green Network. August 17, 1993. Hatfield, Mass. Telephone interview, April 21, 1996.

Lydia Herbert. New York Green activist. August 10, 1993. Syracuse, N.Y.

Tricia Hoffman. Feminists for Animal Rights. June 6, 1993. Santa Monica, Calif.

Marti Kheel. Cofounder, Feminists for Animal Rights. June 3, 1993. San Francisco.

Ynestra King. Ecofeminist activist and author. October 8, 1993. New York City.

Erica Bremer Kneipp. Ecofeminist activist. August 1, 1994. Plainfield, Vt.

Winona LaDuke. White Earth Land Recovery Project. August 3, 1993. Duluth, Minn.

Stephanie Lahar. Ecofeminist educator. August 23, 1993. South Burlington, Vt.

Linda Martin. 1992 U.S. Senate candidate, Hawai'i Green Party; D.C. Clearinghouse coordinator for 1996 Nader presidential campaign. Honolulu. May 27, 1993.

Cathleen McGuire. Cofounder, Ecofeminist Visions Emerging (EVE). September 1, 1994. Minneapolis.

Susan Meeker-Lowry. Economist and author. August 24, 1993. Montpelier, Vt.

Ross Mirkarimi. San Francisco commissioner on the environment; Green activist. June 3, 1993. San Francisco.

Lowell Nelson. Left Green Network; Green Party of Minnesota. April 23, 1996. Minneapolis.

Gloria Orenstein. Ecofeminist author. June 6, 1993. Santa Monica, Calif.

John Rensenbrink. Cofounder, Green Politics Network. November 8, 1993. Bowdoinham, Maine.

Ira Rohter. Co-chair, Hawai'i Green Party. May 28, 1993. Honolulu.

Julia Scofield Russell. Founder, Eco-Home Network. June 6, 1993. Santa Monica, Calif.

Constantia Salamone. Feminist-vegetarian and green activist. Telephone interview. April 11, 1996.

Lorna Salzman. New York Greens activist. Telephone interview. June 1996.

Catriona Sandilands. Ecofeminist theorist and Green activist. August 1, 1994. Plainfield, Vt. Telephone interview, August 7, 1996.

Laura Schere. Anarchist feminist. April 29, 1996. Minneapolis.

Vandana Shiva. Ecofeminist author and activist. March 11, 1994. Minneapolis.

Joel Sipress. Duluth Area Green Party cofounder. June 5, 1996. Minneapolis.

Charlene Spretnak. Ecofeminist and Green activist and author. June 5, 1993. Moss Beach, Calif.

Penelope Starr-Karlin. Ecofeminist activist. June 6, 1993. Santa Monica, Calif.

Brian Tokar. Social ecologist. November 9, 1993. Plainfield, Vt.

Karen Warren. Ecofeminist philosopher. September 13, 1993. St. Paul, Minn.

Laura Winton. Left Green Network Clearinghouse coordinator. April 20, 1996. Minneapolis.

Toni Wurst. Hawai'i Green Party, O'ahu co-chair. May 27, 1993. Honolulu.

Notes

Introduction

1. Peter Singer, *Animal Liberation: A New Ethics for Our Treatment of Animals* (New York: Avon Books, 1975).

2. Aviva Cantor, "The Club, the Yoke, and the Leash: What We Can Learn from the Way a Culture Treats Animals," *Ms.* (August 1983): 27–29. Feminists for Animal Rights continues to publish a newsletter and can be contacted at P.O. Box 16425, Chapel Hill, N.C. 27516.

3. That experience is the foundation for the ideas articulated in "Ecofeminism and Wilderness," *Environmental Ethics* 19 (Spring 1997): 5–24.

4. Bill Devall and George Sessions, *Deep Ecology: Living as if Nature Mattered* (Salt Lake City: Gibbs M. Smith, 1985).

5. Judith Plant, ed., *Healing the Wounds: The Promise of Ecofeminism* (Philadelphia: New Society, 1989).

6. Rachel Carson, *Silent Spring* (Boston: Houghton Mifflin, 1962); Léonie Caldecott and Stephanie Leland, eds., *Reclaim the Earth: Women Speak Out for Life on Earth* (London: Women's Press, 1983).

7. The principles of feminist research outlined here are drawn from several sources: Liz Stanley and Sue Wise, *Breaking Out: Feminist Consciousness and Feminist Research* (Boston: Routledge and Kegan Paul, 1983); Mary Margaret Fonow and Judith A. Cook, "Back to the Future: A Look at the Second Wave of Feminist Epistemology and Methodology," 1–15, Patricia Hill Collins, "Learning from the Outsider Within: The Sociological Significance of Black Feminist Thought," 35–59, Maria Mies, "Women's Research or Feminist Research? The Debate Surrounding Feminist Science and Methodology," 60–84, Joan Acker, Kate Barry, and Johanna Esseveld, "Objectivity and Truth: Problems in Doing Feminist Research," 133–53, in *Beyond Methodology: Feminist Scholarship as Lived Research*, ed. Mary Margaret Fonow and Judith A. Cook (Bloomington: Indiana University Press, 1991); Maria Mies, "Towards a Methodology for Feminist Research," 117–39, in *Theories of Women's Studies*, ed. Gloria Bowles and Renate Duelli Klein (London: Routledge, 1983).

8. Stanley and Wise, *Breaking Out,* p. 48.

9. This term was created by Patricia Hill Collins.

10. See Appendix E for a complete list of the interviews.

11. Charlotte Bunch, "Not by Degrees: Feminist Theory and Education," 240–53, in *Passionate Politics: Feminist Theory in Action* (New York: St. Martin's Press, 1987).

12. For that documentary, I remain grateful to Charlotte Bunch, who agreed to describe her four-part model for me on videotape.

Chapter 1

1. Judith Plant, ed., *Healing the Wounds: The Promise of Ecofeminism* (Philadelphia: New Society, 1989).

2. For an overview of influential texts and direct actions of ecofeminism in the United States, see Appendix A.

3. Susan Griffin, *Woman and Nature: The Roaring Inside Her* (San Francisco: Harper and Row, 1978); Mary Daly, *Gyn/Ecology: The Metaethics of Radical Feminism* (Boston: Beacon Press, 1978); Rosemary Radford Ruether, *New Woman/New Earth: Sexist Ideologies and Human Liberation* (New York: Seabury, 1975); Elizabeth Dodson Gray, *Green Paradise Lost* (Wellesley, Mass.: Roundtable Press, 1979); Carolyn Merchant, *The Death of Nature: Women, Ecology, and the Scientific Revolution* (San Francisco: Harper and Row, 1980).

4. See Karen Warren, "Toward an Ecofeminist Ethic," *Studies in the Humanities* 15:2 (1988): 140–56.

5. Ariel Salleh, review of *Staying Alive: Women, Ecology, and Development,* by Vandana Shiva, *Hypatia* 6 (Spring 1991): 206–14.

6. See Françoise d'Eaubonne, "Feminism or Death," 64–67, in *New French Feminisms,* ed. Elaine Marks and Isabelle deCourtivron (Amherst: University of Massachusetts Press, 1980).

7. See Carol Adams, *Ecofeminism and the Sacred* (New York: Continuum, 1993), p. xi.

8. Salleh, review of Shiva, *Staying Alive,* p. 206.

9. Interview, New York City, October 8, 1993.

10. Interview, Moss Beach, Calif., June 5, 1993. The article Spretnak refers to is Robin Quinn, "Mothering Earth," *Ms.* 16 (September 1987): 86.

11. See Vera Norwood, *Made from This Earth: American Women and Nature* (Chapel Hill: University of North Carolina Press, 1993); Charlotte Nekola and Paula Rabinowitz, eds., *Writing Red: An Anthology of American Women Writers* (New York: Feminist Press, 1987).

12. See, for example, Thomas Szasz, *EcoPopulism: Toxic Waste and the Movement for Environmental Justice* (Minneapolis: University of Minnesota Press, 1994), and Laura Pulido, *Environmentalism and Economic Justice* (Tucson: University of Arizona Press, 1996).

13. Michael Goldfield, *The Decline of Organized Labor in the United States* (Chicago: University of Chicago Press, 1987), p. 16.

14. This description of the Women's Pentagon Action is based on the following sources: Tacie Dejanikus and Stella Dawson, "Women's Pentagon Action," 282–91, in *Fight Back! Feminist Resistance to Male Violence,* ed. Frédérique Delacost and Felice Newman (Minneapolis: Cleis Press, 1981); Gina Foglia and Dorit Wolffberg, "Spiritual Dimensions of Feminist Anti-nuclear Activism," 446–61, in *The Politics of Women's Spirituality,* ed. Charlene Spretnak (New York: Anchor Books, 1982); Rhoda Linton and Michele Whitman, "With Mourning, Rage, Empowerment, and Defiance:

The 1981 Women's Pentagon Action," *Socialist Review* 12 (May/August 1982): 11–36; Ynestra King, "If I Can't Dance in Your Revolution, I'm Not Coming," 281–98, in *Rocking the Ship of State: Toward a Feminist Peace Politics*, ed. Adrienne Harris and Ynestra King (Boulder, Colo.: Westview Press, 1989).

15. Foglia and Wolffberg, "Spiritual Dimensions," p. 458.

16. King, "If I Can't Dance," p. 289.

17. The Unity Statement was reprinted in full in Spretnak, *Politics of Women's Spirituality*; King, "If I Can't Dance"; and Dejanikus and Dawson, "Women's Pentagon Action"; and was excerpted in Pam McAllister, ed., *Reweaving the Web of Life: Feminism and Nonviolence* (Philadelphia: New Society, 1982), and Léonie Caldecott and Stephanie Leland, eds., *Reclaim the Earth: Women Speak Out for Life on Earth* (London: Women's Press, 1983).

18. Dejanikus and Dawson, "Women's Pentagon Action," pp. 286–90.

19. Ibid., p. 289.

20. Ibid., p. 290.

21. Ibid., p. 289.

22. On the WomanEarth Feminist Peace Institute, see Noël Sturgeon, *Ecofeminist Natures: Race, Gender, and Transnational Environmental Politics* (New York: Routledge, 1997).

23. See Rachel Bagby, "A Power of Numbers," 91–95, in *Healing the Wounds*, ed., Plant; Lindsy Van Gelder, "It's Not Nice to Mess with Mother Nature: An Introduction to Ecofeminism 101, the Most Exciting New 'ism' in Eons," *Ms.* 17: (January/February 1989): 60–63.

24. Starhawk, *The Spiral Dance: A Rebirth of the Ancient Religion of the Great Goddess* (San Francisco: HarperCollins, 1979), and *Dreaming the Dark: Magic, Sex, and Politics* (Boston: Beacon Press, 1982).

25. Sturgeon, *Ecofeminist Natures*, p. 117; see also Luisah Teish, *Jambalaya* (San Francisco: HarperCollins, 1985).

26. James Mellaart, *Çatal Hüyük* (London: Thames and Hudson, 1967).

27. Elizabeth Gould Davis, *The First Sex* (Baltimore: Penguin Books, 1971); Mary Daly, *Beyond God the Father* (Boston: Beacon Press, 1973); Sheila Collins, *A Different Heaven and Earth: A Feminist Perspective on Religion* (Valley Forge, Pa.: Judson Press, 1974); Merlin Stone, *When God Was a Woman* (New York: Harcourt Brace Jovanovich, 1976); Marija Gimbutas, *The Gods and Goddesses of Old Europe, 7000–3500 B.C.* (Berkeley: University of California Press, 1974).

28. See Davis, *First Sex*, pp. 64, 95–96, 161–62.

29. Spretnak, *Politics of Women's Spirituality*, p. 396.

30. Charlene Spretnak, "Toward an Ecofeminist Spirituality," pp. 127–32, in Plant, *Healing the Wounds*; Charlene Spretnak, "Ecofeminism: Our Roots and Flowering," 3–14, in *Reweaving the World: The Emergence of Ecofeminism*, ed. Irene Diamond and Gloria Feman Orenstein (San Francisco: Sierra Club Books, 1990); Charlene Spretnak and Fritjof Capra, *Green Politics: The Global Promise* (Santa Fe, N.M.: Bear and Co., 1984); Charlene Spretnak, *The Spiritual Dimension of Green Politics* (Santa Fe, N.M.: Bear and Co., 1986).

31. Interview, Portsmouth, N.H., August 21, 1993.

32. Peter Singer, *Animal Liberation: A New Ethics for Our Treatment of Animals* (New York: Avon Books, 1975); Tom Regan, *The Case for Animal Rights* (Berkeley: University of California Press, 1983); Peter Singer, ed., *In Defense of Animals* (New York: Blackwell, 1985).

33. Carol Adams, "The Oedible Complex: Feminism and Vegetarianism," in *The Lesbian Reader* (Berkeley: Amazon Press, 1975), pp. 145–52; Laurel Holliday, *The Violent Sex: Male Psycho-*

biology and the Evolution of Consciousness (Guerneville, Calif.: Bluestocking Books, 1978). Grass-roots activist Constantia Salamone deserves recognition as the first second-wave feminist to address animal liberation. She published the New York City–based *Majority Report* in the early seventies, and the ideas in her numerous flyers and workshops on sexism and speciesism can be found in her few publications (see Chapter 4, note 35).

34. Aviva Cantor, "The Club, the Yoke, and the Leash: What We Can Learn from the Way a Culture Treats Animals," *Ms.* (August 1983): 27–29. Peter Singer defines "speciesism" as "a prejudice or attitude of bias toward the interests of members of one's own species and against those of members of other species," and he compares its logic to the logic of sexism, racism, and heterosexism; see *Animal Liberation*, p. 7.

35. Alice Walker, "Am I Blue?" "Not Only Will Your Teachers Appear, They Will Cook New Foods for You," and "Why Did the Balinese Chicken Cross the Road?" in *Living by the Word* (New York: Harcourt Brace, 1981); Marjorie Spiegel, *The Dreaded Comparison: Human and Animal Slavery* (New York: Mirror Books, 1988).

36. Interview, Louisville, Ky., July 9, 1994. See Carol Adams, *The Sexual Politics of Meat: A Feminist-Vegetarian Critical Theory* (New York: Continuum, 1990); see also Catherine A. MacKinnon, *Feminism Unmodified: Discourses on Life and Law* (Cambridge: Harvard University Press, 1987).

37. Edward Abbey, *Desert Solitaire: A Season in the Desert* (New York: Ballantine Books, 1968); *The Monkey Wrench Gang* (Philadelphia: Lippincott, 1975).

38. Interview, Willits, Calif., February 26, 1995. See also Judi Bari, *Timber Wars* (Monroe, Maine: Common Courage Press, 1994).

39. See Lois Gibbs, *Dying from Dioxin* (Boston: South End Press, 1995).

40. See Joanie Furio, "Toxic Tampons," *Ms.* 3 (November/December 1992): 80–81, and Ellen Bass, "Tampons," 51–53, in *Healing the Wounds*, ed. Plant.

41. Terry Tempest Williams, "The Clan of One-Breasted Women," in *Refuge* (New York: Vintage Books, 1991), pp. 281–90.

42. See Liane Clorfene-Casten, "The Environmental Link to Breast Cancer," *Ms.* 3 (May/June 1993): 52–55, and her recent book, *Breast Cancer: Poisons, Profits, and Prevention* (Monroe, Maine: Common Courage Press, 1996); Joan D'Argo and Joe Thornton, "Breast Cancer: The Chlorine Connection," Greenpeace Chlorine Campaign; and Judy Brady, ed., *One in Three: Women with Cancer Confront an Epidemic* (Pittsburgh: Cleis Press, 1991).

43. Spretnak, "Ecofeminism."

44. Interview, St. Paul, Minn., September 13, 1993.

45. Interview, Claremont, Calif., October 26, 1995.

46. Val Plumwood, "Feminism and Ecofeminism: Beyond the Dualistic Assumptions of Women, Men and Nature," *The Ecologist* 22 (January/February 1992): 13.

47. Lee Quinby, "Ecofeminism and the Politics of Resistance," in *Reweaving the World*, ed. Diamond and Orenstein, p. 123.

48. Karen Warren, "The Power and the Promise of Ecological Feminism," *Environmental Ethics* 12 (Summer 1990): 142–43.

49. Karen Green, "Freud, Wollstonecraft, and Ecofeminism: A Defense of Liberal Feminism," *Environmental Ethics* 16 (Summer 1994): 117–34; quotations from pp. 132–33, 124. Green displays a profound misreading of ecofeminist arguments: for example, she persistently asserts that "ecofeminist[s] claim that feminism and deep ecology are conceptually linked" (p. 117), that "feminism

implies deep ecology" (p. 121), and that "deep ecology requires (hence implies) feminism" (p. 122), when many ecofeminists have critiqued deep ecology at length for its androcentrism. Moreover, Green's concluding citation from Mary Wollstonecraft is thoroughly speciesist and would be immediately rejected by any "animal" ecofeminist, and Green's uncritical celebration of reason would be proved groundless in light of Val Plumwood's critique of reason and its role in creating and maintaining the "master model" (see *Feminism and the Mastery of Nature* [New York: Routledge, 1993]). Green's shortcomings—and by extension, the shortcomings of liberal feminism as a suitable environmental ethic—are most evident, however, on the topics of population and capitalism.

50. Ecofeminist analyses of "population" include Maria Mies and Vandana Shiva, "People or Population: Towards a New Ecology of Reproduction," 277–96, in *Ecofeminism* (London: Zed Books, 1993); Greta Gaard and Lori Gruen, "Ecofeminism: Toward Global Justice and Planetary Health," *Society and Nature* 2:1 (1993): 1–35; H. Patricia Hynes, *Taking Population Out of the Equation: Reformulating I = PAT* (North Amherst, Mass.: Institute on Women and Technology, 1993); Chris Cuomo, "Ecofeminism, Deep Ecology, and Human Population," 88–105, in *Ecological Feminism*, ed. Karen Warren (New York: Routledge, 1994). The most comprehensive and accessible analysis of population is still Betsy Hartmann, *Reproductive Rights and Wrongs: The Global Politics of Population Control and Contraceptive Choice* (New York: Harper and Row, 1987).

51. I attended the World Women's Congress along with Stephanie Lahar and Lori Gruen and participated in drafting and circulating the statement calling for an end to factory farming, animal experimentation, and rainforest beef. Stephanie Lahar has also commented on the barriers to participation at the congress, in "Report on the World Women's Congress for a Healthy Planet," *Regeneration* 3 (Spring 1992): 13, 21.

52. The NGO forum was held in Huairou, about an hour's travel from Beijing, where the UN conference was taking place. Fortunately, this strategy, which was designed to put some distance between the activist NGOs and the official representatives, was not entirely effective.

53. See Zillah Eisenstein, *The Radical Future of Liberal Feminism* (New York: Longman, 1981).

54. Griffin's lesbianism, though well known at the time, was openly discussed on a panel at the Modern Language Association convention in San Francisco in December 1975. Her remarks were later published in "Lesbians and Literature," *Sinister Wisdom* 1 (Fall 1976): 20–33, and collected in her volume of early work, *Made from This Earth* (New York: Harper and Row, 1982). I address an ecofeminist critique of heterosexism in "Toward a Queer Ecofeminism," *Hypatia* 12 (Winter 1997): 114–37.

55. Sally Gearhart's lesbian utopia, *The Wanderground* (Watertown, Mass.: Persephone Press, 1978), along with Monique Wittig's *Les guerrières* (London: Women's Press, 1977), are listed in an appendix of Caldecott and Leland, *Reclaim the Earth*, under "Suggested Further Reading Relating to Eco-feminism," so it's clear that early ecofeminists recognized and claimed the influence of lesbian feminism on ecofeminism. To date, the only explicitly ecofeminist utopia written by an ecofeminist author is Starhawk, *The Fifth Sacred Thing* (New York: Bantam Books, 1993), which depicts pansexuality, an acceptance of all varieties of gender identity, and nonmonogamy as part of its utopian vision. Another, earlier work listed in *Reclaim the Earth*'s appendix, Marge Piercy's *Woman on the Edge of Time* (New York: Ballantine Books, 1976), shares Starhawk's perspective on sexuality and relationships. In my entry "Ecology and Ecofeminism" in *The Lesbian Encyclopedia*, ed. Bonnie Zimmerman (New York: Garland Press, forthcoming), I expand on the lesbian roots of ecofeminism.

56. Recently, Griffin stated that she would consider herself an ecofeminist; see David Macauley, "On Women, Animals, and Nature: An Interview with Eco-feminist Susan Griffin," *APA Newsletter on Feminism and Philosophy* 90 (Fall 1991): 116–27.

57. This discussion of radical and cultural feminisms is taken from two works by Alice Echols: "The New Feminism of Yin and Yang," 439–59, in *Powers of Desire: The Politics of Sexuality*, ed. Ann Snitow, Christine Stansell, and Sharon Thompson (New York: Monthly Review Press, 1983), and *Daring to Be Bad: Radical Feminism in America, 1967–1975* (Minneapolis: University of Minnesota Press, 1989).

58. Echols, *Daring to Be Bad*, p. 243.

59. Interview, August 21, 1993.

60. Josephine Donovan, "Animal Rights and Feminist Theory," 167–94, in *Ecofeminism: Women, Animals, Nature*, ed. Greta Gaard (Philadelphia: Temple University Press, 1993).

61. Interview, San Francisco, June 3, 1993.

62. Andreé Collard with Joyce Contrucci, *Rape of the Wild: Man's Violence against Animals and the Earth* (Bloomington: Indiana University Press, 1989).

63. Irene Diamond, *Fertile Ground: Women, Earth, and the Limits of Control* (Boston: Beacon Press, 1994).

64. Cathleen and Colleen McGuire offer a clear discussion of the differences between radical rationalist feminism and radical cultural feminism, along with the aspects of each that have been adopted by ecofeminists. See "Grassroots Ecofeminism: Activating Utopia," in *Ecofeminist Literary Criticism: Theory, Interpretation, and Pedagogy*, ed. Greta Gaard and Patrick Murphy (Chicago: University of Illinois Press, 1998), n. 24.

65. J. J. Bachofen, *Myth, Religion, and Mother Right* (1870; repr. Princeton: Princeton University Press, 1967); Robert Briffault, *The Mothers*, 3 vols. (1927; repr. New York: Macmillan, 1952).

66. Riane Eisler, *The Chalice and the Blade* (San Francisco: HarperCollins, 1987); Carol Adams, ed., *Ecofeminism and the Sacred* (New York: Continuum, 1993); Rosemary Radford Ruether, ed., *Women Healing Earth: Third World Women on Ecology, Feminism, and Religion* (Maryknoll, N.Y.: Orbis Books, 1996).

67. See two essays by Heather Eaton: "Earth Patterns: Feminism, Ecology, and Religion," *Vox Feminarum* 1 (September 1996): 7–18, and "Liaison or Liability: Weaving Spirituality into Ecofeminist Politics," *Atlantis* 21 (Fall 1996): 109–22.

68. Eaton, "Liaison or Liability," pp. 114–15.

69. Ibid., p. 115.

70. Alice Walker, *In Search of Our Mothers' Gardens: Womanist Prose* (New York: Harcourt Brace Jovanovich, 1983), p. xi.

71. Interview, San Francisco, June 5, 1993.

72. Interview, October 8, 1993.

73. Janet Biehl, *Rethinking Ecofeminist Politics* (Boston: South End Press, 1991); "What Is Social Ecofeminism?" *Green Perspectives* 11 (October 1988): 1–8.

74. See my review in *Women and Environments* (Spring 1992): 20–21; Val Plumwood, "The Atavism of Flighty Females," *The Ecologist* 22 (January/February 1992): 36; Douglas Buege, "Rethinking Again: A Defense of Ecofeminist Philosophy," 42–63, in *Ecological Feminism*, ed. Warren.

75. Interview, Plainfield, Vt., August 1, 1994.

76. Gray, *Green Paradise Lost*, p. 42.

77. See, for example, Victoria Davion, "Is Ecofeminism Feminist?" 8–28, and Buege, "Re-

thinking Again." Janis Birkeland has voiced a radical cultural ecofeminist defense of gender as a primary category of analysis for ecofeminism and captures the feeling level of many grassroots ecofeminist activists; see her "Neutralizing Gender," *Environmental Ethics* 17 (Winter 1995): 443–44, and "Disengendering Ecofeminism," *The Trumpeter* 12 (Fall 1995): 178–80.

78. *Heresies* 13 (Spring 1981), *New Catalyst* 10 (Winter 1987/88), *Woman of Power* 9 (Spring 1988), *Studies in the Humanities* 15:2 (1988), *Hypatia* 6 (Spring 1991), *APA Newsletter on Feminism and Philosophy* 90 (Fall 1991), *Society and Nature* 2:1 (1993), *Alternatives* 21 (April/May 1995), *NWSA Journal* 9 (Fall 1997), *Frontiers* (Winter 1998).

79. This is not to imply that all three branches of radical environmentalism developed at the same time. In fact, Murray Bookchin began developing social ecology in the late 1950s and early 1960s; deep ecology received its start from Arne Naess' 1973 essay ("The Shallow and the Deep, Long-Range Ecology Movement: A Summary," *Inquiry* 16[1973]: 95–100) but was also very influenced by social ecology (see Chapter 3).

80. Steve Chase, ed., *Defending the Earth: A Dialogue between Murray Bookchin and Dave Foreman* (Boston: South End Press, 1991).

81. The following essays advanced the debate between ecofeminism and deep ecology: Ariel Salleh, "Deeper than Deep Ecology: The Eco-Feminist Connection," *Environmental Ethics* 6 (Winter 1984): 339–45; Michael Zimmerman, "Feminism, Deep Ecology, and Environmental Ethics," *Environmental Ethics* 9 (Summer 1987): 21–44; Jim Cheney, "Ecofeminism and Deep Ecology," *Environmental Ethics* 9 (Summer 1987): 115–45; Warwick Fox, "The Deep Ecology–Ecofeminism Debate and Its Parallels," *Environmental Ethics* 11(Spring 1989): 5–25; Jim Cheney, "The Neo-Stoicism of Radical Environmentalism," *Environmental Ethics* 11(Winter 1989): 293–325; Marti Kheel, "Ecofeminism and Deep Ecology: Reflections on Identity and Difference," 127–37, in *Reweaving the World,* ed. Diamond and Orenstein; Michael Zimmerman, "Deep Ecology and Ecofeminism: The Emerging Dialogue," 138–54, in *Reweaving the World,* ed. Diamond and Orenstein; Val Plumwood, "Nature, Self, and Gender: Feminism, Environmental Philosophy, and the Critique of Rationalism," *Hypatia* 6 (Spring 1991): 3–27; Robert Sessions, "Deep Ecology versus Ecofeminism: Healthy Differences or Incompatible Philosophies?" *Hypatia* 6 (Spring 1991): 90–107; Ariel Salleh, "The Ecofeminism/Deep Ecology Debate: A Reply to Patriarchal Reason," *Environmental Ethics* 14 (Fall 1992): 195–216; Ariel Salleh, "Class, Race, and Gender Discourse in the Ecofeminism/Deep Ecology Debate," *Environmental Ethics* 15 (Fall 1993): 225–44; Val Plumwood, "The Ecopolitics Debate and the Politics of Nature," 64–87, and Chris Cuomo, "Ecofeminism, Deep Ecology, and Human Population," 88–105, in *Ecological Feminism,* ed. Warren; Deane Curtin, "Dogen, Deep Ecology, and the Ecological Self," *Environmental Ethics* 16 (Summer 1994): 195–213; Deborah Slicer, "Is There an Ecofeminism–Deep Ecology 'Debate'?" *Environmental Ethics* 17 (Summer 1995): 151–69. Slicer's perceptive essay effectively marked the end of the "debate"; although essays on the differences between ecofeminism and deep ecology continue to be published, activists in both groups seem to have ended the debates by refusing to discuss them any further. The differences, however, have not been resolved.

82. Val Plumwood reviews and critiques the three forms of the deep ecological self, in "Deep Ecology and the Denial of Difference," 165–89, in *Feminism and the Mastery of Nature* (New York: Routledge, 1993).

83. Interview, October 8, 1993.

84. See Greta Gaard, "Misunderstanding Ecofeminism," *Z Papers* 3:1 (1994): 20–24.

85. Kathryn Paxton George's essay, "Should Feminists Be Vegetarians?" *Signs* 19 (Winter

1994): 405–34, was critiqued by Carol J. Adams (221–25), Josephine Donovan (226–29), and Greta Gaard and Lori Gruen (230–41) in a series of responses titled "Comment on George's 'Should Feminists Be Vegetarians?'" *Signs* 21 (Autumn 1995). The format of the journal allowed the original author to have the "last word," in "Reply to Adams, Donovan, and Gaard and Gruen" (242–60).

86. For this misinterpretation, see Beth A. Dixon, "The Feminist Connection between Women and Animals," *Environmental Ethics* 18 (Summer 1996): 181–94. The editors at *Environmental Ethics* were much more open to ecofeminist concerns, and our responses appeared just two issues later. See Greta Gaard, "Women, Animals, and Ecofeminist Critique," 439–41, and Lori Gruen, "On the Oppression of Women and Animals," 441–44, *Environmental Ethics* 18 (Winter 1996).

87. Interview, October 8, 1993.

Chapter 2

1. Susan Faludi, *Backlash: The Undeclared War against American Women* (New York: Crown, 1991).

2. See Barbara Epstein, *Political Protest and Cultural Revolution: Nonviolent Direct Action in the 1970s and 1980s* (Berkeley: University of California Press, 1991), and Edward Walter, *The Rise and Fall of Leftist Radicalism in America* (Westport, Conn.: Praeger, 1992).

3. Fritjof Capra, *The Turning Point* (New York: Simon and Schuster, 1982).

4. See Christa Daryl Slaton, "Quantum Theory and Political Theory," 41–63, and Gus di-Zerega, "Integrating Quantum Theory with Post-modern Political Thought and Action: The Priority of Relationships over Objects," 65–97, in *Quantum Politics: Applying Quantum Theory to Political Phenomena,* ed. Theodore L. Becker (New York: Praeger, 1991).

5. For example, Susan Griffin, *The Eros of Everyday Life: Essays on Ecology, Gender, and Society* (New York: Doubleday, 1995).

6. Books written or published during the 1970s or early 1980s which have been cited by Green writers as influencing the start of the Green movement include Alvin Toffler, *Future Shock* (New York: Random House, 1970) and *The Third Wave* (New York: Bantam Books, 1980); E. F. Schumacher, *Small Is Beautiful: Economics as if People Mattered* (New York: Harper and Row, 1973); Barry Commoner, *The Closing Circle* (New York: Knopf, 1971); Marilyn Ferguson, *The Aquarian Conspiracy: Personal and Social Transformation in the 1980s* (Los Angeles: Tarcher, 1980); Ernest Callenbach *Ecotopia* (London: Pluto Press, 1978); Amory Lovins, *Soft Energy Paths* (New York: Harper and Row, 1977); Mark Satin, *New Age Politics: Healing Self and Society* (Vancouver, B.C.: Fairweather Press, 1978); Carolyn Merchant, *The Death of Nature: Women, Ecology, and the Scientific Revolution* (San Francisco: Harper and Row, 1980); Harry Boyte, *The Backyard Revolution: Understanding the New Citizen Movement* (Philadelphia: Temple University Press, 1980); Hazel Henderson, *The Politics of the Solar Age* (New York: Doubleday, 1981); Murray Bookchin, *The Ecology of Freedom* (Palo Alto, Calif.: Cheshire Books, 1982); Charlene Spretnak, ed., *The Politics of Women's Spirituality* (New York: Anchor Books, 1982); and Capra, *Turning Point.* See Spretnak and Capra, *Green Politics,* pp. 194–95 (see note 7, below), for a list of books. Books on Black Power, American Indian sovereignty, animal rights, gay/lesbian or labor issues are rarely mentioned in such lists.

7. Fritjof Capra and Charlene Spretnak, *Green Politics: The Global Promise* (Santa Fe, N.M.: Bear and Co., 1984). As Spretnak and Capra explain in their introduction to the 1986 edition

(Santa Fe, N.M.: Bear and Co.), the first edition of *Green Politics* listed their names alphabetically, and from that listing readers assumed Capra was the primary author. To correct this misunderstanding, they reversed their names in the second edition to reflect the fact that "Charlene originated the idea for this book, conducted most of the interviews, and wrote most of the text, including the updating and the American chapters" (p. xviii). All page references are to the 1986 edition and are cited directly in the text.

8. In North America, the first Green party was formed in British Columbia in 1983.

9. Because the focus of this book is limited to the U.S. context, readers who are interested in the international Green movement are encouraged to consult a variety of other works. On the German Greens, see Rudolph Bahro, *Building the Green Movement* (Philadelphia: New Society, 1985) and *From Red to Green: Interviews with "New Left Review"* (London: Verso, 1984); Petra Kelly, *Fighting for Hope* (Boston: South End Press, 1984), *Nonviolence Speaks to Power* (Honolulu: Spark M. Matsunaga Institute for Peace, 1992), and *Thinking Green: Essays on Environmentalism, Feminism, and Nonviolence* (Berkeley: Parallax Press, 1994). On the British Greens, see Jonathon Porritt, *Seeing Green* (Oxford: Blackwell, 1984), and Derek Wall, *Getting There: Steps to a Green Society* (London: Green Print, 1990). Finally, for a compilation of European Green platforms, interviews, and essays, see Mike Feinstein, *Sixteen Weeks with European Greens* (San Pedro, Calif.: R & E Miles, 1992).

10. The sixty-two people who attended the founding meeting were Patch Adams, Bruce Bebe, Georgia Berland, James F. Berry, Harry Boyte, Robert Brothers, Linda Bullard, Catherine Burton, Philip Capo, Tyrone Cashman, Steve Chase, Guy Chichester, Daniel Chodorkoff, Jane Coleman, Robert Conklin, Betty Didcoct, Michael Eliseuson, Caroline Estes, Gary Fife, Chino Garcia, John and Sara Gerding-Oresic, Robert and Diane Gilman, Gloria Goldberg, Gerald Goldfarb, Guy Gran, Linda Grey, David Haenke, Howard Hawkins, Ron Hughes, Tini Joukowsky, Robert Koehler, Jeff Land, Karen Lehman, Eleanor Le Cain, David Levine, Michael Luick, Peter Lumsdaine, Bill Maclay, John Marks, Ella McDonald, Paul McIsaac, John Milton, Pat and Gerald Mische, Magaly Rodriguez Mossman, Richard Perl, Wendy Hunter Roberts, Mark Russo, Mark Satin, Ray Segal, Charlene Spretnak, Robert Swann, Nan Swift, Robert Theobald, Rachel Tilsen, James Turner, Eric Utne, Zan White, Lavinia Wittenberg. Special thanks to Howie Hawkins for locating this list in his Green archives.

11. Brian Tokar, *The Green Alternative* (San Pedro, Calif.: R & E Miles, 1987), pp. 28–29, 52. According to Charlene Spretnak, Tokar's account fails to mention that it was the same five-member organizing committee that attended NABC and participated in the one-time Green Movement Committee discussions. This omission obscures the continuity between Spretnak's and Tokar's accounts (Charlene Spretnak, personal communication, August 24, 1997).

12. Ibid., p. 52.

13. John Rensenbrink, *The Greens and the Politics of Transformation* (San Pedro, Calif.: R & E Miles, 1992), p. 129; hereafter cited as *Transformation*.

14. Appendix C is a complete listing of the Ten Key Values, which can also be found in Spretnak and Capra's 1986 revision of *Green Politics*.

15. Christa Slaton, "The Failure of the United States Greens to Root in Fertile Soil," 83–118, in *Research in Social Movements, Conflicts, and Change: The Green Movement Worldwide*, ed. Matthias Finger (London: JAI Press, 1992), p. 98.

16. Ibid., p. 108.

17. Ynestra King, "Coming of Age with the Greens," *Z Magazine* (February 1988): 16.

18. Mark Satin, "Last Chance Saloon," in *New Options for America: The Second American Experiment Has Begun* (Fresno: California State University Press, 1991), pp. 19, 35.

19. Howie Hawkins, "North American Greens Come of Age: Statism vs. Municipalism," *Society and Nature* 1:3 (1993): 180–218. Hawkins's essay originally appeared in *Our Generation* 23 (Winter 1992).

20. Rensenbrink, *Transformation*, p. 98.

21. Phil Hill, "U.S. Greens Grow beyond the Grass Roots," *The Guardian* 43(September 18, 1991): 2.

22. Joseph Boland, Amy Belanger, Diana Spalding, and David Shlosberg, "Healing Rifts: Community and Organization in the Fifth Greens Gathering," *GroundWork* (Fall 1992): 48–51.

23. Keiko Bonk, "Growing Up Politically: The Courage to Act," *Green Horizon* 4 (October/November 1995): 1, 5.

24. King, "Coming of Age," pp. 16, 19. Estimates of the attendance at the 1987 gathering vary considerably. According to King, fifteen hundred people attended (p. 16). According to Satin, "Last Chance Saloon," there were about four hundred registrants, and no more than two hundred additional people stopped in for a workshop or two. Satin's estimate is corroborated by Jon Li, who suggests that about six hundred fifty people attended the gathering (Jon Li, Yolo County Green Party Council, "Defacto Green Leadership," 1992, 8 pp.). Finally, Rensenbrink states that "over 600 people" attended (*Transformation*, pp. 179–80).

25. King, "Coming of Age," p. 16.

26. Ibid., pp. 17, 18.

27. Charlene Spretnak, *The Spiritual Dimension of Green Politics* (Santa Fe, N.M.: Bear & Co., 1986).

28. King, "Coming of Age," p. 19.

29. See, for example, Jay Walljasper, "The Prospects for Green Politics in the U.S.," *Utne Reader* 23 (September/October 1987): 37–39.

30. Depending on which report in note 24 is accurate, the 1988 "Greening the West" gathering could arguably be considered more important than the Amherst gathering because of the greater number of people in attendance. Nevertheless, the national movement developed more directly from decisions made during and after the Amherst gathering.

31. Information about the gathering is drawn from the preconference announcement—"Greening the West Conference, Sept. 30–Oct 2," *Green Synthesis* 27 (April 1988): 15–16, and from the reports on the gathering. See Theresa Shimer, "A Movement in Process," *Green Synthesis* 29 (December 1988): 1, 3; "'Greening the West' Regional Gathering," *Green Letter* 4 (Fall 1988): 29–30; and Robert Koehler, "To Be or Not to Be Political," *Green Synthesis* 29 (December 1988): 1, 3–4, 12–13.

32. Koehler, "To Be or Not to Be Political," p. 1. The story of Ken Kesey and The Merry Pranksters is told in Tom Wolfe, *The Electric Kool-Aid Acid Test* (New York: Farrar, Straus and Giroux, 1968).

33. Epstein's remarks in this presentation were based on her research for a book that would be published three years later; see *Political Protest and Cultural Revolution: Nonviolent Direct Action in the 1970s and 1980s* (Berkeley: University of California Press, 1991).

34. Koehler, "To Be or Not to Be Political," p. 4.

35. *Green Letter* (Fall 1988): 30.

36. These names, which are only a partial listing, are taken from the program for the Am-

herst gathering, titled "Building the Green Movement: A National Conference for a New Politics, Thursday–Tuesday, July 2–7, 1987." For this information, I am indebted to Chaia Heller for saving her program.

37. These remarks are taken from the conference report in *Green Letter* 3:6 (1987): 7–9.

38. "Prospectus for Three-Fold Follow-Up of Amherst National Green Gathering," *Green Letter* 3:6 (1987): 15.

39. The genesis of the SPAKA process is contested: according to Howie Hawkins, Rensenbrink proposed the idea at the first IC meeting after the Amherst gathering, and it met with approval under the assumption that the idea would be forwarded to the locals for discussion. Instead, as Hawkins reports, "it was sent by Rensenbrink to the CoC's national publication, *Green Letter*, as a final decision. Thus, without any grassroots debate, program writing, in addition to fighting over structure, became the preoccupation at the national level. The style in which this decision was made came to characterize the functioning of the right wing of the Greens over the next few years." See Hawkins, "North American Greens Come of Age." Hawkins articulates a Left Green perspective, which is explored in greater depth in Chapter 3. For a different view of the SPAKA process, see John Rensenbrink, "Green Praxis: The Genesis of a National Program," 177–97, in *Transformation*.

40. John Rensenbrink, "Actualizing the Vision: Towards a Green Program for America," *Green Letter/In Search of Greener Times* 4 (Summer 1988): a–b; "Inclusivity and What It Means for the Eugene Gathering," *Green Letter/In Search of Greener Times* 4 (Fall 1988): 36–37; "SPAKA Update," *Green Letter/In Search of Greener Times* 5 (Spring 1989): 31; "Ready for the 90s? SPAKA Is a Key," *Green Letter/In Search of Greener Times* (Summer 1989): 23.

41. Li, "Defacto Green Leadership." Though unnamed, Li and his efforts are cited in Rensenbrink, *Transformation*, pp. 182–83.

42. Jeff Land, "Introduction to the SPAKA Process," *Green Synthesis* 29 (December 1988): 8–9.

43. See John Powers, "Eco-Politics: The Greens Are Right. But Is That Enough?" *L.A. Weekly* 11 (July 14–20, 1989): 20–22, 25–28; Bharat Patankar, "Monochromatic Green Gathering," *Race & Class* 31 (October/December 1989): 68–73; and Christian Thurner, "Economics of the U.S. Greens," *Capitalism, Nature, Socialism* 2 (June 1991): 26–29.

44. For these analyses, see Powers, "Eco-Politics"; Patankar, "Monochromatic Green Gathering"; and Satin, "Last Chance Saloon."

45. Not coincidentally, Brown was also a contributor to the first ecofeminist anthology ever compiled; see "Roots: Black Ghetto Ecology," 73–85, in *Reclaim the Earth: Women Speak Out for Life on Earth*, ed. Léonie Caldecott and Stephanie Leland (London: Women's Press, 1983).

46. This description of the consensus process used at Eugene is taken from Margo Adair and John Rensenbrink, "SPAKA: Democracy at Work," *Green Letter/In Search of Greener Times* (Autumn 1989): 3–5.

47. Powers, "Eco-Politics," p. 22.

48. See Christa Slaton and John Rensenbrink, "The Theory, Practice, and Results of the Ongoing SPAKA Ratification Process," *Green Letter* (Spring 1990): 45–47; Christa Slaton, "Greenroots Politics: The Evolution of the SPAKA Process," *Green Letter* (Summer 1990): 49–51.

49. Slaton, "Greenroots Politics," p. 51.

50. This reconstruction of the Left Green perspective on events is taken from an interview with Lowell Nelson (April 23, 1996); Li, "Defacto Green Leadership"; and Howard Hawkins,

"Greens' National Conference Takes Positive Directions," *Left Green Notes* 5 (November/December 1990): 12–13. For a slightly different accounting of events, see Rensenbrink, *Transformation*, pp. 189–97. Hawkins estimates attendance at two hundred; Rensenbrink estimates three hundred.

51. Hawkins, "Greens' National Conference."

52. Daniel Solnit, "Power and Process: Notes on a Dysfunctional Pattern in the Greens," *Green Letter* 6 (Winter 1990): 30–31. According to Solnit, the dysfunctional pattern took the form of the patriarchal family: the people in leadership were perceived (and perceived themselves) in parental roles, and the conference participants perceived themselves in the role of children. The leaders felt "'harassed and unappreciated' by childish, irresponsible behavior," while the participants felt "'chastised and talked down to' with authoritarian lectures."

53. Ibid., p. 31.

54. Slaton, "Failure of the United States Greens." Slaton's findings were later contested (though not persuasively); see William H. Keyser, "The Failure of Green Academics to Take Root in Democratic Soil: A Reply to Christa Daryl Slaton," 285–317, in *Research in Social Movements, Conflicts, and Change* (London: JAI Press, 1995).

55. Hawkins, "Greens' National Conference," p. 12.

56. Margo Adair, "Green Growing Pains: Third National Green Gathering," *Green Letter* 6 (Winter 1990): 28–29.

57. Mark Satin, "You Don't Have to Be a Baby to Cry," 170–81, in *New Options for America: The Second American Experiment Has Begun* (Fresno: California State University Press, 1991); quotations from pp. 180–81.

58. The keynote is reproduced in its entirety in Walt Bresette, "We Are All Mohawks," *Green Letter* 6 (Winter 1990): 2–3, 49–50.

59. See Kwazi Nkrumah, "Red, Black, and Green," *Green Letter* 6 (Winter 1990): 31, 35.

60. Lynette Lamb, "What's Taking American Greens So Long?" *Utne Reader* 43 (January/February 1991): 142–43.

61. Hawkins, "Greens' National Conference," p. 13.

62. John Rensenbrink, "After Estes Park: Thinking Ahead to the Next Crisis," *Green Letter* 6 (Winter 1990): 34–35.

63. The structure proposed by the working group, complete with diagrams, is described in Dee Berry, Charlie Betz, Greg Jan, and David Perry, "Green Restructuring Process Approaches Ratification," *Green Letter* (Spring 1991): 46–49.

64. Charles Betz, "Green Party Organizing Committee Meets," *Green Letter* (Spring 1991): 36.

65. Charles Betz, "Restructuring Proposal Passes Overwhelmingly: New Greens Structure Supports Movement/Party Integration," *Green Letter* 7 (Summer 1991): 48–49.

66. Dee Berry, "Reflections on the Greens Structure: A Critique of the Restructuring Process and the Approved Document," *Green Letter* 7 (Summer 1991): 50–51.

67. Howie Hawkins, "The Green Gathering in Elkins, West Virginia: You Should've Been There," *Left Green Notes* 10 (November/December 1991): 6–18.

68. In view of the tensions surrounding the question of structure and the movement/party debates, the reports on the gathering are again surprisingly upbeat. Joseph Boland, "The Greens at Elkins: Taking Action, Building Multi-cultural Community," *Green Letter* (Fall 1991): 41, 50, 57, and Brian Tokar, "The Greens: To Party or Not?" *Z Magazine* 4 (October 1991): 42–46.

69. "Rationale for Launching a Green Politics Network," *Greens Bulletin* (March 1992): 45–

46. The thirteen signatories included Tony Affigne, Dee Berry, Greg Gerritt, Mindy Lorenz, John Rensenbrink, Barbara Rodgers-Hendricks, Christa Slaton, and Betty Zisk.

70. Joseph Boland, Amy Belanger, Diana Spalding, and David Schlosberg, "Healing Rifts: Community and Organization in the Fifth Greens Gathering," *GroundWork* (Fall 1992): 48–51.

71. Joseph Boland, "From Post-Patriarchal Values to Feminism," Green Gathering '92 Report Draft (September 1992). Boland's draft contained more details of the gathering but was incorporated with drafts from other writers, and the shorter composite piece was published in *GroundWork* later that fall.

72. These descriptions are taken from the trifold oblong flyer designed by AWOL members to publicize the march. Not surprisingly, one section of the flyer adapted text originally included in *The Wall Street Action Handbook* (1990). For a description of the Wall Street Action, see the section on the Left Green Network in Chapter 3.

73. Tad Simons, "Seeing Green," *Twin Cities Reader* (August 12–18, 1992): 14–15.

74. Diana Spalding, "The Greens National Gathering," *Z Magazine* 5 (November 1992): 54–56.

75. "Welcome, Greens!" *Star Tribune* (Wednesday, August 5, 1992): 14A.

76. Boland et al., "Healing Rifts," p. 51.

77. Mark Weiner, "Greens Add Color to Grass-Roots Politics," *Syracuse Herald-Journal* (August 13, 1993): B1–B2.

78. Howie Hawkins, "Green Party Challenges," *Z Magazine* 7 (October 1994): 23–27. Though Hawkins reports that fifty persons attended the Boise gathering, other internal reports count only twenty-six people.

79. The idea for the change was proposed by Jodean Marks of the Women's Caucus and cosponsored by Aimee Glidden and Sue Nelson. From their perspective, the national Green Action Plan was a top-down formulation of ideas from prominent Greens, without broad input or support from locals. Bottom-up formulation of national action campaigns seemed more in keeping with the grassroots character of the Greens. See *Greens Bulletin* (June/July 1993): 47. The proposal was accepted, and the new direct action networks were described in *GroundWork* 4 (March 1994): 32.

80. Two months before the July gathering, these speculations along with an overview of the Greens' history appeared in Howie Hawkins, "Can the Greens Unite for 1996?" *Z Magazine* 8 (May 1995): 10–14.

81. Information on the New Mexico Greens is based on Bill Bradley, "Building the Santa Fe Greens," *Z Magazine* 8 (June 1995): 14–16.

82. Cris Moore, "The 1995 National Green Conference," *Green Politics* (Winter '95): 3. For another report on the gathering, see Alex Chis, "Greens Meet in New Mexico," *Independent Politics* (September/October 1995): 4–5.

83. See Bonk, "Growing Up Politically."

84. These descriptions are taken from a memo first posted to the Greens U.S.A. online forum on June 9, 1995, but also distributed at the Albuquerque gathering. Signatories of the proposal included Tom Cadorette from the Green Party of Virginia and the G/GPUSA; John Rensenbrink, Greg Gerrit, Jonathan Carter, and Linda Martin of the GPN; Hank Chapot of the Green Party of California; Cris Moore of the New Mexico Green Party; and Blair Bobier of the Pacifica Party in Oregon.

85. For the views of many G/GPUSA members, see Don Fitz, "Political Issues Reappear to Greens," *Greens Bulletin* (September/October 1995): 19–24.

Chapter 3

1. I draw most heavily from two works by Sidney Tarrow: "National Politics and Collective Action: Recent Theory and Research in Western Europe and the United States," *Annual Review of Sociology* 14 (1988): 421–40, and *Power in Movement: Social Movements, Collective Action, and Politics* (Cambridge: Cambridge University Press, 1994).

2. Arthur J. Schlesinger, Jr., *The Cycles of American History* (Boston: Houghton Mifflin, 1986).

3. Marta Fuentes and Andre Gunder Frank, "Ten Theses on Social Movements," *World Development* 17 (1989): 179–91; quotation from p. 179.

4. Andre Gunder Frank and Marta Fuentes, "On Studying the Cycles in Social Movements," *Research in Social Movements, Conflicts, and Change,* vol. 17 (London: JAI Press, 1994), pp. 173–96.

5. See Frances Fox Piven and Richard Cloward, *Poor People's Movements: Why They Succeed, How They Fail* (New York: Vintage Books, 1979), p. 36.

6. Tarrow, *Power in Movement,* p. 18.

7. Ibid., pp. 153–69.

8. The concepts of consensus formation and consensus mobilization are developed in Bert Klandermans, "The Formation and Mobilization of Consensus," *International Social Movement Research* 1 (JAI Press, 1988): 173–96.

9. The concept was first presented in Charles Tilly, *From Mobilization to Revolution* (Reading, Mass.: Addison-Wesley, 1978). The description of various forms of protest over the past two centuries appears later, in Charles Tilly, "Speaking Your Mind without Elections, Surveys, or Social Movements," *Public Opinion Quarterly* 47 (1983): 461–78.

10. Tarrow, *Power in Movement,* pp. 33–35.

11. Ibid., p. 8.

12. Ibid., pp. 141, 142.

13. Ibid., p. 157.

14. Piven and Cloward, *Poor People's Movements,* p. 2.

15. Ibid., p. 15.

16. Frances Fox Piven and Richard Cloward, *Why Americans Don't Vote* (New York: Pantheon Books, 1988), p. xxv.

17. The *fundi/realo* distinction (both terms created and defined by the *realos* alone) within the West German Greens is discussed in Charlene Spretnak and Fritjof Capra, *Green Politics: The Global Promise* (Santa Fe, N.M.: Bear and Co., 1984). For a retrospective on the rise and decline of the West German Greens during the 1980s, see Janet Biehl, "From Movement to Parliamentary Party: Notes on Several European Green Movements," *Society and Nature* 1:3 (1993): 158–79.

18. These numbers are taken from Howie Hawkins, "Can the Greens Unite for 1996?" *Z Magazine* 8 (May 1995): 10–14.

19. These tendencies are distinguished in Howard Hawkins, "The Politics of Ecology: Environmentalism, Ecologism, and the Greens," *Resist Newsletter* 217 (July/August 1989): 1–2, 4–6. Hawkins also includes the movements of populist environmentalism and environmental justice in his analysis, but these movements were never present in the U.S. Green movement, an absence that explains the movement's predominantly white and middle-class composition. The radical ecology movement is usually distinguished through comparison with the mainstream environmental movement, largely composed of the "group of ten" mainstream environmental organizations: the Na-

tional Wildlife Federation, Sierra Club, Natural Resources Defense Council, World Wildlife Fund, Environmental Defense Fund, Audubon Society, Izaak Walton League, Wilderness Society, Environmental Policy Center, and Friends of the Earth. For more information on the "group of ten," see Robert Gottlieb, *Forcing the Spring: The Transformation of the American Environmental Movement* (Washington, D.C.: Island Press, 1993), chap. 4.

20. Bill Devall, "A Spanner in the Woods: An Interview with Dave Foreman," *Simply Living* (Manley, NSW, Australia) 2:12 (1987): 40–43. Murray Bookchin describes his experience at the Amherst gathering in his essay "Which Way for the U.S. Greens?" *New Politics* 2 (Winter 1989): 71–83. The tensions at the Amherst gathering can also be approached through a gendered analysis: among the male ecologists present, the most significant debate seemed to address the differences between social ecology and deep ecology, whereas among the women, the debate that did not surface was the tension between social ecofeminism and cultural ecofeminism. Each debate contained an aspect of the spirituality versus politics debate. Each debate also reflected the cultural geography of the United States: the East Coast, and specifically New England, was the center of intellectual, political, and leftist thought as articulated by social ecologists and social ecofeminists, whereas the West Coast, and specifically California, was the home of those emphasizing the importance of spirituality, psychology, and New Age tendencies as expressed by cultural ecofeminists and deep ecologists. Inevitably, the debates between the male environmentalists received more prominence at the gathering. Although both Bookchin and Janet Biehl published critiques of deep ecology in a special issue of *Kick It Over*, and the ecofeminist critique of deep ecology received attention in academic journals such as *Environmental Ethics*, the necessary debate between the two branches of ecofeminism (social and cultural) was never fully articulated. On the differences within ecofeminism, see Chapter 4.

21. For a recent discussion and interpretation of the Ten Key Values, see Dan Coleman, *Ecopolitics: Building a Green Society* (New Brunswick: Rutgers University Press, 1994).

22. These principles were published later that fall; see "Toward a New Politics: A Statement of Principles of the Vermont and New Hampshire Greens," *Our Generation* 20 (Fall 1988): 22–53.

23. Spretnak and Capra, *Green Politics*, pp. 30–31.

24. "Toward a New Politics," p. 28.

25. Of course, many Greens protested that the 1996 Nader presidential campaign violated the last remaining principle that had united the various Green groupings. For a fuller discussion of democracy and the Nader campaign, see Chapter 6. For a comparison of the pillars, values, and principles of the various Green groups, see Appendix D.

26. "Toward a New Politics," p. 51.

27. Ibid., p. 36.

28. Ibid.

29. Ibid., pp. 31–33. More is said about feminism and ecofeminism in Chapter 4.

30. Information on the First Continental Conference of the Left Green Network is drawn from activist interviews and from the published *Report on the First Conference of the Left Green Network*, Ames, Iowa, April 21–23, 1989.

31. Northern California Greens, "Time for a Reality Check," *Green Letter* 4 (Fall 1988): 35.

32. Danny Moses and Charlene Spretnak, "A Consideration of GCoC History," *Green Letter* 5 (Spring 1989): 37–39.

33. See, for example, Eric Chester, "Toward a Left Green Politics: The Iowa Conference,"

Resist Newsletter 217 (July/August 1989): 3, 7, and Howard Hawkins, "Left Green Network Holds First Conference," *Green Letter/In Search of Greener Times* (Autumn 1989): 50.

34. Lorna Salzman, "Is the Left Green Network Really Green?" *Green Synthesis* 31 (June 1989): 9–11.

35. Ibid., pp. 9, 10, 11. It seems that both Salzman's and the Left Greens' choice of terminology reveals more about the roots of their activism and the different audiences they are addressing than it does about their ultimate vision of a just and sustainable society in harmony with nature. "Biocentrism" reconnects humans with nature from an ecological perspective, which fits neatly with Salzman's roots in environmental activism. "Ecological humanism" reconnects humans with nature from a social perspective, which is best suited to the Left Green Network project of "greening the Left."

36. Salzman, "Left Green Network," p. 11.

37. Margo Adair and John Rensenbrink, "SPAKA: Democracy at Work," *Green Letter/In Search of Greener Times* (Autumn 1989): 3–5.

38. Tom Athanasiou, "A Green Orthodoxy?" pp. 6, 10–11; Janet Biehl, "Adherence to Principles," pp. 6, 11–12; and Carl Boggs, "Why the Left Green Network Is Necessary," pp. 6, 12–14, *Green Synthesis* 32 (October 1989). Athanasiou has since left the Greens and most recently has published *Divided Planet: The Ecology of Rich and Poor* (Boston: Little, Brown, 1996).

39. Biehl, "Adherence to Principles," p. 12.

40. Boggs, "Left Green Network," p. 13.

41. Charlene Spretnak, "Improving the Debates," *Green Synthesis* 33 (March 1990): 3–6.

42. Spretnak does not name "leftist politics" but rather phrases the debate as taking place between "spirituality vs. ?" Her discussion of this debate addresses the Left Green rejection of spirituality as apolitical, a rejection she believes is offensive to the many activists whose spirituality empowers their politics—Quakers, Buddhists, Christians, Jews, Pagans—as well as to those Hispanics and African-Americans whose communities have been influenced by the strong political presence of religion.

43. Brian Tokar, "Shut Down Wall Street for Earth Day!" *Green Synthesis* 33 (March 1990): 13–14.

44. Many of these details are taken from the *Earth Day Wall Street Action Handbook*.

45. These details on the history and evolution of the Wall Street Action are taken from Paul Glavin, "Opposition and Statecraft in the Greens," *Regeneration* 1 (Summer 1991): 3–8.

46. Those organizations include Alliance for Nonviolent Action (Ontario), Amis/es de la Terre (Québec), Antioch Greens (Ohio), Ascutney Greens (Vt.), Bhopal Action Resource Center, Big River Earth First! (Mo.), Boulder Green Alliance (Colo.), Central Vermont Greens, Clamshell Alliance, Columbia Students in Solidarity with Nicaragua, Diné Green Alliance (N.M., Ariz.), Ecological Front (Mass.), Eleutheros Productions (N.Y.), Environmental Project on Central America, Food Not Bombs, Hudson Valley Federation of Coops (N.Y.), Huron Valley Greens (Mich.), Left Green Network, Love Canal Homeowners Association, Mobilization for Survival, National Toxics Campaign, National Toxics Campaign Fund, Neither East nor West (N.Y.), New England Green Alliance, New Options Newsletter, New York Marxist School, Ocean Beach Greens (Calif.), Orange County Greens (N.C.), People for a Socially Responsible University (U. Mass.), Pioneer Valley Greens (Mass.), Putney Greens (Vt.), Red Balloon (N.Y.), Relocation Assistance and Information Network (Pa.), Sabotage Bookstore Collective (N.Y.), Seeds of Peace, Socialist Party U.S.A., Stop the Slaughter Coalition (Vt.), Student Action Union, Tampa Bay Greens (Fla.), Vermont All Species Project,

Vermont Pledge of Resistance, Vermonters Organized for Cleanup, War Resisters League, Wisconsin Greens, Youth Greens.

47. Joshua Nessen, "Take It to Wall Street: A View from the Barricades," *Left Green Notes* 3 (July/August 1990): 1, 36–39.

48. For this information and other reports on the action, I am particularly indebted to Laura Schere, who saved minutes from the planning meetings and clippings from all these papers.

49. Tokar is author of *The Green Alternative* (San Pedro, Calif.: R & E Miles, 1987) and *Earth for Sale: Reclaiming Ecology in the Age of Corporate Greenwash* (Boston: South End Press, 1997), an activist both inside and outside the Greens, and a regular contributor to *Z Magazine*. Tokar's articles on the action are "Shut Down Wall Street for Earth Day!" "After Earth Day," *Green Letter* 6 (Summer 1990): 10, 41; and "Radical Ecology on the Rise," *Z Magazine* (July/August 1990): 12–18.

50. Tokar, "Shut Down Wall Street," p. 14; Tokar, "After Earth Day," p. 10.

51. Tokar, "After Earth Day," p. 41.

52. Tokar, "Radical Ecology," p. 18. Another report on the Wall Street Action from an older Green activist explains, "I felt like it was 1968 and looked at the young people, who were me and my gang, back then. I counted the people of my generation, and came up with five, including myself." Overcoming what she sees as her own "ageism, classism, and racism," the writer reports that she is "honored to have run with the people with the purple hair." Like Tokar, she sees the action as the start, rather than the apex, of a movement and concludes that "the youth are on the move again. After all, they are us, twenty years ago." See Theresa Freeman, "Running on Wall Street," *Green Letter* 6 (Summer 1990): 11.

53. Details on events of the gathering are taken from the LGN Conference Report, which appeared in *Left Green Notes* 3 (July/August 1990): 13–23.

54. The Burlington Greens local dissolved in January 1991, and a letter from Janet Biehl, Murray Bookchin, and Gary Sisco (the LGN clearinghouse coordinator), tendered their resignation from the LGN and the GCoC, claiming they "believe that the U.S. Greens are no longer a fruitful area for us to act politically" [*Left Green Notes* 6 (February/March 1991) :7]. Later Biehl and Bookchin rejoined the LGN, although they had no local with which to affiliate ["Letter," *Left Green Notes* 7 (April/May 1991): 4]. They resigned again later that year.

55. For these details on the inner workings of the Left Green Network, I am indebted to Lowell Nelson.

56. On the car bombing, Earth First! activism in northern California, and Bari's work, see Judi Bari, *Timber Wars* (Monroe, Maine: Common Courage Press, 1994).

57. Details about Redwood Summer are taken from the mailings from Earth Action Network, dated July 1990 and August 1990.

58. The process and outcome of "Greens for Democracy" is discussed in Chapter 2.

59. "Greens for Democracy," *IC Bulletin* (September 1990): 13–14.

60. Howard Hawkins, "Grassroots Greens Beckon Left," *The Guardian* 42 (May 9, 1990): 8–9. This article is the first of at least four articles Hawkins wrote over the next five years in an attempt to persuade the Left to join the Greens; the effort was never very successful. Here the confidence with which Hawkins writes about Greens for Democracy suggests that the group has already met and formed a plan; thus, the idea must have originated either with the New England Green Alliance, which had a strong overlap of Left Green members and which sent out the Call for the Left Green Network, or with Hawkins himself. Hawkins has clearly been a major theorist and spokesperson for the Left Green Network.

61. Howard Hawkins, "Clearinghouse Report," *Left Green Notes* 3 (July/August 1990): 6–9; "Can the GCoC Practice the Grassroots Democracy It Preaches?" *Left Green Notes* 4 (September/October 1990): 13–14, 30–31; "Greens' National Conference Takes Positive Directions," *Left Green Notes* 5 (November/December 1990): 12–13.

62. Information on the ECOnomics drafts is taken from Christian Thurner, "Economics of the U.S. Greens," *Capitalism, Nature, Socialism* 2 (June 1991): 26–29.

63. Ibid., p. 29.

64. Howard Hawkins and Lowell Nelson, "Program of the Left Green Network," *Left Green Notes* 7 (April/May 1991): 5–7, 20–21. In these discussions of the platforms of the GCoC and the LGN, I am deliberately choosing not to delve into substantial analyses or discussion of program planks or political philosophy; I believe such a discussion would take me too far afield from my purpose here. For an overview of the differences among the various Green groups, see Appendix D, which charts the migration of Green values from the West German Greens, through the Green Committees of Correspondence, the Left Green Network, and the Youth Greens, listing each group's core principles. Elaborating on the meaning and implications of those principles through platform writing served as a unifying process for each group's members, inviting discussion of differences and mutual education as well as creating a product that could be used to inform newcomers about each group's Green vision. The GCoC Platform is still available from the G/GPUSA Clearinghouse in Blodgett Mills, N.Y.

65. Many Left Greens contributed their ideas for revision. Here my discussion is based on three specific critiques: Members of the Northern Vermont Greens, "Critique and Proposed Amendments to the Hawkins-Nelson Draft" (July 1, 1991); Murray Bookchin and Janet Biehl, "A Critique of the Draft Program of the Left Green Network," *Green Perspectives* 23 (June 1991): 1–8 (quotations from pp. 6, 7); and Frank Girard, "Toward a Revolutionary Left Green Network," *Regeneration* 1 (Summer 1991): 16–18.

66. See Laura Schere, "Feminism, Ecology, and Left Green Politics," *Left Green Notes* 9 (August/September 1991): 30–31, and Janet Biehl, "Ecofeminism and the Left Greens: A Response to Laura Schere," *Left Green Notes* 10 (November/December 1991): 22–26.

67. Interview with Lowell Nelson, Minneapolis, April 29, 1996.

68. Howard Hawkins, "U.S. Greens on the Threshold," *Left Green Notes* 8 (June/July 1991): 11–12, 20.

69. Howie Hawkins, "The Green Gathering in Elkins, West Virginia: You Should've Been There," *Left Green Notes* 10 (November/December 1991): 6–18.

70. These excerpts are taken from "Youth Caucus Statement: October 21, 1988," *Green Letter/In Search of Greener Times* 4 (Fall 1988): 33, and Bob Long, "Green Youth Caucus," *Green Synthesis* 29 (December 1988): 9.

71. "Antioch Greens Update," *Green Letter* 4 (Fall 1988): 37.

72. "Youth Caucus Statement," *Green Synthesis* 30 (March 1989): 3–4.

73. Kate Fox and Paul Glavin, "The Politics of Imagination and Struggle," *Record of Antioch College* 46 (June 2, 1989): 8–9; Andy Jacobson, "The Youth Greens," *Green Synthesis* 32 (October 1989): 3–4.

74. See Northern California Greens, "Time for a Reality Check," and "Did Someone Say 'Reality'?" *Green Letter* (Summer 1989): 27; the Youth Greens' response was "Youth Greens Concerned," *Green Letter/Greener Times* (Winter 1989): 39.

75. "Youth Greens Concerned."

76. Details about allied Earth Day demonstrations are taken from Laura Schere, "Radicals Rock Earth Day," *The Guardian* 42 (May 9, 1990): 8.

77. Kate Fox, "On the Conference," *Youth Green Newsletter* (Winter 1990): 15, 18–19.

78. Charles Betz and Katie Kadwell, "On Organization and Personal Politics," *Youth Green Newsletter* (Winter 1990): 11–14.

79. Laura Schere and Paul Glavin, "Report on Youth Green Conference," *Left Green Notes* 4 (September/October 1990): 21–23.

80. "Youth Greens Active across the Continent," *Green Letter* 6 (Summer 1990): 24–25, 34; Eric Jacobson, "The Emerging Identity of the Youth Greens," *Left Green Notes* 4 (September/October 1990): 24; Eric Odell and Charles Betz, "Catalyzing a New Student Movement," *Green Letter* 6 (Winter 1990): 14.

81. The acronym AWOL originated during the Persian Gulf protests and was originally intended to parody conservative rhetoric about defending the "American Way of Life." The meaning of the acronym was revised for every occasion, however, becoming "Anarchists Waltzing over Lenin" and "Anarchists with Oblong Leaflets" as the situation demanded (Laura Schere, interview, Minneapolis, April 29, 1996). The acronym exemplifies the spirit of the Youth Greens.

82. Jessica Bernstein, "Report on the National Student Environmental Conference," *People for a Socially Responsible University* 11 (October/November 1990): 8–9; Leslie Fraser, "Green Wave on Campus," *Nuclear Times* 8 (Winter 1990–91): 5.

83. Jason Serota-Winston, "In Search of a Strategy; Or, Fellow Sailors! Where Is the Boat Going?" (Summer 1991); Paul Glavin and Eric Jacobson, "Which Way for the Youth Greens? Theory, Education, and Direct Action! (Just a) Discussion Paper" (Summer 1991); Matthew Moore, "Where's the Revolution? An Open Letter to the Youth Greens" (September 27, 1990); Eric Jacobson, "How about a Little Campaign with Your Organization?" (December 1990).

84. Joe Foss, Northland Greens, "A Letter of Consideration for the Youth Greens," *Youth Green Newsletter* (Spring 1990): 2, 27.

85. Serota-Winston, "In Search of a Strategy."

86. Eric Odell, "Ageism in the Greens," *Green Letter* 7 (Fall 1991): 48.

87. Citations taken directly from the presentation text by Laura Schere and Paul Glavin.

88. Lowell Nelson, "Ups and Downs of Incinerator Battles in Minnesota," *Regeneration* 2 (Fall 1991): 15–16, 18.

89. Twin Cities Greens also sent a copy of their letter to the GCoC Clearinghouse, and it was published in the next *IC Bulletin* (May 1990): 20.

90. Paul Glavin, "Youth Greens Fifth Continental Conference," *Left Green Notes* 10 (November/December 1991): 20–21.

91. Paul O'Bannion, "AWOL Fights Nuclear Power in Minnesota," *Left Green Notes* (1992): 1, 11–12.

92. Paul Glavin, "Out of the Dustbin of History," *Free Society* 1 (Fall 1991): 3–5; Paul O'Bannion, "Tracing Our Descent: Anarchism, Ecology, and the Fight for a Free Society," *Free Society* 4 (1995): 22–27.

93. O'Bannion, "Tracing Our Descent," p. 25.

94. Jim Richmond, "The Inter-Regional Committee Meets," *Green Letter* (Winter 1989): 37. A major figure in the founding of the Green Politics Network and in the SPAKA process that

culminated in the Greens' national platform, Rensenbrink describes the history of the U.S. Green movement, including the conflicts of party and movement activists up through the 1991 gathering at Elkins, in *The Greens and the Politics of Transformation* (San Pedro, Calif.: R & E Miles, 1992), hereafter cited simply as *Transformation*.

95. Rensenbrink, *Transformation*, p. 131.

96. "Reintegrate the Green Party Organizing Committee into the Green Committees of Correspondence," *Left Green Notes* 3 (July/August 1990): 8.

97. See John Rensenbrink, "Are Greens Ready for Politics?" *Green Synthesis* 33 (March 1990): 14; "Taking the Next Step beyond Boulder: Inter-movement and Multicultural Organizing—A Call for Help," *IC Bulletin* (September 1990): 34–36; and "After Estes Park: Thinking Ahead to the Next Crisis," *Green Letter* 6 (Winter 1990): 34–35.

98. John Powers, "Eco-Politics: The Greens Are Right. But Is That Enough?" *L.A. Weekly* (July 14–20, 1989): 20–26.

99. "Don't Divide the Greens! A Response to Restructuring Working Group's Proposal," *IC Bulletin* (March 1991): 13–17.

100. "Restructuring Proposal Passes Overwhelmingly," *Green Letter* 7 (Summer 1991): 48–49.

101. Dee Berry, "Reflections on the Greens Structure," *Green Letter* 7 (Summer 1991): 50–51.

102. For reports of this meeting, see Rensenbrink, *Transformation*, pp. 132–33, and Charlie Betz, "Green Party Organizing Committee Meets," *Green Letter* 6 (Spring 1991): 36.

103. Resenbrink, "Transformation," p. 263.

104. Phil Hill, "U.S. Greens Grow beyond the Grass Roots," *The Guardian* 43 (September 18, 1991): 3.

105. John Rensenbrink, "Green Activists Need to Come Down to Earth," *The Guardian* 43 (October 9, 1991): 18.

106. John Rensenbrink, "Green Story: Recollection of Things Past," *Green Horizon* (newsletter of the Green Politics Network) 2 (July 1993): 3. In this essay, Rensenbrink refers to the Greens/Green Party U.S.A. as G-USA instead of G/GPUSA, the more common usage. His choice of acronym thereby resists the compromise at Elkins, which added the name of "Green Party U.S.A." to the Greens' organization.

107. The thirteen founding members of the GPN were Tony Affigne, Dee Berry, Blair Bobier, Greg Garritt, Ben Kjelshus, Mindy Lorenz, Ron Natoli, John Rensenbrink, Barbara Rodgers-Hendricks, Christa Slaton, Janette Taylor, Terri Williams, and Betty Zisk. At least five of the thirteen (Affigne, Lorenz, Rensenbrink, Slaton, Zisk) were university professors, and four of the five were political scientists.

108. "Rationale for Launching a Green Politics Network," *Greens Bulletin* (March 1992): 45–46. In the same issue of the *Greens Bulletin*, Jodean Marks published a comment, "On the Green Politics Network," in which she observed that "a parallel organization competes, and does not cooperate," and that "an independent network that aims to promote and represent Green politics can only lead to confusion among the public and division among ourselves" (p. 48).

109. Rensenbrink, "Green Story," p. 6.

110. Mike Feinstein, "Report on the Green Parties of the West Conference," *Green Politics News* 9 (March 1993): 4–6. The GPN's newsletter, launched by Barbara Ann Rodgers-Hendricks in June 1992, shifted to an editorial board format in June 1993 and was renamed *Green Horizon*.

111. "Draft Articles of Confederation of the Green Parties of the United States, dated December 28, 1992," *Green Politics News* 9 (March 1993): 8.

112. Sam Smith, "Further Adventures in Green Land," *Progressive Review* (April 1993): 4–6.

113. This account of New Politics '94 is based on Linda Martin, "Fifty Green and Third-Party Activists Meet at GPN's New Politics '94 Conference," *Green Horizon* 3 (October/November 1994): 2, 8.

114. Linda Martin was quoted in *The Nation* (June 26, 1995) and again in Howie Hawkins, "Independent Progressive Politics," *Z Magazine* 9 (March 1996): 18. This report on Third Parties '96 is drawn from Hawkins, "Independent Progressive Politics"; John Rensenbrink, "Will 'Third Parties '96' Lead to an Alliance?" *Green Horizon* 4 (October/November 1995): 1, 6–7; and Walt Sheasby, "Third Parties '96: Birds of a Feather . . ." *Synthesis/Regeneration* 10 (Spring 1996): 32–33.

115. Greg Guma, "No Way to Build a Movement," *Toward Freedom* (August/September 1995).

116. "An Open Letter to Third Parties '96 from the Interim Continuations Committee of the National Independent Politics Summit," January 31, 1996. Signatories to the letter included Rick Adams, Claire Cohen, Ron Daniels, Marsha Feinland, Mary France, Ted Glick, Howie Hawkins, Arthur Kinoy, Sandra Rivers, James Vann, Inila Wakan, and Linda Wambaugh.

117. John Rensenbrink, "Response to NIPS," February 26, 1996; Hank Chapot, "Response to NIPS," February 27, 1996.

118. Rensenbrink, "Response to NIPS."

119. See Dee Berry, "Report on the People's Progressive Convention," *Green Politics News* 4 (September 1992): 3–4, and letter from Vera Bradova, *Green Politics News* 7 (December 1992): 8.

Chapter 4

1. Ynestra King, "Coming of Age with the Greens," *Z Magazine* (February 1988): 19.

2. Charlene Spretnak and Fritjof Capra, *Green Politics* (Santa Fe: Bear & Co., 1984), p. 151.

3. Kelly assessed the shortcomings of the West German Greens in "Open Letter to the German Green Party," 149–59, in Petra Kelly, *Nonviolence Speaks to Power,* ed. Glenn D. Paige and Sarah Gilliatt (Honolulu: Center for Global Nonviolence Planning Project at the University of Hawaii, 1992). Spretnak's memorial for Kelly is appended to Petra K. Kelly, *Thinking Green! Essays on Environmentalism, Feminism, and Nonviolence* (Berkeley: Parallax Press, 1994), pp. 151–54.

4. This narrative for the origin of the Ten Key Values is from Charlene Spretnak, personal communication, August 23, 1997.

5. Howard Hawkins, "North American Greens Come of Age: Statism vs. Municipalism," *Society and Nature* 3 (1993): 204–5.

6. Charlene Spretnak, ed., *The Politics of Women's Spirituality* (New York: Doubleday, 1982), and *The Spiritual Dimension of Green Politics* (Santa Fe: Bear & Co., 1986); Mark Satin, *New Age Politics: Healing Self and Society* (New York: Dell, 1978), and *New Options for America: The Second American Experiment Has Begun* (Fresno: California State University Press, 1991).

7. Since cultural ecofeminism is not the sole form but rather one of several branches of ecofeminism, Spretnak's words here may be read as accurate descriptions of her own intellectual development. See "Ecofeminism: Our Roots and Flowering," pp. 3–14, in Irene Diamond and Gloria Feman Orenstein, eds., *Reweaving the World: The Emergence of Ecofeminism* (San Francisco: Sierra Club Books, 1990).

8. Satin's analysis of social problems shifts the responsibility away from social, economic, and political structures (including capitalism and statism) to an examination of individual psychology,

attitudes, values and beliefs. In his chapter "New Age Critique of Marxism" in *New Age Politics*, for example, Satin rejects "Marxist arrogance and self-righteousness" and explains that "capitalism (as we know it today) and also socialism (as we know it today) can more usefully be seen as symptoms of our problems. . . . If we are able to break out of the Prison (i.e., begin to change our consciousness) and convert our monolithic institutions to biolithic ones, then capitalism would or at least could be humane. (Same with socialism)" (p. 273).

9. After *ecology* and *social responsibility*, the other two of the Four Pillars, *nonviolence* and *grassroots democracy*, already articulated feminist values developed from participation in the peace movement, the environmental movement, and the movements to stop battering and domestic violence. The feminist emphasis on interpersonal and community relationships as the appropriate locus of power (and the antileftist opposition to naming all forms of capitalism as a problem or socialism as a solution) can be seen in the values of *decentralization* and *community-based economics*. The phrase *postpatriarchal values* emphasizes specific ways of behaving that had previously been devalued as feminine: cooperation, relationships, feelings, an emphasis on process, a valuing of the means as well as the ends, and a valuing of "the inner life." The "feminine" concern for others and for inclusivity can be seen in the value *respect for diversity*, and a concern for the well-being of children and grandchildren is articulated in the values *global responsibility* and *future focus*. Overall, the Ten Key Values reflect a shift in valuation, from a masculinist, patriarchal style of politics to a politics based on values traditionally associated with women's sphere.

10. Because radical feminism was formed out of a reaction against experiences in the New Left, it does not offer a substantial critique of oppressions other than gender. See Ellen Willis, "Radical Feminism and Feminist Radicalism," 91–118, in *The Sixties without Apology*, ed. Sohnya Sayres, Anders Stephanson, Stanley Aronowitz, and Fredric Jameson (Minneapolis: University of Minnesota Press, 1984).

11. Janet Biehl, "What Is Social Ecofeminism?" *Green Perspectives* 11 (October 1988): 4.

12. My purpose in Chapter 1 was to articulate many of these heretofore unexamined distinctions among ecofeminisms, and in the present chapter I examine some of the foundations for an alliance between cultural ecofeminism and deep ecology, as well as distinctions between social ecofeminism and deep ecology. The distinctions between social ecofeminism and social ecology have not been explored.

13. The exchange took place in a single journal; see Kirkpatrick Sale, "Ecofeminism—A New Perspective," *The Nation* (September 26, 1987): 302–5, and Ynestra King, "What Is Ecofeminism?" *The Nation* (December 12, 1987): 702, 730–31. King rejects labeling the various branches of ecofeminism, seeing such labeling as a divisive tactic rather than a helpful analytic tool; yet because she identifies herself as both an ecofeminist and a social ecologist, I admit to taking liberties here by identifying her as a social ecofeminist. Indeed, no other branch of ecofeminism describes her position so well.

14. Sale, "Ecofeminism," p. 702. Just as Marti Kheel has argued against the use by ecofeminists of the term "testify" (based on its sexist origins in the practice of men swearing by their testicles), and Carol Adams has deplored the use of the word "denigrate" (for its racist association of defaming with "blackening" and its root in the word *niger*, or black), I take this opportunity to argue against the words "hybrid" and "amalgam" in describing the roots of ecofeminism. "Hybrid" has connotations of genetic engineering and the human control of nature through the forced cross-breeding of two disparate species or varieties. Similarly, "amalgam" specifically refers to the combi-

nation of mercury with a "softening" agent—leaving an ecofeminist no doubt as to whether it is ecology or feminism that is the "softer"—and the toxicity of mercury, whether in lakes or in dental fillings, has been conclusively proved and hence does not offer a suitable metaphor for ecofeminism.

15. For Plant's work on bioregionalism, see Judith Plant, "Revaluing Home: Feminism and Bioregionalism," 21–23, in *Home! A Bioregional Reader*, ed. Van Andruss, Christopher Plant, Judith Plant, and Eleanor Wright (Philadelphia: New Society, 1990); Judith and Christopher Plant, *Turtle Talk: Voices for a Sustainable Future* (Philadelphia: New Society, 1990); and Judith Plant, "The Circle Is Gathering," 242–53, in *Healing the Wounds: The Promise of Ecofeminism* (Philadelphia: New Society, 1989).

16. King, "What is Ecofeminism?" p. 702.

17. Ibid., p. 730. Laura Schere, personal communication, October 1996.

18. King, "What Is Ecofeminism?" p. 731.

19. Janet Biehl, "An Eco-Feminist Looks at Deep Ecology," *Kick It Over* (special supplement) 20 (Winter 1987/88): 2A.

20. Ibid., pp. 2A-4A (quotation from p. 4A). Though initially positioning herself as a social ecofeminist, Biehl later believed cultural ecofeminism was taking over all of ecofeminism and found it necessary to disassociate herself from the movement entirely. Her book *Rethinking Ecofeminist Politics* (Boston: South End Press, 1991) is thus a social ecologist's critique of cultural ecofeminism, which Biehl mistakes for the sole form of ecofeminism and hence refers to it not as *cultural* ecofeminism but simply as "ecofeminism." Like the debate between Sale and King or numerous other essays, too much ink has been wasted in struggles over the "one true ecofeminism" by writers who fail to recognize the various distinct branches of thought within ecofeminism. Biehl's book has been criticized by several ecofeminists for its use of straw woman arguments, for its omissions of ecofeminist authors whose work directly disproves Biehl's theory, and for its conclusion that ecofeminism should be abandoned in favor of social ecology, the supposedly all-inclusive political theory that respects unique identities while affirming reason and the universal "human." See my review in *Women and Environments* (Spring 1992): 20–21; Val Plumwood, "The Atavism of Flighty Females," *The Ecologist* 22 (January/February 1992): 36; Laura Schere, "Feminism, Ecology, and Left Green Politics," *Left Green Notes* 9 (August/September 1991): 30–31; and Douglas Buege, "Rethinking Again: A Defense of Ecofeminist Philosophy," 42–63, in *Ecological Feminism*, ed. Warren.

21. See Marilyn Frye, "Oppression," 1–16, in *The Politics of Reality* (Trumansburg, N.Y.: Crossing Press, 1983).

22. Biehl, "Eco-Feminist Looks at Deep Ecology," p. 3A.

23. Ibid., p. 4A.

24. The collaborative writing process for developing the Greens' national platform was created by John Rensenbrink in collaboration with Christa Slaton and Margo Adair. The process was notable for its difficulties: many groups failed to respond to their coordinators, some coordinators dropped out entirely, and others had to write up their sections alone. It was an example of choosing a supposedly feminist, democratic method of writing for its politics rather than for its suitability to the writing situation. Of course, the Greens have not been alone in this: in 1991, the same year the final draft of the Greens' national platform was approved, the World Women's Congress, sponsored by the Women's Environment and Development Organization, met in Miami to draft a Women's Action Agenda for presentation at the UN Conference on Environment and Development in Rio de

Janeiro the following summer. As one ecofeminist reported, there were "not many opportunities for the majority of Congress participants to contribute to or develop the agenda, which began as a draft written by a smaller group of international women leaders—who were hand-picked to insure strong representation of developing countries—the week before the Congress. There was some criticism of this format because it created feelings of hierarchy and power among the Congress participants." See Stephanie Lahar, "Report on the World Women's Congress for a Healthy Planet," *Regeneration* 3 (Spring 1992): 21.

25. "Consensus and Community: An Interview with Caroline Estes," 235–41, in *Healing the Wounds,* ed. Plant.

26. Telephone interview, June 26, 1996.

27. See John Powers, "Eco-Politics: The Greens Are Right. But Is That Enough?" *L.A. Weekly* 11 (July 14–20, 1989): 20–22, 24, 26, 28.

28. Howie Hawkins, "The Politics of Ecology: Environmentalism, Ecologism, and the Greens," *Resist* 217 (July/August 1989): 6.

29. Barbara Epstein, *Political Protest and Cultural Revolution: Nonviolent Direct Action in the 1970s and 1980s* (Berkeley: University of California Press, 1991), esp. pp. 85–91.

30. Telephone interview, June 26, 1996.

31. See Noël Sturgeon, *Ecofeminist Natures: Race, Gender, and Transnational Environmental Politics* (New York: Routledge, 1997).

32. I am indebted to Charlene Spretnak for copies of these statements and for the attributions she wrote for each section or statement.

33. Sturgeon, *Ecofeminist Natures.*

34. "Ecofeminism," *Green Letter/Greener Times* (Autumn 1989): 39. The crossover between academic and activist ecofeminists can be seen in the fact that the contact person for the working group on ecofeminism, Karin Herrmann, also participated in the founding meeting of the Ecofeminist Caucus for the National Women's Studies Association in Baltimore in June 1989.

35. See Chapter 5 for a more detailed discussion of animal rights activism (and its failure to take hold) within the Greens. Salamone's essays include "The Prevalence of the Natural Law within Women: Women and Animal Rights," 364–7, in *Reweaving the Web of Life: Feminism and Nonviolence,* ed. Pam McAllister (Philadelphia: New Society, 1982); "Feminist as Rapist in the Modern Male Hunter Culture," *Majority Report* (October 1973); "The Knowing: The Masculist and Moralistic Philosophical Animal 'Rights' Movement Can Never Become Part of the Larger Merging Nature Movement until it Accepts and Absorbs Deep Ecologist/Feminist Processes, Visions, Rituals, and Passage," *Woman of Power* 9 (Spring 1988): 53; "Loving the World: Animal Rights, Deep Ecology, and the Goddess," *One Earth* 9 (Autumn 1989).

36. Adair and Howell coauthored the essay "Women Weave Community," 35–41, in *Circles of Strength: Community Alternatives to Alienation,* ed. Helen Forsey (Philadelphia: New Society, 1992), and the pamphlet *The Subjective Side of Politics* (San Francisco: Tools for Change, 1988). Adair is also known for her essay "Will the Real Men's Movement Please Stand Up?" 55–66, in *Women Respond to the Men's Movement,* ed. Kay Leigh Hagan (New York: HarperCollins, 1992).

37. Paul Stark, "Why Detroit Summer?" *Green Letter* 7 (Fall 1991): 2–3.

38. Chaia Heller, "Down to the Body: Feminism, Ecology, and the Evolution of the Body Politic," *Society and Nature* 2 (1993): 142.

39. First published in *Renewing the Earth*, ed. John Clark (London: Green Print, 1990), Heller's essay "Toward a Radical Ecofeminism: From Dua-Logic to Eco-Logic" is available to U.S. readers in the journal *Society and Nature* 2:1 (1993): 72–96. Heller has also published her essay "For the Love of Nature: Ecology and the Cult of the Romantic," 219–242 in *Ecofeminism: Women, Animals, Nature*, ed. Greta Gaard (Philadelphia: Temple University Press, 1993). Most recently, she has developed her theory of social ecofeminism in *The Revolution That Dances* (Aigis Publications, forthcoming). Based on interviews with Ynestra King and Chaia Heller, I am persuaded that the theory of social ecofeminism was first developed by King but was named by Heller; at a copy shop in Vermont, Heller ran into Biehl, who was duplicating the aforementioned essay and who then asked Heller if she might use the term publicly. Though her request for permission seems a bit tardy, it is only fair to note that Biehl had already credited Heller in a footnote as the originator of the term "social ecofeminism."

40. Kate Fox and Paul Glavin, "The Politics of Imagination and Struggle," *Record of Antioch College* 44 (June 2, 1989): 8–9.

41. April Cope, "Heller, Eco-Feminists Conflict with Greens," *Record of Antioch College* 46 (June 2, 1989): 5. On the back of the student newspaper issue reporting on the conference was a full-page ad titled "The Green Man's Guide to Meeting Women." The text read, "Opening lines every Green man should know: 'Sometimes, I'm ashamed to be a man', 'I really respect eco-feminism', 'Yeah, I went to Antioch'." At the bottom was the line, "Let the critique of patriarchy work for you," and below that, "To order, call 1-800-BOOKCHIN have credit card ready." The anti-ecofeminist hostility at Antioch was not necessarily unique to the Youth Greens, however, and needs to be placed in historic context as part of an overall antifeminist backlash that was growing on campuses across the United States at that time.

42. Cope, "Heller, Eco-Feminists," p. 5.

43. The Women's Pentagon Action is described in Chapter 1. See also Ynestra King, "If I Can't Dance in Your Revolution, I'm Not Coming," 281–98, in *Rocking the Ship of State: Toward a Feminist Peace Politics*, ed. Adrienne Harris and Ynestra King (Boulder, Colo.: Westview Press, 1989).

44. "Women's Caucus Report," *Left Green Notes* 3 (July/August 1990): 17.

45. Laura Schere's critique of the December 1990 Youth Greens gathering in Knoxville was mailed to Youth Greens as part of an informational packet in the spring or summer of 1991.

46. Maura Dillon, "Anarchism, Feminism, and Building a Movement," *Left Green Notes* 5 (November/December 1990): 8–9, 11.

47. The favorable review of Biehl's book, written by Kelly Stoner, appears in *Left Green Notes* 7 (April/May 1991): 11. Transcripts of Schere's and Sandilands's presentations, along with the revised "women's liberation" principle, were published in *Left Green Notes* 9 (August/September 1991); see Kate Sandilands, "They Don't Call Us a Movement for Nothing: A Preface to the (New) Left Green Principle on Women's Liberation," p. 29, and Laura Schere, "Feminism, Ecology, and Left Green Politics," pp. 30–31.

48. Cora Roelofs, "Left Green Process and Projects Starter Kit," *Regeneration* 3 (Spring 1992): 20.

49. The most detailed information available on the GPOC's pre-gathering meeting is presented in Howie Hawkins, "The Green Gathering in Elkins, West Virginia: You Should've Been There," *Left Green Notes* 10 (November/December 1991): 6–18. I have taken the liberty of deleting

Hawkins's pejorative "self-styled" from "eco-feminist" in the description of Terri Williams; moreover, throughout this chapter I take the position of accepting, not challenging, every woman's self-description. My goal here is to explore correlations between the various forms of ecofeminism and the various political tendencies within the Greens. Although I argue that certain versions of ecofeminism lead to political positions and strategies that are undemocratic, I believe it contradicts the fundamental insights of feminism to engage in discussions of who is and who is not a "true ecofeminist."

50. Christa Daryl Slaton, "The Failure of the United States Greens to Root in Fertile Soil," 83–117, in *Research in Social Movements, Conflicts, and Change: The Green Movement Worldwide,* ed. Matthias Finger (London: JAI Press, 1992) (quotations from pp. 101, 114).

51. Telephone interview, June 11, 1996.

52. "Women's Statement on Sexism and Division in the Greens," *Greens Bulletin* (March 1992): 47.

53. Ann Foland, Aspen Olmstead, Martha Percy-Meade, Syracuse Greens, "Change 'Post-Patriarchal Values' to 'Feminist Values,'" *Green Tidings* 4 (August 8, 1992): 9.

54. The remarks of "Sunshine Sam" appeared in *Green Tidings* on August 9, 1992, the day after the motion was introduced; they were quoted in Joseph Boland's report on the gathering, which was later revised and coauthored with Amy Belanger, Diana Spalding, and David Shlosberg as "Healing Rifts: Community and Organization in the Fifth Greens Gathering," *GroundWork* (Fall 1992): 48–51.

55. Joseph Boland, "From Post-Patriarchal Values to Feminism," draft notes later condensed and published as "Healing Rifts."

56. Diana Spalding, "The Greens National Gathering," *Z Magazine* 5 (November 1992): 54.

57. Ibid., p. 55.

58. Boland et al., "Healing Rifts, " p. 48.

59. Margaret Elysia Garcia, "Whatever Happened to Green Feminism?" *Z Magazine* 9 (March 1996): 20–21.

60. Ibid.

61. Telephone interview, May 1996.

62. Interview, Big Island of Hawai'i, May 23, 1993.

63. Quoted in "Keiko Bonk-Abramson: A New Green Officeholder Interviewed on Her Campaign and Green Justice," *Green Politics* 2 (Spring 1993): 10.

64. A transcript of Keiko Bonk's keynote was printed as "Growing Up Politically: The Courage to Act," in the GPN newsletter, *Green Horizon* 4 (October/November 1995): 1, 5.

65. Ibid., p. 5.

66. Ibid.

67. Quoted in Don Chapman, "A Still-Green Politician: Hawai'i Greens Co-Chair Linda Martin Is New to Politics, but She Brought Recognition to Her Party," *Midweek Magazine* 9 (November 11, 1992): A10.

68. Ibid.

69. Interview, Honolulu, May 27, 1993.

70. Dee Berry, *The Challenge of the Greens: Making the Spiritual-Political Connection* (pamphlet), February 12, 1989, 25 pp.

71. Dee Berry, *A Green Story* (pamphlet), circa 1988, 15 pp.

72. Ibid., pp. 13–14.

73. Berry, "Challenge of the Greens," n.p.

74. Anne Goeke, "A Way of Being Gylany Green" (pamphlet), n.d. See also Riane Eisler, *The Chalice and the Blade* (San Francisco: HarperCollins, 1987). Here is a good example of the problem with cultural feminism, and cultural ecofeminism: combining the distorted characteristics of gender will not create a whole, balanced person, and it's rather like expecting the combination of Marilyn Monroe and Clint Eastwood to create a balanced individual. The critique that socialist feminists and social ecofeminists have made is that liberation involves not a world of balanced gender but one that is postgender.

75. Telephone interview, July 8, 1996.

76. Earth Spirituality Caucus, "Greens USA Integrate Earth Spirituality," *Greens Bulletin* (June/July 1994): 16–17.

77. Charlene Spretnak, "Improving the Debates," *Green Synthesis* 33 (March 1990): 5.

78. Ibid., p. 17.

79. Telephone interview, July 8, 1996.

80. Quoted in Jennifer Kopf, "Speaker Urges Grassroots Link of Ecology, Feminism," *Intelligencer Journal* (Lancaster, Pa.), (March 12, 1996): B-2.

81. Anne Goeke, personal communication, June 23, 1996.

82. Goeke, "A Way of Being Gylany Green," n.p.

Chapter 5

1. Margo Adair, "Beyond Personality Politics and Process Problems," *Green Letter* 4 (1988): 1, 7; David Perry, "The Birthing of a Movement: On Divisiveness and Differences in Green Politics," *Synthesis* 27 (April 1988): 3–8.

2. Adair, "Beyond Personality Politics," p. 7.

3. Perry, "Birthing of a Movement," p. 8.

4. My phrasing here alludes to Gloria Steinem's *Revolution from Within: A Book of Self-Esteem* (Boston: Little, Brown, 1992), an exceptionally important and accessible argument about the relationship between external social structures of oppression and internalized oppression in the form of lowered self-esteem. In her last chapter, Steinem makes the connection among ending oppression, healing the earth, and restoring value to the human self and argues for the relevance of ecofeminism: "There is now a body of theory and groups in almost every country that see the relationship of humans to nature as the paradigm for our relationships to each other, and also equate our view of nature with our view of the inner self" (p. 295). Steinem's book was criticized by socialist feminist reviewers as lacking in political relevance.

5. Steve Chase, ed., *Defending the Earth: A Dialogue between Murray Bookchin and Dave Foreman* (Boston: South End Press, 1991).

6. Bookchin's central ideas are articulated in *The Ecology of Freedom: The Emergence and Dissolution of Hierarchy* (Palo Alto, Calif.: Cheshire Books, 1982); *Our Synthetic Environment* (New York: Colophon, 1974); *The Limits of the City* (Montreal: Black Rose Books, 1980); *Toward an Ecological Society* (Montreal: Black Rose Books, 1984); *The Rise of Urbanization and the Decline of Citizenship* (San Francisco: Sierra Club Books, 1987); and *Remaking Society: Pathways to a Green Future* (Boston: South End Press, 1990). Naess's essay launching the deep ecology movement is "The Shallow and the Deep, Long-Range Ecology Movement: A Summary," *Inquiry* 16 (1973): 95–100.

7. Michael Tobias, ed., *Deep Ecology* (San Marcos, Calif.: Avant Books, 1984); Bill Devall and George Sessions, *Deep Ecology: Living as if Nature Mattered* (Salt Lake City: Gibbs M. Smith Books, 1985).

8. Dave Foreman's comments in *Simply Living* 2:2 (1987) are quoted in Murray Bookchin, "Social Ecology vs. Deep Ecology," *Kick It Over* (special supplement) 20 (Winter 1987): 4A-8A. This article is probably the closest available transcript for Bookchin's keynote address at the Amherst gathering.

9. Miss Ann Thropy, "Population and AIDS," *Earth First!* (May 1, 1987): 32. The column's authorship has been attributed to Chris Manes.

10. The basic principles of deep ecology are presented and discussed in Devall and Sessions, *Deep Ecology,* pp. 70–76.

11. "Social Ecology vs. Deep Ecology," *Synthesis* 26 (December 1987): 16–20; "The Deep Ecology vs. Social Ecology Debate Continued," *Green Synthesis* 28 (September 1988): 3–5; Murray Bookchin, "A Reply to My Critics," *Green Synthesis* 29 (December 1988): 5–7; Arne Naess, "Finding Common Ground," *Green Synthesis* 30 (March 1989): 9–10; Joanna Macy, "Deep Ecology Notes," *Green Synthesis* 30 (March 1989): 10; Mike Wyatt, "Humanism and Ecology: The Social Ecology/Deep Ecology Schism," *Green Synthesis* 32 (October 1989): 7–8; Charlene Spretnak, "Improving the Debates," *Green Synthesis* 33 (March 1990): 3–6.

12. For essays addressing ecofeminism and deep ecology, see Chapter 1, note 81. After 1991, the debate between deep ecology and social ecology had ceased to be of interest in the Greens, but academic philosophers continued to work out the fine points of difference in journals such as *Hypatia* and *Environmental Ethics;* see also Karen Warren, ed., *Ecological Feminism* (New York: Routledge, 1994). Ecofeminist philosopher Deborah Slicer may have brought the debate to a conclusion by observing that there never had been a debate, since a debate requires that each side listen and respond to the other; according to Slicer, deep ecologists had never listened to ecofeminists. See "Is There an Ecofeminism–Deep Ecology 'Debate'?" *Environmental Ethics* 17 (Summer 1995): 151–69.

13. See Ynestra King, "What is Ecofeminism?" *The Nation* (December 12, 1987): 702, 730–31; Janet Biehl, "It's Deep, but Is It Broad? An Eco-Feminist Looks at Deep Ecology," *Kick It Over* (special supplement) 20 (Winter 1987): 2A–4A.

14. Spretnak's statement on the politics of ecofeminist spirituality, particularly responding to Biehl's misreading of Spretnak's work, was widely circulated among ecofeminists and finally published in the *Ecofeminist Newsletter* 4 (Summer 1993): 3–4.

15. King, "What Is Ecofeminism?" p. 702.

16. See Chaia Heller, "Toward a Radical Ecofeminism: From Dua-Logic to Eco-Logic," *Society and Nature* 2:1 (1993): 72–96, quotation from pp. 94–95.

17. Janet Biehl, "The Politics of Myth," *Green Perspectives* 7 (June 1988):1–6, and *Rethinking Ecofeminist Politics* (Boston: South End Press, 1991).

18. John Rensenbrink, *The Greens and the Politics of Transformation* (San Pedro, Calif.: R & E Miles, 1992), pp. 238–39; hereafter cited as *Transformation.*

19. Dee Berry, "Notes from a Green Spiritual Feminist," *Green Horizon* 3 (April/May 1995): 3, 6. Berry is also the author of "The Challenge of the Greens: Making the Spiritual-Political Connection" (transcript of a speech delivered in Dallas, February 12, 1989).

20. Anne Goeke, "Thoughts about Earth Spirituality," *Green Horizon* 3 (April/May 1995): 1.

21. Charlene Spretnak, "The Politics of Women's Spirituality," 393–98, in *The Politics of Women's Spirituality,* ed. Spretnak, (New York: Anchor Books, 1982).

22. Spretnak, "Improving the Debates," p. 6. Curiously, the religions Spretnak wants to welcome into the Greens are indeed patriarchal.

23. For a social ecofeminist critique of population, see Janet Biehl's *Kick It Over* essay, p. 3A; for a social ecologist critique, see Murray Bookchin's *Kick It Over* essay, p. 7A; for a cultural ecofeminist critique, see Charlene Spretnak, "Ecofeminism: Our Roots and Flowering," 3–14, in *Reweaving the World: The Emergence of Ecofeminism,* ed. Irene Diamond and Gloria Feman Orenstein, (San Francisco: Sierra Club Books, 1990); for a "neither Left nor Right" critique, see Rensenbrink, *Transformation,* pp. 172–73; and for a Left Green critique, see Dan Coleman, "The Specter of Population Growth," 11–22, in *Ecopolitics: Building a Green Society* (New Brunswick: Rutgers University Press, 1994). The Greens' debate on population was articulated through "The Population Question: Three Views—Bill McCormick, Charlie Keil, and Murray Bookchin," *Green Synthesis* 36 (August 1992): 7–9, with McCormick and Keil urging an examination of population limits once the social justice concerns had been addressed, and Bookchin denouncing the racism and classism of population control ideology in general. For more recent ecofeminist critiques of population, See Chapter 1, note 50.

24. Rensenbrink, *Transformation,* p. 173.

25. Spretnak, "Ecofeminism," p. 12.

26. Brian Tokar, "Exploring the New Ecologies: Social Ecology, Deep Ecology, and the Future of Green Political Thought," *Alternatives* 15:4 (1988): 31–43, and "Ecological Radicalism," *Z Magazine* 1 (December 1988): 84–91. Each essay reprints a portion of the other; my citations are taken from the *Z Magazine* issue (quotations from pp. 89–90).

27. What I call here the "cultural geography of ecofeminism" is a perspective that evolved collaboratively during a telephone conversation with Stephanie Lahar sometime in 1990. Stephanie (located in Burlington, Vt., and having studied with Bookchin) and I (born in Hollywood, Calif., and raised in the San Fernando Valley, where I enjoyed a feast of spiritualities) developed our analyses based on both theory and experience. For the relationship of ecofeminism to the nonviolent, direct action antinuclear movement, see Barbara Epstein, *Political Protest and Cultural Revolution* (Berkeley: University of California Press, 1991).

28. One example of the potential compatibility between animal liberation theory and the Green movement is the fact that philosopher Peter Singer, author of *Animal Liberation: A New Ethics for Our Treatment of Animals* (New York: Avon Books, 1975), has worked within the Australian Green Party and has even run for office as a Green.

29. Debbie Domal, interview, Minneapolis, April 13, 1995.

30. Ecofeminist philosopher Val Plumwood addresses the experience of being prey, and the implications for ecofeminist theory, in her short story, "Human Vulnerability and the Experience of Being Prey," *Quadrant* (March 1995): 29–34. Marti Kheel has analyzed the "holy hunter" in her essay "License to Kill: An Ecofeminist Critique of Hunters' Discourse," 85–125, in *Animals and Women: Feminist Theoretical Explorations,* ed. Carol J. Adams and Josephine Donovan (Durham: Duke University Press, 1995).

31. For an example of the Left's anthropocentric inability to recognize animal oppression, see Susan Meeker-Lowry, "Challenging the Meat Monopoly: Massive Corporate Control of Land and Farmers," *Z Magazine* 8 (March 1995): 28–35. The article offers a thorough critique of the meat industry, analyzing the oppression of the workers, the local economies, the water and soil pollution,

and the risks to human health for consumers; it remains completely silent on the central reason the meat industry exists at all—the animals themselves, and the belief that whatever pain or death they suffer is justifiable if it serves human ends. Meeker-Lowry even states, "I'm not advocating that we stop eating meat" (p. 34). As an author, however, she is not alone in this inability to examine speciesism: the editors at *Z Magazine* published the article without comment and refused to print letters protesting the article's omission of animal oppression from its list of concerns.

32. Kim Bartlett, "Different Shades of Green: The Politics of Animal Liberation," *Animals' Agenda* 7 (November 1987): 12–13, 16.

33. Ynestra King, "Coming of Age with the Greens," *Z Magazine* (February 1988): 16–19.

34. Charles Allen Dews, "Towards a Green World," *Animals' Agenda* 9 (January 1989): 45.

35. Ibid., p. 57.

36. Sharon Seidenstein, "Cattle Grazing on Public Lands," *Green Letter* 4 (Spring 1988): 8–11.

37. John Mohawk, "Animal Nations and Their Right to Survive," *Green Letter* 4 (Fall 1988): 20.

38. Billy Ray Boyd, review of *The Dreaded Comparison: Race and Animal Slavery*, by Marjorie Spiegel, *Green Letter* 4 (Fall 1988): 16–17, 24. Boyd is author of *The New Abolitionists: Animal Rights and Human Liberation* (a 24–page pamphlet), and the book *For the Vegetarian in You* (San Francisco: Taterhill Press, 1987).

39. Ibid., p. 24.

40. The anthropocentric tradition of animal sacrifice in religion was first challenged by Sally Abbott, "The Origins of God in the Blood of the Lamb," 35–40, in *Reweaving the World*, ed. Diamond and Orenstein. Marti Kheel has frequently observed the plea-bargaining belief that "if animals are killed . . . human beings will be allowed to live," a belief inherent in Western patriarchal religions and more recently manifested in patriarchal science through the practices of animal experimentation. See Marti Kheel, "From Heroic to Holistic Ethics," 243–71, in *Ecofeminism: Women, Animals, Nature*, ed. Greta Gaard (Philadelphia: Temple University Press, 1993). "Animal" ecofeminists have criticized other ecofeminists who advance the deep ecological belief that hunted animals "offer themselves" to the hunter: see my "Ecofeminism and Native American Cultures: Pushing the Limits of Cultural Imperialism?" 295–314, in *Ecofeminism*, ed. Gaard.

41. Mark Linenthal, "A Green Who Hunts," *Green Letter* 5 (Spring 1989): 23–24.

42. Billy Ray Boyd, "Beyond the Hunt: An Ex-hunter Responds," *Green Letter* (Summer 1989): 14–15.

43. Gayle Hudgens, interviewing John Robbins, "Food Choices and the Green Agenda," *Green Letter* (Summer 1989): 3–4, 36–37. See also John Robbins, *Diet for a New America* (Walpole, N.H.: Stillpoint Publishing, 1987).

44. Rick Whaley, "Food and Politics," *Green Letter* 6 (Summer 1990): 8–9.

45. Whaley describes these struggles against the racism and neocolonialism of rural Wisconsinites in detail, in Rick Whaley with Walter Bresette, *Walleye Warriors: An Effective Alliance against Racism and for the Earth* (Philadelphia: New Society, 1994).

46. As of 1996, most of the founding members of the Ecofeminist Task Force have still not returned to NWSA, though our absence is due more to the struggles with racism at the 1990 Akron conference than it is to the rejection of our vegetarian conference meal proposal.

47. "Readers Angered by 'Poem for Lettuce,'" *Green Letter* 6 (Winter 1990): 46, 52.

48. Debbie Anderson, Letter of Resignation, *Greens Bulletin* (March/April 1996): 10.

49. See, for example, Carol Grunewald-Rifkin, "The Greening of Animal Rights," *Animals' Agenda* 12 (September/October 1992): 36–39; Anna E. Charlton, Sue Coe, and Gary Francione,

"The American Left Should Support Animal Rights: A Manifesto," *Animals' Agenda* 8 (January/February 1993): 28–34; and Adam M. Roberts, "NAFTA: No Aid for the Animals," *Animals' Agenda* 8 (September/October 1993): 12–13.

50. Greens are culturally, more than economically, middle class; that is, many Greens come from middle-class backgrounds but do not live their lives according to those economic aspirations. Thanks to Brian Tokar for reminding me of this (personal communication, November 7, 1996).

51. The predominance of white, middle-class people in the Greens has been noted by Youth Green Charlie Betz in "Joining Ecology with Social Justice," *Crossroads* (April 1992): 41–44, and by Kwazi Nkrumah, "'Green Justice' and the Green Movement," *Green Politics* 2 (Spring 1993): 1, 3. Nkrumah observes that even the international Green movement has "middle-class origins" but explains that "most new social movements of any type tend to develop among the middle class first, especially among intellectuals." In the United States, diversifying a movement with white, middle-class origins is made more difficult by the class and racial stratification of U.S. society.

52. This account of the Greens' founding meeting is taken from Danny Moses and Charlene Spretnak, "A Consideration of GCoC History," *Green Letter* 5 (Spring 1989): 37–39. Whereas Moses and Spretnak say "almost no people of color" participated in the founding conference, Howie Hawkins reports that "the sixty or so people who attended were virtually all upper middle class and white," "authors connected with academia or nonprofit educational corporations," and "more New Age than New Left," and that "only a handful were grassroots activists." See Howie Hawkins, "North American Greens Come of Age: Statism vs. Municipalism," *Society and Nature* 1:3 (1993): 180–218. Charlene Spretnak, however, says that at least half were grassroots activists, invited for that very reason (personal communication, August 23, 1997).

53. Charlene Spretnak and Fritjof Capra, *Green Politics: The Global Promise,* 2d ed. (Santa Fe, N.M.: Bear & Co., 1986), p. 229.

54. B. R. Douglas, "Greening the U.S.," *Nonviolent Activist* (October/November 1989): 7.

55. "First National Green Gathering," *Green Letter* 3 (Fall 1987): 7.

56. Margo Adair, John Faustini, Terrie Schultz, Jess Shoup, and Charlene Spretnak, "The 'Greening the West' Regional Gathering," *Green Letter* 4 (Fall 1988): 29–30.

57. Eric Chester, "Toward a Left Green Politics: The Iowa Conference," *Resist Newsletter* 217 (July/August 1989): 3, 7.

58. Jay Walljasper, "The Prospects for Green Politics in the U.S.," *Utne Reader* 23 (September/October 1987): 39.

59. Margo Adair, "Toward Diversity," *Green Letter* 5 (Spring 1989): 8, 20.

60. Quoted in Adair et al., "Greening the West," p. 30.

61. Richard Grow, "Greening the West: A Critique," *Green Letter* 5 (Spring 1989): 9, 21–22.

62. Bharat Patankar, "Monochromatic Green Gathering," *Race & Class* 31 (October/December 1989): 68–73.

63. In the spring 1989 issue of *Green Letter* (vol. 5), the following reprinted articles appear: Jesus Sanchez, "The Environment: Whose Movement?" pp. 3–4, 14–16 (repr. from *California Tomorrow*); Jason W. Clay, "Genocide in the Age of Enlightenment," p. 13 (repr. from *CS Quarterly*); Kathryn J. Waller, "A Question of Survival: Black Farmers Struggle to Keep Land," pp. 5–6 (repr. from *Sojourners*), and "A Time to Cast away Stones," pp. 7, 18 (repr. from *Southern Changes*); Jon Christensen, "A Different Kind of Bean Field," pp. 7, 19–20 (repr. from *High Country News*).

64. Brian Tokar, "The Greens: To Party or Not?" *Z Magazine* 4 (October 1991): 42–46.

65. Johann Moore, "Gay and Green," *Green Letter* 7 (Fall 1991): 44.

66. Eric Odell, "Ageism in the Greens," *Green Letter* 7 (Fall 1991): 48.

67. After the Nader presidential campaign, New York's vice-presidential Green candidate, long-time civil rights activist Muriel Tillinghast, was promoted to co-convenor of the Green Council after only a few months in the Greens.

68. See James Boggs, with intro. by Sharon Howell, "Rebuilding Detroit," *Green Letter* 4 (Fall 1988): 6, 22; Roberto Mendoza, "Stop the Wars on Young People of Color," *Green Letter* 6 (Spring 1991): 14–15; Detroit Summer Coalition, "Detroit Summer '92," *Green Politics* 2 (Summer 1992): 6; "Detroit Summer Takes Off," *Green Letter* (Spring 1992): G-5; Sharon Howell, "Detroit Summer: On the Move," *GroundWork* (Spring 1992): 24, 40.

69. Marie Bloom, "500 Years of Resistance: Lenni-Lenape/Delaware Indians and Allies Confront the Myth of Christopher Columbus," *Green Letter* 7 (Fall 1991): 15, 23.

70. "Shutting Down Columbus Day in Colorado," *Green Politics* 1 (Fall 1992): 8; Diana Spalding and Dean Myerson, "500 Years of Resistance in Denver," *Green Politics* 2 (Spring 1993): 1, 8.

71. David Ellison, "The Northeast Ohio Greens and the 500 Years Campaign in Cleveland: Lessons in the Do's and Don't's of Multi-racial Coalition-Building," *Green Politics* 2 (Fall 1992): 6.

72. Whaley with Bresette, *Walleye Warriors*, p. 97.

73. Walt Bresette, "We Are All Mohawks" (keynote address at the 1990 Green gathering), *Green Letter* 6 (Winter 1990): 2–3, 49–50 (quotation from p. 50).

74. Joseph Boland and Amy Belanger, with Diana Spalding and David Shlosberg, "Healing Rifts: Community and Organization in the Fifth Greens Gathering," *GroundWork* (Fall 1992): 48.

75. Cris Moore, "The 1995 National Green Conference," *Green Politics* 4 (Winter 1995): 3.

76. Two recent texts exploring the race and class diversity of grassroots environmental justice activists are Laura Pulido, *Environmentalism and Economic Justice: Two Chicano Struggles in the Southwest* (Tucson: University of Arizona Press, 1996), and Thomas Szasz, *Ecopopulism: Toxic Waste and the Movement for Environmental Justice* (Minneapolis: University of Minnesota Press, 1994).

77. See "Lesbian and Gay Caucus Statement" and "Get Used to It: Fighting Heterosexism," *Free Society* 1 (Fall 1991); "Responses to L/G Caucus' Statement" and "Queer Feminist Insert," *Free Society* 1 (Winter 1992). The journal continued, but the Youth Greens no longer existed. See Chapter 3 for a fuller discussion of the Youth Greens.

78. "Intimacy and Partnership," *Green Letter* (Autumn 1989): 39–40.

79. Johann Moore, "Gay and Green," *Green Letter* 7 (Fall 1991): 44.

80. Johann Moore, personal correspondence, May 12, 1996.

81. Lavender Greens, San Francisco, "California Green Party: Lesbian/Gay Working Platform Outline," *Greens Bulletin* (November 1991): 9.

82. Johann Moore, "The Lesbian, Bi-Sexual, Gay, Queer Caucus Organizes," *Green Politics* 2 (Spring 1993): 11.

83. Patti Myers, "Cheers for Queers: An Overview of the Civil Rights Needs of Lesbians and Gay Men," *Green Politics* 5 (Spring 1996): 1, 8.

84. Moore, personal correspondence, May 12, 1996.

85. Fortunately, the queer press is beginning to fight back. See, for example, Rick Nelson, "The Myth of Gay Affluence," *Q Monthly* [Minneapolis] (September 1996): 10–13.

86. For a brief discussion of the evolution of the economics plank at Eugene, see Christian Thurner, "Economics of the U.S. Greens," *Capitalism, Nature, Socialism* 2 (June 1991): 26–29.

87. See Michael Goldfield, *The Decline of Organized Labor in the United States* (Chicago: University of Chicago Press, 1987).

88. See David Croteau, *Politics and the Class Divide: Working People and the Middle-Class Left* (Philadelphia: Temple University Press, 1995).

89. See Judi Bari, *Timber Wars* (Monroe, Maine: Common Courage Press, 1994).

90. Michael Albert and Robin Hahnel, *Looking Forward: Participatory Economics for the Twenty-First Century* (Boston: South End Press, 1991). The book is directed toward lay readers; for a more in-depth discussion of economics, see Albert and Hahnel, *Quiet Revolution in Welfare Economics* (New Jersey: Princeton University Press, 1990).

91. See Susan Meeker-Lowry, *Economics as if the Earth Really Mattered* (Philadelphia: New Society, 1988) and *Invested in the Common Good* (Philadelphia: New Society, 1995); Roy Morrison, *We Build the Road as We Travel* (Philadelphia: New Society, 1991).

92. See Marilyn Waring, *If Women Counted: A New Feminist Economics* (San Francisco: HarperCollins, 1988). More recently, Chris Beasley has developed a theory of feminist economics that critiques masculinist theories though it is not inclusive of ecological economics; see *Sexual Economyths: Conceiving a Feminist Economics* (New York: St. Martin's Press, 1994).

93. See Maria Mies and Vandana Shiva, *Ecofeminism* (London: Zed Books, 1993); Vandana Shiva, *Staying Alive: Women, Ecology, and Development* (London: Zed Books, 1988); Maria Mies, *Patriarchy and Accumulation on a World Scale* (London: Zed Books, 1986).

94. Many of the presentations from that conference are collected in Bob Walter, Lois Arkin, and Richard Crenshaw, eds., *Sustainable Cities: Concepts and Strategies for Eco-City Development* (Los Angeles: Eco-Home Media, 1992).

95. Sale is well known for his book *Dwellers in the Land: The Bioregional Vision* (San Francisco: Sierra Club Books, 1985).

96. The bioregional quiz was compiled by Leonard Charles, Jim Dodge, Lynn Milliman, and Victoria Stockley and published in *Coevolution Quarterly* 32 (Winter 1981): 1. It was made widely available through its appearance in Devall and Sessions, *Deep Ecology* (1985) and was later republished in *Home! A Bioregional Reader*, ed. Van Andruss, Christopher Plant, Judith Plant, and Eleanor Wright (Philadelphia: New Society, 1990), pp. 29–30.

97. Gene Marshall, "The Bioregional Approach to Social Change," *Green Synthesis* 35 (March 1992): 10–11.

98. Judith Plant, "Revaluing Home: Feminism and Bioregionalism," 21–23, in *Home!* ed. Andruss et al. See also *Healing the Wounds: The Promise of Ecofeminism* (Philadelphia: New Society, 1989).

99. These problems are pointed out in Robyn Eckersley, *Environmentalism and Political Theory: Toward an Ecocentric Approach* (Albany: State University of New York Press, 1992), and articulated from an ecofeminist perspective by Michelle Summer Fike and Sarah Kerr, "Making the Links: Why Bioregionalism Needs Ecofeminism," *Alternatives* 21:2 (1995): 22–27.

100. King, "What Is Ecofeminism?" p. 730.

101. See, for example, Betty Zisk, John Rensenbrink, and Carla Dickstein, "Staying Alive: Local Green Group Maintenance for the Long Haul," *Green Letter/In Search of Greener Times* 4: 1: j, k, l; Betty Zisk, "Green Organizing," *Green Letter* 4 (Fall 1988): 31; Brian Tokar, "Toward a More Vital Grass-Roots Green Politics," *Green Letter* (Summer 1989): 16–17; and Sharon Howell, "Building a Green Movement," *Green Letter* 6 (Summer 1990): 4–5, 37–38.

102. This pattern was observed in Charlie Betz, "Joining Ecology with Social Justice," *Crossroads* (April 1992): 41–44.

103. Jamie Sayen, "A Clearcut Challenge in Maine Vote," *Earth Island Journal* 11 (Summer 1996): 23.

104. Bill Bradley, "Building the Santa Fe Greens," *Z Magazine* 8 (June 1995): 14–16; Cris Moore, "Green Victory in New Mexico!" *Green Politics* 5 (Spring 1996): 7.

105. In addition to my own experience in both the Lake Superior Greens and the Duluth Area Green Party, I compiled this information from personal interviews with David Conley, Jan Conley, and Joel Sipress, who was a key organizer of the mall sprawl campaign.

106. See "California Green Party: Discussion and Debate," in *Green Letter* 6 (Summer 1990), which includes Carl Boggs, "Why the California Greens Should Wait to Have a Party," pp. 14, 42–43; Kent Smith, "The Green Party Takes Off," p. 41; Sue Nelson, "The Instant State Green Party," pp. 13, 41; Mike Feinstein, "A Strategic Argument for the Formation of the Green Party of California," pp. 14, 43–44; and Bob Long, "A Response to Carl Boggs: Why the California Greens Should *Not* Wait to Have a Party," p. 15. Boggs's position was based on research for his book-length study *Social Movements and Political Power: Emerging Forms of Radicalism in the West* (Philadelphia: Temple University Press, 1986).

107. Boggs, "California Greens," p. 43.

108. Betz, "Joining Ecology," p. 43.

109. Bob Long, "Green Party of California Must Build Solidly," p. 5; Tom Stafford, "Greening the Political Scene," p. 3; David Spero, "Green 'Movement' Unexists: Green Is an Electoral Concept," p. 11; Greg Gerritt, "An Ecological Analysis of the Development of the Greens," p. 23, all in *Regeneration* 4 (Fall 1992).

110. See Lynn Margulis and Rene Fester, eds., *Symbiosis as a Source of Evolutionary Innovation: Speciation and Morphogenesis* (Cambridge: MIT Press, 1991).

111. Eric Chester, "Independent Political Action and Revolutionary Politics," *Regeneration* 4 (Fall 1992): 13–14.

112. Diana Balot Frank, "Electoralism a Diversion from Community," *Regeneration* 4 (Fall 1992): 28–29, 37.

113. Ed Jahn, "The Problem with Elections," *Regeneration* 4 (Fall 1992): 6.

114. See Lawrence Goodwyn, *The Populist Moment: A Short History of the Agrarian Revolt in America* (New York: Oxford University Press, 1978).

115. Howie Hawkins, "The Greens and the New Movement for Independent Politics," *Regeneration* 4 (Fall 1992): 18.

116. Hawkins, "Greens and the New Movement," p. 17.

117. Sulaiman Mahdi, "A Movement-Party or a Party-Movement?" *Regeneration* 4 (Fall 1992): 36–37.

118. Hawkins, "Greens and the New Movement," p. 17.

119. Frank Girard, "Elections: The Long and the Short Term Views," *Regeneration* 4 (Fall 1992): 24–25.

120. Frances Fox Piven and Richard Cloward, *Poor People's Movements: Why They Succeed, How They Fail* (New York: Vintage Books, 1979); Audre Lorde, "The Master's Tools Will Never Dismantle the Master's House," 110–13, in *Sister Outsider* (Trumansburg, N.Y.: Crossing Press, 1984).

121. For an excellent critique of the addictive structure of white Western culture, see Chellis Glendinning, *My Name Is Chellis and I'm in Recovery from Western Civilization* (Boston: Shambhala Books, 1994).

122. Christa Daryl Slaton, "The Failure of the United States Greens to Root in Fertile Soil," in *Research in Social Movements, Conflicts, and Change: The Green Movement Worldwide,* ed. Matthias Finger, London: JAI Press, 1992), p. 116.

123. Don Fitz, "Developing a Green Organizational Structure," *Regeneration* 4 (Fall 1992): 30–31.

Chapter 6

1. Anne Phillips, *Engendering Democracy* (University Park: Pennsylvania State University Press, 1991). If one considers prepatriarchal history, Goddess cultures of the Neolithic, or indigenous cultures throughout the ages, one gets a very different idea about the origins and practices of democracy.

2. On the democratic practices of feminism's second wave, particularly its successes and shortcomings, see Anne Phillips, "Paradoxes of Participation," 120–46, in *Engendering Democracy;* on the democratic structures of feminism's second wave, see Myra Marx Ferree and Patricia Yancey Martin, eds., *Feminist Organizations: Harvest of the New Women's Movement* (Philadelphia: Temple University Press, 1995).

3. This summary of Green democracy is based on four texts of the U.S. Green movement: Charlene Spretnak and Fritjof Capra, *Green Politics: The Global Promise* (Santa Fe, N.M.: Bear & Co., 1984, 1986); Brian Tokar, *The Green Alternative* (San Pedro, Calif.: R & E Miles, 1987, 1992); John Rensenbrink, *The Greens and the Politics of Transformation* (San Pedro, Calif.: R & E Miles, 1992); and Daniel Coleman, *Ecopolitics: Building a Green Society* (New Brunswick: Rutgers University Press, 1994).

4. Don Fitz, "Green Self-Organization: Dissolving Old Social Systems to Build New Ones," *Green Letter* 6 (Spring 1991): 40–41.

5. See Richard L. Grossman and Frank T. Adams, *Taking Care of Business: Citizenship and the Charter of Incorporation* (Cambridge, Mass.: Charter, 1993).

6. Christa Slaton, "Greenroots Politics: The Evolution of the SPAKA Process," *Green Letter* 6 (Summer 1990): 49.

7. Margo Adair and John Rensenbrink, "SPAKA: Democracy at Work," *Green Letter* (Autumn 1989): 3.

8. Phillips, "Paradoxes of Participation," pp. 126–27.

9. Most recently, Jo Freeman ("Joreen"), "The Tyranny of Structurelessness," has been reprinted in *Communities Directory: A Guide to Cooperative Living* (Langley, Wash.: Fellowship for Intentional Community, 1995), pp. 124–25. As Freeman explains in the afterword to *Feminist Organizations,* the essay was originally written in 1970 as a term paper for a political science course; the professor rejected it because there were no citations, though as Freeman explains, there was no literature to cite. She later revised the essay when there had been more studies on organizational structures and submitted it to social sciences journals, which rejected it on the grounds that it "added nothing new to the literature." Apparently, academic professors and journal editors are not always the best judges of an essay's value, since Freeman's essay has become one of the most widely

reprinted articles from the feminist second wave. (See Jo Freeman, "From Seed to Harvest: Trans-formations of Feminist Organizations and Scholarship," 397–408, in *Feminist Organizations*, ed. Ferree and Martin.)

10. Adair and Rensennbrink, "SPAKA," p. 3.

11. Andrew Light has developed a theory for an ecological identity that would use the frame-work of identity politics; see "Ecological Identity? In Search of a Concrete Communitarianism," paper presented at the Radical Philosophy Association Conference, November 14–17, 1996, Purdue University.

12. Chantal Mouffe, "Feminism, Citizenship, and Radical Democratic Politics," 369–84, in *Feminists Theorize the Political,* ed. Judith Butler and Joan Scott (New York: Routledge, 1992).

13. Brian Tokar has also told the story of the Nader campaign; see "The Nader for President Fiasco," *Z Magazine* 9 (November 1996): 26–30. Tokar and I were writing our narratives at the same time, and though we cover slightly different aspects of the Nader campaign, we have similar perspectives on this issue.

14. Nader made his early reputation through his book *Unsafe at Any Speed* (New York: Grossman, 1965), which challenged the safety of the Chevrolet Corvair and American cars in gen-eral. Unlike Nader, Greens had never made speed limits a priority in any local or statewide cam-paign.

15. Fourth of ten points in Nader's Concord Principles, the "new democracy tool box" em-phasizes six measures that would protect voters from "having their voting powers diluted." Nader discusses the Concord Principles in "Reinventing American Democracy: Democratic Revolution in an Age of Autocracy," *Boston Review* (March/April 1993): 8–10, 12. For a free copy of the Concord Principles, enclose a self-addressed stamped envelope with your request and send to Concord Prin-ciples, P.O. Box 19312, Washington, D.C. 20036.

16. Tokar, "Nader for President Fiasco," describes in greater detail the national electoralists' efforts to bring the Nader campaign to states that originally did not want it; see esp. p. 29.

17. Seattle SPAKA, "Leadership: A Question of Community Responsibility," *Green Letter/In Search of Greener Times* (Autumn 1989): 43.

18. See John Rensenbrink, "Leadership among the Greens: Learning by Doing," 198–213, in *Greens and the Politics of Transformation* (quotation from p. 200). Rensenbrink discusses the role of Green leadership in a national presidential campaign on pp. 207–8.

19. Adair's booklet, *From Leadership to Empowerment: Creating Collaborative Contexts* (1993), was widely available among the Greens; the booklet had originally appeared as an article in *Communities: A Journal of Cooperative Living* 80/81 (Spring/Summer 1993). Many Greens were also familiar with a feminist model of leadership through the work of Bruce Kokopeli and George Lakey and their booklet *Leadership for Change: Toward a Feminist Model* (Philadelphia: New Society, n.d.).

20. Keiko Bonk, "Growing Up Politically: The Courage to Act," *Green Horizon* 4 (October/November 1995): 1, 5.

21. Kwazi Nkrumah, personal communication, August 18, 1996, national Green gathering, UCLA.

22. Ralph Nader, speaking on the David Frost Special, PBS Transcript #38, October 21, 1994.

23. Greens have not been unanimous in their views on initiative, referendum, and recall; as many Greens have observed, the process has also been used by conservative groups to challenge and sometimes eliminate environmental legislation and human rights for minorities. It is one of many

examples of the fact that democratic processes need to be upheld in conjunction with correctives to ensure outcomes that maintain or increase social and ecological justice.

24. Nader, "Reinventing American Democracy," p. 8.

25. Quoted in "Nobody's Nader," by Wesley J. Smith, *Mother Jones* (July/August 1996): 61.

26. Ralph Nader, "The Concord Principles: An Agenda for a New Initiatory Democracy" (February 1, 1992).

27. Nader refused to comment on reproductive choice when interviewed on the Phil Donahue Show in March 1996; he later refused to comment on same-sex marriage, saying he would not address "gonadal politics." Such positions showed the limitations of Nader's democracy.

28. Ralph Nader, interviewed on Pacifica Radio's "Democracy Now," by Amy Goodman and Larry Bensky, March 27, 1996. Broadcast on KPFK FM 90.7, Los Angeles, at 9:00 A.M.

29. For this discussion of liberalism, liberal democracy, and the feminist critiques thereof, I have drawn from several sources: Mary Dietz, "Context Is All: Feminism and Theories of Citizenship," 63–85, in *Dimensions of Radical Democracy: Pluralism, Citizenship, Community,* (London: Verso, 1992); Alison M. Jaggar, *Feminist Politics and Human Nature* (Totowa, N.J.: Rowman and Allanheld, 1983); and Phillips, *Engendering Democracy.*

30. See Carole Pateman, *The Sexual Contract* (Cambridge: Polity Press, 1988), and *The Disorder of Women* (Cambridge: Polity Press, 1989).

31. A notable exception is Iris Marion Young, best known for her book *Justice and the Politics of Difference* (Princeton: Princeton University Press, 1990).

32. Dietz, "Context Is All," p. 73.

33. Ibid., p. 75.

34. Chantal Mouffe, "Feminism, Citizenship, and Radical Democratic Politics," 369–84, in *Feminists Theorize the Political,* ed. Judith Butler and Joan Scott (New York: Routledge, 1992) (quotation from p. 378). See also Chantal Mouffe, "Democratic Citizenship and the Political Community," 225–39, in *Dimensions of Radical Democracy,* ed. Mouffe.

35. Ynestra King, "Coming of Age with the Greens," *Z Magazine* (February 1988): 19.

36. I allude to an important essay by Murray Bookchin, "The Left That Was: A Personal Reflection," *Green Perspectives* 22 (May 1991): 1–9.

37. Biehl's critique of Athenian democracy appears in her essays "Women and the Democratic Tradition: Part I," *Green Perspectives* 16 (June 1989): 1–7, and "Women and the Democratic Tradition: Part II," *Green Perspectives* 17 (August 1989): 1–6. Note that Biehl did not repudiate ecofeminism until 1991, so these essays can be read as articulations of her social ecofeminism.

38. Biehl, "Women and the Democratic Tradition: Part II," p. 5.

39. The exclusionary strategies involved in this construction of reason are described cogently in Val Plumwood, *Feminism and the Mastery of Nature* (London: Routledge, 1993).

40. Bookchin, "The Left That Was," pp. 2, 8.

41. Janet Biehl, "Ecofeminism and the Left Greens: A Response to Laura Schere," *Left Green Notes* 10 (November/December 1991): 22–26. For a fuller discussion of this issue, see Chapter 4.

42. See, for example, Marti Kheel, "From Heroic to Holistic Ethics: The Ecofeminist Challenge," 243–71, in *Ecofeminism: Women, Animals, Nature,* ed. Greta Gaard (Philadelphia: Temple University Press, 1993).

43. Mouffe, "Feminism, Citizenship, and Radical Democratic Politics," pp. 372, 379.

44. Ernesto Laclau and Chantal Mouffe, *Hegemony and Socialist Strategy: Toward a Radical Democratic Politics* (London: Verso, 1985).

45. For a sampling of Sandilands's work, see "Ecofeminism and Its Discontents: Notes toward a Politics of Diversity," *The Trumpeter* 8 (Spring 1991): 90–96, and "Political Animals: The Paradox of Ecofeminist Politics," *The Trumpeter* 11 (Fall 1994): 167–72. For her work with the Greens, see "Radical Democracy: A Contested/ing Terrain," *Synthesis/Regeneration* 5 (Winter 1993): 14–16; "They Don't Call Us a Movement for Nothing: A Preface to the (New) Left Green Principle on Women's Liberation," *Left Green Notes* 9 (August/September 1991): 29; and "Ecology as Politics: The Promise and Problems of the Ontario Greens," 157–73, in *Organizing Dissent: Contemporary Social Movements in Theory and Practice,* ed. W. K. Carroll (Toronto: Garamond Press, 1992).

46. See Catriona Sandilands, "The Good-Natured Feminist: On the Subject of Ecofeminism and the Quest for Democracy," Ph.D. dissertation, York University, January 1996.

47. Catriona Sandilands, "From Natural Identity to Radical Democracy," *Environmental Ethics* 17 (Spring 1995): 90.

48. Ibid., pp. 78, 85.

49. Sandilands, "Political Animals," p. 168.

50. Sandilands, "Natural Identity," p. 82.

51. Ibid., p. 84.

52. Mouffe, "Feminism, Citizenship, and Radical Democratic Politics," p. 379.

53. Sandilands, "Natural Identity," p. 89.

54. See Mouffe, "Feminism, Citizenship, and Radical Democratic Politics," pp. 234–35.

55. Sandilands is currently developing a concept of citizenship that would be compatible with an ecofeminist theory of radical democracy (personal communication, August 7, 1996).

56. "Has Democracy Failed Ecology? An Ecofeminist Perspective," *Environmental Politics* 4 (Winter 1995): 134–68. See also Val Plumwood, "Feminism, Privacy, and Radical Democracy," *Anarchist Studies* 3 (1995): 97–120.

57. As ecofeminists have observed, the dualisms that form the conceptual framework of the master model in Western culture are reinforced when connections are made among the devalued halves: for example, the constructed similarities between women and animals or between nonwhite humans and the erotic merely serve to reinforce their dual subordination. See Greta Gaard, "Toward a Queer Ecofeminism," *Hypatia* 12 (Winter 1997): 114–37.

58. This problem is well documented in Mark Dowie, *Losing Ground: American Environmentalism at the Close of the Twentieth Century* (Cambridge: MIT Press, 1995), as well as in Urvashi Vaid, *Virtual Equality: The Mainstreaming of Gay and Lesbian Liberation* (New York: Doubleday, 1995).

59. Plumwood, "Has Democracy Failed Ecology?"

60. The theory of the master model is developed in Plumwood, *Feminism and the Mastery of Nature.*

61. Mies and Shiva do not refer to Plumwood simply because their book appeared before hers. See Maria Mies and Vandana Shiva, *Ecofeminism* (London: Zed Books, 1993).

62. Marilyn Waring, *If Women Counted: A New Feminist Economics* (San Francisco: HarperCollins, 1988).

63. A notable exception to this generalization can be found in the work of Carol Adams, who has begun exploring the uses of rights-based language in the defense of women and animals. See *Neither Man nor Beast: Feminism and the Defense of Animals* (New York: Continuum, 1994) and Carol Adams and Josephine Donovan, eds., *Animals and Women: Feminist Theoretical Explorations* (Durham: Duke University Press, 1995).

64. In "Ecofeminism and Wilderness," *Environmental Ethics* 19 (Spring 1997): 5–24, I have offered a description of an "ecofeminist ecological self as political animal," one that goes beyond the feminist conceptions of self-in-relationship, which have tended both to be anthropocentric and to overlook the problem that the individual's identity can be subsumed in or subordinated to the relationship. An ecofeminist notion of identity has been evolving for nearly a decade, and the articles and texts addressing this topic are almost too numerous to list. For a start, see Janis Birkeland, "Ecofeminism: Linking Theory and Practice," 13–59, in *Ecofeminism: Women, Animals, Nature,* ed. Greta Gaard (Philadelphia: Temple University Press, 1993); Josephine Donovan, "Ecofeminist Literary Criticism: Reading the Orange," *Hypatia* 11 (Spring 1996): 161–84; Marti Kheel, "Ecofeminism and Deep Ecology: Reflections on Identity and Difference," 128–37, in *Reweaving the World: The Emergence of Ecofeminism,* ed. Irene Diamond and Gloria Feman Orenstein (San Francisco: Sierra Club Books, 1990); Patrick Murphy, *Literature, Nature, and Other: Ecofeminist Critiques* (Albany: State University of New York Press, 1995); Plumwood, *Feminism and the Mastery of Nature;* and Karen Warren, "The Power and the Promise of Ecological Feminism," *Environmental Ethics* 12 (Summer 1990): 125–46.

65. Plumwood, *Feminism and the Mastery of Nature,* p. 142.

66. Ecofeminist philosopher Lori Gruen is developing an ecofeminist ethic that transcends the rhetoric of instrumental/intrinsic value.

67. See Carol Adams, *The Sexual Politics of Meat: A Feminist-Vegetarian Critical Theory* (New York: Continuum, 1990).

68. Lori Gruen and I have perceived WEDO as advancing a form of liberal ecofeminism, in that the spokespersons for the organization emphasize the linked oppressions of women, nature, the colonized, and the poor, and they seek to incorporate these excluded categories into the international framework of rights, economics, and other legal considerations. Others have suggested that WEDO is not ecofeminist at all but rather combines feminism and environmentalism in a liberal strategy for inclusion. To date, the only written critique of WEDO that I am aware of appears in Noël Sturgeon, *Ecofeminist Natures: Race, Gender, and Transnational Environmental Politics* (New York: Routledge, 1997). For international readers, or those U.S. citizens who resisted memorizing and repeating the pledge of allegiance, here is the original pledge of allegiance unrevised by WEDO: "I pledge allegiance to the United States of America, and to the republic for which it stands, one nation, under God, indivisible, with liberty and justice for all." The phrase "under God" was not part of the original pledge but was added during the McCarthy era of the 1950s.

69. Plumwood, "Has Democracy Failed Ecology?" pp. 155–60.

70. These ideas and others are developed in Michael Albert and Robin Hahnel, *Looking Forward: Participatory Economics for the Twenty-First Century* (Boston: South End Press, 1991).

71. Plumwood suggests this in "Has Democracy Failed Ecology?" but it has also been suggested by several poets and novelists concerned with ecology and democracy; see, for example, Marge Piercy, *Woman on the Edge of Time* (New York: Ballantine Books, 1976); Gary Snyder, "Four Changes," in *Turtle Island* (New York: New Directions, 1969, 1974); and Starhawk, *The Fifth Sacred Thing* (New York: Bantam Books, 1993).

72. On the reason/erotic dualism, see Gaard, "Toward a Queer Ecofeminism."

73. Information on the IPPN is drawn from Howie Hawkins, "Independent Progressive Politics," *Z Magazine* 9 (March 1996): 15–20, and "Independent Progressive Politics Network," *Z Magazine* 9 (June 1996): 17–21.

74. Drawing on her experiences in the revolutions of Cuba and Nicaragua, Margaret Randall makes this point very clearly in regard to feminist organizations, in her book *Gathering Rage: The Failure of Twentieth-Century Revolutions to Develop a Feminist Agenda* (New York: Monthly Review Press, 1992).

Conclusion

1. Ynestra King, "Coming of Age with the Greens," *Z Magazine* (February 1988): 19.
2. Ibid., p. 17.
3. Ibid., p. 16.
4. Actually, Nader is an Arab-American, and his sexuality remains undeclared; the fact that he is thus *passing* for white and heterosexual has been a topic of considerable discussion among the more radical Greens.

Index

deep ecology (*cont.*)
    bate, 48, 182, 291n. 81; and ecological wis-
    dom, 97; and hunting, 49, 148; social eco-
    feminist critique of, 147–51. *See also under*
    social ecology
Dejanikus, Tacie, 20
Deming, Barbara, 22
democracy, 9–10, 64, 87, 135, 138, 267, 280;
    and citizenship, 234, 244, 247–48, 249–55,
    259; ecological, 255; grassroots, 86, 97, 98,
    101, 212; grassroots democracy, and the
    Greens, 230–34; and identity, 234; liberal,
    10, 243, 246–48, 250; participatory democ-
    racy, and feminism, 229, 233; radical, 10,
    105, 269; social, 113, 114; and social move-
    ment organization, 93; "trickle-down de-
    mocracy," 245. *See also* Ten Key Values
Democratic Party, 54, 99, 100, 128, 170, 171,
    212, 222, 235
Detroit Summer. *See under* Green Action Plan
Devall, Bill, 3, 63, 96, 102, 180
Dews, Charles Allen, 119, 155, 190, 208
Diamond, Irene, 24, 39, 63, 153, 154
Dietz, Mary, 247
direct action, in social movements, 91–92; as
    principle of Left Greens, 101; as principle of
    Vermont New Hampshire Greens, 97
Donovan, Josephine, 24, 38

Earth Day Wall Street Action, 106–10; hand-
    book for, 108; and Left Green Network,
    101, 106, 121; scenarios for, 108; and social
    ecofeminism, 160; and Women's Pentagon
    Action, 160; and Youth Greens, 120, 121–
    22, 127, 129. *See also* Redwood Summer
Earth First! 111, 122, 123, 180, 181, 215; jour-
    nal of, 96
Earth Spirituality Caucus/Network, of GCoC
    and GPN, 174–75, 183
Earthwise Education Center, 82, 206
Eaton, Heather, 39–40
Echols, Alice, 36–37
ecofeminism: and animal liberation, 153, 154;
    and bioregionalism, 217–18; chronology of,

271–73; and citizenship, 247, 249–55, 258,
259–62; and democracy, 248–63; and economics, 215–16; as feminism's third wave,
31; future of, 41–42, 47, 51, 253, 266; and
Green Politics Network, 74; and the Greens,
61, 64, 96, 249; and identity, 258; and Left
Greens, 99, 114; life experiences leading to,
29–31; paths of activism leading to, 15–31;
and radical democracy, 159–63, 251; roots
of, 7–8; social ecology and deep ecology,
distinguished from, 154; and social movement theory, 94–95; as a term, 12–15, 157–
58; theoretical branches of, 8, 31–47; as
theory in process, 32; and Vermont and
New Hampshire Greens, 97, 99; and white
women, 13, 22, 41; and women of color, 13,
22, 40–41; and Youth Greens, 118. *See also*
"animal" ecofeminism; cultural ecofeminism; ecofeminist activism; social ecofeminism; spiritual/cultural ecofeminism
ecofeminist activism: in Earth Day Wall Street
Action, 9, 160; in the GPN, 169–76; in the
GPOC, 163–66; in Green movement, 8–9,
140–57, 162, 166–69, 178, 180, 208, 265; in
international Green movement, 140; in Left
Greens/Youth Greens, 157–62; WomanEarth
Feminist Peace Institute, 9, 21–22, 41, 140,
153–54; Women and Life on Earth conference, 3, 11, 18, 47, 158; Women's Pentagon
Action, 9, 11, 18, 47, 158, 160; Women's
Pentagon Action, and Unity Statement, 19–
21, 160. *See also* Ecofeminist Visions
Emerging; Feminists for Animal Rights
Ecofeminist Caucus, of National Women's
Studies Association, 3, 11, 194, 308n. 34
Ecofeminist Perspectives conference, 145–
46
Ecofeminist Visions Emerging (EVE), 46–
47
ecological humanism, 97, 101, 147–48
ecological wisdom, 58, 97, 142, 181, 212. *See
also* Ten Key Values
ecology, as a core Green value, 97, 142. *See
also* Ten Key Values